WOLFGANG GOETHE

WOLFGANG GOETHE

BY

GEORG BRANDES

Authorized Translation From the Danish

BY

ALLEN W. PORTERFIELD

VOLUME II

FRANK-MAURICE, INC.
NEW YORK   MCMXXV

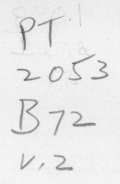

CONTENTS

iv CONTENTS

CONTENTS

WOLFGANG GOETHE

WOLFGANG GOETHE

CHAPTER I

CHRISTIANE VULPIUS—*Römische Elegien*

AFTER Goethe's return home he lived in a world of Roman reminiscences. He was "the aristocratic Roman," as Herder half jestingly, half satirically called him. He fused Roman memories with fresh Weimarian impressions of his happy life with Christiane Vulpius in his collection of poems entitled *Römische Elegien*. This was the first pretentious work he wrote after his return and in order to mislead the curious he gave his beloved the Roman name of Faustina which, scarcely by accident, sounds like the feminine form of Faust. In the original sketch her name was Christina.

There was nothing of the Roman woman in Christiane herself. Her uninterrupted friendship for Goethe lasted twenty-eight years. Born June 1, 1765, she was twenty-three years old in 1788. Her father had been an official copyist in Weimar, but during his later years he fell an incurable prey to drink and eventually died of intemperance. Her brother was a capable official and energetic reviser of dramas. He had made a name for himself by his robber novel entitled *Rinaldo Rinaldini*, a work which enjoyed an enormous popularity, greater in-

7

deed than any single work of his illustrious brother-in-law.

Goethe's ardent yearning for Christiane was the point of departure of the union. It gradually developed into affectionate resignation such as a more distinguished man can cherish for an unpretentious and dependable woman friend who does not possess the excellence of training enjoyed by her protector. Goethe gave her a care-free existence. She appreciated him even though she did not understand him. By her living with him she was subjected to humiliations from those about her. She never failed to maintain a feeling of distinct and unwavering gratitude toward him. She had felt that she was too good to be cast aside after Goethe's first desire had been satisfied, and Goethe found her too good to be treated in this way. In the little poem entitled *Gefunden* he tells how, while taking a walk one day, he found a little flower out in the forest:

> Im Schatten sah ich
> Ein Blümchen stehn,
> Wie Sterne leuchtend,
> Wie Äuglein schön.

His first impulse was to pluck it; it asked: Was I created only to be plucked and then left to wither and decay?

> Ich grub's mit allen
> Den Würzlein aus,
> Zum Garten trug ich's
> Am hübschen Haus.

He replanted the flower and it grew and put forth branches and flowers.

The poems *Morgenklage* and *Der Besuch* are

on love. They tell how she absented herself from
a tryst where she was expected with longing and
yearning and how, at a certain visit, he took her by
surprise as she lay sleeping and did not have the
heart to disturb her. Goethe's charming portrayal
of Christiane, half lying and half sitting, asleep in
the corner of the divan, with her head against the
pillow, resembles strongly an illustration of the
poem.

Christiane was in no sense of the word distinguished though she was not on that account vulgar.
She possessed to a rather remarkable degree the
attractions of youth and beauty. She had what the
French call *la beauté du diable*. She appeared better full face than profile. She was, as the *Römische
Elegien* inform us, a brunette whose dark hair fell
luxuriously down over her forehead while short
locks curled about her pretty neck and loose un-
braided hair stood up from her crown. She was a
child of the people and liked that type of amusement
which attracts a young girl of her social class. She
was especially fond of dancing, a passion she never
lost until well on in years. She did not bother herself about reading and was a poor correspondent.
She amused herself by talking, attending social affairs and the theatre and associating with actors
and actresses. The daughter of a factory worker,
she followed her father's example. Though she
never led a really dissolute life, she liked a glass
of good wine; indeed she had no objection to two
or three of them.

She made her protector's home charming and attractive, though she was a poor economist, especially in her later years when, racked with physical

pain, she paid so little attention to the details of
housekeeping that Goethe became financially embarrassed. She never regarded herself as his equal;
she always addressed her Lord and Husband offi-
cially as *Sie* or *Herr Geheimrath*. Even after the
marriage had been legalized she submitted to all
the slights to which the society of Weimar took
pleasure in subjecting her. It was not until 1811,
when her son August had grown up and had received a title that, zealous of his rights as a legitimate citizen, she became pugnacious, even grossly
critical; she forbade Bettina admission to her home,
even though she came accompanied by her husband.
In fine, she made it known that she was a genuine
Geheimrätin.

One sees the various women in Goethe's life in
various positions and situations: Friederike when
she runs across the meadow under the open sky,
Charlotte Buff cutting bread and butter for her little
brothers and sisters, Lili at the ball, Charlotte von
Stein at her country place or at court, Christiane in
bed as a young woman, as an older woman in the
kitchen or on walks out to Belvedere.

As the years passed by, she became quite stout.
The women of Weimar, especially Charlotte von
Schiller, called her *die dicke Ehehälfte*. But when
younger, she exercised, by reason of her solid and
exhuberant figure, her sprightly and loving eyes,
a sort of sensual bewitchery over Wolfgang Goethe,
then almost forty years old. The mere thought of
embracing her filled him with extreme delight.
Neither daily life in the company of each other, nor
months of separation, nor five periods of pregnancy
(1789, 1791, 1793, 1795, 1802) were able to cool

his ardor or effect his estrangement, even though he never conceived his domestic fidelity as being unconditional. Of the five children, three sons and two daughters, only the first born survived. The others were born dead or lived only a few weeks. The sensual attraction is in time transformed into conventional marital affection: the sweetheart becomes the housekeeper, the housekeeper becomes the wife.

We have a letter from Schiller, the authenticity of which is not absolutely assured since the original has not been preserved. Its reliability, however, in substance in the part quoted is beyond question. At the close of the century, Schiller wrote to Count Schimmelmann concerning Goethe's relation to Christiane. Schiller's views on this subject coincide entirely with those of his wife, who was of noble birth. After having praised and defended Goethe from every conceivable angle—as an intellectual force, as a poet, as a scientist, and as a man— Schiller says:

I wish I could also fully justify Goethe with regard to his domestic relations just as I could confidently do with regard to his literary and civilian relations. Unfortunately, however, he has come, owing to some false conceptions of domestic happiness and because of a solicitous fear of the marriage vow, into a situation which oppresses him and makes him unhappy in his own home, and from which, alas, he is too weak and gentle-hearted to disentangle himself. This is the sole blot on his escutcheon; it harms no one but himself, however, and even it comes from a quite noble trait of character.

Goethe adopted the same Fabian policy here that he had employed in his literary activity. He postponed getting married so long that when he did finally make up his mind, the people of Weimar looked upon Christiane as having been irreparably compromised. It was only with extreme difficulty that she was admitted to the society of Weimar; she was never received at court. If he wished to marry her he should have done so when he took her into his home. As it was, he endured the drawbacks incident to having a woman around without a single one of the advantages that a formal union with her would have procured for him, and especially for her. Had the marriage been solemnized earlier, his son, August, would have escaped the stigma of being of illegitimate birth, a stigma that was for a considerable time a decided hindrance on his journey through life.

II

The *Römische Elegien* constitute a most charming cycle of poems. An exact knowledge of the German language is, to be sure, indispensable to unqualified enjoyment of them. When, some time ago, the *Elegien* were praised by Taine, a Frenchman who chanced to be present asked what they really were. The great critic gave this off-hand reply: *Des pastiches d'après Properce.* That they are just this Goethe himself never denied. By way of defending them and the Venetian epigrammes, he writes the introduction to *Hermann and Dorothea:*

Also das wäre Verbrechen, dass einst Properz mich begeistert,
   Dass Martial sich zu mir auch, der Verwegne, gesellt,
Dass ich die Alten nicht hinter mir liess, die Schule zu hüten.
   Dass kein Name mich täuscht, dass mich kein Dogma beschränkt.

But for all this the elegies are abundantly original. They begin by giving a few somewhat buoyant pictures of Rome, its gripping monuments, proud palaces and venerable walls, with a reference to the genius of the city. All of this glory and all of this magnificence are without meaning to the poet until he has found the one who to him personifies the city and gives it voice. He soon finds her; and then he finds joy. She gives him a place of refuge where he is in peace from politics and news, from ladies and gentlemen of the smart world. She herself is not a lady; she is not ashamed of receiving help from this doughty stranger. She yields without hesitation. But despite her hasty sacrifice, for which she had a precedent in the gods and goddesses of olden times—Venus with Anchises, Luna with Endymion, Rhea Sylvia with Mars—she has both her chastity and her pride. She loves the man to whom she has yielded. She is a widow with a little boy; she must be cautious; she must try to avoid the malicious gossip of the town. Consequently the lovers conceal their mutual understanding as well as they can. *Opportunity* is one of the goddesses they now worship.

With the freedom of the Roman poets, but with a different and more artistic spirit than, for example, Ovid, Goethe depicts the caresses that the poet gives and receives. No Roman of ancient days ever surpassed such verses as these:

Dann versteh' ich den Marmor erst recht; ich denk' und vergleiche,
   Sehe mit fühlendem Aug, fühle mit sehender Hand.

The close of the elegy is jocose and unforgetable:

Wird doch nicht immer geküsst, es wird vernünftig
    gesprochen.
Ueberfällt sie der Schlaf, lieg' ich und denke mir viel.
Oftmals hab' ich auch schon in ihren Armen gedichtet
    Und des Hexameters Maas leise mit fingernder Hand
Ihr auf dem Rücken gezählt. Sie athmet in lieblichem
    Schlummer,
    Und es durchglüht ihr Hauch mir bis ins Tiefste die
    Brust.

Once again he glorifies Rome and the climate of
Italy. In the seventh elegy we find almost precisely
the same words that were quoted above (page 343)
touching on Goethe's return home. These verses
were written at the same time as the letter to Herder, though they contain a picture of the grey sky
of the North, its fog and darkness, its formlessness
and poverty of color. It is a distant, uncomfortable
memory which serves as a foil to the brilliance of
the present. In the fifteenth elegy he prefers a complete tribe of southern fleas to the mists in the
mopish North.

Concerning Faustina he makes the remark—it
corresponds to what was said above regarding Christiane's grace—that during her childhood and ado-
lescence she was regarded as neither pleasing nor
beautiful. It is even so with the flower of the grape-
vine—a simile that is quite felicitous—in that it
lacks forms and color, but it brings forth grapes
that ripen and mature both men and gods.

A strong and vigorous, though sensuous, feeling
of happiness is expressed through a profound sympathy for the illustrious dead, from Alexander and
Caesar down to modern times: they are only shades,

and are never warmed in the embrace of woman.
There is an exquisite depiction of his quiet, happy,
domestic life with his sweetheart while the noise
and confusion from the outside Roman world pene-
trate to the pair and suggest to the poet themes for
amusement and passionate devotion. He hears the
cheerful voices of the harvesters as they come home
on the Flaminian Way. When they approach the
Porta del Popolo he complains that Rome no longer
celebrates Ceres as the goddess of grain, and seizes
upon this opportunity to tell of the nocturnal mysteries which were transplanted from Eleusis to
Rome, the secrets of which were, in reality, the incidents of a love-affair between Ceres and a demi-
god. There is a good deal of mythology in all of
the poems; in all of the myths there is a good deal
of eroticism. But there is neither an excess of erudition nor a superfluous tone of boldness and vulgar
sensuality in them. Grace is never forgotten:

> Euch, o Grazien, legt die wenigen Blätter ein Dichter
> Auf den reinen Altar, Knospen der Rose dazu.

If there is no reference to any other Roman god,
Amor at least receives abundant attention; and
whenever Goethe delineates the sweetheart, he
avails himself of the touch by which he characterises
—a bit monotonously—Christiane: the locks about
her precious head as she lies in bed, her head resting on his arm:

> Find' ich die Fülle der Locken an meinem Busen, das
>   Köpfchen
> Ruhet und drucket den Arm, der sich dem Halse bequemt.

There is constant and dolorous reference, not simply
in the elegies which were excluded from the familiar

collection, the ones now generally published with the poem entitled *Das Tagebuch*, but also in the elegies of which Goethe approved, to sexual diseases— which were happily unknown to ancient times. The abhorrence with which they are mentioned is unmistakable. The fear of infection is characterised as the most venomous foe of pleasure. His own beloved is lauded in unequivocal words. Convinced as he is of her fidelity, he fears no danger from this source.

We may assume that Goethe was incited to write these poems by his correspondence with Karl August. In February, 1788, he received a letter from the Duke containing, among other observations, the report that a case of sickness from which the latter had suffered had been different and more nefarious than Goethe had supposed. Moreover, and peculiarly enough, it contained a challenge to Goethe to go in for a life of vigorous erotic enjoyment. Goethe replied (Rome, February 16):

I was good-natured enough, on the reading of your letter which the courier brought me, to think of hemorrhoids, and now I see that the neighborhood has suffered. Let us hope that all the evil will be eliminated from the body once for all by this annoying inoculation. I shall not fail to defy the evil spirits through the application of the mysterious *sigillo*. . . . You write so convincingly that one would have to have a *cervello tosto* not to be enticed into the alluring garden of flowers. It seems that your good thoughts of January 22 have dispatched their influence direct to Rome, for I could tell you of a number of exquisite walks I have latterly taken. This much is certain, and you, as a *doctor longe experimentissimus,* are perfectly correct in your assertion that a moderate indulgence such as that of which you spoke tones up the mind and brings the body into a state of precious equilibrium. As I have experienced more than once in my life, just as I have also felt the irritation, when I have deviated from the broad way and was about to set out on the narrow path of abstinence and certainty.

The passage in the letter is significant by way of characterising the freedom of speech that obtained at that time between the Prince and the Poet and by way of showing the unqualified confidence that each had in the other. The introduction to the eighteenth elegy reminds one of the letter:

Eines ist mir verdriesslich vor allen Dingen, ein Andres
　Bleibt mir abscheulich, empört jegliche Faser in mir,
Nur der blosse Gedanke.　Ich will es Euch, Freunde,
　　gestehen;
　Gar verdriesslich ist mir einsam das Lager zu Nacht;
Aber ganz abscheulich ist's, auf dem Wege der Liebe
　Schlangen zu fürchten, und Gift unter den Rosen der Lust.

But however much the elegies may have been experienced, partly in Rome, partly in Weimar, they nevertheless remind not infrequently of Roman pictures; and they are just as reminiscent of Ovid as of Propertius. There seems to me to be no doubt at all but that Goethe, in his fifteenth elegy with its portrayal of a scene in an *Osteria,* has imitated Ovid's fourth elegy in the first book of his *Amores.*

The word *Osteria* is, to be sure, quite modern, though the scene that is depicted is Old Roman. Ovid tells how the beloved, accompanied by her husband, after having taken her place at the table, is requested to write fond words in the wine that has been spilled. Tibullus does nearly the same in his fourth elegy on Delia. She too is asked to write words of cunning in the wine. Goethe has his heroine, accompanied by her uncle, take her place at

the table, where the top is moist from wine that
has been spilled. And then she writes a Roman
numeral *Four* by way of indicating the hour of
rendezvous for the following day.

Some of these short poems are merely little jokes
and intended as such. There is one in which the
lover remains away because he believes he sees the
stern uncle in the garden before the house. What
he sees is the scare-crow. In another he tells of his
detestation of the barking of dogs in general, but
his delight at hearing a certain definite dog, the dog
of his neighbor, bark, for he is thereby apprised
of the coming of his sweetheart. In others, the nineteenth for example, which depicts the danger that
threatens from *Fama,* the goddess of rumor, Goethe, in order to set forth the hostility that naturally
obtains between *Fama* and *Amor,* has so interwoven
and interfiltered two old, well-known myths that
we wish with all our heart that he would drop mythology once for all and adhere to actual life. Even
in the works of Pindar and Ovid the introduction
of an excessive amount of mythology makes the enjoyment of their poetry a difficult task. And when
a modern poet incessantly harks back to the myths
and legends of long ago, the effect produced may
be tiresome, lifeless and ineffectual.

Nevertheless, the last little poem dedicated to
Verschwiegenheit, is a charming bit of lyric poetry.
It is the companion poem to the one that cautioned
against *Fama.* In this case, as indeed generally,
the poet's own words come into play: *Dichter lieben
nicht zu schweigen—wollen sich der Menge zeigen.*
So it comes about that he who would not confide
in his lady friend lest she might disapprove of his

manner of living, nor in his gentleman friend lest he
might become his rival, and who is too advanced in
years and experience to feel that it is judicious to
proclaim his secrets to the forests and the fields,
entrusts them to the form of the distich and em-
bodies them in ancient verse, just as he might de-
posit a precious treasure in a jewel box:

Dir, Hexameter, Dir, Pantameter, sei es vertraut,
Wie sie des Tags mich erfreut, wie sie des Nachts mich
    beglückt.

All in all, it must be said that, just as Goethe in
his *Iphigenie auf Tauris* succeeded in imitating Euri-
pedes and vivifying his theme with that particular
spirit of humanity which predominated at the close
of the eighteenth century, he succeeded equally well,
in his *Römische Elegien,* in imitating and bringing
down to modern times the three Latin poets whom
he jestingly calls the Triumvire of Rome—Tibullus,
Catullus, and Propertius.   And he created, incidentally, a worthy and more nearly modern counterpiece
to their erotic lyricism.   There are just a few pages
of the *Römische Elegien,* only twenty elegies in all,
whereas Ovid's *Amores* alone consists of a half hundred poems of cognate species.   Goethe's poems
constitute a complete and well rounded whole. They
are saturated with the sensual feeling of happiness
and a warm, perhaps a little easy-going and massive, sensuality, which, in contrast to that of the
poems of olden times, is distinctly heathen.   It actually enjoys its indifference toward ascetic prescrip-
tions, an attitude of which the writers of antiquity
knew nothing.
    It is practically unnecessary to tell of the indigna-

tion felt by the fine ladies of the day at the *Frech-heiten* in the *Römische Elegien*. Nor need we report on the manner in which the virile guardians of Zion went out after these poems with tongs of fire, with fire and tongs.

CHAPTER II

SECOND SOJOURN IN VENICE: *Venezianische Epigramme*

IT so happened that Goethe had an opportunity, earlier than he had anticipated, of seeing Italy for the second time, or more accurately, one city in Italy, Venice. The Duchess Anna Amalie, accompanied by a number of people, Herder among others, had been living for some while in Italy, and Goethe had expressed a desire to call on her. It was accordingly arranged that he should meet her in Venice and accompany her home. At the latter part of March, 1790, after a journey of eighteen days from Jena, he arrived in Italy. The Duchess having been delayed in Naples, he staid at first alone in the City of the Doges until the beginning of May, and then with the Duchess and her entourage until some time in June.

The fruit of this sojourn was the *Venezianische Epigramme,* interesting in themselves, but doubly interesting as the counterpart to the *Römische Elegien.* Though written in the same metre, they are in direct contrast to the spirit of the elegies, which are peaceful, enrapture by everything ultra-montane, the product of contentment; the epigrammes are quarrelsome, dissatisfied with the piggishness and bigotry of Italy, sharp and caustic against the foreign as well as the domestic.

21

Much of this is owing to the fact that Goethe started on his journey a few months after the birth of his son, August. His home was then unusually attractive. He missed Christiane bitterly, by day as well as by night. He did not realize how indispensable she had become to him until this separation, the first since their union. Under these circumstances, the Italy he had idolized just a few years before now lost its attraction; and captious as he was, he saw only its shady side. He suffered from dishonesty, selfishness and extortion on the part of the foreigner, and especially on the part of the Hierarchy, which, only a few days ago, had played an insignificant rôle in his joy over the South. In the Rome of which he had written his elegies, Christiane had been the central point; in the Venice in which he was now engulfed, there was no Christiane:

Schön ist das Land, doch ach! Faustinen find' ich nicht
    wieder.
Das ist Italien nicht mehr, das ich mit Schmerzen verliess.

In these epigrammes we catch fleeting glimpses of the cynicism which the last letter to the Duke betrays. It is a wholesome cynicism; in its intolerance of hypocrisy and bigotry it calls things by their right names. They show the poet unsusceptible to the world of beauty in Venice, and so dejected in spirit that poetic creation is difficult. It is also noteworthy that in these epigrammes, and here only, Goethe is occupied, while producing, with the production itself. He speaks again and again, in a way that does not exactly entertain the reader, of the book into which the verses are introduced and raises the question as to whether a given epigramme

is excellent or inferior, impudent or humble. We
are not accustomed, in the case of Goethe, to be
led through the kitchen; we are rather used to being
conducted at once to the elaborately furnished din-
ing room where the bounteous meal stands ready.

The disagreement with and aversion toward
Christianity, which we observed in the *Italienische
Reise,* has reached its climax in the *Venezianische
Epigramme.* He attacks Christianity under the
rubric of *Schwärmerei*—transcendental enthusiasm.
Some of these observations are as harmless as this
one:

> Mache der Schwärmer sich Schüler wie Sand am Meere
> —der Sand ist Sand; die Perle sei mein, Du, o vernünftiger
> Freund!

Others reveal a feeling of violent hostility. We
quote but one:

> Jeglichen Schwärmer schlagt mir ans Kreuz im dreissigsten
>   Jahre!
> Kennt er nur einmal die Welt, wird der Betrogne der
>   Schelm.

Imagine, by way of comparison, what the mockers
of religion produced during the days of the Renaissance! Aretino himself was certainly not naïve;
but his sarcastic little poems are naïve and innocent
when measured by Goethe's standard. Take, for
example, this epigramme (quoted from memory):

> Qui giace Aretin', poeta Tosco.
> Chi parlo' mal' d'ognun', fuor' di Christo,
> Scusandosi cosi: Non lo cognosco.

A more direct address is given to many of these
epigrammes that attack priests, bigots and palmers

(Nos. 6, 9, 11, 15, 17, 19, 21, 49, 57, aside from those excluded from the collection). They give evidence of a blending of human sympathy with stupidity, of delusion unmasked by a man of the world, of contempt for the ignorance and loquaciousness of the masses. They also pour vitriol on that old inclination on the part of the masses to accept every untruth that glitters as gold.

The pronounced and inescapable appreciation of the defects of the German language as a medium of poetic expression to which these epigrammes give ample testimony, is of unusual significance. That German, as compared with the other languages of the leading countries of Europe in Goethe's day, was uncultivated there can be no doubt. It was Goethe himself who elevated German to the position of a world language. In his poetry he placed it almost at once on a level with Italian, French, and English. With regard to prose, German was even further behind the other languages. Goethe's own prose was not infrequently prolix and heavy. He himself, however, does not list these defects of his mother-tongue that were disagreeable to him. It is more than likely that he had reference, not so much to the lack of historic development from which German suffered, as to its ponderous syntax, its throwing the verb back to the very close of a relative proposition, with the result that the reader is obliged to go through several lines before he can tell whether the person that constitutes the subject of the discussion has been murdered or embraced.

In our own day, German scholars and interpreters have endeavored to explain away the meaning of the twenty-ninth epigramme; they have tried to

make it appear that the material therein referred to
was not the German language at all. Such a deduc-
tion is the outcome of the patriotism that blinds and
deludes. For the epigramme reads as follows:

Vieles hab' ich versucht, gezeichnet, in Kupfer gestochen,
   Oel gemalt, in Thon hab' ich auch Manches gedruckt,
Unbeständig jedoch, und nichts gelernt noch geleistet:
   Nur ein einzig Talent bracht' ich der Meisterschaft nah:
Deutsch zu schreiben. Und so verderb' ich unglücklicher
      Dichter
   In dem schlechtesten Stoff leider nun Leben und Kunst.

Compare this with the following, and its meaning
is clear:

Was mit mir das Schicksal gewollt? Es wäre verwegen,
   Das zu fragen; denn meist will es mit Vielen nicht viel.
Einen Dichter zu bilden, die Absicht wär ihm gelungen,
   Hätte die Sprache sich nicht unüberwindlich gezeigt.

Aside from this collection of epigrammes there
is still another from the same period and inspired
by the same mood. In it there is no lament over
the German language in and of itself. But the
poet gives expression to his regret that German is
so little known abroad. He defends himself in a
humorous way against the charge that he writes
on inappropriate topics. He contends that not one
man outside of Germany understands a word of
what he is saying:

"Wagst Du Deutsch zu schreiben unziemliche Sachen?"
      Mein Guter,
Deutsch dem kleinen Bezirk leider ist Griechisch der Welt.

In our day such a remark made with regard to
a writer in one of the Northern languages would

seem natural, though it seems quite unnatural when applied to German, spoken in Europe alone by at least eighty million people and by perhaps twenty million outside of Germany. At that time the situation was totally different. Goethe himself was the first German to be translated on a large scale, rarely of course in verse and least frequently of all in verse that can be read with enlightening pleasure.

A number of these Venetian poems revolve around the poet's visits to *Osteria* or booths where acrobats and jugglers made merry with their arts. With genuine rapture he returns again and again to the portrayal of a little girl by the name of Bettina who stood on her head, walked on her hands, was tossed up into the air from the hands of her father, threw a *salto mortale,* and so on. A number of epigrammes are also dedicated to some charming and attractive little girls, who sought out acquaintances on St. Marks Place or the Piazettas and enticed strangers to follow them. They are compared to the lizards of the South that run quickly up and down the walls and then suddenly disappear in the cracks and crevices. The satisfaction with which the description is carried out contains a definite challenge, of the same kind that Byron and Heine, after Goethe, delighted in making, to bourgeois dignity and self-righteousness. Goethe has here, by way of exception, apparently started with the intention of vexing. In one of his epigrammes he has directed the question, in order to make his meaning quite distinct, to himself as to whether he saw nothing but jugglers and sinners, men and

women, and as to whether he was not admitted to
good society. He replies:

Gute Gesellschaft hab' ich gesehn; man nennt sie die gute,
Wenn sie zum kleinsten Gedicht keine Gelegenheit gibt.

In the very midst of all this material that chal-
lenges there is one epigramme that has a peaceful,
beneficent effect: it is the one in which Goethe expresses his cordial gratitude to Karl August. It is
totally devoid of exaggeration, keeps down to this
earth, and lists with approval the profane and secular things for which he feels indebted to his Duke.
What good has it done his renown, what benefit
has he derived from the fact, that he has been imitated in Germany and read in France? No emperor
has inquired after him! No king has concerned
himself about him! No other prince has cared for
his needs:

Klein ist unter den Fürsten Germaniens freilich der meine;
    Kurz und schmal ist sein Land, mässig nur, was er vermag.
Aber so wende nach innen, so wende nach aussen die Kräfte
    Jeder! Da wär's ein Fest, Deutscher mit Deutschen zu
        sein.
Doch was priesest Du Ihn, den Thaten und Werke ver-
        künden?
    Und bestochen erschien deine Verehrung vielleicht;
Denn mir hat er gegeben, was Grosse selten gewähren,
    Neigung, Musse, Vertraun, Felder und Garten und Haus.
Niemand brauch' ich zu danken als Ihm, und manches
        bedurft' ich,
    Der ich mich auf den Erwerb schlecht als ein Dichter
        verstand.

Beside this unique poem of praise for Weimar's
Duke there runs an entire series of epigrammes
that revert to praise of Christiane, with the repeated

assurance that in her he has obtained happiness—
the happiness for which he longed—and he has obtained it completely. All in all one cannot say that
Goethe was pretentious or exacting; that he was
quite easily satisfied is more nearly the whole truth.

CHAPTER III

THE FRENCH REVOLUTION: GOETHE'S ATTITUDE TOWARD IT—*Der Grosskophta*: THE AFFAIR OF THE NECKLACE

GOETHE had begun his career with the youthful, revolutionary and rebellious aversion to the nobility and the princes that is natural to a son of the people. But so far as he personally was concerned, he lifted himself up above the petty caste in which he was born; he became superior to the middle-class society of the Germany of his day. He had found in time an outlet, a field of activity, and possibilities for development at the court of a prince who, though subordinate, was nevertheless sovereign. Goethe had come to see how the good and fruitful can be accomplished when and if the doughtiest and cleverest has his hand on the helm.

Moreover, his life had taught him how much importance—and how little—can be attached to the judgment of the masses.

He had grown to be forty years old and, as La Rochefoucauld has said, he who has lived for forty years without having come to detest men has never loved them. Goethe had loved men. And though he can in no sense of the word be called a misanthrope, he had been made painfully familiar with the ignorance, the envy, the prejudice of the human

29

horde. He had come to see that, as a rule, the opinion of the majority is either a display of stupidity, or a manifestation of rudeness. He had come to cherish the settled conviction that what the masses want can never be anything else than food and drink and general well-being. He could not appreciate the righteous demand on the part of the poor that they be allowed to earn their daily bread without becoming slaves in the attempt. The word liberty had to a large degree lost its charm for him. The time was now far distant when he and his young comrades on the *Frankfurter Gelehrte Anzeigen* characterised themselves as those to whom the name of political liberty had such a sweet sound (*so süss schallt*).

Like all ambitious and ingenious spirits, Goethe had from the very first felt an unrestrained longing for liberty. This explains why the action in *Götz* is being constantly interrupted with toasts to liberty. But his life had taught him how differently different people understand liberty. He had seen that it can be longed for personally or socially or artistically or politically. Refractoriness, free thinking, defiance of social customs, opposition to art, radicalism—all of these bore a direct relation to the general concept of liberty. There was the individual who longed for freedom from the religious and political point of view, but opposed the same principle in art. There was the other who longed for it in art, but rejected it in politics and religion. Liberty indeed was somewhat like a chemical element that may or may not enter into composition with other elements, such as nationalism and democracy. It was made the opposite of coercion, but not the opposite of a voluntary subjection to such coercion as that of moral discipline, or that of metrics, or social forms, or reasonable law: *Und das Gesetz nur kann uns Freiheit geben.*

At the beginning, he too had regarded liberty as being one with personal unruliness. But he had been called to educate the Duke of Weimar, and thereby himself.

Then came the French Revolution. The storming of the Bastille, as a symbolic action, caused general rejoicing in the minds of all liberty-loving men throughout Europe; and it did actually inaugurate the great deeds that followed. When closely examined, however, it was a pitiable and contemptible affair. The Bastille had long since ceased to be the prison of despotism. Its few remaining inmates were confessed criminals. The one hundred and twenty disabled soldiers that guarded it were brave and noble veterans. Its commandant was a humane man and an officer of superior honor. They who rushed in when the guards kindly opened the doors were blood-thirsty ruffians. If the practical signal for the Revolution was an ill omen, the theory that was proclaimed was no better. Sièyes posited this presumptuous statement regarding the third estate: "It is nothing; but it is to be everything." Goethe obviously had a vivid idea as to what was to be expected from and of the citizenry.

At the same time he received the impression that the age was venal; that it had its price for every buyer; that it was at the disposal af anyone whose audacity and arrogance would speculate on its bigotry; that those who would could lead it around by the nose. By the populace, however, he was poles removed from understanding the lowest stratum of society. The clergy had prepared men's minds to believe anything, quite regardless as to whether it was credible or not, and to manifest the most humble respect for the cultivators and spokesmen of all that was most glaringly at odds with sound judgment and reasoned intentions.

Goethe follows the life of Cagliostro and looks into the family history of the Balsamos in Palermo as well, for he learns that the son, Giuseppe Balsamo, who disappeared after having perpetrated a number of mad pranks, and the notorious Count Cagliostro are identical. He studies the history of the Balsamos and investigates even their correspondence with the same thoroughness that he is wont to employ in studying a plant family in botany. He observes with alert interest the triumphs over credulity celebrated by the boldest adventurers and humbug-makers known to modern times. He investigates the way in which deceived, semi-deceived and deceivers study these people and flout sound common sense. It captivates him to follow Balsamo's metamorphosis from the obscure beginning up to and through succeeding stages of Marchese Pellegrini and Count Cagliostro. He indulges at the same time his inveterate proneness to mystification when he secures an introduction to the Balsamos by claiming, without hesitation, to be an Englishman, delegated to bring a letter from Cagliostro, then living in London.

After the affair of the necklace, the immediate precursor of the Revolution in France, had aroused the suspicion of the masses, shaken the throne and exposed the criminal gullibility of the society that centred about the French court, Goethe wove his impressions of the lawsuit together with the impressions of Cagliostro, and wrote his drama entitled *Der Grosskophta*. It is admittedly a weak, unsatisfactory product, though by no means either thin or void.

Consequently, he did not take an especially vigorous delight in liberty when the Revolution broke out. He understood it as little as did Taine or Nietzsche after him. For him it was merely an eruption of envy and avarice. He did not perceive the earthquake; the great historical pulse in it all passed by him unnoticed, unregarded.

Long before the Revolution actually began, the citizenry of France knew precisely what it wished to substitute for the then prevailing feudal monarchy. It wished to abolish absolute power and the rapacious lordship of the nobility. It was republican in its way of feeling; but it wanted the propertied classes to rule. If it hated the Catholic Church it was not because of an inborn hostility to religion but because the Church made common cause with the rulers in fleecing the people. Long before the Revolution broke out the peasant class also knew precisely what it wanted. It wanted the land that it cultivated in chronic hunger, martyred to the point of despair from the taxes it had to pay to the State, the impost it was forced to contribute to the landed proprietors, the tithes it had to raise for the clergy, and the villeinage imposed by all three in union one with another. The ever-increasing distress into which the people sank gave rise to a spirit of rebellion and brought to the fore the very necessity of a well-known law of nature.

It was far too petty then, when, in the first unsuccessful piece Goethe wrote against the spirit of
the Revolution, *Der Bürgergeneral,* he has the story
revolve around the fact that one man wants to have
access to the pantry of another, to steal his loppered
cream and put his sugar on it. In this way "the sweet
and sour cream of Liberty and Equality" are supposed to be mixed in the right proportions. Here,
as in the imperfect and incomplete but interesting
drama entitled *Die Aufgeregten,* the rebels demand
absolutely nothing that is justified.

We have pointed out above that Goethe took all
his themes from his own time, or from the Antique
and the Renaissance. Especially do his themes belong to the period from 1789 to 1799, from his
fortieth to his fiftieth years. *Der Grosskophta, Die
Aufgeregten, Das Mädchen von Oberkirch, Der
Bürgergeneral,* and *Unterhaltungen deutscher Ausgewanderter* are all based either on the theories or
the effects of the Revolution. *Die natürliche Tochter* depicts the civic order of things such as existed
previous to the Revolution, events that took place
when Goethe was about twenty-four years old. In
this group belongs also *Hermann und Dorothea* in
which the Revolution forms the background and sets
the action in motion. Among his most valuable
works on the Revolution, and written at the time of
it, must be mentioned also his excellent monograph,
Die Campagne in Frankreich (1792).

Goethe's correspondence shows that he sympa-
thised with the people in their sufferings. Their
lot in the days preceding the Revolution was not
easy. On April 3, 1782, he wrote: "The curse
of being obliged to waste the very marrow of the

country makes the maturing of pleasure an impossibility." On June 20, 1784, he wrote: "The poor people have to carry the bundle and little difference does it make whether it is too heavy on the one side or the other." In the *Venezianische Epigramme* we find this vitriolic comment on the conservatives in Germany:

Jene Menschen sind toll, so sagt Ihr von heftigen Sprechern,
Die wir in Frankreich laut hören auf Strassen und Markt:
Mir auch scheinen sie toll; doch redet ein Toller in Freiheit
Weise Sprüche, wenn ach! Weisheit in Sklaven verstummt.

Heartily displeased as he was at the imitations of the French Revolution on German soil, he was also worried over the reaction that Jacobinism in France was evoking in Germany.

Though the Minister of the little Duchy of Sachse-Weimar was intensely interested in the affairs of the commonalty and tried in many ways to improve them, he never really had a clear idea as to the burden of injustice under which the poor were laboring in a kingdom like the France of that day. He was consequently in error as to the justice with which the elementary powers in France arose in rebellion.

As a whole, the elementary, the basic, in history did not appeal to Goethe. He appreciated only the humanly great as it confronted him in *personal form*. Just as he derived his conception of the Renaissance from such real personalities as Raphael, Cellini, Reuchlin and his own heroes, Götz and Egmont, just so did he appreciate the Revolution only when he stood face to face with its executor, Napoleon Bonaparte. The great strength in the powers

of the Revolution left him untouched. For him the
Revolution was the inorganic, the disorderly, the
break in that chain of evolution of which he came
very near being the first discoverer. When the
Revolution started in 1789, he was more engrossed
with the ideas of evolution than at any other period
of his life. Order was for him what we call composition, but composition in development. In the
vegetable kingdom he had seen the root develop
into a stem, the stem transformed into a leaf, and
the leaf re-formed into a flower. In the animal
kingdom he had seen the vertebrae transformed into
the bones of the skull. In no case had there been
a sudden leap; it was all merely a matter of transition. In geology he had followed the slow, mil-
lenial changes and had passionately combatted the
doctrine of a sudden, volcanic overturning.

As such a sudden, volcanic overturning the Revolution filled him with horror.

II

The first of Goethe's works immediately connected
with the French Revolution is *Der Grosskophta,*
1791. It is especially important because of its direct
bearing on contemporary events. After the fashion
of *Clavigo,* it deals not only with individuals who
were still living but with events that had taken place
quite recently; some of them had become closed
issues only five years before. It is the famous story
of the necklace that Goethe has dramatized.

The Cardinal of Rohan appears under the name
of *Der Domherr.* Jeanne de St. Remy de Valois,

Countess of Lamotte, is known as *Die Marquise*. She was the adventuress who took advantage of the Cardinal's zeal in order to ingratiate herself into the favor of Marie Antoinette, and who inveigled him into buying the necklace at a cost of over a million and a half. Her tool, Nicole le Guay, called d'Olivia, who was disguised as the Queen and represented her at the nocturnal meeting in the palace garden of Versailles, is known as *Die Nichte*. And the leading character is introduced simply as *Der Graf*, though the Count of Cagliostro himself had nothing to do with the affair. He was imprisoned because of his intimate association with Rohan. His name is mentioned but once, as "Rostro." The remaining characters, as is the case with *Die natür-liche Tochter*, are nameless. Goethe's unhappy fondness for abstractions, connected with his preference for types, is responsible for the fact that the *dramatis personae* are given rank, such as the Colonel, the Knight, the Dean, the Count, and nothing more; it does not follow, however, that they display the individuality which the rank implies. As to the style, it leaves much to be desired. As to the drama itself, it is well constructed, dramatic, and certainly theatrical, unsympathetic though it may be as a work of art.

The drama portrays a colossal swindler who calls to his aid belief in spirits and conviction of the reasonableness of miracles in order to impress those about him and thereby gain power, though it is not clear from the drama what he does or wishes to do with this power. Without having any direct connection with him, though supported by him, we have the operation of an unscrupulous pair: There

is the Marquis who seduces his niece that has been
trained to appear partly as an innocent girl in a
Masonic ceremony, partly as the Princess in some
relation to the Dean; and there is the Marquise,
the shrewd, keen-sensed malefactress who pulls the
wires. Since the young niece is not at all inclined
to serve as the tool for repeated frauds, she tells
the Knight, in whom she has confidence and for
whom she feels affection, of her wretched position,
prays to him for help, and betrays the entire intrigue
to the ruling Prince. The drama closes with the
imprisonment of the culprits.

The conduct of the Knight is not very chivalric.
Since the entire action concerns so unexciting and
flat an affair as the pilfering of a necklace by a pair
of cut-throats and their deception in dealing with
an admitted dunderhead, and since there is not one
glimpse of humor or comedy in the drama, it must
be set down as a failure.

But this does not prevent it from being a substantial contribution to the psychology of unctuous
prophets and their gullible adherers. Among Goethe's contemporary friends, Lavater believed firmly
in Cagliostro; in this way the phenomenon came
personally near to Goethe himself. When he wrote
his drama the Cardinal of Rohan was only fifty-
seven, Cagliostro only forty-eight. He explained
to his followers that he was in actuality eighty, but
by using an elixir which he sold in bottles, he looked
as though he were forty.

Since the poet originally planned to treat the
theme as a text for an opera, he wrote a few verses
under the rubric of *Kophtische Lieder*. They contain in condensed form the action of the entire

drama.   Let us look at the first lines of one of these
poems:

> Thöricht, auf Bess'rung der Thoren zu harren!
> Kinder der Klugheit, o habet die Narren
> Eben zum Narren auch, wie sich's gehört!

Or examine the following lines from the second of
these songs:

> Auf des Glückes grosser Wage
> Steht die Zunge selten ein.
> Du musst steigen oder sinken,
> Du musst herrschen und gewinnen
> Oder dienen und verlieren,
> Leiden oder triumphiren,
> Amboss oder Hammer sein.

Compare the great skill of such verses with the
affectation and sentimentality that characterise the
monologue in prose from the *Grosskophta*.   The
Dean speaks:

A profound stillness prophesies to me my immediate good
fortune.   I hear not a sound in these gardens which otherwise, owing to the kindness of the Prince, are open to all
pleasure seekers, and on pleasant evenings are frequently
visited by a lonely, unhappy lover, and even more frequently
by a joy-crowned, loving couple.   I thank thee, divine light,
that thou seest fit to envelope thyself to-day in a quiet veil!
Thou delightest me, O brisk wind, thou threatening, murky
rain-clouds, that thou wardest off the frivolous folk who
generally swarm back and forth through these paths, fill the
arbors with laughter, and rob others of their sweetest joy
without securing any genuine joy for themselves.   O ye
beautiful trees, how ye seem to have grown in the last few
summers!

It would appear that there lay in German prose
a hidden temptation for Goethe to go over to the

Kanzleistil of emotion. Here, as in *Die Geschwister*, he evokes and justifies the question: Was the fault inherent in the language, or was it his own? The language, we dare not forget, was undeveloped in his day. We have already seen that, in the *Venezianische Epigramme*, he laid the blame on the language; on the German language.

CHAPTER IV

THE FRENCH REVOLUTION: *Der Bürgergeneral;*
Das Mädchen von Oberkirch

THE following little drama, *Der Bürgergeneral,*
is the product of Goethe's activity as director of
the Weimar Theatre. A number of unpretentious
French dramas, in German versions, had been performed in Weimar and Scapin, who had received
in German the ill-sounding name of "Schnaps," was
played with marked success by a certain Herr Beck
who had come to Weimar in 1793. Goethe created
the Scapin-figure of this drama for him, and chris-
tened it "Schnaps." There is, incidentally, this peculiarity about awkward German farces: In order
to evoke laughter from the plain people, they pooh-
pooh probability, whereas laughter is excited in the
farces of other civilized nations through inconsis-
tencies that are really born of an unimpeachable
inner logic.

In a country town that belongs to a liberal, refined, young nobleman, there lives an exceedingly
happy newly married couple, Görge and Röse.
Schnaps comes to Röse's father, Märten, and informs him that the renowned Jacobins in Paris have
heard of his cleverness, and in order to win him
over to the cause of freedom and equality have just
appointed him Citizen's General. As proof of all

41

this, he has in his possession a tri-colored cocarde and a regimental coat, which, in reality, he had stolen from a French soldier who had been taken prisoner. The real purpose of his visit, which Görge had welcomed in no way, is to get a square meal free of charge. He breaks open the cupboard in the house and finds a large plate of loppered milk. While the coming revolution is being proclaimed in the village, he regales himself with milk, cream, sugar, and rye-bread. But just as he is consuming his repast, Görge appears on the scene and gives him a sound trouncing. The cries and screams call the attention of the district judge to the unusual proceedings. That functionary hastens up to the scene of activity and, finding the cocarde and the uniform in the house, is on the point of arresting its occupants. But the sensible nobleman appears in time and adjusts such embarrassments as have arisen.

That does not in truth seem to have much connection with the French Revolution; and yet it does: The entire drama is interspersed with references to it. Schnaps demands that Märten shall be free and equal; he imagines he already sees the people dancing around the tree of liberty. When Märten tells the nobleman that Schnaps first acted kindly toward him only later to break open the cupboard and take whatever he wanted, the nobleman replies: "Just like his comrades! In the provinces, where his type have carried on their work of devastation, and where gullible idiots at first rejoiced over what was taking place, they began with compliments and promises and ended with violence, theft, and banishment of the high-minded people."

It has a rather depressing effect to feel that Goethe saw nothing in the Jacobins but criminals, and that in order to give a poignant portrayal of their character he could think of nothing better than the appropriation by force of a bottle of loppered milk. Moreover, it is distinctly aggravating to think that he wasted his time writing this insipid nonentity and left the serious and in some ways significant drama of the Revolution from the same year, *Die Aufgeregten,* lie as a fragment. The middle and conclusion of it are only hurriedly sketched. It is a lasting pity that he did not finish it instead of *Der Burgergeneral.*

Die Aufgeregten is well planned, gives an excellent impression of the echo made by the Revolution in a rustic village, and contains some interesting characters, one of whom especially stands out clear and distinct among Goethe's heroines.

An estate is being managed by an intelligent Countess on behalf of her young son. For no less than forty years the peasantry have litigated against the estate, which demands soccage and the up-keep of certain roads. The peasants consider themselves exempt on the ground that an agreement had been entered into which limited the rights of the Countess and protected them. But the document has in some unexplained way disappeared. If the Countess had only herself to take into consideration, she would have dropped the case long ago for the sake of humanity. But since she is merely the administratrix of her son she feels duty bound to have the case brought up before the court at Wetzlar.

In the meantime the ideas of the Revolution have reached the neighborhood, and the peasantry is

aroused by a certain "Tinker Politician." He is the
grandson of Holberg's [1] politicaster and makes
himself out as such. He is called Breme von Bremenfeld, is a barber and a surgeon, holds himself in
high esteem both professionally and politically, and
unites Hermann von Breme's conviction of his unusual ability as a political leader with Gert West-
phaler's smooth loquaciousness. He is really superior to the latter in that he has a measure of talent
as an orator. Goethe has amused himself by having
him use expressions in one of his speeches which remind of Antony's oration in Shakespeare's *Julius
Caesar.*

We are introduced to an entire galaxy of personages. There are a couple of young girls of the burgher class, one of whom, Breme's daughter, is in
love with a young baron who pays her importunate
court; there are a number of peasants; there is the
tutor of the Countess's young son who is excellently
portrayed, in just a few strokes, as a Jacobin fanatic; there is an intelligent and deserving councillor
who is the spokesman of Goethe's own ideas and
who, somewhat like Goethe, inspires respect because
of his bearing; and there is the Countess's young
daughter Friederike who, though only half grown,
is a sportswoman full of family pride, veracious,
determined, a hater of nonsense and effusive bu-

[1] Holberg wrote "Den Politiske Kandestöber" in 1722, one of
the most fruitful years in the history of Northern literature. The
comedy has thirty characters as contrasted with the fifteen in *Die
Aufgeregten*, a title that Goethe gave his play only after much
deliberation and hesitation. He had at first decided to call it
"Breme von Bremenfeld." Had he done so, its relation to Holberg's comedy would have been more evident. Holberg's influence
on Goethe is even more pronounced than Brandes' comments
would lead one to believe.   —TRANSLATOR.

reaucracy. On hearing that the cringing officer is suspected of having made off with the lost document, but that countless difficulties are in the way of a definite settlement of the affair, she levels her gun at his head and would have shot him down without any more ado had he not been frightened into making a clean confession and telling where the document could be found.

There is in her something that we rarely find in Goethe's characters—inveterate energy and indiscriminate resoluteness. The action itself is diverting; the spirit of the play is humane; the jocular conception of the German revolutionists is quite free from rancor. It is moreover interesting to see a Holbergean character taken over and varied by Goethe. It is only a pity that in one single scene this character is lifted out of the comic style where it belongs by poetic right: This is where Breme uses the most fearful expressions in abusing his daughter because she refuses to be his blind tool against the Baron, whom he wishes to capture and lock up. Such a move is a novel and unmotivated testimony to the fact that the comedy was not Goethe's strong point.

It is also unfortunate that the excellently planned drama of the Revoultion, *Das Mädchen von Oberkirch,* the manuscript to the introductory scenes of which was not found until 1895, remained a fragment. The little that was worked out gives an exalted idea of the rest of which only an indistinct glimpse can be derived from the outline as found among Goethe's papers. The action takes place in Strassburg during one of the first years of the Revolution, and is introduced by a conversation between two people of noble birth. The Countess, whose estates have been plundered, sits knitting in her apartment in the city, when her nephew, the Baron, enters and tells her of her sons and daughters who have emigrated but who have escaped only with their lives. The sons are in the army [in Coblenz, then], the daughters have found a quiet place of refuge; they embroider and sew in order to make their living.

After a great deal of hesitation and self-evoked argument the Baron comes out with a statement telling just why he has appeared: He intends to get married and to marry out of his class. The Countess is shocked; but she becomes rebellious when she learns that the object of his choice is her own lady in waiting or companion, Marie. The Baron shows that his conduct is not simply the outcome of warm feeling; it is the result of good politics as well. Under the present threatening conditions he will do best to marry a woman from the people. Moreover, Marie is the Countess's foster-daughter rather than her servant. The conversation is interrupted by Pastor Manner, a young preacher, whose assistance the Baron needs as an offset to the aunt. Marie has really all sorts of virtues: She is pretty without being arrogant, amiable without being coquetish, obliging without being self-humiliating. But when it becomes evident that Manner is also seriously in love with Marie, the latter emphasizes the political uselessness, even the unreasonableness, of the intended union, to which the Baron, as we in time learn, has as yet not acquired the consent of his beloved. The powers that be (in Manner's words: the rabble) will pay no attention to such a marriage. The Baron would, to be sure, not free himself from suspicion by this course, but he would make Marie also seem a fit subject for distrust.

The outline of the play contains only a few local names and designations, hardly thirty words in all, exclusive of the verbs. I believe I catch a glimpse of just this much from this fact: It is Manner and not the Baron to whom Marie feels drawn. As one of the common people, she is favored by the *sanssculottists*. Moreover, it is her beauty that brings it about that she figures in the Cathedral as the goddess of reason, in which capacity she is worshipped and adored. But the rôle is contrary to her nature; she protests against the ideas whose interpreter she has been forced to become. She is thrown into prison and the two men who love her take common counsel as to how she can be rescued. This is a guess and is not meant to be anything more; but it seems to me that the words of the outline support it.

To the group of plays from the Revolution there belongs finally the larger and more significant work entitled *Die natürliche Tochter*. But since it was not planned until 1799, and not completed and produced until 1803, discussion of it must be postponed. It shows evidence of a complete change in the poet's dramatic style.

CHAPTER V

Die Campagne in Frankreich, 1792: GOETHE ON THE BATTLE FIELD—*Reineke Fuchs*

IF we wish to see Goethe at his freshest and happiest as a student of the Revolution, we have to read his *Campagne in Frankreich*, 1792. Though the book was not published until 1820, it consists exclusively of his diary which he kept on the field during the action. It is a notable piece of work because of the ease and calm with which it is written.

In July, 1790, shortly after his second return from Italy, he had accompanied Karl August to Silesia where the latter took part in the manouvres while Goethe himself spent most of his time studying Kant and Osteology. When the Duke, in 1782, participated in the campaign of the Allied Powers against revolutionary France, Goethe (after one visit in Frankfort and another in Mayence) followed Karl August to the front, and met him at the close of August in Longwy. The campaign was an absolute failure; it was abandoned when the French were victorious at Valmy. The retreat of the Allied Powers was an affair of sheer dissolution. Goethe realized, in person and at first hand, how completely he had underestimated even the outward strength the French Revolution could develop. The impression, however, did not lessen his aversion.

The feature of it all that especially gratifies the reader of his diary is his perfect equanimity coupled with his insatiable desire for knowledge. Nothing escapes him. No optical phenomenon such as the refraction of a colored shard in a fen—which evokes a treatise on the science of color. No rare osteological phenomenon, nor any mineralogical one either, fails to receive due and disciplined attention from him. During the battle at Valmy he studies the beautiful spec. s of stone found in the neighborhood. During the sie, of Mayence he searches in the charnel house among the decayed bones: "The best ones had already fall into the hands of the surgeons."

He narrates and portrays with vividness. One sees one's self the young girls who received the Allied forces in Verdun, and about whom Victor Hugo has sung. Goethe seems not to have learned th terrible fate that was subsequently in store for them. He depicts the bayonet squad as it rushes headlong down a steep declivity, like a waterfall; and he does so with a clarity which no other author, whose specialty was the depiction of the visible (Théophile Gautier for example), has ever surpassed.

Goethe did not experience cannon fever. He gloried in the fact that every danger tended only to make his mind more bold, even rash. Amid the thunder of the cannon he calmly rides up to Fort La Lune. He studies his condition and is satisfied with his pulse while under fire. Still he notices that something unusual is taking place within him: "It is as if one were in a very hot spot and were so completely permeated by the heat that one feels one's self in complete harmony with the surrounding element."

On September 19, 1792, we have a remarkable utterance from him. He tells how in the morning everyone thought only of bayonetting and gobbling up all the Frenchmen, and how he himself felt absolute confidence in an army such as that commanded by the Duke of Brunswick. After the unsuccessful attack, however, each man fought for himself; dependence upon one's neighbor was out of the question. Finally someone called out to Goethe asking him what he had to say since it had become a custom for him to be the enlivening element in the party. He replied: "From today and from this place there begins a new epoch in the history of the world, and you can say that you were present."

The incident has been regarded with suspicion. Some have felt that it was a later fabrication, a parallel observation having been found in the diary of a German officer, a diary, incidentally, which Goethe borrowed while elaborating his own monograph. But he must have used the expression; for he tells in his book on the siege of Mayence that the officers who heard this prophecy afterwards believed that it had been literally fulfilled, for the French abolished at that time the old Catholic calendar. His remark, as he himself emphasizes, naturally has a quite different meaning. Even before the battle of Valmy Goethe felt that a new era was dawning.

At no time does he appear to better advantage. He portrays his various experiences, his weariness and hunger, his longing for a bed and something to eat, his blind confidence in the fate that seizes him while in the midst of all manner of infectious diseases, his joy on receiving his trunk and with it his manuscript on the science of colors. He makes some quite discriminating remarks on the difference in the character of the Prussian and the Austrian non-commissioned officer, expresses his thoughts concerning a monument from the age of the Antonies which he sees now for the second time, and discusses his relation to the philosophy of Hemsterhuis. This latter inspires him to set forth straightway his own definition of the beautiful. It runs in this vein: "The sight of the law-abiding animate in its greatest activity and perfection which goads us on to re-production and brings us to feel that we are animate and in the greatest of activity ourselves." The definition has been declared to be ingenious; if so, it may also be described as droll.

Die Belagerung von Mainz gives a profound impression of Goethe's innate humanitarianism and personal courage. When Mayence is taken and—together with the French garrison—the Germans, who, as republicans, had aided the French, file out, the common people became of course enraged at these German republicans. Just in front of Goethe's house there is seated on horseback a tall, handsome man; at his side is his sweetheart in man's attire and likewise very beautiful. He is an architect suspected of pillaging and incendiarism. The rabble rush upon them in the attempt to injure them.

Thereupon Goethe, who has been watching from his window, springs down into the street and tells them to halt in such a commanding tone that they immediately desist from further attacks. Goethe succeeds in saving the life of the man that had been threatened.

To a friend who cannot forbear saying that, with

actual danger to himself, he has saved the life of a stranger, perhaps of a criminal, Goethe makes the remark that has been quoted time out of mind: "There is simply something in my nature that makes me rather commit an injustice than submit to disorder."

The expression is constantly being twisted so as to mean just the opposite of what Goethe indubitably had in mind. Thus, not long since, the celebrated German General Keim used it against the Goethe League as evidence that Goethe would have found the judicial murder of the Spaniard Francisco Ferrer wholly justifiable. Quite the contrary; he pleads here for the utmost clemency; and he understands by any injustice that he may be obliged to commit the tempering of justice with mercy, or the allowing of mercy to pass for justice.

The remark shows how far removed he was from bloodthirstiness toward the revolutionists, who were in truth directly contrary to his innermost being.

After the conquest of Mayence, Goethe turned back, visited his brother-in-law, Schlosser, in Heidelberg and his mother in Frankfort. Frau Aja was now living in pecuniary embarrassment because of the war tax which the French army under Dumouriez had levied on the city. She was forced to sell her wine cellar, her books and her paintings. Goethe was not yet financially able to save her from this loss and privation.

II

After his return to Weimar Goethe took in hand a bit of work which was of a quite different nature from anything that had formerly engaged his attention: He began a revision of a folk poem, the old beast epic on the cunning of the fox, in hexameters, just as it had been treated when the oldest parts of it were written in Latin in the tenth, eleventh, and twelfth centuries (*Ecbasis, Isengrimus, Reinardus Vulpus*). The French redactions of the thirteenth century had greatly expanded the material; the Dutch *Reinaert* was made the foundation for all later versions in German. In 1752 Gottsched had published the prose translation which Goethe undertook to versify under the title: *Heinrichs von Alkmar Reincke der Fuchs.*

The exercise in writing hexameters which the *Römische Elegien* and the *Venezianische Epigramme* had given Goethe, together with the inclination that he had gradually developed to see preëminence in ancient art forms, beguiled him into the oddity of choosing the hexameter as the cloak for the naïveté and satire of the Middle Ages. Form and substance do not in this case coincide, they do not harmonize. The hexameter is ill adapted to the German language and has on that account been practically abandoned in our day.

It was dissatisfaction with the age and perhaps embitterment over the complaint against Louis XVI which caused Goethe to have recourse to the old beast saga: "Had I hitherto," he writes in the *Campagne in Frankreich,* "been obliged to surfeit myself to the point of loathing with street, market, and mob scenes, it was really inspiring to look into this mirror for courts and regents. For though the human race is even here quite naturally portrayed in its unfeigned brutishness, everything happens, if

not in an exemplary, at least in a jocund way, and
good humor is nowhere impaired."

It is a diligent piece of work Goethe has done;
so far as the very art of language is concerned it
is quite and entirely worthy of him. Oehlenschläger,
however, who translated it into Danish in 1806,
used exorbitant language when he said: "In my
estimation, *Reineke Fuchs*, in Goethe's version, is
the most beautiful imitation we have of the Homeric
poems."

Though the work was revised by Goethe's aesthetic friends—Knebel, Wieland, Herder—before
being sent to the publisher, a few linguistic and
metrical rough spots have remained. A verse
such as

Fehlet Euch alles im Hause, so gebt eine Maus her—mit
        dieser
Bin ich am besten versorgt.

cannot be acquitted of the charge of an awkward
dactyl: *Maus her mit*. In a verse such as the following,

Selbst verschont ich des Königs nicht, und mancherlei Tücken
    Uebt ich kühnlich an ihm

the meaning has been reduced to haziness for the
sake of the meter; for it is obvious that the unblem-
ished prose of it would be: *Sogar des Königs verschont ich nicht.*

There are passages in which Goethe did not exercise sufficient care in comparing the old texts, with
the result that negligible but amusing errors have
crept in, for the familiar reason that one of his
predecessors made them only to be imitated by an-

other and later. In *Reinaert,* for example, we read
een paer Kerspetten; in *Reineke* we read, as the
result of an error in imitation, *gude Kersebern.*
Kerspetten are waffles; *Kersebern* are cherries. Goethe
the therefore refers in his work to this queer menu:

So ging inch mit ihm und bracht' ihm behende Kirschen
und Butter.

We understand full well Goethe's delight in ap-
propriating and reproducing all the old popular experience and wisdom of the animal fables, so much
of which applied to his own time, indeed to all times.
It makes delightful reading. We are highly amused,
by way of illustration, when the fox devotes his eloquence to picking at the Pope's legates, abbots, pre-
lates and nuns, and when the badger replies: "Uncle,
I find it quite remarkable that you confess the sins
of the others: No one would make a better monk
than you."

And how imperishable is that story of the peasant
and the serpent! The former found the latter
caught in a trap—and freed his potential foe after
he had taken a quite solemn oath never again to
harm him. A short while elapsed, and the serpent,
beginning to feel the inconvenient pangs of hunger,
would strangle the man and devour him. The man
complained; the serpent indulged in a political
affirmation:

"Das ist mein Dank? Das hab ich verdient?" So rief er.
    "Und hast Du
Nicht geschworen den theursten Eid?"—Da sagte die
    Schlange:
"Leider nöthiget mich der Hunger; ich kann mir nicht
    helfen;
Noth erkennt kein Gebot, und so besteht es zu Rechte."

That is the political morality of the twentieth century, just as it was of the twelfth century.

Throughout the entire work, large in volume and poetic in content, Goethe has interpolated but two brief passages in which he has given expression to his personal convictions: The one is quite in the spirit of the poem of the Middle Ages, which never lacked a reason to see the clergy in a culpable light; in the other, Goethe voices his aversion to all revolutionists. These few lines have been attacked with imbecile violence as grating against the fundamental tone of the old beast epic; and they have been defended with a zeal that is in no way less exaggerated. They are found in the eighth song, lines 152-160, and lines 171-177. The passage on the clergy runs as follows:

Freilich sollten die geistlichen Herrn sich besser betragen,
Manches könnten sie thun, wofern sie es heimlich vollbrächten;
Aber sie schonen uns nicht, uns andere Laien, und treiben
Alles, was Ihnen beliebt, vor unsern Augen, als wären
Wir mit Blindheit geschlagen; allein wir sehen zu deutlich,
Ihre Gelübde gefallen den guten Herren so wenig,
Als sie dem sündigen Freunde der weltlichen Werke behagen.

Apart from the solemnity of the style, there is really nothing to prevent this from having stood in the old folk poem. Goethe's lines on the men of the Revolution sound undeniably more modern:

Doch das Schlimmste find' ich den Dünkel des irrigen Wahnes
Der die Menschen ergreift, es könne Jeder im Taumel
Seines heftigen Wollens die Welt beherrschen und richten.
Hielte doch Jeder sein Weib und sine Kinder in Ordnung,
Wüsste sein trotzig Gesinde zu bändigen, könnte sich stille

Wenne die Thoren verschwenden, in müssigem Leben er-
       freuen!
Aber wie sollte die Welt sich verbessern? Es lässt sich ein
       Jeder
Alles zu und will mit Gewalt die Andern bezwingen
Und so sinken wir tiefer und immer tiefer in's Arge.

These two short passages contain literally everything there is of Goethe himself in *Reineke Fuchs*.
It cannot be denied that they express not merely a
pronounced indifference to politics, but an excessive
insusceptibility to the revolution that was then taking place in the minds of the people. They express
also a certain underbred satisfaction with existing
circumstances. This is seen most clearly in the conservatism to which the latter quotation gives voice.

CHAPTER VI

SCHILLER AND BAGGESEN; SCHILLER AND DEN-
MARK — SCHILLER'S YOUTH; SCHILLER AND
VOLTAIRE; SCHILLER AND CAMPISTRON —
SCHILLER AS HISTORIAN AND PHILOSOPHER
—BEGINNING OF THE FRIENDSHIP BETWEEN
GOETHE AND SCHILLER

IN 1790, Jens Baggesen visited Friedrich Schiller in Jena. In June, 1791, he received, through a note from Countess Schimmelmann, wife of the Minister of State, the unfounded news concerning Schiller's death, fourteen years before it occurred. Though Baggesen, smitten as he was with all the mawkish sentimentality of the age, exaggerated the expression of his grief (in his language it was despair for which he asks Providence to forgive him), the effect of the rumor made a profound impression, not merely on Baggesen himself, but on all the men and women who at that time stood highest in cultured Denmark.

Count Schimmelmann and his wife, also the Danish minister at The Hague, Schubart and his wife, who had previously planned to go on an excursion from Copenhagen to Hellebaek, now united to celebrate Schiller's memory at this beautiful spot, at that time isolated and charming because of its very wildness. Baggesen and Sophie von Haller, together with the above mentioned company, betook themselves to the home of Count Schimmelmann at Sölyst, where the Emilie fount now flows. Baggesen,[2] without the slightest foreboding of the unpleasant news, had latterly been so completely taken up with Schiller that when he opened his trunk he found that the books which he had sent on ahead for recreation in bad weather consisted almost exclusively of the works of Friedrich Schiller.

They had planned to sing Schiller's *Ode to Joy* under the most agreeable circumstances. Now they had to listen in abject sadness to a recital of it by Baggesen. He began: *Freude, schöner Götterfunken, Tochter aus Elysium.* The clarinets, flutes and horns joined in. They sang the chorus, the ecstatic hymn of human love, the expression of a stronger faith in a loving Province in fact than Schiller maintained in daily practice:

Seyd unschlungen, Millionen!
Diesen Kuss der ganzen Welt.
Brüder! Ueberm Sternenzelt
Muss ein lieber Vater wohmen.

Baggesen had written several verses in German in honor of Schiller and promised on oath to live true to his spirit. Then four young couples of youths and maidens, clad in white and crowned with blossoms, entered and danced as shepherds and shepherdesses.

---

[2] Baggesen was captivated, soul and body, by the *Sturm und Drang* movement in Germany. He adored Voss and worshipped Klopstock. He considered himself a disciple of Wieland and married Albrecht von Haller's granddaughter. His friendship for Reinhold lasted until his death. But before Schiller he bowed in reverent admiration. If his grief at the news of Schiller's alleged death seems extraordinary it was in keeping with his life. It was difficult for him to seem or be unaffected. —TRANSLATOR.

The following day Baggesen read aloud scenes from *Don Carlos,* passages from the unfinished history on the defection of the Netherlands, and poems such as the *Götter Griechenlands* and the *Künstler.* In Hellebaek, the very name of which reminded of Hellas, they felt hellenically disposed:

> Unser todter Freund soll leben,
> Alle Freunde, stimmet ein!
> Und sein Geist soll uns umschweben
> Hier in Hellas' Himmelhain.

Owing to the condition of his lungs, Schiller had in reality been near death's door. And just as the unsubstantiated report of his demise reached Copenhagen, the true enlightenment came bearing on the wretched economic plight in which the poet was slowly but surely pining away. Then it was that the two Danish friends with German training, two men who had been brought into an alliance by the familiar *Weltbürgergeist,* Duke Frederick Christian of Augustenborg and Count Ernst Schimmelmann, agreed to assure Schiller an annual pension of 1000 talers (3600 marks) for the coming three years. With this aid the poet could resume his work. It would otherwise most probably have been closed with *Don Carlos.* (It is difficult to refrain from the thought that had Schiller died at the age of eighty-five instead of forty-five, and had he reaped the modern harvest in the way of royalties from his dramas, Mr. Rockefeller's income would hardly have surpassed his.)

At the close of 1791 he wrote to Körner:

I at last have time to read and collect and work for eternity. Before the three years shall have elapsed, I can find a position in Denmark, or the Mayence plan shall have materialized, and then I shall be fixed or the rest of my life.

He cherished unbroken gratitude toward his two benefactors, though he never saw them. His desire to visit Copenhagen was prevented only by ill health.

At the expiration of the three years, in June, 1794, Schiller met a fate that was better than an appointment in Denmark would have been: He made the intimate acquaintance of Goethe.

When twenty years old, Fritz Schiller, as a poor, distressed, and defiant student at the Karlsschule in Stuttgart, had caught a glimpse of Goethe who, as a handsome, stately young *Geheimrat,* dressed in court costume, and accompanied by Karl August, had paid the school a brief visit. Nine years had in the mean time passed by, years of poverty and passion, endured under the pressure of petty military despotism, in rebellious moods, in erotic joy and anguish, in an eternal struggle for mere existence, carried along by an ambition that was only partly satisfied.

Schiller had come to Weimar in 1787; Goethe was then in Italy. During the Christmas of 1784 he had made the acquaintance of Karl August in Darmstadt, and had given public readings from his own works before the local court. He read the first act of his *Don Carlos* to the Duke himself, privately. His reward for this was the bestowal of the title of *Herzoglicher Weimarischer Rat.* When Goethe returned from Italy, Schiller was out in the country, at Volkstädt, near Weimar.

He had become attached to the Lengefeld family, was patronized by the mother, and attracted by the two daughters, Caroline von Beulwitz, and Charlotte, who afterwards became his wife. Schiller was eager to make Goethe's acquaintance; he felt certain he would see him at the home of Frau von Stein at Kochberg. It lay but a short distance from Volkstädt. He was quite unaware that Goethe returned from Italy with the conviction that Schiller's influence was a power inimical to his own efforts. Nor did he realize that Goethe was no longer an habitue of Kochberg, and that he was destined never again to become such. Schiller was hurt; he was offended; he could not understand why Goethe failed to take the slightest notice of his presence: It was such a short distance from Weimar to Volkstädt. He might, however, have known that his criticism of *Egmont* was ill inclined to open the way to Goethe's traditionally locked heart.

In September, 1788, however, the wanderer chanced to go on a visit to Frau von Lengefeld in Rudolstadt, and there met Schiller. In addition to the three Lengefeld women, Frau Herder, Frau von Stein, and Frau von Stein's mother were also present. Goethe was courteous; but he did not have anything to do with Schiller personally.

Schiller wrote to Körner concerning the first meeting with this man whom he had admired for so long:

The first sight of him lessened to a marked degree the exalted opinion I had formed with regard to his striking and beautiful figure. He is of medium height, unbending, and walks erect. His face is unfeeling, though his eyes are expressive, vivacious. You like to look at him. Though he is serious, there is something benevolent and good in his mien. He is a brunett, and seems to be much older than he really is according to my count. His voice is exceedingly agreeable, his power of narration is marked by fluency, intellectuality, and vivacity. You like to listen to him, and when he is in a good humor, which was more or less the case on this occasion, he speaks willingly and in an interesting way. Our acquaintance was quickly made, and without the least coercion. The company, to be sure, was so large, and the others were so eager to engage him in conversation, that I had no opportunity to be with him for any length of time, nor to speak with him on any but general topics. He speaks gladly and passionately of Italy. What he told me concerning Italy gave me a most striking and vivid picture of the land and the people.

What is not said, though it is implied, is the fact that Schiller was bitterly disappointed. He had hoped for some remark from Goethe which would show that he recognized his worth as a poet; Goethe discoursed on Italy. In the autumn, Schiller moved to Weimar. Goethe avoided him with such infinite care that Schiller never had a single chance to see him. But there he was, without a position, with marked ability and, as it would seem, with very poor prospects. Goethe recommended him for a vacant professorship at the University of Jena. The chair of history at Jena had been made vacant through the call of its former incumbent to Göttingen. That was a neat way by which Goethe could remove Schiller from Weimar. In December, 1788, Schiller accepted the call, incident to which he paid his respects to Goethe, hoping that he might finally approach the grand master on this occasion. Goethe's minister acknowledged the call; he confined his conversation exclusively to the professorship at Jena and was most profuse and voluble in the expression of his desire to see Schiller succeed in his new post. There was no fixed stipend attached to the position when Schiller entered upon the duties of his office in May, 1789. In January, 1790, the Duke granted him an annuity of two hundred thalers. In February of the same year Schiller married Charlotte von Lengefeld. In January, 1791, he had a violent tubercular attack. On the road to recovery, he suffered a relapse that brought him face to face with death. Then it was that help came from Denmark.

II

Schiller's letters to Körner from February and March, 1789, betray the dissatisfaction, even desperation, which Goethe's kindly negative deportment had evoked in the poet who was his junior by ten years.

He writes:

To be near Goethe often would make me decidedly unhappy. He never has moments during which he pours out his heart even to his most intimate friends; he is not to be got hold of; I believe he is an inordinate egotist. . . . He is benevolent, but only as a god, without giving of himself —which appeals to me as being consistent and carefully deliberated behavior intended to make effective the keenest enjoyment of egotism. Men should not allow any such creature to rise up among them. Because of all this I dislike him, though I love his mind with all my heart and think very highly of him. . . .

He has awakened in me a queer blending of hatred and love; a feeling not dissimilar to that which Brutus and Cassius must have cherished toward Caesar. . . .

I prefer to let you know me precisely as I am. This person, this Goethe, is forever in my way, and he reminds me all too often that fate has treated me unkindly. How gently his genius has borne him up above fate! How I have had to fight up to this very moment!

That Schiller's fate had been unspeakably hard in comparison with Goethe's admits of no doubt. But in order to appreciate the instinctive aversion which he felt toward Goethe, we must first become clear as to how Schiller conducted himself, spiritually, at this particular period of his life; nor must we overlook the huge gulf that lay between his mental point of view and that of Goethe.

With his first play, *Die Räuber,* unbaked though it was, Schiller as a born dramatist had produced the most effective drama of the German stage. As the author of this drama, published in 1781, and the next two plays of the next three years, *Fiesco* and *Kabale und Liebe,* Schiller belonged, heart and mind, to the period of Storm and Stress. All three plays are in prose; in all of them the rhetoric and bombast were in keeping with the style of the period; in all of them there was abundant strength.

In *Die Räuber* there was a breath of world history. This drama by a young man who, up to this time, had lived to see nothing but the detestable and petty tyranny in the military academy at Stuttgart, preludes the revolution that was soon to shake Europe. Franz Moor was the old form of State's "tyrant"; Brother Karl was the man with the sympathetic heart, discovered and depicted by Rousseau. The two brothers together personified the social forces of the eighteenth century in clash and conflict with each other during the French revolution. Otherwise nearly everything in the play was unreal. If we except the robbers, whom Schiller copied from his own comrades, the remaining characters belong either to the realm of shades (as Amalia and the old Moor), or to the theatrical stock in trade (as

Daniel and Hermann). Karl Moor was the prize
work of a youthful imagination; Franz Moor was
a combination of Edmund the wicked brother of
Lear, Iago, and Richard III.

The part of the drama which deals with the
rivalry between two brothers, the one good, the
other bad, was a common theme of the period. We
have but to recall Klinger's *Die Zwillinge* and Leisewitz's *Julius von Tarent* (1776). The latter was
Schiller's most immediate prototype. Julius corresponds to Karl Moor, Guido to Franz, Blanca to
Amalia. The horrors are heaped up even more
strongly, in that Guido murders Julius, while the
Prince, their father, who corresponds to the old
Moor, puts his own wicked son to death.

But the spirit of revolt itself and the dramatic
tempest motif were Schiller's own; and it was he
who created Karl Moor as the champion of humanity. He rejects and abandons a degenerate society and throws down the gauntlet to its laws.

In *Fiesco* Schiller had shown himself less dependent upon models; he had indeed made marked technical progress. His tragedy had an admirable
vigor. In the leading character he had created an
interesting and more consistent personality than his
previous hero. With the exception of Muley Has-
san, the other male characters are of little account,
while the women are just as unreal as Amalia.

In *Kabale und Liebe* Schiller had attacked primarily the caste system. Begun in captivity and
continued through adversities and humiliations, the
drama was written in the most unhappy period of
the poet's life. It was a *bürgerliche Tragödie* similar to other bourgeois tragedies of the age; the

most immediate prototype in this case was Gemmingen's *Der deutsche Hausvater;* but as a love tragedy it surpassed them all. At the close, however, the characters in the play disintegrate under Schiller's inept hands. He caused the righteous young lover to poison his sweetheart because of a silly suspicion. Nevertheless, he has given us a picture of his own age, just as it was, gloomy and sinister, but so strong and in certain respects so true, that the play even to this day belongs to the fixed repertoire of the German theatre.

With his early productions, Schiller had been on the way to establishing a national theatre. His persons came near to being individuals. His prose was continually growing better. With his next work, *Don Carlos,* he started out on an entirely different road upon which he continued until his death. His talent was Europeanized; he gave up Shakespeare as a model and put himself in the power of the French—with constant protest against them. In this he simply followed Lessing's example, who, with praise for Shakespeare and words of contempt for the tragedy-writer Voltaire, had produced his masterpiece, *Nathan der Weise,* as a pupil of Voltaire and in Voltaire's spirit. When Schiller gave up prose and began to write verse, he seemed to have forgotten what he had previously learned, and went in for glittering rhetoric. At the same time he supplanted his individuals with types.

The first prose sketch of *Don Carlos* written in Bauerbach, has not made much progress over *Kabale und Liebe.* As this was a *Familiengemälde* in a private home, just so is *Don Carlos* a *Familiengemälde* in a royal household. The leading character in this case, the young prince, has been a Ferdinand on a higher social plane, with higher potentialities, and was to be a hero after Schiller's young heart. In like manner, Princess Eboli, in the original sketch, was to have been Lady Milford in duplicate, only raised to a higher degree. On April 14, 1783, Schiller wrote to Reinwald from Bauerbach: "If I dare use the expression, Carlos gets his soul from Shakespeare's Hamlet, his blood and nerves from Leisewitz's Julius, and his pulse from me."

In the finished drama, however, Don Carlos, in consequence of a change in plan and because of the introduction of Marquis Posa into the plot, is only a shadow of his friend, only a shadow of the man who was originally to have been his intimate and confidant. Posa dominates the entire play. Carlos is toned down into an ideal youth in love with his blameless stepmother. The drama is drawn out to immeasurable length. The plot and action, worked over and revised through fully five years, became confusion worse confounded.

It was Dalberg, the intendant of the theatre in Mannheim, who, as early as the spring of 1782, drew Schiller's attention to the theme. It was Dalberg who, in 1783, had Schiller appointed to the post of theatre poet in Mannheim. But in Mannheim French taste prevailed; French literature was read and there, more than anywhere else, tribute was paid to Wieland. Dalberg, who valued French drama and underestimated Shakespeare, demanded the revision of *Fiesco* so that it would be in accord with the prevailing taste, and in harmony with the ideals of Wieland. This demand had such an influence upon Schiller that his spiritual development from the point of view of the drama became thoroughly French. All French tragedies were written in verse; the theme of *Don Carlos* was precisely the sort the French liked. It was akin to Racine's *Mithridate* and *Phèdre*. Schiller cherished a profound respect for Racine. And when illness hindered him in his original intention, he translated *Phèdre* into German verse. He wrote to Dalberg on August 24, 1784: "Secretly I also entertain a more than feeble hope of sometime performing an important work for the German stage by transplanting the classical plays of Corneille, Racine, Crébillon, and Voltaire to our own territory."

Voltaire's influence upon the German drama of the eighteenth century had been overwhelming. He was more easily understood than his less realistic predecessors. The philosophic optimism with which the Germans had become familiar through the philosophy of Leibniz and Wolff had prepared the people's minds for him. They liked the dramatic conflict in his works; it resulted in spiritual progress and moral improvement, even though the hero lost his life thereby. In his works, the leading persons from the time of Louis XIII and Louis XIV were modernized by an ingrafting of such sentimentality as Rousseau and Diderot had glorified and had taught the Germans to admire. His dramas were *Tendenzdramen;* they made propaganda for the cause of freedom in religion and politics, shrieked abhorrence at fanaticism, at the Inquisition, at superstition, and at fire and brimstone in the service of the oppressed in faith. No hero can have thoughts more akin to Voltaire than Schiller's Marquis Posa. All these youths *à la* Schiller in the later tragedies, who are noted in German textbooks as distinctly Germanic, the very ones whose idealism, like that of Max Piccolomini, is supposed to be national, are none other than heroes of the *Sturm und Drang* period who have felt the cosmopolizing influence of Voltaire.

Weisse, Cronegk, Brawe blazed the path that Schiller followed. When Schiller revised *Don Carlos,* he stood at the parting of the ways. Should he follow Shakespeare and Goethe, or Voltaire and Lessing? His philosophic-poetic *naturel* made the choice for him. He simply could not set up the human and the concrete as a point of departure after the fashion of Shakespeare and Goethe, and then have this transformed into poetry. Owing to his deep-seated preference for abstract ideas, he proceeded from thought and poetry to the human. His creative works consisted in giving thoughts a framework and then clothing the framework. He always proceeded from an idea, just as Voltaire and Lessing had done.

His Posa is certainly at the same time the most Voltairesque and the most Schilleresque of his creations. He incarnated himself with all his ideal yearnings in the Spanish *Marquis.* In his mind's eye, nevertheless, he had a distinctly French model for his *Don Carlos* in Campistron's *Andronic.*

The Greek emperor Colojanus Palaeologus has robbed his son Andronicus of his beloved, Irene of Trapezunt, and married her himself, just as Philipp II has robbed his son, Don Carlos, of his beloved, Elizabeth of Valois, and taken her in marriage.

Depuis près de deux mois qu'on épousant Irène
L'Empereur s'est lié d'une nouvelle chaîne
Qu'enlevant la Princesse à son fils malheureux
D'une fois tant jurée il a rompu les nœuds.

The son, like Don Carlos, is beloved everywhere
throughout the empire, but nowhere more than by
the rebellious Bulgarians, with whose messenger he
fraternizes and whose wish it is to have him for their
leader, just as the rebellious Netherlanders appeal
to Don Carlos to be their ruler.

Il s'est de tout l'Empire attiré l'amitié,
Vous voyez qu'il soutient les rebelles Bulgares
Chaque jour l'envoyé de ces peuples barbares
L'entretient.

The Prince, just as Don Carlos, merely wishes
to come to the help of the oppressed:

Léonce, vous verrez, avec combien de zèle
Des peuples opprimés je défends la querelle. . . .
Qu'on me laisse partir, que jaille en Bulgaire!

When he encounters the rejection of his desire
to go to the maltreated and rebellious province, he,
like Don Carlos, will travel in secret. The emperor
condemns him to death. He can choose his way of
meeting death, so he has his veins opened in the
bath. The innocent Empress takes poison.

What is so noteworthy here is the fact that this
old French play from the close of the seventeenth
century is, despite its Byzantine name, founded upon
the self-same source which inspired Schiller, namely,
Abbé de Saint Réal's *Dom Carlos, Histoire Es-
pagnole*. Campistron himself made this statement
in an older preface which is not prefixed to the

drama, and which I did not discover until the above
was written.

It was the impossibility of placing the characters
of the Spanish court on the stage in Paris which
forced the poet to disguise it as Byzantine.   This
explains why Schiller resorted to the old drama, and
accounts for the fact that the most original character in his *Don Carlos,* Marquis Posa, in his most
original situation, in the scene with Philipp II, has
already been portrayed in the French text.   Let
us compare Léonce's appeal to the Emperor with
Posa's celebrated appeal to Philipp, in the tenth
scene of the third act:

> Fais si bien, juste ciel, que ma plainte le touche!
> Tout un Peuple, Seigneur, vous parle par ma bouche;
> Un Peuple qui toujors à vos ordres soumis,
> Fut le plus fort rempart contre vos Ennemis. . . .
> Cet heureux temps n'est plus; ces guerriers intrépides
> Sont en proye aux fureurs de gouverneurs avides;
> Sous des fers odieux leur coeur est abbatu,
> La rigueur de leur sort accable leur vertu;
> Tout se plaint, tout gémit dans nos tristes Provinces;
> Les chefs et les soldats, et le peuple et les princes.
> Chaque jour sans scrupule on viole nos droits,
> Et l'on compte pour rien la Justice et les Lois.
> En vain nos ennemis à nos peuples soutiennent,
> Que c'est de votre part que leurs ordres nous viennent.
> Non, vous n'approuvez point leurs sanglants attentats.
> Je dirai plus, Seigneur, vous ne les savez pas.
> Ah! si pour un moment vous pouviez voir vous même
> Pour quels coups on se sert de votre nom suprême;
> Que ce saint nom ne sert qu'à nous tyranniser,
> Qu'à mieux lier le joug qu'on nous veut imposer;
> Alors de vos sujets moins Empereur que Père
> Vous ne songeriez plus qu'à finir leur misère.

In a letter to Körner, February 12, 1788, Schiller
tells of an argument which he had with Wieland.

When the conversation centered upon French taste, Schiller offered to make each individual scene of any French writer of tragedy, whosoever he be, truer and at the same time better. (This recalls Lessing's boast in the *Hamburgische Dramaturgie*): "Name me one play of the great Corneille, which I dare not undertake to improve. He (Wieland) brought up my *Carlos* in order to refute me, *since just in this particular instance I perpetrated the very fault which I had censured in the French*." As may be seen, Wieland had a critical eye for the affiliation of Schiller's tragedies with the French. More than this, Fritz Jacobi cracked the only joke in his life on *Don Carlos*. He called the drama "a cold palace, where there is the smell of an overheated stove."

If Schiller's creative powers as a poet were hereafter for some time at a standstill, it was owing to the fact that he turned to the study and writing of history. He had always been philosophically inclined. Hardly since the days of Lucretius had any poet been philosophic to such a high degree. Poems such as *Die Götter Griechenlands*, 1788, *Die Künstler*, 1789, and *Das Ideal und das Leben*, 1795, reveal a philosophic gift of high order that has espoused poetry and begotten a beautiful art of narration.

But even now we can see from what has been said concerning Schiller how sharply Merck's expression to Goethe fitted him: "You try to give the real a poetic form. *The others* try to make the so-called poetic real"—which furnished Merck with an unfavorable testimonial.

III

As a historian and philosopher no less than as a
poet Schiller belonged mind, heart and soul to the
eighteenth century; and what is more, he continued
to hold out against the influence of intellects, which
in the eighteenth century prepared the way for the
nineteenth.

From 1786 to 1791 he had buried himself with
inspired zeal in the study of history; and because
of this very fact he attained at the close of his life
as a poet that reality which stands so decidedly at
odds with his original Rousseau-like point of view
and imparts to his later works a merit that is rare.

But his conception of history and historiography
was poles removed from Herder's.　In the first
place, he did not write the history of peoples but of
leading characters; in the second—and more important—his fundamental view was teleological:　It
sought and found the end and aim.　His serious
interest in history had been aroused by Kant's *Idee
zu einer allgemeinen Geschichte in Weltbürgerlicher
Absicht* and his *Bestimmung des Begriffs einer Men-
schenrace*, both of which interpreted the past in advance of experience.　Schiller felt (rationalistically
and withal poetically) that the task of the historian
was to impart to that which has been handed down
a higher harmony.　Never losing hold of the optimism which began in the age of enlightenment, he
believed that history contains a sort of divine judgment:　*Die Weltgeschichte ist das Weltgericht;* and
he reshaped history in accordance with this basic
point of view.　Like Voltaire, he wrote history with

a philosophic end in view and with artistic vividness. The History of Charles XII by Voltaire was and remained his model for historical depiction. He put his own ideas and those of his age into the struggles of the past. This method was not so successful in converting the Thirty Years War, with its religious fanaticism, into a struggle for freedom of thought; it adapted itself better to the rebellion of the Netherlands, despite the fact that at bottom this revolution lay fully as distant from the contemporary struggle on the part of the German intellectual aristocracy against Lutheran orthodoxy.

Schiller began his study of Kant's philosophy with the *Kritik der Urtheilskraft,* published in 1790, hence with that particular part of Kant's *Kritik* which must have interested him most, the *Aestetik.* And when he received that year a small sum of money from Denmark, he decided (as he told his friend Körner January 1, 1792) to use the three years, in which freedom from economic pressure was assured him, in entering into the teachings of the philosopher of Königsberg. Kant had insisted that the idea of beauty was purely subjective, dependent upon mere personal taste; Schiller tried to look upon beauty as real, tangible, and defined it as freedom of appearance (*Freiheit in der Erscheinung*): Nothing is self-determined; everything stands in a position of reciprocal dependence, though the value of an entity rests upon the degree in which it approaches freedom. Since beauty has nothing to do with the thing, but with its appearance, things are beautiful in so far as they seem free. To be sure this definition was not real; for whether things seem free or not, depends naturally upon the observer. The definition, however, made a profound impression upon the age.

Noteworthy for Schiller's philosophic striving was the fact that, over against Kant's definition of joy resulting from beauty, namely, *disinterested agreeableness* from which a deep gulf separated the aesthetically pleasing from the useful, he tried, in the spirit of former times, to emphasize the mutual interdependence of art and morality. In the wake of Shaftesbury, he contended that aside from the beauty of the human form, which awakens disinterested approval, there is still such a thing as *winsomeness:* beauty in movements, and the movements are not beautiful unless they express a feeling or an idea, therefore something moral. Then there is *dignity,* another expression for something moral, that is to say, for the exaltation which signifies the victory of man over his lower nature.

In conformity with his assertion concerning the inseparability of beauty from ethics, Schiller attacked the rigid distinction which Kant, with his categorical imperative, had made between pleasure and duty. He deprived duty of its harshness and also made its fulfillment a joy. There is grace in the epigramme:

Gerne dien' ich den Freunden, doch thu' ich es leider mit
 Neigung,
Und so wurmt es mich oft, dass ich nicht tugendhaft bin.

He repudiates Kant, in so far as his desire leads toward a full, harmonious life, and that can only be approached by *man's aesthetic education,* that is to say, by the discipline of the mind to the beautifying and evaluating of the beautiful. The cultivation of

beauty liberates from low sensuousness on the one
hand, and from the sovereignty of calculating reason
on the other.

The art of poetry especially is the true fountain
of youth:

Glaubt mir, es ist kein Märchen! die Quelle der Jugend, sie
  rinnet
Wirklich und immer. Ihr fragt, wo? In der dichtenden
  Kunst.

But the art of poetry was of a double nature, for
modern poetry had to have its peculiar characteristics as over against ancient, and Schiller had to assure the justification of his poetry as over against
that of Goethe: Poetry was therefore partly naïve,
partly sentimental. He approached these two conceptions, not by the road of experience, but *à priori,*
and here as little as anywhere else did he concern
himself to the slightest degree with the conception
of an historic development. (See John G. Robert-
son: *Schiller. After a Century*).

IV

In Jena, Batsch had founded a "naturalistic
society" with splendid collections and valuable apparatus. Goethe took pleasure in attending its periodical meetings. Once in the year 1794 he met
Schiller there. They left accidentally at the same
time. In the course of the conversation that spun
itself out between them, Schiller remarked with reference to the lecture that had been held, that such
a piecemeal method of dealing with nature could
not attract the layman. This was water on Goe-

the's wheel; he replied that this manner of observing nature was hardly more satisfactory for the initiated, and that there existed still another way of portraying nature, namely as working and living, as striving from a whole to individual parts. Schiller did not rightly understand, did not clearly see, how such could proceed from experience.

They came to Schiller's house; the conversation enticed Goethe in. He depicted for Schiller the metamorphosis of plants in a general way, making clear to his mind a sort of symbolic plant. Schiller listened attentively, but shook his head and replied: "That is not an experience; that is an idea." Goethe was nonplussed, became slightly offended, and felt that they had neared the crossroads where their paths lay apart. Schiller's insistence upon freedom toward nature in his essay on *Anmut und Würde* entered his mind and he said: "It is at least pleasing to me to have ideas without knowing it and to see them with my own eyes." Schiller replied politely, as a cultured Kantian, who stood in the presence of an obstinate "realist" (as Goethe called himself). But neither of them gave in. What was for the one a matter of experience was for the other an *à priori* idea.

The initial step toward a closer relationship had however been taken. The personal attraction that emanated from Schiller's noble and striving nature, from his exalted mind and immensely fertile intellect, did not fail of its influence. And when his wife, whom Goethe had admired from her childhood on and who in turn had grown up in reverence for him, did what lay in her power to effect an enduring understanding between the *disocuri*, between these two

great souls who had for so long remained at a safe
distance from each other, then it was that the feeling of unalloyed friendship began to take root in
both of them. In their spiritual views they could
be compared to two hemispheres which could and
should fit perfectly together each one complement-
ing the other.

And just at this time Schiller wished to start one
of those journalistic enterprises by which he tried,
on several occasions, to eke out an existence. Having assured himself of the necessary coöperation of
Fichte and Wilhelm von Humboldt, he next sought
to win Goethe as a collaborator. This was essayed
in a quite nice and profoundly reverential letter
dated June 13, 1794, to which Goethe replied most
graciously: "It will afford me genuine pleasure to
join your society." By August 23, the relationship
had developed so far that Schiller, in a letter which
fills four printed pages, was in a position to open up
his heart to Goethe and show him how well and
thoroughly he understood him.

He traced the contrast between Goethe and himself back to a contrast between quickness of perception and discriminating understanding (intuition and
analysis). A man with Goethe's mental equipment
had no reason to borrow from philosophy; on the
contrary, it could learn from him. Philosophy could
merely dismember what is given it; but genius was
the power that gives. Goethe sought for the necessary in nature but by the most difficult road in that
he strove to create the individual from the whole.
From an understanding of the simplest organisms
he came to the point where he could understand the
most highly developed organism, man, ascended

from All-Nature's building materials. It was "a grand and heroic idea," which showed full well how completely his mind controlled his conceptions and confined them in one beautiful unity.

If Goethe had been born in Greece or in Italy, he would have been surrounded from birth by a world that is beautiful and an art that idealizes. As it was, he had to create a Greece from within himself. In the space of time during which the young soul is being formed, he had been surrounded by imperfect forms and by a harsh, northern climate; he had already assimilated his unamiable environment when his victorious genius detected the lack and proceeded to make amends. He had been forced to devote himself to remoulding the less desirable world that had forced itself upon his powers of imagination, and this could come about only in accord with guiding concepts. Consequently he who had been wont to move from a basic view to abstractions, was now forced to pursue the opposite road, to transform conceptions into views and thoughts into feelings, because he as a genius could create only from feeling and view.

This, wrote Schiller, was his conception of Goethe's spiritual mode of progression, and Goethe himself knew best whether he was right. But what Goethe could not know—because genius is always a secret unto itself—was the full harmony existing between his own philosophic instinct and the oldest and purest results of inquiring reason. One would think that there must be a sharp distinction between the speculative mind, which proceeds from unity, and the intuitive which proceeds from variety. But if speculation sought experiences with pure and stead-

fast mind, then intuition in turn sought the law with
free and independent mental power. They met each
other half way.

Intuition had, to be sure, to do only with individual beings, speculation only with species. But
if intuition was ingenious, it produced individuals
with typical characteristics; and if speculation was
no less ingenious, it never lost sight of the experience that comes from seeing, but produced class beings with a potentiality for life and a clear relation
to reality. Quickness of perception on the one hand
and thoroughness of investigation on the other were
perfect complements.

Thus Goethe and Schiller each had his field of
activity defined; and despite Schiller's profound
sense of modesty, he felt assured of nearness to
Goethe by virtue of his marked creative ability. It
was here, too, that he felt called upon to tell Goethe,
once for all, how that long conversation between
them had set his world of ideas in motion.

Goethe replied to his letter with genuine cordiality. In his life too that conversation had left its
tidal mark. He had once more had opportunity to
appreciate the honesty and rare earnestness in everything that Schiller did or wrote. But it is not Schiller alone who is to be benefited by the coöperation;
Goethe is also to come out of it with renewed energy and clarified vision. There is so much in him
that is dark, hazy, unfixed, hesitating.

In his reply, Schiller blessed the fate that had
finally brought them together. How wise it was to
let chance take its course! He had often wanted
to come nearer to Goethe; now they had met each
other just at the right moment. He himself was

a hybrid. His imagination interfered with his
world of thought; cold reason disturbed his writing of poetry. And in addition to all of this, illness
had threatened to destroy his physical strength just
at the time he was beginning to make full and correct use of his mental powers.

It was in this connection that he accepted an invitation from Goethe to spend several weeks at his
home in Weimar. On his return to Jena he was
quite overwhelmed by the mass of ideas his great
friend had awakened in him. It would take a great
deal of time merely to unravel and disentangle
them; but he confidently hoped that not one of them
would be lost.

Such, then, was the introduction to the unbroken
coöperation between two of the most prominent
men of modern times. A union more beautiful, and
more productive of the results that endure, can be
referred to in only the rarest of instances throughout the history of the entire world.

CHAPTER VII

THE BEGINNING OF *Wilhelm Meisters Lehrjahre;*
SCHILLER'S ENTHUSIASM — WISDOM IN *Wilhelm Meisters Lehrjahre*—CLASS DIFFERENCES
IN *Wilhelm Meisters Lehrjahre*—CHARACTER
PORTRAYAL IN *Wilhelm Meisters Lehrjahre*

SHORTLY before Goethe had made Schiller's more
intimate acquaintance he had taken in hand the
frayed manuscript of *Wilhelm Meister* with the
idea of revising it. In June, 1794, he finished the
first two books. He thereupon sent Herder a copy
of the first book and invited him to dinner in order
to hear his opinion. But he was painfully discon-
certed when Herder proved to be exceedingly vexed,
even "appalled," at the beginning of the novel.
Herder wrote to a sanctimonious woman friend:
"These Mariannas and Philinas, this whole business
in truth, I detest." He hoped that the poet in the
course of the novel would brand both of these
women as worthy of contempt. But if they were
introduced in this fashion at the beginning, the hero
would thereby be besmirched throughout the rest
of his life. So spiritually cramped had Herder become that he took pleasure in nothing of which he
could not approve morally.

How refreshing it was then for Goethe to receive
the inspired gratitude of Schiller, when *he* received

the beginning of the novel, immediately upon its publication. Goethe lamented the fact that his relation to Schiller had not been established before the publication was started. Schiller devoured the introduction with rapture and found absolutely nothing in it which did not stand in perfect harmony with the work as a whole, and the entire work was considered admirable. Disheartened by Herder's lack of understanding, Goethe had sent Schiller the book with anxiety and distrust. The effusive homage of his friend set his mind at ease, just as it filled him with a desire to complete the elaborate work so soon as possible.

Indeed Schiller gave him far more than mere encouragement; he gave him ideas as well. A reciprocal fructification between these two great minds was called into being. Goethe later wrote in this connection: "For me that was a new springtime in which everything germinated joyously and sprang forth from the seed which opened and from the branches whose leaves burst forth."

The theme around which *Wilhelm Meisters Lehrjahre* revolves wholly and entirely is one with which no novel in the literature of the world had previously dealt. It was a conception unknown to earlier times and one that has become almost foreign to modern times. The theme was Education. As a rule novels treated adventure or love or the struggle for one of various aims such as the winning of a sweetheart or the liberating of a prisoner or the overcoming of an obstacle or the conquering of an enemy. This novel treated education.

Rousseau's *Emile* had turned upon training; that was something quite different from education. Even

in ancient times people had believed in training.
Education in the sense in which the word was formed
and conceived of in Germany at the close of the
eighteenth century was something radically different.

We see nowadays that there was an age, such as
Goethe has created, the interests of which centred on
this point, an age in which neither money nor social
position nor pleasure nor power nor knowledge was
the aim, but proper development of the soul in accord with its inborn ability and innate power.

We see a youth groping about through life and
being formed into what he is actually capable of
being and becoming, and what the name connotes,
a Master.

The question arises whether fortunate environment is not the first, last and sole condition that can
guide a man to a lofty goal. The answer is more or
less negative. There is no doubt but that the circumstance of birth is the initial point of departure
from which the goal is indicated and by which we
are directed to it. But between the beginning and
the end much will be wanting in case education, and
nota bene early education, does not make a man
what he can become. It is entirely possible that the
individual to whom we ascribe genius would be in a
far worse position than he who possessed only general qualities, for the highly gifted can be misguided
much more easily, he can be thrust aside on false
roads much more forcefully and completely, than
he whose talents are smaller, whose gifts belong
more nearly to the class that we call average.

The hero asks somewhere whether genius cannot liberate itself and heal unaided the self-inflicted

wound. "By no means"—it is said—"or at most
only in part." No one is to imagine that he can
overcome the first impressions of youth. He who
has grown up in praiseworthy freedom, in concourse
with good men, and whose master has taught him
what he needs first in order to understand more
readily that which is to follow; he who has learned
what he never needs to forget, never needs to un-
learn, will come to lead a more worthy life than he
who has allowed his original powers of youth to be
led into delusions from which he is afterwards
obliged to free himself.

He whom fate takes charge of is to be extolled
as fortunate, says Wilhelm: It trains each one according to its way. Fate, we are told, is a superior
but expensive tutor. I would always prefer to be
beholden to a human master's reason. For wise
fate has an especially clumsy organ through which
it works. This organ is chance. Chance seldom
executes accurately and dependably what fate has
once decided upon.

In response to Schiller's plea, Goethe appended
in the latter part of his book a more penetrating
explanation of the symbolic expressions *apprentice*
and *master*. We are told that this depends, relatively, upon education. The majority wish merely
a household remedy in order to attain prosperity,
a mere prescription by which to attain wealth and
good fortune.

From the very beginning the hero of the novel
is a seeker; he fancies that others can give him
what after all can come only from himself. He is
without particular character, a football of persons
and circumstances. But he is at heart—as is said of

him in time—"as arrogant as Scipio, as liberal as
Alexander, infatuated, too, now and then, but not
rancorous toward his rivals." This last virtue is,
however, not an especially noteworthy one since he
rarely has rivals and the few that he does have are
fairly harmless. Goethe has imbued Wilhelm with
his own longing for harmonious development, his
own striving to make headway in the larger life of
this world and of art. And, albeit the fact is never
expressly stated in so many words, and though Wilhelm himself almost seems to be overlooked, he has
also given his hero that intriguing amiability which
wins women without fail. Marianne and Natalie,
Philine and Mignon, Aurelie, the Countess and
Therese, each succumbs in turn. It is Wilhelm's
own nature and not the extraneous and never fail-
ing power that gradually and in due time leads him
along the path that is right.

Lacking experience as he does, the hero places
an inordinate value on the experience of others and
on the results that follow therefrom. He fairly
gathers and garners up opinions and thoughts, retains in his memory the true intermingled with the
false, and follows strange lights as guiding stars.
This man's bitterness and that man's icy contempt
infect him. The most dangerous personality for
his type of independence is Jarno, who reminds us
of Merck. Jarno passes correct and accurate judgment upon individual occurrences, but he generalizes thcm so that they become false in the end.
Jarno acts, however, as a beneficent force. His
enemies speak incessantly of his restless head and
his sharp tongue. But why? Because the anthropo-
morphic rabble stands in mortal fear of brains. If

they only knew how frightful a monster stupidity is, they would fear it—and not brains!

Wilhelm is exposed to the delusions of the striver; and particularly to the delusion of seeking education where for him there is no education. He is exposed also to the idea of imagining that he can acquire a talent—the talent for acting—for which he has absolutely no natural aptitude. He feels that the time he has spent in trying to become an actor lies behind him as an infinite emptiness, since nothing from this period has become a part of him. His error is grievous. Everything with which he comes in contact leaves its mark upon him. Everything contributes, unnoticed, to his education as to to the education of all.

The sole danger for all of us lies in the desire to give an account of our own stewardship; in this way we become either arrogant or depressed. The safest method to pursue is always to perform the task that most immediately confronts us. The education he has in mind is freedom from prejudice. "I hate the French language with all my soul," says Aurelie. The reply is: "How can one hate a language to which one owes the greatest part of one's development, to which even now we must still owe a great deal before our existence can acquire form."

The education he has in mind is contrasted with bourgeois morality and the claims of bourgeois society. Toward the close of the novel (Book 8, Chapter 1) Wilhelm cries out: "How superfluous is all this moral strictness since nature, in her good way, moulds us for the highest we are to become. Woe to every kind of education which destroys the most effective means to true education and interests us in the final aim, instead of making us happy while on the road itself."

The education he praises is contrasted first with the orthodox and then with pious education in general. In the section on "the fair soul" there is developed, in contrast to orthodoxy, the purest religious life of the emotions, an existence which is purity not merely in itself, but which imparts purity to its surroundings, a nature whose independence is proved in the impossibility of assimilating something which does not harmonize with the noble and amiable spirit that lies at its root. But where Natalie, the niece of the woman who is entitled "the fair soul," is described, the former's earthly being is portrayed (without emphasis) as of a higher mould than the fair nature of the other, which was moulded so conscientiously that it became overrefined. We become acquainted with Therese before we become acquainted with her friend, Natalie. Therese has the cleanliness of a Dutch woman in everything physical and spiritual, in all her relations, external and internal. Jarno once denied her the three beautiful graces, Faith, Hope and Charity; for her, he said, knowledge took the place of Faith, confidence that of Hope, steadfastness that of Charity. She herself admits that she knew nothing higher than clarity and cleverness until Natalie's richer being overcame her and inspired her. When in Therese's presence we feel simply the happiness that comes from acquaintance with a being so serene.

Natalie, on the contrary, is portrayed as a creation of a more ideal sort; her harmony, due to her lofty education, is richer; her love of harmony is innate. We conceive of Therese as the good spirit of the house, as the sensible woman who, aside from other accomplishments, is well versed in counting and reckoning. Natalie's education carries along with it ingenious quickness of perception. With regard to the great fundamental question in the book, as to whether one should let nature take its course and thereby go astray, or whether one, where possible, should anticipate and ward off the danger, she has nothing to say; such a question is foreign to her mind. She thinks neither of delusions nor of dangers; she simply does not see such things. But everywhere among men, she sees a need, a want: she sees it in the case of the child who cannot even stand on its feet, and in the woe of the old man who has lost his strength. What her eye is trained by nature to detect, is the quiet craving for activity, the inclination for a talent, gifts along a hundred different lines. She sees what no one has drawn her attention to; she seems also to have been predestined to see only this. And wherever she observes a lack or a want, she is ready with a substitute, a remedy, an aid. She has, until she becomes acquainted with Wilhelm, never loved passionately though she has always loved.

Great stress is therefore put upon what her brother Lothario says at the close of the book. "It is incredible what *an educated person* (note how flat this expression has become in our day, this expression which then signified a new world) can do for himself and for others, when, unconscious of any desire to dominate, he has the disposition to become the guardian of many, leads them to do at the right time what they all would gladly do, and directs them to the goal which the majority keep well enough in view, though they themselves miss the road. . . . My sister, Natalie, is a vivid example of this type of individual. The method of procedure that nature has ascribed to this fair soul will always remain unattainable. She surely deserved this title of honor far more than many others, indeed, I dare say *even more than our noble aunt, who in her time was the fairest nature known to our circle.*" Fräulein von Klettenberg was the model for this aunt.

II

Though Wilhelm develops from within, he is both guided and punished by fate. He does, in time, penance for everything, including the insignificant, and for all errors in judgment and action. Just as there is bitter cruelty in the fate which pursues Faust in that the dissipation of a few nights results in the homicide of Gretchen's mother, her brother, her child and herself, so is there cruelty in the fate that pursues Wilhelm unwilling ever to let him go.

When eighteen years of age, he had had an affair with an actress by the name of Marianne. He sees a man slink away from her house; he finds an incriminating note in her scarf. He deserts her, innocent though she is, without questioning her, or listening to her, or even so much as letting her know his address. He allows her to be condemned and bear her child alone and deserted; the truth is not made known to him until her death when it is too late for reparation.

Accompanied by a number of actors, he comes

to the castle of the Count; a mild infatuation ensues
between him and the Countess. A frivolous Baroness, who wishes to involve the Countess in an unpleasant affair, disguises him by dressing him up in
the Count's housecoat and placing him in the latter's
chair. The Count enters; he imagines he sees his
double at his desk; he loses control of himself; he
becomes sanctimonious, Quakerish, simple-minded.
On one single occasion, and then just as she is taking
leave of him, the fair young Countess presses Wilhelm to her bosom. The act is of momentary dura-
tion but she so bitterly regrets this unique outburst
of passion that a mad idea finds lodgement in her
brain: She has pressed a locket which she has been
in the habit of wearing against her breast; a can-
cerous sore that will completely undermine her
health has developed from it. It is a morbid fancy;
but it transforms her; it ruins her.

Goethe wished to show here how cruelly life
itself punishes and avenges and consequently how
superfluous moral preaching is. He emphasizes
this theory with special force where Wilhelm feels
called upon seriously to moralize for Lothario,
whom he does not know personally but whose behavior toward the actress Aurelie seems to him
in the highest degree reprehensible.

Aurelie has told Wilhelm the history of her life.
Once upon a time she contracted a rationalistic marriage. When her husband was at death's door, she
became acquainted with the distinguished Lothario.
In company with some Frenchmen, he had fought
with marked distinction under Lafayette in the
American colonies. He approached her with quiet
demeanor, with open kindliness, and talked so sym-

pathetically about himself, that she rejoiced to see herself for the first time rightly appreciated. She says concerning Lothario, for whom Karl August's brother, Konstantin, is the model: "He seemed accustomed to feminine favor; that attracted my attention; he was not in the slightest way flattering or obtrusive; that made me carefree." In this way Goethe prepares us for the impression Lothario is to make: "With each rôle that I played, I always felt as though I were praising him and speaking in his honor; for this is the way my heart felt, it made no difference what I said." And when they applauded her playing, there was a cry within her: "That I owe to him." When Lothario leaves her, she seeks death. Like Ophelia and Emilie Galotti, she plays her own misery and desertion; but she feels this so keenly she would just as willingly play unclad. Then she dies in despair over the loss of Lothario.

The dying woman has charged Wilhelm to give her last greeting to her faithless lover. Indignant as he is, he prepares a strong upbraiding speech in true pharisaical fashion. He arrives at Lothario's castle where he meets him surrounded by a few highly cultured men, conspicuously worldly wise and somewhat hard-hearted, one of whom, Jarno, is as full of contempt for man as Wilhelm is full of ignorance of men. More than this, an exalted little sweetheart, Lydia, is found in Lothario's presence.

Lothario has nothing to do with Wilhelm, taken up as he is with other affairs (a duel which a deserted sweetheart has foisted upon him out of rage at a third whom he has preferred. . . . Lothario's sweethearts seem innumerable). There lives also in his neighborhood the woman (Therese) who is his secretly chosen bride, but from whom, because of a tragic misunderstanding, he lives apart. He looks upon her as the daughter of a person with whom he had an alliance during a journey. In her love and adoration for him, she regards everything he does in a favorable light and concedes him everything, even all of his inclinations toward other women.

Wilhelm cannot bring himself to deliver his speech; he is overcome by the man's superiority and straightforwardness. In truth, Lothario, in the novel represents the masterful personality in full action. With him all is survey, activity on a large scale, and incessant advance. He carries every one along with him. Wherever he is, he has a world unto himself. His nearness inspires and enflames. He acts not merely upon the individual, but upon the whole, not merely on the adjacent, but on the remote as well. He is, to put it briefly, the genius of the novel.

In direct contrast to him, we have a portrayal of an old physician who influences only the most immediate circumstance, merely creating a means to activity, not imparting activity itself. Perhaps Lothario destroys in one day what it took the physician years to build up; but perhaps Lothario imparts in one day power to replenish a hundredfold what has been torn down.

Furthermore, Wilhelm cannot bring forth his accusation, for the Countess is Lothario's sister, while Lothario is too magnanimous to rebuke Wilhelm. The hero feels by no means sufficiently guiltless to cast the first stone. The models, incidentally, for the Count and Countess were Count and Countess Werthern, the latter of whom was Karl August's intimate friend and the sister of Freiherr von Stein, the restorer of Prussia.

Wilhelm is enthusiastic about Lothario. When Lydia and he are on the way to Therese, he exclaims: "Oh Fräulein, what a man he is, and what men are those who surround him!" His admiration for Therese augments his admiration for Lothario: "It is only natural that such a distinguished man should attract the souls of remarkable women. How widely the influence of real manhood and the character of worthy beings extends!"

Wilhelm finally succeeds in beginning his speech in honor of Aurelie, though in a modified form: "I intended to criticize you bitterly," and so on. But he is unable to reply to these simple words of Lothario: "Most assuredly does my behaviour deserve censure. I should not have exchanged my friendship toward her for love. Alas! She was not lovable when she loved; and that is the greatest misfortune that can befall a woman." Wilhelm then merely remarks, quite tolerantly, that we cannot always avoid the blameworthy, cannot always avoid the fact that our points of view and methods of acting are turned aside from their sane and natural course.

Goethe has once more elaborated the thesis that life itself avenges and punishes adequately. Instead of composing sermons to mortify others, it were better for the preacher to deliver his sermons into the mirror. Preaching is unnecessary; unnecessary too is the repentence and absorption in religious books, such as Lydia indulges in when she meets with adversity.   Therese, who speaks for Goethe, does not see how anyone can believe in a God who appeals to us through books and stories; for does not the heart reveal everything?   For her the moral is not a sickening medicine but a rational and whole- some diet.   To moralize otherwise is to imitate the rustic barber who parts everybody's hair with the same comb.

Superficial, prejudiced and idiotic readers have concluded from such expressions that the moral standard of this book is not what it should be—of this book which can be called "The Wisdom of Wolfgang Goethe" with even more justice than that volume entitled "The Wisdom of Jesu Sirach." Take, for example, the inexorable severity displayed in the portrayal of Wilhelm's relation to Mignon. Of itself it is beautiful; but it is cruel.   The child loves him and he the child; yet he becomes her murderer.

Owing to the frivolous talk of Philine and other young girls, the idea becomes irresistibly attractive to Mignon of spending a night with her beloved, with never a thought of anything other than a lovers' tryst.   But just as she is on the point of entering Wilhelm's room, she sees with dismay that a rival has forestalled her.   Philine locks the door. The child feels a hitherto unknown, even unsuspected anguish.   Her heart, which had been throbbing with longing and anticipation, stops beating; it stands perfectly still; it feels like a lump of lead in her bosom.   When Wilhelm is eventually betrothed to Therese, and Mignon sees how the latter hurries to meet him and embrace him, she grasps at her heart, falls with a cry to the ground, and dies.   And thus Wilhelm, through no fault of his own, becomes her murderer.

There is a passage in the book which throws radiant light on the fate of characters of this sort. Wilhelm once promised the company of actors to stand by them through thick and thin. When the time, however, comes that he feels he must leave them, he suffers acute pangs of conscience at the thought of breaking his vow. He is blind to the fact that his presence is quite superfluous; he is unaware that not a one of the actors took his promise seriously.

In this connection the author points to the current belief that our circle would feel an immeasurable loss at our departure. The gap is easily filled; we discover how dispensable and easily replaced we are. "One should never promise," says Wilhelm.

The intelligent Frau Melina replies to this: "We consider it a disgrace to ourselves not to keep a given promise. But, alas! a good man promises with his mere existence, with his mere presence, far too much. The confidence he evokes, the expectations he awakens, are infinite. He is and remains the debtor without knowing it."

In this way we see that, although the crux of the novel lies in the intellectual, not in the moral, since it centers upon the problem of *Meisterschaft,* no moral question is omitted. The book revolves about education as an intellectual, and especially as an artistic process. It is in this sphere that it contains the results of penetrating experience and exhausting rumination. It is more than Old Testament-like wisdom that we read in the *Lehrbrief* (after an introduction with the quotation from Hippocrates:

Art is long, life short, judgment difficult, opportunity fugitive:

> Mimicry is instinctive; but that which we should imitate is not easily recognized. The remarkable is seldom found; less seldom payed tribute to. The distant entices us; not the steps which lead to it; with the summit before our eyes, we often go astray. Only a part of art can be taught; the artist needs the whole. Who knows but the half, always goes wrong and chatters a great deal; he who possesses the whole wishes only to work and talks seldom or slowly. The halfway ones have neither secrets nor strength. *Their knowledge is like baked bread, tasteful and satisfying for one day; but flour cannot be sown, and seed is not supposed to be ground.* . . . The spirit in which we act is the highest. Conduct is conceived and reproduced only by the spirit.

It is for the sake of clearness, upon which Schiller insisted during the process of elaboration, that this distinctive life wisdom has been introduced into the novel. For the book has undoubtedly suffered from the fact that it was worked out after an entirely different plan from that according to which it was originally designed. There was a good and simple intention in the fact that the main section concerned itself with actors and histrionics, since poetry and dramaturgy were supposed to be Wilhelm's real calling. That his attempt at poetry should be mere dilettantism, his enthusiasm for the dramatic profession only a whim, his demeanor as an actor devoid of all talent, is disconcerting. Wilhelm seems thereby somewhat incapable of taking his fate into his own hands.

The fruitlessness of striving after arbitrary independence is thrown therefore into sharp relief. "What we would gladly hold, we must let go, and undeserved benefits intrude." The feeling for what one might term the rush of life's stream as over against the growing man's power to swim begets a melancholy belief in fate.

Just as Wilhelm originally wavers between the calling of business and that of art, just so does he subsequently waver. He is helpful, good, unprejudiced, but weak in character; determinable and undetermined. Wilhelm once spoke in the presence of Jarno with bitterness and despondency. Jarno's reply is unforgetable: "It is well and good that you are vexed and bitter. It would be still better, if you would become really enraged."

With this "really enraged" the character of the man is supposed to be laid bare. But the ideal that flits before our eyes is the complete mastery of life, ennobled with harmonious education. There is not one glimpse of political trend, not to mention political ambition or feeling for the state. The mind alone shall be freed. Of other freedom there is no mention. Will in this far-reaching novel of education is an unknown and unnamed power.

III

The background of the novel is the condition and color of society as it existed in the eighteenth century; as it existed in the eighteenth century preceding the Revolution and preceding Rousseau. Class distinctions ran deep; marriage duties were taken quite lightly. When Wilhelm feels attracted to the Countess he forgets that she is far above him in birth and rank. Of this lapse of memory we are informed; we are not informed, however, of the discrepancy in etiquette that arises from the fact that the Countess is married. Indeed the distinctions in the various ranks of society are so keenly felt that the aristocratic, while at dessert, discourse on "dogs, horses, and actors." It is characteristic of the age that the abbots speak more immorally than the actors. The abbot says, by way of illustration, in the coolest sort of way: "The Baron had a little affair with a lady which caused much more sensation than was really necessary, for she merely wished to make too great use of her triumph over a rival."

The general thesis of the novel is, that in Germany as it existed at that time the nobleman alone can develop himself personally and harmoniously. The burgher is too dependent; his personality is lost. The nobleman can have influence; the burgher can only work. The nobleman alone can experience the interesting. Beyond the pale of higher society the interesting can only be experienced on the stage. The ideal of middle-class happiness, as portrayed by Wilhelm's brother-in-law, held no attraction for him. Werner does not yearn for luxury; he merely asks for rational enjoyment. Precious stones make no appeal to him; he wants interest-bearing capital. He wants to earn money. He will live economically and well. Though he does not wish any superfluous wardrobe, what he has is to be of the very best. Wilhelm, whose sole desire is to educate himself, after the fashion of the best noblemen of that day, exclaims: "Why should I manufacture good iron when I myself am full of slags? Why try to put my house in order when I am at odds with myself?"

Since he does not enjoy the freedom inherent in and common to the best society, he is drawn to the freedom that goes with the dramatic profession.

Though a surrogate, it is better than nothing. As
an actor he can, if only on the stage, have all manner of experiences—moods, feelings, sights, and so
on. But it is not only the life of the stage that
attracts him; he is taken up with the gipsy-like freedom associated with the stage and its devotees.

Goethe manifests a certain predilection for *al
fresco* scenes such as the theme requires. The actors arrive at the Count's castle. The wind blows
through the high gateway. In total darkness, rain
and cold, they shiver and shudder; the women are
frightened, the children weep. Finally they place
a few bundles of fagots in a huge fireplace. It is
only for show. The smoke blows out and fills the
room; the fire leaps forth in crackling flames; they
fear that the castle will be endangered. It is a
scene such as could be introduced into Théophile
Gautier's masterful *Capitaine Fracasse,* written long
afterwards, which opens with a description of the
Castle of Misery at which a band of travelling
players arrives.

Or follow with Goethe the roving troupe, wandering through the forest in war time, with long
hunting knives in embroidered straps and pocket-
pistols in their belts! The women are slowly drawn
forward in the wagon; an actor goes along at its
side, whistling. Wilhelm himself wanders along,
constantly accompanied by the tight-rope dancer,
Mignon, and the erratic old harpist in his long cloak.
The cloak is tucked in his belt; he carries the harp.
They camp over night after the fashion of hunters
and charcoal burners. Their strange clothing and
weapons gives them the appearance of foreigners.

What is all this but the youth's longing for free-

dom from all ensnaring ties? What else but the
love for the fatherland and native-land of all artists,
that old gipsyland to be found everywhere and situated nowhere? What else but love for the saun-
tering life in contrast to the fixed life, the life beset
with pursuits and aims!

Wilhelm severs his connection with the troupe
of actors and buys himself an estate near Lothario.
His brother-in-law, Werner, informs him that people know of his life with dissolute young noblemen
and actresses—an indisputable reference to the ru-
mors which Klopstock believed concerning Goethe's
initial relation to Karl August. Wilhelm replies
by expressing his utter indifference to public opinion.

If we compare, however, the hero as he appears
in the novel with the Wilhelm of the *Sendung* we
see that Goethe has forced him back within and
confined him to a much more delimited field, just
as he did with Torquato Tasso in the final form
of the drama. Originally Wilhelm was to found a
national German theatre; and there was the material
in him to do so. Later on Goethe subtracted all
such ability from Wilhelm and the plan naturally
failed. Tasso likewise, as originally conceived, was
to enjoy the position of friend and peer to his prince.
But in the finished work he fell from this height and
was made as unlike his poet as possible.

IV

Goethe's ability to develop characters was extraordinary. No one has produced a galaxy of
personages of more pronounced individuality than
he. Since at the bottom and basis of his own char-

acter, however, the nature-growing, nature-binding
is more marked than the life of volition and practical energy, his women stand out clearer and more
forcible than his men. Even his aged Faust has not
one doughty deed to look back upon.

In contrast to this his women are unforgetable.
This is true not merely in *Wilhelm Meister* but in
the earlier works. And yet, at the very time that
Wilhelm Meister was being finished we note a retrogression even in his ability to depict women.
Mignon and Philine, both creations of the earlier
Sendung, are shown in *situations;* they have a more
vigorous influence than some living persons of our
acquaintance. Therese and Natalie, on the contrary, are merely *described.* The descriptions reveal uncommon psychological finesse, but we do not
see them. We merely read about them.

Just as Gretchen's character is depicted in five
monologues, and Clärchen's in two short ditties,
Mignon's likewise is set forth to its very depths
through the instrumentality of a few songs. We
have *Heiss mich nicht reden,* which expresses the
mysterious element in her nature; *So lass mich
scheinen, bis ich werde,* which voices her premonition of an early death; *Nur wer die Sehnsucht kennt,
weiss was ich leide,* which acquainted us with her
longing; and *Kennst Du das Land,* more widely
known than any of the others and through which she
utters her ardent longing for a life in common with
her lover on Italian soil.

Few of Goethe's characters have imprinted themselves more sharply on man's mind, drawn as it is
with firm and simple strokes. She is invested from
the very beginning with the mixed impression of a

boy and a girl that she makes when she appears in her silk jacket with slashed sleeves and long, black, curly hair. She is not described; she is revealed. She seems to be only twelve or thirteen years old. Her brow is mysterious; her mouth is true-hearted and frank, though a bit too compressed for a girl of her age and inclined to twitch to one side.

Later we become acquainted with her heteroclitic actions. She springs up and down the stairs, slides over the banisters, or sits perched up on a wardrobe. She has a way of her own of greeting people; Wilhelm she greeted with folded arms. Furthermore, her language is distinguishable by its mixture of French, German and Italian, though we are not supplied with illustrations. Mention is made of her clothing, patched but clean, not, however, in detail, as when Therese or Natalie is described. The monumental expression has been found.

From an artistic point of view, Philine is an even more remarkable character. She is all life from the top of her head to the tip of her toes, on which hang her high-heeled slippers; they flap back and forth. She too is depicted through everything that she does and says; she too portrays herself in a matchless song:

> Singet nicht in Trauertönen
> Von der Einsamkeit der Nacht,
> Nein, sie ist, o holde Schönen,
> Zur Geselligkeit gemacht.

In contrast to the clear-cut, glowing Mignon, Philine is the epitome of charming exuberance and lazy, likeable frivolity. Goethe alone among German poets has succeeded in making such a woman lifelike and lovely. When Heine attempts to depict a character of this sort, he invariably becomes impudent and the character becomes a mere doll. He does not possess Goethe's Prometheus-like powers, nor his innocent Paganism.

Philine is revealed slowly and gradually. Wilhelm catches sight of a well-shaped woman. Her blond hair falls unloosened about her neck. She is seen in a window and has him ask for flowers. Stroke connects stroke—with a long intermission— until the graceful character moves before our eyes. She is cleverly sketched by the art which makes us see how many dislike her, and how many she cajoles. She is mischievous and roguish, but seldom condescends to be coquetish.

Goethe has made his Wilhelm somewhat ridiculous by the excess of virtue he unfolds when he finds her slippers in his room. But Mignon is anything but ludicrous when, after having danced as a maenad to the sound of her tambourine, she, madly jealous of Philine, bites Wilhelm in the arm. Because of her very aversion, Aurelie paints Philine with the most certain strokes of the brush, so that she seems doubly entrancing: "How contrary she is to my nature, to my inmost being, even down to the slightest details. Her brown eyes and blond hair, which my brother finds so fascinating, makes no appeal to me whatever. The scar on her forehead is so repellent to me, so indicative of something base, that I always want to draw back ten paces from her." "Her deportment is culpable," says Wilhelm, "but I must do justice to her character." "Character!" shrieks Aurelie, "do you believe that such a creature has character? Ah you men! I

know every one of you.   You are worthy of just
such women!"

This flaming hatred and naïve jealousy depict
Philine even more vividly than the longing she awakens.   She is sweet frivolity in feminine form, the
true Eve.   A charming creature is she, enveloped
in her magnificent blond hair hanging about her
bright face with its kiss-thirsty mouth, unforgetable
because of the beaming humor and the joyousness,
lightheartedness, and changeableness of her nature.
There radiates from her an atmosphere of deeply
subjugating voluptuousness.

She and Mignon complement each other by contrast.   Mignon, the child of a southern clime, with
her dark eyes, is the direct counterpiece to Philine.
Her beauty is stern and cold, her being smouldering
passion, her lot in life the abuse of fate.   She is
bound to her protector by the magic of gratitude
and a childish affection.   She is the child who all at
once feels that she is no longer a mere child.   While
Philine seeks Wilhelm at night time to give him a
hearty embrace, Mignon crawls in at night to stay
with him as a dog at his feet.   So it is that she is
suddenly seized with awakening passion, and is
speedily consumed by it.

Philine seems to have sprung from Goethe's
brain.   But the impression of all the seventeen years
in which he struggled with the novel seem concentrated in the figure of Mignon.   The conception of
her figure arose, in all probability, when a company
of rope dancers visited Weimar in 1777.   The song
Kennst Du das Land is from 1782.   The poem *An
Mignon,* addressed to Maddalena Ricci, the beautiful Milanese, is of considerably later date.   Th·

poem *Euphrosyne* was inspired by the actress Christiane Neumann, Becker by marriage, who stood so close to Goethe's heart. It portrays her as a child in relation to Goethe. Written in the year 1798, it depicts Christel Becker in a situation which recalls Mignon, and with the use of a Mignon-like expression, she "seeks her teacher, her friend, her father."

Goethe upbraids Madame de Staël somewhere for considering Mignon an episodic figure; he even goes so far as to say that she it is, on the contrary, around whom everything revolves. She is the burning longing for a life in complete resignation and an overardent enthusiasm requited with love; she is the hope for deep passion in deep happiness; she is a being from a higher world, at once elf and maid of a southern clime—a child of the copse with acrobatic grace and angelic goodness. But just as Shakespeare's Othello and Beaumarchais's Figaro and Hugo's Hernani are essentially known to the public at large as characters in the operas of Verdi and Mozart and Rossini, just so does the European and American public know Mignon and Philine merely from the operatic stage as creations of Ambroise Thomas.

CHAPTER VIII

Die Bekenntnisse einer schönen Seele

A CENTRAL point of the large circle of women in the book is occupied by the figure of a sort of Protestant nun, the refined canoness, portrayed in the sixth book, which is incorporated in the novel as an episode.

Bekenntnisse einer schönen Seele is Goethe's unique attempt to portray a religious existence. With this exception, not only in the novel but elsewhere as well, Goethe eludes the religious. The society in the tower is meant as a kind of substitute for what the church was in former days, that is to say, it is to be taken symbolically: It is a higher society without traditions and without dogma though it serves as a substitute for Providence and the clergy.

This explains the introduction of an entirely new poetic cult, of a new ritual with its choir and antiphonal choir and ceremonies without ceremonial, in *Wilhelm Meisters Lehrjahre* on the occasion of the death of Mignon; likewise in *Die Wahlverwandtschaften* at the burial of Ottilie.

In the confessions of a fair soul Goethe attempts to depict also the beauty and poetry of a pious disposition. With this end in view, he took up the notes and events in the life of Fräulein von Klettenberg, reviewed and revised them to suit his purpose, though he adhered so exactly to his material that

all the events related and all the personalities depicted are reproduced true to reality.

The title, "The Confessions of a Fair Soul,"
sounds in our ears a bit emotional and sanctimonious. But these notes have nothing to do with the
sanctimonious or the emotional.

The young woman whose development into Moravian religiosity and inspired pietism we follow
here has originally a rather healthy nature, clear,
intelligent and refined as she is. She is more nearly
bold than timid. She is at first worldly, though
almost incorporeally inclined—a nature fond of
reality, in which, however, the lasting conception
can be developed of living in inner communion with
her God. But this religious propensity is brought
on by several hemorrhages, the first of which takes
place as early as her eighth year.

Her unusual thirst after knowledge and her powers of conjecture date from the first awakening of
her reason. If she takes medicine, she wants to know
the origin of the herb from which the medicine
is made. When she learns to cook it is a feast for
her to cut up a chicken or a pig. Her father dilates
to her on splanchnological activities as though he
were lecturing to a student. Her childlike wish is
to get hold of a little sheep in which there is concealed an enchanted prince. She becomes acquainted
with a boy while dancing, with whom she begins to
fall in love: "Now I really have the little sheep
for which I wished." They write to each other and
rave about each other until they are separated.

The old French language teacher warns her. In
a composition written under a fictitious name she
related the story of her affair with this young chap.

The teacher says: "The good Phyllis had better
take care; that can easily become serious." Offended, she asked him what he means by *serious;*
he gives the half-grown girl some advice that is far
too straightforward and plain.   Blushing deeply,
she contends that Phyllis is a demure young girl.

Now she becomes acquainted with a crowd of
young people, happy-go-lucky young men without
any real education.   These were the German court
people "and this class had at that time not the
slightest *Kultur.*"   The majority of them led improper lives, and their conversation with her concerned itself with indecencies.   This offended her
and made her act coldly toward them; at times their
impropriety became shameless, whereupon she answered them rudely.

The old language teacher had, moreover, solici-
tously explained to her that not merely a girl's virtue
but her health as well was in danger from inter-
course with such men.   She depicts her horror for
them, her anxiety when one of them comes near her:
"I guarded myself from any glass or cup from which
they had drunk, indeed even from the chair from
which one of them had risen."   In this way she
soon feels isolated, spiritually as well as physically.
For the understanding of the soul this is important,
because it shows us how, through fear of contagion
thus ingrafted on the nature of a refined woman,
the joy from a sensuous life is at once disturbed at
its source.

Now follows the acquaintance and friendship
with an excellent young man, Narciss.   When he,
quite unblameworthy, because of an outburst of jealousy in a gathering, is felled by a blow and the thrust

of a sword, and she binds up his wound, the feeling which she in her quiet mind had nourished for him, bursts out like a flame struck by the air.

She thinks now and then of God, but always puts him off with only a ceremonious visit and then always wears fine clothes: her virtue, her honor, her special merit. But He seems not to have noticed her in this finery. She does not take this especially to heart; she has what she needs, health and well being; her contention is that God is not concerned further with her, because she herself is not much occupied with Him. Here begins this "most delicate interchange of the subjective and the objective" which for Goethe is the clear mark of religiosity.

She refers Narciss to her father, and they become engaged. She receives all her education from him. Good came of the association, according to her conception, in that "the submission so necessary and fitting for the feminine sex began" when she as betrothed strove to adapt herself to the wishes of her lover. In the meantime, however, they become totally at odds concerning the limits of propriety. She wishes to be safe and grants no freedom; he finds this "diet" quite severe, praises her principles and seeks at the same time to undermine them. But she always keeps the warning of the language teacher before her.

In the meantime she has become a little better acquainted with God; she was thankful to Him for giving her this man who was so dear to her. She complained to Him about that which made her solicitous, and did not notice that she herself had yearned and wished for this very thing. But when the whole world, with the exception of Narciss, was

dead for her, she was often lonely in society, and
complete isolation was most agreeable to her, because in it were developed her powers for convers-
ing with God concerning her feelings and thoughts.
God and love did not cross each other.   Her love
fitted in with the whole plan of creation.   In vain
did Narciss give her books which derided everything
invisible and supernatural, including even yearning
for knowledge on the part of woman.   She became
conscious of self-contradiction in the last instance:
"Like all men he mocked at learned women and
nevertheless educated me continually."

It is a question of his gaining promotion to an
office.   She prays to God about this in his behalf.
He is, however, not appointed, and she conceives
it as her religious duty to be satisfied therewith,
since this mishap also must be intended for her real
good.   And now the mildest emotions enter into
her soul; she feels that with the aid of heaven
everything can be accomplished.   He has less power
of resistance against this adversity than she; consequently she must console him.   And the milder and
the sweeter the inner experiences have been up to the
present, all the more often does she seek to prolong
them and find consolation where she has found it
so often.

The most of us are acquainted with experiences
of this sort, particularly from the days of our youth.
The impulse to prayer is a natural one and is awakened moreover by our environment.   In the beginning there is not a shadow of a doubt but that the
prayer is addressed to an unqualifiedly receptive
being.   Gradually, in the case of not a few, the
consideration of and for this being decreases, or

it disappears entirely. In the place of real prayer there arises a state of composure, of inner calm. The soul releases itself from tormenting anxiety and solicitude, seeks an inner, central point, finds its balance little by little and enjoys the feeling that it is being supported. Its poise is so much the surer because it believes it is being borne. It does not conceive of poise otherwise. It calls to mind those tribes of people who believe that the earth rests upon a tortoise and an elephant.

Since the soul is in this way concentrated in devotion, in prayer, in purpose, it will not suffer itself to be disturbed by temptation or torn by disappointment and sorrows. It feels itself purified, free, happy, far cleaner and stronger than when it was cowed, merged into everything that befell it, and lay broken-hearted and discouraged. It takes delight in its purity and independence. It rejoices in its strength, for it has moments when it swells with power. All this is still purely human, so to speak.

But in the case of many people, especially women, the personality feels that it is not merely supported, but comprehended, seen, observed. It finds itself face to face with the Invisible, the Almighty, the All-Good, which wills only its good, its very highest good. And then it feels irresistibly strong, for it has God with it and behind it in its struggles, and at the same time it feels infinitely humiliated, for it receives not the slightest measure of strength from itself. But it can move mountains.

Mere tendency towards God makes the soul happy. It seeks for itself its inner life after the fashion of one who is sensitive to cold, and wishing to become warm, seeks the fire. A shadow, a hindrance of some sort may, nevertheless, intervene.

And thus it happens in this instance to the narrator. She asks herself why her soul feels at times so repressed, so retarded in its efforts to attain unto the lofty heights that stand out as her spiritual objective. She discovers that the prime difficulty lies in her distracting and dissipating occupation with unworthy things. She would much prefer to deprive herself of all social life, of dancing and playing and of whatever else made up a part of the social customs and pleasures of her day. She would like to withdraw from all such amusements and diversions entirely. But by such action she offends Narciss who stands in incessant fear of ridicule. For his sake then she endures all these things, which in her heart she regards as folly, harmful folly. But the thought of them and her attitude toward her present life give her more and more concern.

She is going on twenty-two years old. The innocent pleasures appear to her no longer innocent. Furthermore, she knows of higher joys, of joys that strengthen in adversity and give comfort in misfortune. The struggle in her soul is soon ended. Even though there be something in her which causes her to yearn for sensual pleasures, she can no longer enjoy them aright. Just as he who is fond of wine, she argues, takes no pleasure in drinking it when he stands by a full cask in the cellar where the mephitic air is on the point of stifling him. Narciss has apparently been unable to conquer her senses. There is in her not merely a decisive measure of solicitude; there is also an element of real disgust at his erotic longing.

She is sufficiently unprejudiced not to condemn in any way a worldly life in others. She is not unmindful of the fact that a given food may in and of itself be healthy, though it is harmful to her. There is, at the same time, no use to try to induce her to commit an act on the ground that it is not immoral for others. In this way, the gap between the betrothed becomes wider and wider, until they are separated. She still loves him, but she no longer feels the need of him. She breaks with him. And now that she is free, and there is no longer any secret of her unctuous dread of diversions, she feels even less than ever the need to conceal her great love for art and science. She paints; she reads; and she finds an abundance of congenial society.

Another hemorrhage and prolonged physical weakness produce a renewed intensification and pressure of piety. She feels happy at knowing that just as certain as respiration is a sign of life, just so certain is she not without God in this world. She feels as if she were near Him, as if she stood before Him. But she heartily disapproves of Lavater's appeals to the orthodox to give publicity to examples of real grantings of prayer. She feels that just as momentous as each inner experience has been at the critical moment, just so flat, unessential, ineffectual, and improbable would the narrative sound if she were to quote single details. What she dares say is that she never returned empty-handed when she sought God in trouble and in need.

But she has never for a second feared Hell; the idea of an evil spirit and of a place of martyrdom after death could nowhere find a place in her range of ideas. Nor does she know at all the thing called

sin. But through communion with the invisible
Friend she perceives the sweetest enjoyments of all
her life power. The impulse to enjoy these good
fortunes becomes so great that she gladly relinquishes everything that might interfere with it.

At this period she makes a new and significant
acquaintance in her development. She becomes acquainted with Philo (the later minister and chancellor K. von Moser) a man of heart, wit, and
talent, but a man who wades in feminine favor and
constantly seeks new relations with women. In her
eyes he is a Wieland-like "Agathon" living a life
of enjoyment. They become attached to each other;
he is tempted to give this nun-like creature his complete confidence. She anxiously forebodes "fearful
external and internal complications" for him and
becomes lost in melancholy over him.

She thereupon suddenly hears an inner voice:
"You are no better than he," and is startled.
Throughout an entire year she feels capable of all
degrees of wickedness, murder, theft, and voluptuousness. It is the human, weakly erotic sympathy
in the mature woman. She *will* not in her heart be
considered better than he; she understands his temptations and faults. That voice is the voice of blood,
of the instinct of love, which wakes for the last time
and drives her over into faith, faith which is essentially love. For she herself says: "Such is not
cured by the practice of virtue but by faith."

Now what is faith? How can it help her accept
the story of a past event as true? Faith must be
a condition in man's own mind; she therefore implores the Almighty: "Give me faith!"

One day she was leaning over a table hiding her

tear-stained face in her hands. What did she feel then? It was as though a gust of wind, a blast, were bringing her to the cross on which Jesus died. "It was a gust of wind," she says, "I can call it nothing else, *just like that by which our soul is borne to a faraway lover,* an approach which to all appearances is far more natural and truer than we suppose." From this moment on she knew what faith was.

In addition to inner clarity, equanimity, and fulness in her soul there now comes emotionalism. To the poise, freedom, and purity of the soul in the moral domain, to this consecrated naïveté, is added ecstasy which in her nature is nothing more than the transfer of the stifled erotic longing to the realm of religion. She feels a power to arise that is wholly new to her: "In such presentiments, words fail us." . . . Just so does a love-sick woman also speak. Her expression coincides letter for letter with that from the lips of a girl who is deeply in love, and whose love is reciprocated. "I could rise up above that which formerly menaced me, just as a bird, singing and without difficulty, flies up over the fastest stream opposite which a dog remains standing with fretful barking."

Now in place of the poise of peace, the security of ecstasy like that of a somnambulist enters her mind. When she finally attempts to give a conception of her condition, she writes: "I no longer remember a prayer. Nothing appears to me in the form of a law. It is an instinct which leads and directs me aright. I follow my conviction with liberty, and know as little of limiting destinies as of remorse." This is, as we see, the quiet and humble expression of a free person. It is what the Russian advanced *Intelligentsia* calls the immediate condition.

What especially attracted and profoundly fascinated Goethe is evidently the fact that the moral striving in this case is overcome in a way that renders ethics superfluous. It is nevertheless most interesting to observe the incessant intermingling of that which actually takes place in the soul, and the reflection of the soul's agitations, resulting as it does in the phantastic representation of a hovering, as it were, in the metaphysical world.

The same thing happens here that happens at a familiar and frequently performed physical experiment. An object that obeys all the laws of earthly existence, including the law of gravity, (a person, for example, who lies stretched out on a table) appears, because of a false conception that is itself conditioned by law, to be floating in the air as a supernatural, celestial phantasm. But if this figure be beautiful, it is just as beautiful even though it in reality be bound to the earth and its floating be a mere illusion.

Without one word by way of interpretation, without having written one sentence in his own name, without having set down one single idea that could flected in this same woman's mind, floating freely in the vast celestial expanse near her divine redeemer.

Moralists even to this very day have not entirely not have come just as well from the orthodox Moravian woman, Goethe has pictured the soul of a fair and noble woman both as it is, subservient to all conditions of earthly existence, and as it is, respent their rage on *Wilhelm Meister*. Vischer, Germany's greatest aesthetician, wrote concerning the novel a few years before his death: "One does not need to be a *Bierphilister* in order to inquire whether it is in the nature of things that an eighteen-year-old shop boy becomes a happy father. Not that a poet dare not say as much, but this situation calls for a final act in which his old man, who hears about it, at least locks him up for a week on bread and water. . . . And on Philine the poet dwells certainly with more satisfaction than logic demands."

Vischer's conception does not glitter with wit nor his mode of expression with finesse; at any rate he should not have entirely forgotten the detailed dwelling upon the confessions of the Moravian woman, these confessions which give the work so heavy a counterbalance to Philine's roguishness.

Among contemporaries it was Schiller who could best evaluate the confessions; be praises them because they avoid the "trivial terminology of devotion." This section, which accentuates so strongly the abrogation of law, accords harmoniously with the spirit of the entire work of which the confessions are but one single link. The spirit in *Wilhelm Meister* proceeds in truth from the dissolution of duty's harsh claim and the defense of freedom along the lines of beautiful naturalness. The spirit of the novel teaches that the road to freedom is through the gateway of beauty.

Hence the embitterment over the work on the part of the pious, the moral, the sanctified, the earlier friends, men and women. Hence the scandals of Klopstock, Stolberg, Claudius, Jacobi, and Schlosser. Hence the remark of Frau von Stein that there

are some "beautiful thoughts" in the book, but that
"wherever Goethe has experienced something of
the noble feelings in human nature, he attaches to
them a little dirt." Hence Herder's exclamation at
"a certain unclean spirit in the book," his purifying
himself from complicity, his insistence that Goethe
no longer troubles himself about "the good, the
noble, the moral grace," until he comes near setting
his own humanity based on morality up against Goethe's based on beauty. The latter wrote concerning
this in one of his letters to Schiller: "And in this
way, the old, half true, Philistine hurdy-gurdy melody buzzes without ceasing, to the tune that art shall
recognize the moral law and subordinate itself to
it. It has always done the first and must do so . . .
If it did the second, it were lost, and it were better
to hang a mill stone about its neck and drown it than
to let it slowly give up the ghost as the outcome
of acquiescence in this utilitarian platitude."

It was not fortuitous that Goethe entitled that
insertion "the confessions of a *fair* soul." The
beauty of the life of the soul is the central thought
of the entire work. It is psychological. A type of
psychic beauty such as is portrayed here in the lower
religious form is, according to Goethe's intention,
supposed to appear in a more complete, purely human form in the person of Natalie. Lothario, consequently, at the close of the novel, when Therese
relinquishes Wilhelm to Natalie, pronounces the
above-quoted judgment on Natalie's conduct, which
is regarded as an unattainable model. He calls
her "this beautiful soul" and adds: "Indeed she
deserves this appellation of honor more than many
others, *even more than our noble aunt herself.*"

In *Wilhelm Meister,* Book VIII, Chapter 5, we have a portrayal of Natalie's castle. Sphinxes of granite guarded the main entrance to the great hall, "the hall of the past." The doors, of Egyptian style, are somewhat narrower at the top than at the bottom, while their iron wings prepare us for a sombre, even horrible sight. One was therefore pleasantly surprised on entering the hall to see that art and life had abolished every touch of death and the grave. Not even the sarcophagi and urns round about made a disheartening or disturbing impression. Everything gleamed with marble and azure; all this splendor was effective from a purely architectural point of view. Directly opposite the entrance, on a splendid sarcophagus, was a marble statue of a stately man resting on a cushion. He held a scroll in his hands which he seemed to be studying with marked attentiveness. On it were inscribed the words: *Remember to Live!*

Remember to Live! That is the complete *Wilhelm Meister* in three words. It is Goethe's laconic *memento vivere* flung out in happy defiance and quiet sublimity against all concerned with the opposite. It is the challenge to inflated piety and the *memento mori* of Christianity.

Remember to Live! What does it mean? Not that we are to scrape together as many sensual enjoyments as possible. It means that we are to get the best out of our lives. What did the expression *to live* mean to Goethe? To him it signified the preservation of the beauty of the soul that leads to freedom. Never to feel one's self as a mere means to an end, but as one who does not need the law.

CHAPTER IX

DEFECTS IN GOETHE'S NARRATIVE ART

GOETHE'S art of narration is distinctly inferior to his unique lyric power and his ability to depict characters. He composes his novels after the old-fashioned pattern. He depends far too much on the effect of surprises, remarkable coincidences and romantic circumstances. His epic style, antiquated from the beginning, becomes more so as he grows older. It is this that intimidates the half-educated from the study of his narratives.

Even the unprejudiced reader finds it odd that he should begin his *Wahlverwandtschaften* with a sentence like this: "Eduard—thus we call a rich Baron in his prime—had spent a fine April afternoon in his garden." Not even an admitted bungler would begin a novel with such a sentence to-day. He would do anything to avoid a parenthesis after the first word, nor would he dream of introducing a *we* at the very outset and thereby detract from the unhampered manipulation of the name and general content.

No matter how fresh and vivid the narration of *Wilhelm Meisters Lehrjahre* may be at times, the reader is repelled at other times by the method of elaboration. We demand of the modern author that he understand his business and be able to depict everything that should be depicted. To use the

word "indescribable" or admit that "such no pen
can describe," is a manifestation of weakness at
odds with writing in the twentieth century. But
Goethe constantly refers to his lack of ability. On
the occasion of Wilhelm's first conversation with the
harpist, we are regaled with the following: "We
might become ever so diffuse and yet we would not
be able to describe the charm of the hasty conversation if we attempted to reproduce the remarks of
our friend with the adventuresome stranger."

Occasionally Goethe even promises to tell the
reader something on another occasion: "The master
of horse would like very much to learn the origin
and life history of Friedrich; the latter then related
an adventure he has already told on a number of
occasions and with which we intend to make our
readers acquainted at another time." Or take this
instance further on in the novel: "Wilhelm wrote
down many such conversations, and we will, since
we dare not break off the narrative so often, present it to our readers at another opportunity; it is
entirely likely that they will be interested in such
dramaturgic attempts."

A fire breaks out in the course of the novel during
which the harpist, who seems to have become insane,
wants to murder Wilhelm's child with a knife.
Mignon prevents him from so doing. Wilhelm
hurries away after the non-plussed harpist, entices
him into a summer house and, Goethe writes, "carried on with him a remarkable conversation, which,
however, in order not to pain our readers with dis-
connected ideas and solicitous feelings, we prefer to
suppress rather than to give at all, to say nothing
of setting it forth in detail."

It is by this inartistic means that Goethe holds
back the secret in the harpist's life, disagreeable as
it is, until the very close of the novel. He has been
passionately in love with his sister Sperata without
once suspecting his blood relationship to the young
girl. Mignon is his daughter by Sperata. Begotten
in incest, she was later on abducted by the tight rope
dancers. The harpist was loath to part with his
sweetheart, even after he had learned precisely who
she was; and not once had he been willing to admit
of any break in the love between brother and sister
—until he and she were separated from each other
by force.

We and the characters in the novel learn of this
secret, with its romantic by-product and the incredible impression it leaves, when it is far too late to set
in motion a real play of feelings. It is suppressed
when it might well be suspected and related when
it is entirely superfluous.

A peculiar result of the constant intrusion of the
narrator is defective diction as soon as direct discourse becomes necessary. Goethe has manifestly
laid inadequate stress on distinguishing and individ-
ualising. While Martha in *Faust* speaks after the
fashion of an old matchmaker, Marianne's maid
and confidant, old Barbara, talks like a book. We
do not see her for ourselves; her language is abstract
and literary. How wholly different, how much better, Voltaire portrays such an old crone, even when
she appears in one of his admittedly didactic novels
of philosophic intent! "And Felix?" Wilhelm asks.
The woman of many years replies: "Your son
by this lovable girl, whose sole misfortune was that
she loved too tenderly . . . I am not going to run

off! Wait and I will fetch you a document that will cause you both joy and sorrow."

What produces the strangest effect of all in Goethe's method of narrating is the trite pretense on the part of the author that he himself was the invisible observer of the scenes he sets forth. The very close of the first chapter, with the happy meeting between the two lovers, reads as follows:

Wilhelm entered. With what vivacity she rushed to meet him! With what ecstasy he embraced the red uniform! With what delight he pressed the silken bodice to his breast! Who would dare describe, who would be so bold as to give expression to, the joy of two lovers? The old woman went away mumbling something to herself and we depart with her and leave the two blissful souls alone and undisturbed.

This is amusing and nothing more. The aged but loquacious matchmaker trips away and the invisible narrator follows suit, in *pluralis majestatis,* in order not to cause embarrassment. It is all strange, almost as much so as when Goethe remains in certain tender scenes, of which the novel has a plenty, and joins in the chatter. For example, when Wilhelm and the Countess embrace for the first and last time. Among other observations we are regaled with this one:

"Her head rested upon his shoulder and no thought was given to the locks and ribbons crushed and dishevelled by assuming this position. She put her arm around him; he embraced her tightly, pressed her again and again to his bosom. Oh, that such a moment cannot last forever! And woe to the envious fate which disturbed our friends in this brief moment!" It is evident that the narrator would grant them the complete enjoyment of culpable pleasure.

Most remarkable of all is the style in which the narrator himself declares that he is uncertain as to how the situation appeals to the imagination of the persons depicted. After having practised her ingratiatory arts upon Wilhelm long and in vain, Philine one day sits down by his side, or more accurately speaking, on his lap and caresses him in full view of all who chance to pass by. She derides him because he sits there like a stick, as inanimate as a stone. About to leave him, she says: "Please stay so that I can find my stone man on the bench when I return."

Goethe adds: "This time she did him an injustice; for however much he strove to control himself in her presence he would, *in all probability*, had he been with her in a place convenient for amusement, not have let her fondling go by unheeded." The thoroughness with which this phase of the matter is treated is pedantic, to be quite conservative.

Still queerer, however, is the clumsiness of the style in the depiction of the relation between Wilhelm and Philine the day following the clandestine visit by night to his sleeping chamber. Wilhelm does not know, because of the darkness, which woman it was who had visited him. This is an infringement on one's sense of probability.

A little later we read: "On leaving Philine whispered to Wilhelm: I must have left my slippers behind; please don't lock the door. These words throw him into profound confusion. His surmise that the guest of the previous night had been Philine is strengthened, and the reader is forced to share this opinion, especially since we cannot discover the reasons which made him doubtful and which must have instilled him with another curious misgiving." Reasons, incidentally, which have already been definitely hinted at but which Goethe has forgotten because he wrote the book after too long an intermission. We learn, too, at the close, that Mignon had also intended to do this very thing. It was her plan to sneak into Wilhelm's room on that very same night. According to the original plan it seems that she and not Philine was to pay the visit.

As a superfluous supplement to this bizarre system, as a result of which the author frequently does not know the hero's thoughts and is not always aware of what really takes place, must be added the fact, for modern readers even more antiquated, that others do know what the hero is thinking about, and are aware of what takes place even though it occurs in secret, in the dead of night or within the silent mind. There are, for example, the men in the tower, the secret society of the omniscient, with the abbot at its head. The eighteenth century was, to be sure, the age of Freemasons, Jesuits, Rosicrucians and numerous other secret societies.

It is never chance but reason that directs Wilhelm's fate. When the society of actors is to play *Hamlet* an unknown individual turns up to take the part of the ghost. He slinks away unseen but leaves his veil behind on which the warning, "Flee, young man, flee!" has been imprinted. Wilhelm's guide has considered it high time to wean him away from association with actors. We would hardly anticipate such architecture nowadays in a dime novel.

It finally comes out that Jarno knows even Wil-

helm's secret thoughts, thoughts expressed to no one.
There is, by way of illustration, the motif of the
secret benefactor suspected of being a recruiting
officer, who wants to press him into military service
against his will.   Wilhelm feels poignant grief at
knowing that whatever he does he is watched and
guided.   He had felt that he was unobserved and
free.

Yet what do these imperfections signify in comparison with the breadth of vision and horizon of
the novel as a whole?   What are they in comparison
with its wealth of characters, each unforgetable,
and its depths of knowledge concerning and insight
into the mysterious workings of the human soul?

Though this anticipates the course of development, it is worthy of note in this connection that in
the looser composition of Wilhelm's *Wanderjahre*
the narrator makes himself much more felt.   We
are left with the impression that in those days a
novel was written to be read in the long winter evenings in lonely, isolated homes, the family gathered
around the centre table and regarding the poet as
their personal friend.

In the introduction to the excellent narrative
interwoven at this point, *Der Mann von fünfzig
Jahren,* Goethe discloses to us his initial plan: He
wishes to adapt himself to the custom of the
highly honoured public by entertaining in sections.
He will bring out the present narrative serially.
But then he found an uninterrupted discourse more
suitable to his purpose.

In the novel the hero has translated several verses
of Ovid for a charming young lady.   But as he is
about to give them to her he finds himself in a dis-

tressing situation. The young woman in the poem is depicted as a spider. Should the lady who is to be favored with the translation see an allusion to her own personality she might find the comparison offensive. Then we are regaled with this surprising comment: "We do not know how our friend extricated himself from this difficulty. We must refer the incident to others over which the muses are kind and shrewd enough to cast a veil." That is naïve.

In not a few points Goethe departs from his established prose form of later years. Having commented on the excellence of a certain painter, he says: "In order not to be accused with putting good-natured readers off with vague, empty phrases which they are not in a position to verify, I reproduce the judgment of a connoisseur concerning the work of this artist. For several years he has been studying the works of this painter and of others of the same school." Then we are treated to a section of real or fictitious essays in art criticism.

All form comes to a dead stop when, in the introduction to the *Wanderjahre,* we read: "He [Wilhelm] began to read." But instead of telling us that what Wilhelm read, Goethe says: "But if we find it convenient not to let the good man read further, our friends will hardly take it amiss. . . . Our friends have undertaken a novel and since it has occasionally become more of a didactic poem than is right we find it advisable not to put our readers' patience to a still harder test. The papers shall be printed in another place."

As time went on Goethe's prose thereby lost its clarity and warmth. He could now and then even go over to pure *Kanzleistil* and write *solches* and *dasselbe,* as in the following:

Ist nun das Gras von ihnen geschlagen und zu Heu getrocknet, so werfen sie *solches* von den Höhen in tiefere Thalgründe herab, wo *dasselbe* wider gesammelt . . . wird.

This is due in part to the fact that his powers of observation weakened with age; he fused pictures from memory. It is due also to his inclination to shatter illusions, to reflect the work within the work, a conceit which the German romanticists inherited from him.

In *Die Wanderjahre* Wilhelm meets a painter who has read *Die Lehrjahre.* He is enchanted by the dead Mignon and wishes to paint her in appropriate surroundings. They arrive at "the great sea," by which Goethe—as he tells Eckermann—meant Lago Maggiore. We read: "Couched under the cypresses they saw the laurels rise up, the pomegranates ripen, the orange and lemon trees in bloom, and the fruit at the same time gleam out from the dark foliage."

We feel here Mignon's song of her country; we feel, too, the joy for the strongly picturesque which in later years predominated in Goethe's works, especially in his verse, and which makes the style in the second part of *Faust* so new and surprising, at times even Rembrandtesque.

Whereas Goethe, in the poetry of his youth, was interested mostly in the psychic, his creative writing changes, as years go by, its principle of style and dwells in his old age preferably on that which is revealed to the senses and enriches them in a mysterious way.

CHAPTER X

Voss's *Luise* AND Goethe's *Hermann und Dorothea*

Johann Heinrich Voss, founder of the *Göttinger Hainbund*, friend of Klopstock and Claudius, ardent opponent of Wieland, zealous rationalist, and lover of virtue and the fatherland, had, during his impecunious days as tutor and schoolmaster, assimilated a comfortable amount of philological information. When thirty years of age (1781), he published his excellent translation of the *Odyssey*, followed by many other translations from Greek and Roman antiquity. He was the first German who controlled the hexameter, and made it melodious in the German language.

As early as 1783 he published, as a fragment, the second song of his idyllic poem *Luise;* it did not appear in its entirety until 1795, caused an extraordinary sensation, and met with great success. Voss was living at that time as rector in Eutin, a position which his friend of that period, Fritz v. Stolberg, had procured for him. Since Eutin then belonged to Denmark, Voss had, as Baggesen relates in *Labyrinthen,* "determined to learn Danish." It remained a matter of determination. This and the acquaintance with Baggesen is all the share that Denmark has in him.

Luise became significant for Goethe's production, for immediately after the completion of *Wilhelm*

Meisters Lehrjahre, in September, 1796, he began the elaboration of *his* idyll in hexameters, *Hermann und Dorothea,* which, despite its grandeur and value along other lines, would never have come into existence if Voss's poem had not preceded.

Luise is a vicarage idyll which makes its appeal because the verses are excellently built up with correct, weighty spondees and lightly moving dactyls in a set scheme, where not one accent is false; and which repels because of the bland way in which all family emotions are sugarcoated with sentimentality and saturated with emotional weeping.

There is sympathetic delight in landscapes and a vivid sense for plant and animal life. The landscapes, incidentally, leave a distinctly Danish impression. Since the hero is a country parson, the deism of the poet makes itself felt in ever-recurring prayers of gratitude and incessant laudation of God's dominant, fatherly goodness toward his many and varied creatures, all of which has a decidedly old-fashioned ring. On the other hand, the poet is a militant rationalist. When the wise and good are enumerated, Socrates is not forgotten; nor is Voss's good friend, Mendelssohn. They are listed side by side with the apostles and prophets—somewhat as Oehlenschläger groups together "Jesus on High, Baldur, Socrates."[3]

We have a legend that tells how St. Peter let a Catholic, a Calvinist, and a Lutheran sit outside of Heaven's gates on one and the same bench, while all within sang the praises of one and the same God.

---

[3] Oehlenschläger wrote (1835) a tragedy entitled "Sokrates," the death scene from which was read to him a few hours before he died.   —TRANSLATOR.

The legend begins as follows:

> O Himmelswonne, wir freun uns,
> Alle, die Gutes gethan nach Kraft und redlicher Einsicht,
> Und die zu höherer Kraft vorleuchteten; freun uns mit
>   Petrus,
> Moses, Konfuz, und Homer, dem liebenden, und Zoroaster,
> Und, der für Wahrheit starb, mit Sokrates, auch mit dem
>   edeln
> Mendelssohn! Der hätte den Göttlichen nimmer gekreuzigt.

Though the combination of names in this passage is rather striking, the one in which the greatest plastic artists are catalogued is even more so. It contains the names of Praxiteles, Phidias—and Angelica Kauffmann.

No idyllic poet of ancient times was ever so idyllic as Voss. All the persons are of immaculate character, the men as well as the women, plebeian just like the noble, servants along with the masters. Everything in this parsonage smells good, tastes good, sounds good. The unique disharmony arises when the young parson, about to drink a toast (proposed by Luise's father) to his beloved Luise of eighteen summers, takes hold of his glass so high that it does not quite clink *comme il faut*. Voss's rivals, who do not write such excellent hexameters, receive this gentle dig:

> Tausendmal hab' ich ihn, Sohn, an die Erzuntugend erinnert!
> Klappt nicht immer sein Glas wie ein spaltiger Töpf und
>   des neuern
> Dichterschwarms ungeschliffner Hexameter, welcher daher-
>   plumpt
> Ohne Takt und Musik, zum Aergernis? Kann er nicht
>   anders?

This is the only false note struck in *Luise* and there can hardly be a difference of opinion as to its insignificance. Otherwise everything that takes place is ideal; fortune means good fortune; in so far as there is feeling it is that of joy. The author carries on a bit of coquetry with himself as the poet. The first is when they sing the new song which "our friend in Eutin" composed—he was then in Grünau —a hymn to international brotherhood. The second is when the wedding song is sung in honor of Luise and her bridegroom. It is ascribed expressly to "our Voss in Eutin." It is a rather vapid but well-meant song in praise of marriage.

When Goethe published *Hermann und Dorothea* two years later, the tendency in many circles, especially in those in which Voss's friends were in the majority, was to place *Luise* above the new epic poem. Goethe's effort was referred to as a relatively weak imitation. But neither for enlightened contemporary opinion nor for posterity has there been the slightest doubt concerning the relative value of the two works. Goethe's superiority is incalculable.

If, however, one wishes to get a clear impression of the reawakening of Greek antiquity, as revived by Voss, let him compare the *Der Achtzigjährige Geburtstag,* or his *Luise,* with André Chenier's contemporary revivification of ancient poetry on French soil. Such a comparison will enable us to see why Voss produced the ancient idyll in housecoat and slippers, fitted it out with pious sentimentality and gave it spiritual impetus, while Chenier, his junior by eleven years, born of a Greek mother and permeated with Attic spirit, was throughout free in mind and sober in the expression of emotions, and chaste in style even when erotic. Voss was chaste even in his handling of his material; his passion is merely the Protestant passion of married life. But in his style he is unchaste. There is not a trace of attempt to govern and control the joy of beauty: it smacks and weeps; it is undisciplined and run-away. What Goethe did was to bring an anecdote of the year 1734 down to his own time, transfer it from Salzburg to the Rhine, and incidentally make use of the turmoil of the revolution and the general flight of people *en masse* as a background in the portrayal of the fortunes of private individuals. His poem is marked throughout by the finer and grander elements in his own character just as it reveals his plastic conception of men and situations.

Hermann und Dorothea does not belong to Goethe's most interesting works; it has no great inner wealth; it is without the horn of plenty. But it is grand, classical, clear and on a lofty stylistic level. It strikes the chord upon which half a century later Johan Ludwig Runeberg [4] plays both in his compositions in hexameters and in his individual bits of poetry. It is the first real poetic work on the Fatherland that Goethe wrote since *Götz von Berlichingen*. It is artistic and yet quite simple. It

[4] Brandes has reference, it would seem, to Johan Ludvig Runeberg's (1804-1877) *Hanna* (1836), a charming idyl of Finnish life, written in hexameters. Runeberg was recognized, for a while at least, as second only to Tegnér among Swedish poets. Though born in Sweden, he spent his entire life in Finland, where, as a tutor in small Finnish villages, he became familiar with the life of the people, a familiarity which he used to good purpose in his poetry. Though influenced by the Greeks and Goethe, he was of exceptional originality. He did a great deal to link the country of his birth and the country of his adoption together. He lectured for a while at the University of Helsingfors on Roman literature. His romance in verse entitled "Grafven i Perrho" was awarded the gold medal by the Swedish Academy. He founded the Helsingfors *Morgonblad,* which dealt chiefly with æsthetic and literary questions and exerted a marked influence. —TRANSLATOR.

idealizes types of German men and women. Though
it revolves about the affairs of a small town, it is
a stranger to the outstanding faults of Voss's *Luise,*
though it is probable that with regard to purity and
correctness in versification Voss is superior to Goethe. The latter could occasionally allow a trochee
to stand for a spondee or commit other small sins
against prosodic perfection.

The great public in as well as out of Germany
has had its impression of both Hermann and Dorothea spoiled by Kaulbach's illustrations which, like
Cornelius's of *Faust,* either overlook or blur that
particular feature which constitutes Goethe's peculiar merit: his measured dignity and spiritual temperance which abhor all that is theatrical and avoid
depicted heroism. There is a wholesomeness and
simplicity about *Hermann und Dorothea* that render
affectation impossible. But how affectedly Faust
behaves when, according to Cornelius, he offers his
arm to Gretchen! What figures of Teutonic
strength Hermann and Dorothea have become at
the hands of Kaulbach! They have become super-
naturally big and totally unnatural as types.

Goethe's own strength lies in his holding fast
to the *modesty of nature,* even where he strives
after the typical and representative. We have seen
that his men are not always manly; but his women
are always womanly. In this case the hero is
equipped with an extremely sympathetic, unosten-
tatious manliness, while the heroine makes an even
more sympathetic impression, despite her hardy
courage that enables her to use a sabre so effectively.
But she possesses more penetrating feminine qualities, such as self-sacrificing goodness, easily awak-

ened though earnest affection, and, like the hero,
unqualified humanity. In his ecstatic admiration for ancient literature
Goethe amused himself by giving the nine short
songs into which he divided his idyllic epic names
after the nine books of Herodotus, one for each
of the nine muses. And the muses did not fail him.
First and foremost the work has an exceptionally
wide horizon. Its very first lines give the reader
at once a view out over the fate that has befallen
a train of fleeing refugees, out over the Rhine,
which, powerful stream that it is, constitutes one
of the protective boundaries of Germany designed
by nature. These same lines give a view in on the
daily life of the little town on the Rhine with its
dignitaries, the host and hostess of *Zum goldenen
Löwen,* the Pastor, and the Apothecary. In the way
of thinking and mode of living of the inn-keeper and
his wife we feel that we recognize young Wolfgang's
parents: The father domineering and persevering
in harmless snobbery; the mother clever and unprejudiced. Each is gifted with a good head and a
loving heart. And Hermann has inherited the excellence of both; he is at once sturdy and affectionate. He is also patriotically inspired as no other
of Goethe's young heroes; he bewails the fact that,
as an only son, he was not called to the colors. He
grieves over the fact that Germany is not united
and makes this virile speech:

Wahrlich, wäre die kraft der deutschen Jugend beisammen,
An der Grenze verbündet, nicht nachzugeben dem Fremden,
O, sie sollten uns nicht den herrlichen Boden betreten,
Und vor unseren Augen die Früchte des Landes verzehren,
Nicht den Männern gebieten und rauben Weiber und
    Mädchen!

In clear fashion and unmistakable form Dorothea makes her first appearance before the reader, and before Hermann as well: She is guiding with her long staff the oxen before the heavily laden wagon. We see her walking with stately tread and womanly bearing; she makes the impression of some lofty, consoling power. She alone takes charge of the young mother who lies stretched out on the straw of the wagon. Dorothea appeals to us as the embodiment of care and unselfish devotion, so much so and so strongly that we understand quite well Hermann's involuntary impulse, not merely to surrender to her the linen that the patient needs, but to entrust her with the distribution of all the food and drink given him by his mother for the needy emigrants.

Not a word is used at this first meeting to describe the girl as beautiful or impressive. Through the deep impression, however, that she has made upon the manly youth, and by reason of the ardent desire he manifests to see her again, and to secure her for his parent's home, her figure stands out in the reader's imagination as a charming creation, a captivating creature. Her history and her delineation are put on the lips of the Judge who accompanies the fleeing band.

Goethe has likewise entrusted to the Judge the portrayal of the picture of the times. It is the Judge who says what Goethe has to say regarding the expectations which had been aroused by the outbreak of the Revolution, and which had so quickly been brought to naught. The words are at once passionate and poetic:

Denn wer leugnet es wohl, dass hoch sich das Herz ihm
  erhoben,
Ihm die freiere Brust mit reineren Pulsen geschlagen,
Als sich der erste Glanz der neuen Sonne heranhob,
Als man hörte vom Rechte der Menschen, das Allen gemein
  sei,
Von der begeisternden Freiheit und von der löblichen
  Gleichheit. . . .
Schauten nicht alle Völker in jenen drängenden Tagen
Nach der Hauptstadt der Welt, die es schon so lange
  gewesen
  Und jetzt mehr als je den herrlichen Namen verdiente?
Waren nicht jener Männer, der ersten Verkünder der
  Botschaft,
Namen den höchsten gleich, die unter die Sterne gesetzt
  sind?
Wuchs nicht jeglichem Menschen der Muth and der Geist
  und die Sprache?

In this way the Judge shows, in resentful and
striking words, how the first joy over liberty and
the original faith in popular fraternity was followed
by a succession of keen disappointments, one more
austere than the other. And through the ingenious argument that a conquering enemy can be noble
minded, as in this case it was, but that an army in
retreat, in fear of death, filled with lust for murder
and pliancy in the exercise of violence, is and remains purely bestial, the transition is made to the
portrayal of Dorothea's heroism in her struggle
on behalf of the little girls against the plundering
and rapacious rabble. We still do not know how
she looks; but we do know that she is high spirited.

At last, in the sixth song of the idyl, we have
the description of her, set forth in the most natural
and clever way. The Apothecary has been looking
for the girl among the crowd of fugitives and has

guessed her identity from the old calico and the blue
pillow-slip which she has swathed about the new
born child. Hermann's mother had sent her the
clothing. He next recognizes her red stomacher
which, prettily laced, supports her rounded bosom,
the black bodice and the freshly ruffled frill which
lies gracefully about her chin. Above this he notes
the fine oval of her head and her heavy braids
wound about the silver pin. Though Dorothea is
sitting down, we easily discover the symmetry of her
tall form; and where her skirts stop we perceive
her well shaped ankles. Instinctively and from the
text we feel that her figure is commendable in every
detail.

Here as elsewhere in this genuine masterpiece
the description is revealed in narration. This is
real throughout, and never sentimental, though it
is constantly inspired by emotions; its fundamental
tone is noble. It is real poetry.

It is no wonder that *Hermann und Dorothea*
won the popular favor that was so frequently and
unjustifiably denied Goethe's other works. Here
was not the slightest detail that might give offence
of any kind. Family and fatherland were glorified,
and though every line was written with extreme dignity, nothing was tame or insipid. An unassuming,
everyday theme was treated in a grand and enno-
bling style.

CHAPTER XI

Friendship With Schiller; Collaboration on *Die Xenien*—Collaboration on Schiller's *Balladen*

THE ever-growing friendship with Schiller dominates this period of Goethe's life, though it is well to remember that it was not a friendship between equals. The two had a high regard for each other, but they were what the Romans called *non aequo foedre amantes.* There was the difference in age and the difference in rank. They were perhaps equally drawn to each other, but what Schiller offered was a most zealous incitement to poetic activity, considered by Goethe at the time as highly encouraging. What Goethe contributed was a wealth of ideas which suggested their own form, greatly augmented Schiller's spiritual stock in trade and determined for the time being his productive tendency. While Goethe's circumstances had made him a *grand seigneur,* who worked only when the spirit moved him, Schiller, by natural inclination and because of his economic indigence, was a litterateur who founded magazines, was supposed to supply the copy, and pressed both himself and others to write for them.

This means of producing, under stress and tension, was capital for the hectic, fiery Schiller but was ill adapted to Goethe's nature, which created when it had to but otherwise lay dormant. In a letter to Wilhelm von Humboldt of 1803, Schiller writes of Goethe: "It is deplorable that he allows the familiar habit to get the upper hand. He busies himself with everything possible but is unable to concentrate himself on some one thing." That is said of Goethe!

We meet, consequently, for the first time in Goethe's works with a conspicuous lack of originality in the contributions which Schiller pressed from him for his magazine, *Die Horen*. Under the collective title of *Unterhaltungen deutscher Ausgewanderter,* Goethe submitted a series of tales that are nothing but a rehash of ghost stories, replete with spiritism and exploiting the worn themes of the creaking desk and the enchanted table. They were taken from mediocre French memoirs. It is all an adventure in rebus style with incomprehensible allegories; and in the execution there is at once irksome garrulity and intolerable diffuseness.

The best of the series, the one on the honorable *Prokurator,* is such a tale as was found amusing in the fifteenth century when *Cent nouvelles nouvelles* were in vogue. They appeal to a contemporary as abounding in questionable taste and brutal psychology. In this particular narrative we have to do with the purely outward preservation of virtue on the part of a woman, though the lady in the case would gladly dispense with it altogether. A lawyer, the procurator, goes to the city where he makes the acquaintance of a young woman whose husband, having set out on a long journey, insists that should she be unable to endure her temporary and enforced singleness, she is to choose none but older men as her lovers. She feels a passion for the procurator. But he, long since past the days of early youth and immensely demure, leads her to believe that he has taken a vow that binds him to complete abstinence for many months. Out of love for him, the young woman remains chaste during the time of waiting and the virtuous friend of the family extends the time until the husband returns home. It is such episodes that transpired in an age when no appreciable difference was made between a stable and an alcove. But when published five hundred years later for the moral, we feel repelled.

The tales are set in a frame from the time of the Revolution. As in *Das Mädchen von Oberkirch,* the large family of a Baroness have been obliged to flee from the left to the right bank of the Rhine where they associate with a *Geheimrat,* who, after the fashion of the *Hofrat* in *Die Aufgeregten,* is scrupulously conservative. He comes to blows, argumentative if not physical, with Carl, the nephew of the Baroness, who is strongly in favour of the guillotine and hopes to see it rigidly employed on German soil. In order to preserve calm, stories are told. The narrative which closes the series and which Goethe called *Das Märchen* is held in high esteem in Germany and is indeed excellently adapted to German readers in so far as it gives unlimited opportunity for the development of hermeneutics. After repeated and diligent readings I must confess my absolute inability to find any meaning in this exacting and irritating work, written, as it seems to have been, with the same proneness to give the reader riddles to solve that prompted Goethe

a little later to write his *Weissagungen des Bakis*.
The purpose of art, however, is not to treat the
reader as a burglar in that the cupboards are so
constructed that no fiend can open them unless he
has a half score of ingenious keys and can insert
them at the right place by means of a magic word
known only to the initiated. It seems probable to
me that *Das Märchen* is built up on symbols of Freemasonry, that the Kings—Wisdom, Strength, Light
—correspond to the lodge expressions Wisdom,
Strength, Beauty, and that the King's initiation corresponds to the liturgy of Freemasonry. I have
read from the interpreters that the work is supposed
to signify some such idea as the victory of culture
over nature as raw material. For my part it is a
matter of indifference as to what it means. It is
not a business of art to create complicated and incomprehensible allegories.

Die Horen was not long lived; it lasted only from
1795 to 1797. Subscribers became fewer and fewer.
The organ had from the very beginning found it
-impossible to live up to its name, for according to
its programme it excluded precisely those two topics
that were uppermost in the minds of the people:
religion and politics. A number of its articles
were tiresome, or at least devoid of general interest.
Goethe's contributions could not make good the defects of others. His *Unterhaltungen* did not rise
far above mediocrity. His superb *Römische Elegien* frightened the common bourgeois public, informed as it soon was by the critics that these poems
were immoral. His translation of *Benvenuto Cellini's Life*, a deserving though not perfect work,
called for readers with a yearning sense for the

Italian Renaissance—which was then lacking in the demure German commoner and his wife.

Indefatigable and restless as Schiller was he had, even before *Die Horen* was discontinued, begun a new joint undertaking, the publication of a series of *Musenalmanache*. They continued to appear for six years in succession (1795-1800).

In the year 1796 the *Almanach* brought out Goethe's and Schiller's combined *Xenien* (the Greek word for gifts of the guest), very short poems in hexameters and pentameters in which the allies, according to Schiller's proposal, were to be concerned with everything and everybody that was displeasing to them in the sphere of German letters. The *Xenien* were to be the Doom's Day for contemporary German literature, for magazines, criticisms, publishers, and the public; they were to hurl a mortal blow, a felling shaft against whoever appeared to one of the two great confederates (very frequently to both) as a catch-penny writer, as a perverter of good taste, or a dilettant, or as deceptively bright, or mawkish, or dull, or vain, against anyone who had opposed them, and had made stupid or rancorous attempts upon their work, their souls' redemption.

They opened fire with an attack upon magazines which indeed were truly of no account and stupid, as magazines not seldom are. They ridiculed old-fashioned, honor-crowned poets such as Gleim, Nicolai the Berlin rationalist, hated equally by Goethe and Schiller, adherents to the French Revolution, such as the musician and journalist Reichardt, who had, nevertheless, so long been closely allied to Goethe as the composer of his songs and operettas;

the pious, nonsensical Count Fritz v. Stolberg, who
had passed disparaging judgment on Antiquity as
heathen.   They even extended over the quite young
of the rising generation, those who, like Friedrich
Schlegel, had glorified Goethe at Schiller's expense.
Schlegel incurred this famous Distich:

Was sie gestern gelernt, das wollen sie heute schon lehren,
  Ach was haben die Herrn doch für ein kurzes Gedärm!

The *Xenien* were to a surprising degree joint productions.   The two poets discussed them together,
wrote them together.   One would produce the idea,
the other the form.   And yet, for all that, the majority of those concerned succeeded in finding the
originator.   From a number of them we know definitely by the theme alone who wrote them.   There
is *à priori* no doubt but that the scientific ones are
written by Goethe, the philosophic by Schiller.
Moreover, the style of the two poets is so dissimilar that they cannot, as a rule, be mistaken.   Each
has in this scant form produced a handful of small
masterpieces which no one who has read them can
ever forget.   To be sure, Goethe's are the most
copious, but Schiller's are the keenest, the wittiest,
and have more marked points.   Take, among Schiller's epigrammes, this one on the majority of
scholars:

O wie viel neue Feinde der Wahrheit! Mir blutet die Seele,
  Seh' ich das Eulengeschlecht, das zu dem Lichte sich
    drängt.

Or its counterpiece on science:

Einem ist sie die hohe, die himmlische Göttin, dem andern
  Eine tüchtige Kuh, die ihm mit Butter versorgt.

Or the humorous one on learned societies and their members:

Jeder, sieht man ihn einzeln, ist leidlich klug und verständig;
  Sind sie *in corpore,* gleich wird euch ein Dummkopf
  daraus.

Or the deep and witty one on moralizing dolts:

Herzlich ist mir das Laster zuwider, und doppelt zuwider
  Ist mir's, weil es so viel Schwatzen von Tugend gemacht.
"Wie, du hassest die Tugend?"—Ich wollte, wir übten sie
  alle.
Und so spräche, will's Gott, ferner kein Mensch mehr
  davon.

Nor is it at all difficult to cull out individual epigrammes from among those written by Goethe which rise high up above the personalities and squabbles of everyday life and contain eternal verities. Such, for example, is the one on the investigators who find a reason and aim for everything in nature, and who know full well that the cork tree was created so that bottles could have stoppers:

Welche Verehrung verdient der Weltschöpfer, der gnädig
Als er den Korkbaum schuf, gleich auch die Stöpfel erfand!

Or take this sally created for him who demanded that poetry should have a moral purpose and ethical aim:

"Bessern, bessern soll uns der Dichter." So darf denn auf
  Eurem
Rücken des Büttels Stock nicht einen Augenblick ruhn?

Now all this is excellent. But the great mass of *Xenien* are not up to this standard. So soon as they become personal—and they do so in many, many

places—so soon as they have a distinct address,
attack an old newspaper that no man of today ever
heard of, or an old magazine which can now be
found only in half a score of dusty, muggy copies
in German university libraries, or a novel that none
of us has ever read or even heard mentioned, or a
definite passage in a description of travels by Stolberg that is thoroughly stupid, or a clumsy phrase
in the work of a schoolman like Manso, then they
are absolutely unreadable and impossible. They
are a feast and a festival for Dryasdust, a divine
mouthful for commentators who can write a full
page on each distich. But what are the rest of us
to do with them?

It is difficult in this connection to hold back a
heresy to the effect that this entire personal *Xenien-
Kampf*, in which Germany's two greatest poets invested so much, was simply wasted trouble and
stands as an instructive witness to the tenuous knowledge of men and the enormous naïveté of two prominent writers who always lived in a little provincial
town. They imagined in all seriousness that they
could overcome mediocrity. It never once occurred
to them that mediocrity is omnipotent. They fancied that they could annihilate those they struck
in public esteem; of course they only made them
doubly popular. They deluded themselves into believing that they who were right by reason of special
gifts would receive and enjoy justice from their contemporaries. Schiller was at that time thirty-seven
years old, and Goethe was forty-seven.

The protest that was raised against them, the
sympathy that was nourished for the attacked, the
lampoons that rained down on the heads of those

two demi-gods, and the vats of undiluted dirt that
were emptied on these coryphaei, who believed that
they, like Apollo, could send shafts from the vault
of heaven and each foe would receive his due
amount of mundane punishment, must have taught
them that they had produced no outward effect by
their polemics. The only thing they accomplished
was exercise in the writing of excellent verses of a
certain definite kind for which they no longer had
any use.

In a letter dated November 21, 1795, Goethe ex-
Renan would have said concerning them that they
had too much anger and not enough contempt. Or
to be more accurate: It was Schiller, the younger,
the more pugnacious, the genuine *literateur*, who
felt in his element when he wielded blows on journal-
ists and editors; it was Schiller who carried Goethe
along with him, dragged him down from Olympus,
and induced him to beat away at the heads of daub-
ers and smearers. But the whole enterprise was
energy wasted and time lost. The wretched becomes
stronger by being attacked; it thereby comes to believe that it actually is, and is strengthened in its
dangerous belief that it really exists. As Hegel
says: Only the reasonable is real.

In a letter dated November 21, 1795, Goethe expresses to Schiller a touching assurance that it will
be easy to visualize to the reasonable public the
deranged madness of those who are narrow-minded
and stupid on general principles. By declaring war
on half-measures in all domains, Goethe felt they
could put an end to the secret feud that was being
waged against both of them through the exploita-
tion of silence, misinterpretation, and oppression.
Had there been a reasonable public there would

have been no call for these *Xenien;* and the unreasonable saw in them only blotches on the honor of
the two poets.

II

A collaboration of a far more pleasing and fruitful sort between the two friends was that which
was entirely unpolemic. They laid their themes before each other, discussed them together, and then
gave each other mutual criticism while the poem in
question was being worked out. Their collaboration
stretches out over wide fields. It begins with the
writing of a series of ballads during which each
subjects the ballad in question to the judgment of
the other. Whoever wishes to acquire an exhaustive
idea of what Goethe meant to Schiller in this special
domain should take as an illustration Schiller's work
on the beautiful ballad entitled *Die Kraniche des
Ibykus.*

Schiller first brought the theme to Goethe's attention and told him what he wished to make out of
it. On July 19, 1797, Goethe hopes that the *Kraniche* will soon, while on their annual flight, come
near him. On July 21, Schiller is going to try his
fortune with them. Not until August 17 does he
write to Goethe, after some days' work, as follows:

At last you have *Ibykus.* It is to be hoped that you will
be satisfied with it! I must confess that when I actually
began to work on the material I found more difficulties than
I had anticipated. But it seems to me that I have overcome
the majority of them. The two main points upon which
so much depended seem to me to be these: In the first
place, it was necessary to bring real coherence and connection into the narrative which, in truth, the raw fable does
not have. In the second place it was necessary to create a

certain mood so as to bring out the right effect. I simply could not put the finishing touch to the ballad, when I completed it last evening, and it is a matter of great moment to me that you read it before I finish it, so that I can avail myself of your observations.

It turned out that in this form the ballad appealed to Goethe as being far from perfect; and it is most captivating to see with what docility and talent Schiller uses every reasonable suggestion that was given him by his friend. "The raw fable," as Schiller called the theme, was as follows: Some cranes that have been witnesses to the fact that two murderers fell upon and killed a travelling poet become the agents through which the crime was discovered, in that they reappear over the theatre in which the poet's drama was being performed, so that the robbers, in superstitious terror, confessed their crime.

Goethe wishes to have the beginning of the ballad thoroughly revised, and one can see that Schiller added four entire strophes of eight verses each. And then he wishes to have a strophe added after the one in which the Erynnies on the stage withdrew. Schiller acquiesced. Goethe's letter of August 22 shows that he too laid out a plan for a poem on the same theme. But he gave it up when Schiller finished his sketch, just about as he gave up the idea of treating the legend of *Wilhelm Tell* as an epic when he handed over the material to Schiller for dramatic treatment.

Goethe writes:

Die Kraniche des Ibykus is in my opinion a quite successful bit of work. The transition to the theatre is very beautiful and the chorus of Eumenides is at the right place. Since this turn has been discovered the entire fable can no

longer be thought of without it, and in case I could find
a desire to struggle with the theme, I would likewise be
compelled to take up this chorus.

Now a few remarks. (1) The cranes as birds of passage
should be an entire flock that fly over Ibykus as well as
over the theatre; they come as a natural phenomenon, as
much according to law as the sun or other regular changes
in nature. In this way the miraculous element will be
removed, for they do not need to be the *same* cranes; they
are perchance only a part of the great flying flock, and the
incidental really constitutes in my estimation the mysterious
and odd in the story.

(2) After verse 14, where the erynnies withdraw, I
would insert a verse by way of portraying the mood into
which the contents of the chorus brings the spectators, and
go over from the serious observations of the good to the
indifferent diversion of the ruthless, and in this way let the
moping murderer come with his exclamation stupid, raw,
and high, and yet distinct only to those sitting closest by.
Then there should arise a quarrel between him and those
around him until the populace become aware of what is
taking place, and so on. In this way, as well as in the
flight of the cranes, everything will be done in a natural
fashion and, as I see it, the effect will be increased. As it
is now, the 15th verse begins in too high a voice and too
significantly; we almost expect something different from
what actually takes place. And if you will be a bit more
careful here and there with the rhyme, the rest can easily
be attended to. I wish you all manner of success with this
fortunate work.

In order to obtain more light on the subject,
Goethe returned to the ballad the next day. Since
Schiller had been so successful with the middle part,
Goethe wished to have a few strophes added to
the exposition. As he saw the situation, even the
wandering Ibykus should catch sight of the cranes;
as a traveller he should compare himself with the
wandering birds, just as a guest in a foreign land

compares himself with the birds that are, as it were,
visiting there, and from their flight he should see
a good warning for himself and in this way, while
in the hands of the murderers, appeal to the cranes
as his witnesses. Hereby these birds came to occupy
an exceedingly important place and the impression
of their being could be fused with the impression
of the avenging goddesses in the tragedy. Goethe
emphasized the fact that he himself in his own
sketch had found nothing more that was useful.

But this was by no means negligible. We see at
once how exactly he himself thought the matter
over, and how nobly he had left everything to Schiller that had ever occurred to him concerning this
idea.

The veracious Schiller answers (August 30) with
the confession that he, as a poor observer, knows
in reality nothing about cranes except what he has
read in a few literary comparisons to which they
gave rise. He again avails himself of this opportunity to comment upon the fact that a rich and
vivid experience greatly facilitates poetic invention.
Then (September 7) he makes clear the points in
which he has followed Goethe's suggestions, and
those in which this has not been possible. The exposition is now not so thin, the hero of the ballad
is more interesting, the cranes fill the imagination
of the reader to a much higher degree, and engage
his attention so completely that they are not forgotten when they are seen for the second and last time.

On the contrary, Schiller has not been able to see
his way clear to have only those sitting nearest hear
the exclamation of the murderer and then have the
excitement pass gradually over the entire assembly.

That would weaken the general effect and dissipate
attention just where the expectations were the most
impatient.   He has avoided the miraculous entirely,
a plan that he had in mind, indeed, when he first
worked out his sketch.   A natural occurrence was to
cause the flock of cranes to fly over the theatre.
The drama itself has neither affected nor frightened
the rude murderer; but it has reminded him of his
crime and in this way he is seized by the sudden appearance of the cranes and involuntarily shrieks
out.   Since he sits high up in the amphitheatre,
where the common people sit, he sees the cranes
before they hover over the middle of the theatre.
In this way his exclamation precedes the observation of the cranes by the spectators.   Moreover, his
shriek is heard to a better advantage, in Schiller's
opinion, just because his seat is so elevated.   The
latter is a grave mistake on the part of Schiller,
a mistake which he shares, however, with all who
build tribunes for speakers.   Those who speak or
exclaim are never heard to a better advantage than
when they are at the very bottom of the amphitheatre.

In the course of time Schiller sends his finished
ballad to Böttiger in order to learn from him
whether anything in it is contrary to and inconsistent
with ancient Greek customs and usages.   It seems to
me that Böttiger might have remarked that the
spectators in the Greek theatre never sat, as they
do in Schiller's ballad, close up against each other
on the *benches*, but on the steps of the theatre, and
that even if there existed supports under the stage
that these never could have been just about ready to
break down from the weights of the spectators, who

absolutely never squeezed close in around the stage. But Böttiger found nothing whatsoever that was at odds with Grecian custom, and since Schiller had done his best, he was now quite at ease.

The genesis of *Die Kraniche der Ibykus* is a beautiful example of the artistic seriousness and consciousness with which the two poets worked together solely and alone for art's sake. There was no money to be made by writing a ballad, and very little honor from the writer's contemporaries; and least of all could the unnamed collaborator expect any honor or profit therefrom. In this way, however, a short, irreproachable work saw the light of day, which, like the rest of Schiller's ballads that live in the consciousness of the German people, is an eloquent expression of rare heroism or mysterious justice.

CHAPTER XII

Goethe's *Balladen*—Goethe's Satirical Poems

THERE is no oratory in Goethe's contemporary ballads. But in the best ones at least, there is something that is far better. In the weaker ones, such as the *Der Schatzgräber,* there is a certain amount of instruction, good suggestion and seasoned advice given impressively, in *sotto voce,* whereas Schiller always speaks in a loud, full tone. *Der Schatzgräber* gives in a subdued tone simple rules of living expressed pithily:

> Tages Arbeit, Abends Gäste!
> Saure Wochen, frohe Feste!

A masterpiece of technique, and written with a splendid irony which quite controls the graphic power of imagination, is *Der Zauberlehrling,* the story of the venerable wizard's pupil, the dilettant who, the master being absent, wishes to carry on his arts. But he is not able to exorcise or dispel the spirits he himself has conjured up. It is the ballad of all mimicking bunglers. Goethe found the material in Lucian's *The Liar* and has exploited it in a most fascinating manner. It is artistic and it is instructive. Instead of a mortar, which in Lucian is commanded to fetch some water, Goethe has used nothing more pretentious than an old broom, the idea being that this is an object which comes within the immediate activity of all men.

The effect of the shifting verse accent in the al-

ternate strophes is remarkable. It visualizes at
once the witchery and the unrest in the mind of the
apprentice. Content and form are one when, for
example, the boy cries out to the broom:

> Stehe, stehe!
> Denn wir haben
> Deiner Gabe vollgemessen!
> Ach, ich merk' es! Wehe! Wehe!
> Hab' ich doch das Wort vergessen.

The little cycle, *Der Edelknabe und die Müllerin,
Der Junggeselle und der Mühlbach, Der Müllerin
Verrat, Der Müllerin Reue,* is without exception
graceful, erotic, and written in French spirit. *Der
Müllerin Verrat* is Goethe's version of an old
French ditty which he several years later translated
in its entirety for *Wilhelm Meisters Wanderjahre*
(Book I, Chapter 5).

The German poet has appropriated the roguish
frivolity of the French text; in the later translation
the rendering is somewhat heavy as over against the
flippant content. Compare:

En manteau, manteau sans
chemise,
Non que l'ami pût en man-
quer;
C'est que la sienne lui fut
prise
En lieu charmant à remar-
quer:
Surpris en cueillant une
pomme
Pomme de vingt ans au
moulin,
On l'avait mis nu comme
l'homme
En le chassant de cet Eden.

Woher der Freund so früh
und schnelle,
Da kaum der Tag in Osten
graut?
Hat er sich in der Wald-
kapelle,
So kalt und frisch es ist, er-
baut?
Es starret ihm der Bach ent-
gegen;
Mag er mit Willen barfuss
gehn?
Was flucht er seinen Mor-
gensegen
Durch die beschneiten wilden
Höhn?

From the later translation:

> Gar wunderlich von warmer Stätte,
> Wo er sich bessern Spass versprach,
> Und wenn er nicht den Mantel hätte,
> Wie grässlich wäre seine Schmach!
> So hat ihn jener Schalk betrogen
> Und ihm das Bündel abgepackt;
> Der arme Freund ist ausgezogen,
> Beinah wie Adam bloss und nackt.

It is instructive as furnishing an insight into the nature of the two friends, that, at the same time that Schiller in his ballads was glorifying the haughtiest courage incident to daring deeds (*Der Taucher*), the heroic fidelity that goes through fire and water only to be crucified (*Die Bürgschaft*), chivalry which exposes itself to the talons of lions and tigers but spurns the reward therefor (*Der Handschuh*), shrewdness and heroism coupled with beautiful humility (*Der Kampf mit dem Drachen*), courageousness which effects great achievements and in resignation is content with the sight of the beloved (*Ritter Toggenburg*)—while Schiller was thus engaged, Goethe, by dint of his fondness for the feminine sex, cannot let go of the passionate, returns in these ballads here and there to the rococo tone of his youth, and in the two ballads in which he rises to greatest heights and far above Schiller, is again the eroticist, though in the loftiest and purest style.

Die Braut von Korinth and *Der Gott und die Bajadere,* the two greatest ballads in the German language, were both produced in the first half of the month of June, 1797. After having written them Goethe paid so little attention to them and laid so little stress on them that in a letter to Schil-

ler, June 10, 1797, after both had been finished,
he writes in a purely jesting tone: "Luck to you,
and let your diver be drowned as soon as possible.
It is not bad that just as I have brought my two
pairs into the fire and out of it, you have sought the
opposite element for your hero."

As the main source for the *Die Braut von Korinth,* Goethe availed himself of an anecdote from
a collection of Greek miracles, written by a Lydian
named Flegon, one of Emperor Hadrian's serfs.
This serf published among other things a description of the island of Sicily, and told of Hadrian's
life and exploits. Of his book on miracles a few
fragments are left and among other things one
(unquestionably fictitious) letter from a governor of
a province (procurator) to an official at the imperial
court:

The letter tells how Filinnion, daughter of
Demostratus and Charito, though dead, is secretly
united with Machates, the guest of her family.
The nurse takes them by surprise, sees the young
girl sitting on the young man's couch, calls as loudly
as she possibly can to the parents, and requests them
to get up and see their daughter. Charito is at first
moved; she weeps and declares that the nurse is
beside herself. But finally she goes to the guest
chamber; the couple that have been seen by the
nurse are now sleeping in the dark. She catches
sight of just a few clothes and a profile, and decides
on this account to come again the next morning
and then perhaps take her daughter by surprise.
But when she returns in the morning the young man
is alone. The mother plies him with questions and
in his bewilderment he confesses that Filinnion has

visited him and that the young girl, who longed for him, had said to him: "I come to you wholly without the knowledge of my parents." As an evidence he gives Charito a gold ring that he has received from the young girl and a ribbon that she forgot to bind about her breast when she left. He is forced to promise the mother to show her her daughter, in case she returns. All await her the next night. She comes to the young man, sits down by his bed, eats and drinks. He declines entirely to believe that his friend is dead; he fancies that some one has robbed the deceased of her garments and jewels and sold them to the young girl's father. The parents appear on the scene, recognize Filinnion and, mute with astonishment, embrace her in this condition. But she says to them: "O Father and Mother, how unjustly have you deprived me of the three days during which I had permission to be in my parents' house with your guest! You will have occasion to deplore your curiosity. I return to the place that has been set aside for me. It is not without the will of the Divine that I have come here."—And she falls down to the earth, dead.

The writer of the letter tells that he himself has had the grave opened, has found it empty except for an iron ring and a gold beaker, such as Filinnion had received from Machates on the first night. The young girl's body lay in the chamber of her parents. The young man took his life soon thereafter from grief.

As becomes clear at once, the narrative furnished Goethe with nothing but the crude material. The idea contained in the ballad, its protest against the morals of asceticism, against the placing of the young girl in the convent, is not found in the narrative; and certainly there is no evidence in it of the wild pathos, the tremendous verve, in which the condition of the soul of the two leading characters is placed. And least of all does the narrative contain the wonderful art with which the strophes are composed in that, as is now more and more frequently the case in Goethe's works, there is the seriousness and calm of dignity in the first half and the fiery haste of passion in the second.

More than ten years previous to this, in 1788, Schiller wrote his *Götter Griechenlands* in which he gave expression to precisely the same mood that here seizes Goethe. In Schiller's poem we read:

> Finstrer Ernst und trauriges Entsagen
> War aus eurem heitern Dienst verbannt,
> Glücklich sollten alle Herzen schlagen,
> Denn Euch war der Glückliche verwandt.
> Damals war nichts heilig als das Schöne . . .
>
> Alle jene Blüthen sind gefallen
> Von des Nordens schauerlichem Wehn!
> Einen zu bereichern unter allen,
> Musste diese Götterwelt vergehn.

We read in Goethe's poem:

> Und der alten Götter bunt Gewimmel
> Hat sogleich das stille Haus geleert.
> Unsichtbar wird Einer nur im Himmel
> Und ein Heiland wird am Kreuz verehrt,
> Opfer fallen hier,
> Weder Lamm noch Stier,
> Aber Menschenopfer unerhört.

Grief over the destruction of the old gods is in Schiller's work as deep and genuine as in Goethe's.

But his poem is a poem of thought, singularly distant from life and reality. Though it praises the
world of the senses it contains not the slightest
breath of living sensuality. What an unforgetable
expression has Goethe, on the contrary, given here
to the fiery yearning:

> Heftig fasst er sie mit starken Armen
> Von der Liebe Jugendkraft durchmannt:
> Hoffe doch bei mir noch zu erwarmen,
> Wärst du selbst mir aus dem Grab gesandt!
> Wechselhauch und Kuss!
> Liebesüberfluss!
> Brennst du nicht und fühlest mich entbrannt?

> Liebe schliesset fester sie zusammen
> Thränen mischen sich in ihre Lust;
> Gierig saugt sie seines Mundes Flammen
> Eins ist nur im Andern sich bewusst . . .

When, at the beginning of the nineteenth century,
Wolfgang Menzel led the fashion in German literature and discovered three kinds of personal vanity
and six kinds of tendencies toward voluptuousness,
he saw in *Die Braut von Korinth* "the expression of
that voluptuousness which yearns for the body,
which, even in the terrors of the grave, seeks the enjoyment of the taste of putrifaction in love with
beautiful apparitions." But even this critic found
a public, as this kind of critics always does, which is
as imbecile as themselves and which admires them
for their "morality."

Die Braut von Korinth is a ballad of twenty-eight
stanzas without, however, seeming long. It gives
rather the effect, because of its lively tempo and hurried beat, of marked brevity. It is so charming that

we read it again and again, so complete a painting, so fiery a lyric, so fresh and clear a sketch of life, that it belongs to the not numerous group of eternal works of art.

A companion piece to this, and of the same rank, is the legend written at the same time, entitled *Der Gott und die Bajadere*. This ballad is shorter and more condensed; it has only nine stanzas. But it too was written for eternity.

Goethe took the material from Sonnerat's *Reise nach Ostindien und China in den Jahren* 1774-1781. But to this no one attaches the slightest bit of importance. He has treated, in an amazing Goethe-like way, a theme which, by its very nature, is purely Schilleresque; he has depicted what Schiller invariably poetized as a matter of preference: Heroism which, inspired and of its own free will, elects a lamentable death. But in Goethe's work it is a woman, not a man as in Schiller's *Der Taucher* or *Die Bürgschaft*, who seeks death. Why? Because of a passionate love which is at the same time the flaming ardor of perception and unconditional submission. If there was one theme ill adapted to Schiller's powers it was a loving dancing girl; if there was anything the portrayal of which seemed intended for Schiller rather than Goethe, it was that enthusiasm which seeks self-destruction and leaps into the flames in order not to survive. But Goethe has conquered the theme; it is Raphael-like; and it is written with matchless ease.

The admirable composition of the stanza is more ingenious than that of the sonnet; it is original, too. It seems as though it were adapted to just this sub-

ject and no other. If there be skeptics, let them
be converted to faith by this:

> Bei der Bahre stürzt sie nieder,
> Ihr Geschrei durchdringt die Luft;
> Meinen Gatten will ich wieder!
> Und ich such' ihn in der Gruft.
> Soll zur Asche mir zerfallen
> Dieser Glieder Götterpracht?
> Mein! er war es, mein vor Allen!
> Ach nur eine süsse Nacht!
> Es singen die Priester: Wir tragen die Alten.
> Nach langem Ermatten und spätem Erkalten,
> Wir tragen die Jugend, noch eh' sie's gedacht.

It has always appeared to me as especially effective that the trochees of the first eight lines have
a pronounced tendency to go over into anapests.
But quite overwhelming is the masterliness whereby
the three concluding lines in these nine strophes al-
ternately relate, dance, paint, explain, kiss, scream,
sound the organ, boom, and fly.

II

Less value attaches to the individual satirical
poems that Goethe wrote at this period: *Musen
und Grazien in der Mark,* and *Der Chinese in Rom.*
The former is a persiflage on one now hopelessly
forgotten Schmidt von Werneuchen; the latter is a
quite witty satire on Jean Paul.

The former is of special interest because it is
one of the countless proofs of the aversion Goethe
felt toward the spirit of Mark Brandenburg—the
spirit of Berlin. Goethe's relation to Prussia was
anything but cordial. Even in *Der ewige Jude* there
is an outcry against the Prussian capital:

Hier ist des Landes Mittelthron.
Gerechtigkeit und Religion
Spedieren wie der Selzerbrunn
Petschirt ihren Einfluss ringsherum.

In *Die Vögel* we have this bit of sarcasm inspired by reflection on the Prussian eagle:

In the north there now exists the greatest reverence for the image of the eagle. It can be seen portrayed with well-nigh perfect ubiquity, and the peoples bow before it even when merely carved by a bungler or painted by a dabbler. It is black; there is a crown on its head; it opens its mouth wide; it sticks out its red tongue; it always displays a pair of ready claws. No one can feel wholly at ease who looks upon it.

During Goethe's sole and only sojourn in Berlin, for a few days in May, 1778, in the company of Karl August, he felt so ill-humored that he could never be prevailed upon to repeat his visit. He writes, May 19, 1788, from Berlin to Charlotte von Stein: "This much I can say: The greater the world is, the more offensive the farce becomes, and I can swear that no indecency, no asininity in Jack Pudding lampoons is so disgusting as the carrying-on of the great, the half great, and the puny among each other." His depression of spirits is so lasting that as late as October 30, 1809, he writes to Zelter: "I at least still pass my days in Weimar and Jena, two provincial little towns which God has preserved thus far, though the noble Prussians have tried to devastate them in this way and that."

As a result of this aversion to the general spirit of Berlin we must consider his feud of years standing with Nicolai, who appealed to him as the representative of Berlin. And it is only as a result of this dislike that we can justify a poet of his rank in writing polemics against such a poet as F. W. A. Schmidt.

Under the title *Musen und Grazien in der Mark* he parodied the *Kalender der Musen und Grazien,* published by the book-dealer C. Spener in Berlin, 1795. This came out as a continuation of the former *Neuer Berliner Musenalmanach,* made public by F. W. A. Schmidt and I. C. Bindemann. Through this effort Goethe brought it about that Pastor Schmidt came to be looked upon in the future as the poet of vulgarity and unjustifiably coarse naturalness—if this can be called a result. As is well known, Goethe's closing statement is often quoted to this very day:

> Wir sind bieder und natürlich,
> Und das ist genug gethan.

But was it worthy of Goethe to attack a tiny, insignificant clerical poet who had never done anyone any real harm, and whose verses moreover are not particularly inferior to those of Goethe's model and master Voss, to which he gave the vote of cordial approval a year later? In 1889, Ludwig Geiger published under the same title as Goethe's famous poem a selection of the verses by Schmidt that had been so ridiculed; it turned out that, in reality, they were no worse than poems frequently are.

Der Chinese in Rom, the satire on Jean Paul, is a half-score lines in distich form which Goethe wrote out of irritation over an expression which he considered arrogant, and which had been used by Richter in a personal letter to Knebel. The Chinese finds all the buildings in Rome heavy and squat. He had expected to find small columns of wood, carved work and gildings. Goethe adds, in a rather prosaic way, that it is possible to see in this incident the symbol of many an ultra-enthusiast who compares his aerial chimeras with the eternal coverings of solid nature and calls the healthy sick in order that he may logically ascribe health to his own diseased being.

Poor Jean Paul was not responsible for the fact that he was portrayed as a sort of anti-Pope to Goethe by the people who hated the latter even more than they loved the former. By his writings he had made friends and patrons in Weimar. Wieland regarded him highly and called him the German Yorick and the German Rabelais. The comparison with Sterne has more reason and foundation than that with the great French monk and physician.

Herder commended Jean Paul. For Knebel and Einsiedel his books were favorite reading. Charlotte von Kalb, left in the lurch by Schiller, wrote to him with glowing enthusiasm and had him visit her in Weimar (1796). Hardly had he arrived in June, when he felt an overwhelming fascination in her presence. Since Charlotte stood close to Herder, it followed as a matter of course that Jean Paul associated intimately with the latter. If only for this reason, Schiller and Goethe received the new-comer coolly. For Herder and Wieland formed at this time, in the castle of the Dowager Duchess, a sort of secondary court to that of Karl August's, where people were busied conversationally with heaping abuse upon Goethe and Schiller. Because of jealousy at the friendship between the two, Herder had become exceedingly bitter.

Quite apart, however, from this personal rela-

tion, it was wholly impossible for such a styleless
penman as Jean Paul to stand before the tribunal
of the *Dioscuri*. The mere fact that he larded his
novels with detached ideas and paradoxical figures
which he had jotted down in notebooks for future
use could not fail to have a terrifying effect upon
them. For real antipathy on the part of Goethe
though there was no ground. And the cordiality
in Jean Paul's mind was deserving of a measure of
kindliness and praise from the two noted writers.
Ludwig Börne wrote correctly concerning Jean Paul
on the occasion of his death: "In the countries one
counts only the cities; in the cities only the temples
and towers and palaces; in the houses their masters;
in the various peoples their leaders. . . . Jean Paul
went out into the narrower, more obscure ways and
sought out the town that had been neglected.
Among the peoples he counted the human beings.
In the towns he counted the roofs, and under each
roof the hearts."

But it was not merely Jean Paul's formlessness
that irritated Goethe. It was his indistinct political
liberality and his excessive faith in the rapidity of
political progress that made Goethe tired of his personality and impatient with his art.

CHAPTER XIII

IT is quite within reason to believe that Goethe
had Christiane in mind when he wrote *Der Gott und
die Bajadere.* The rejection the dancing girl suffers in being relegated to the dead, unmarried to
her dead god, the words, "Nur die *Gattin* folgt dem
Gatten," draw the attention of the reader to her.
Goethe wrote at the same time, in the same metre
as *Der Chinese in Rom,* an entire series of short
poems, all of which owe their origin to his happy
domestic life with Christiane.

In *Der neue Pausias und sein Blumenmädchen* he
transferred the scene to ancient Hellas and prefaced
it with a quotation from Pliny in order to conceal
the otherwise patent allusion to the fact that she had
been employed in a flower factory. The quotation
from Pliny runs as follows: "Pausias of Sicyon, the
painter, had fallen in love, as a young man, with
his fellow townswoman, Glycere, who had great
inventiveness in the binding of flower wreaths. They
emulated each other; he became a master at imitation. Finally he painted his beloved, sitting, busied
with a wreath." In the form of a dialogue the first
acquaintance of the two is glorified and her unassuming skill is praised as a talent "at poetizing and
painting with flowers." The way in which they

169

became acquainted is remodelled; and a contest is added during which Pausias protects the girl from an importunate lout, wins in this way her gratitude and finally her herself.

The sight of an apple tree surrounded by ivy, which Goethe saw on his third journey to Switzerland in September, 1797, gave rise to the poem *Amyntas*. It reminded him of the way in which Christiane had become entwined about his life and was drawing nourishment from him, though she had become indispensable to him. Amyntas addresses this poem to his physician Nikias (the eleventh idyl of Theocritus is addressed to a physician of this name). We understand that Nikias has requested Amyntas to practice abstinence and temperance in the presence of his sweetheart, since their living together has had the harmful consequences that he no longer has the slightest bit of energy left for mental work. But he beseeches the physician not to enforce such a stern and rigid cure upon him and compares himself with the apple tree, which begged that the ivy might be retained when the people began to take it away piece by piece:

Nahrung nimmt sie von mir; was ich bedürfte, geniesst sie;
  Und so saugt die das Mark, sauget die Seele mir aus.
Nur vergebens nähr' ich mich noch; die gewaltige Wurzel
  Sendet lebendigen Safts ach nur die Hälfte hinauf. . . .
Nichts gelangt zur Krone hinauf, die äussersten Wipfel
  Dorren, es dorret der Ast über dem Bache schon hin
Ja die Verrätherin ist's! sie schmeichelt mir Leben und
      Güter,
  Schmeichelt die strebende Kraft, schmeichelt die Hoffnung
      mir ab . . .
Süss ist jede Verschwendung; o lass mich der schönsten
      geniessen!
  Wer sich der Liebe vertraut, hält er sein Leben zu Rath?

The thirty-seven distichs printed under the rubric *Sommer* in the little collection entitled *Vier Jahreszeiten* also revolve around Christiane. But the tone is fresher; and the method of presentation is less painful. In one single distich Goethe lays bare the entire secret of his relation to Christiane:

Neigung besiegen ist schwer; gesellet sich aber Gewohnheit
    Wurzelnd, allmählich zu ihr, unüberwindlich ist sie.

The majority of these poems treat such themes as joy over lines discovered in his sweetheart's hands, embraces, kisses, and passion in general. A few of them are serious in tone; two of them are especially so. The first betrays Goethe's occasional doubt as to her fidelity; but it praises at the same time the deep significance of the illusion:

Sie entzückt mich, und täuscht mich vielleicht. O Dichter und Sänger,
Mimen! lerntet Ihr doch meiner Geliebten was ab!

The second affords consolation for the mutability of beauty by emphasizing the beauty of what is past and gone:

Warum bin ich vergänglich, o Zeus? So fragte die Schönheit.
    Macht ich doch, sagte der Gott, nur das Vergängliche schön.

The charming elegy entitled *Metamorphose der Pflanzen* is also addressed to Christiane. In it he attempts to explain to her in the simplest way possible his fundamental idea concerning the development and metamorphosis of the plant; he closes with a personal reference to her and her only. The change of form in the plant is conceived of as sym-

bolic of the growth and change in their love for
each other:

O gedenke denn auch, wie aus dem Keim der Bekanntschaft
    Nach und nach in uns holde Gewohnheit entspross,
Freundschaft sich mit Macht in unserm Innern enthüllte,
    Und wie Amor zuletzt Blüthen und Früchte gezeugt.

It cannot be denied that Christiane's humble
character has been accorded signal honor in Goethe's poems along with the more brilliant and refined women who aroused his passion and enjoyed
his homage.

II

During these years Goethe became more and
more interested in Hellenism. Just as ten years
later Thorvaldsen found it impossible to conceive
of art in any other form than Grecian, and persisted
in making his costumes Greek even though his
themes were modern, just so did Goethe now strive
to write and feel after the fashion and in the spirit
of the Hellenists of olden times. He was unmindful and unaware of the self-contradictory element
in this method of procedure. The Homeric poets,
as all the world must know, never tried to write
precisely as men had felt and written three thousand
years previous to their day.

The factor in Goethe's young days that drew him
to Homer was the straightforward naturalness he
at that time fancied he had found in him. Now,
after his journey to Italy and his association with
Schiller, he detected in the Homeric poems the ultimate laws for the art of poetic portrayal. Up to
this time he had lacked the courage to compete with
Homer. But when F. A. Wolf published his *Prole-*

gomena (1795), which essayed to do away with the
unity in the *Iliad* and the *Odyssey,* and to divide
them into a number of different rhapsodies, and
after Goethe's initial objection to the idea had been
overcome, he no longer found it presumptuous to
vie with the individual Homeric songs. In his elegy
Hermann und Dorothea he paid his homage to
Wolf, and referred to himself as the last of the
Homerides:

Erst die Gesundheit des Mannes, der endlich vom Namen
        Homeros
    Kühn uns befreiend uns auch ruft in die vollere Bahn!
Denn wer wagte mit Göttern den Kampf? und wer mit dem
        Einen?
    Doch Homeride zu sein, auch nur als letzter, ist schön.

At the close of December, 1797, Goethe made a
diligent study of the *Iliad,* for it seemed to him that
between it and the *Odyssey* there still remained sufficient room for an epic poem; and the temptation
to write such a poem was all but irresistible. It
should be done quite in the spirit of the *Iliad.* However unimportant Jean Paul Friedrich Richter may
be when compared with Goethe, it was after all more
natural to write *Leben, Tod und Ehestand des
Armenadvokaten Siebenkäs* (the humorous history
of a mendicant advocate from Jean Paul's own time,
who becomes a bigamist after he has pretended to
be dead in order to rid himself of his wife) than
to try to write a poem "quite in the spirit of the
Iliad."
   From a number of Goethe's individual remarks
we can at least derive a general idea as to how his
epic on the death of Achilles was to take shape.
Achilles knows that his death is imminent, but he

falls in love with the Trojan Princess Polyxena, and
because of his great love for her forgets his fate.
But we no longer know whether, according to Goethe's plan, Achilles was to find love in return and
endeavor to escape the death that had been prophe-
sied for him before Troy by fleeing with Polyxena,
who would then take her life from grief over his
death, or whether Polyxena was to leave Achilles's
love unrequited and betray him to the Trojans,
whereupon he would fall a prey to the arrow of
Paris.

In vain did Schiller give Goethe the wholesome
advice not to take Homer as his model at all but to
mould the material wholly in accordance with his
own nature. Goethe strove—partly by the use of
Homeric adjectives—to come as near as possible
to the Greek poetry of olden times. Finally, after
long hesitation, he began the work. He finished
only the first canto of *Achilleis*. This was written
in March and April, 1799. He never touched the
theme again.

This first canto shows, in the introduction, how
Achilles had had an enormous burial mound erected
on the sea-coast for himself and his friend Patroc-
lus, whose body the falling flames have just consumed. Then we are led to the mansions of the
gods where Hera derides her son Hephaistos for the
industry he has used on the weapons of Achilles,
since the death of the latter is a question of only
a few days. When Thetis makes known her agony
arising from the fate that is quickly to befall her
son, Hera overwhelms the mother with scorn and
jealous hatred because of the passion she has awakened in the heart of Zeus. When the latter speaks

a few words of reconciliation, Hera begans a positive quarrel. But Pallas Athene appears on the
scene, speaks to the goddess, and confesses that
none of the heroes of either the past or the present
have been so dear to her as Achilles. This comes
as a slight surprise, since we have believed up to
this point that Odysseus was her favorite. It is a
matter of great grief to Pallas that Achilles is to
die so young:

Ach, und dass er sich nicht, der edle Jüngling, zum Manne
Bilden soll! Ein fürstlicher Mann ist so nöthig auf Erden.

When Achilles stands in the depth of the grave,
as though at the bottom of a beaker, while the Myr-
midons heap up the earth all round about, Pallas,
in the form of Achilles's friend Antilochus, accosts
him and begins a cordial conversation in order to
encourage him to look upon his fate through eyes
that know not despair. Achilles declares modestly
and composedly that at some time in the future
many passers-by will look upon this mound and say:
"There lies buried by no means the least worthy of
the Achaeans." Pallas replies with enthusiasm:

"Nein, so redet er nicht," versetzte heftig die Göttin;
"Sehet," ruft er entzückt, von fern den Gipfel erblickend,
"Dort ist das herrliche Mal des einzigen grossen Peliden
Den so früh der Erde der Moiren Willkür entrissen."

She felicitates him most heartily on the prospect
of an early death:

Ja, soweit nur der Tag und die Nacht reicht, siehe verbreitet
Sich dein herrlicher Ruhm, und alle Völker verehren
Deine treffende Wahl des kurzen rühmlichen Lebens.
Köstliches hast Du erwählt. Wer jung die Erde verlassen
Wandelt auch ewig jung im Reiche Persephoneia's,
Ewig erscheint er jung den Künftigen, ewig ersehnet.

Athene returns again to her consolatory remarks, saying that the name of Achilles will sound forever from the lips of singers; his renown will become so great that that of other brave men will fade in comparison with his. It is then that Achilles praises friendship as the chief gratification of brave men; and in the expressions he uses it is—it seems to me —clear that Goethe had Schiller in mind and the joy he experienced from the hand clasp of his friend, now that the *Xenien* struggle is over. Achilles says:

Denn mir ward auf der Erd nichts Köstlichers jemals
    gegeben
Als wenn mir Ajax die Hand, der Telamonier, schüttelt,
Abends nach geendigter Schlacht und gewaltiger Mühe
Sich des Siegs erfreuend und niedergemordeter Feinde.

So far as the metrical form, the versification in general, is concerned, the entire work is quite worthy of Goethe. But how little within the range of the great German poet this ancient meter in reality lay is shown by an individual hexameter so awful as this one:

Wilder Amazonen zum Todeskampfe heranführst.

Much ado has been made of the fact that in *Hermann und Dorothea* Goethe had originally rendered the following verse quite unrhythmical by the insertion of the redundant *und*:

Ungerecht bleiben die Männer, *und* die Zeiten der Liebe vergehen.

And time out of mind the amusing answer has been quoted which Goethe gave to the younger Voss when the latter drew his attention to the error: "Let the seven-footed beast stand!" Later, however, he deleted the impossible *und*. But this carelessness is so trifling when compared with the striking lack of sense for the harmony of verse which is brought to light when *Amazonen* has to be pronounced with two false accents: one on *ma* and one on *nen*. This is necessary in order to arrive at anything that even faintly resembles a real hexameter.

CHAPTER XIV

GOETHE'S STUDIES IN OPTICS: BROODINGS OVER
THE NATURE OF COLORS; GOETHE AND NEW-
TON—*Die Farbenlehre:* ITS ADHERENTS AND
OPPONENTS

THROUGHOUT all the years that Goethe and Schiller lived in such close spiritual communion, the
former was always engaged in experiments relating
to the nature of colors; he brooded over the subject
well nigh without interruption. Goethe went
through life with his eyes open. He was ever interested in the weather; he studied its changes, and
made observations concerning them. He gave long
and reasoned attention to the formation of clouds.
The world of color became for him, consequently,
one in which he felt at ease. It had been his wont
to pass in and out of the homes of artists. He himself had sketched and painted. In Italy he had
buried himself in the study of ancient and modern
art. And, as he remarks in §4 of his first *Beiträge
zur Optik,* Italy's natural scenery had disclosed to
his eyes a "fairy-like" harmony of colors.

Even as a young student in Leipzig, he had been
a witness to Winckler's optical experiments that were
undertaken in sympathy with Newton's teachings.

In Italy he had studied the technical side of the art of painting. He had questioned painters as to whether they knew of any guiding principle concerning coloring. They shook their heads. At his request Angelica Kauffmann had made experiments in colors, had painted a picture gray in gray, and then tinted it with a slight superficial coloring; she had also painted a landscape in which all the blue colors were wanting. Color phenomena in the sky had interested him at the same time: green shadows at purple red sunsets, the bluish tinge of distant mountains.

When Goethe returned to Weimar, he borrowed Büttner's excellent set of optical instruments. Büttner had just moved from Göttingen to Jena. Goethe wanted them in order to make some experiments. But as usual he had a great many other schemes on hand just then, and the prisms lay untouched for some time. Büttner became impatient and asked that they be returned. At last he sent a messenger to Weimar to get them. Goethe cast one final look through the prism. It became an epoch-making moment in his life. He knew that white light should be broken and scattered into colors when seen through a prism. He expected consequently to see the white wall of his room taking on colors of the rainbow; but to his surprise it remained white; only where some dark object made a line on the wall was he able to detect more or less distinct colors, and at last the cross piece in the window frame was seen to be brightly colored, while there was no trace of color visible in the light gray sky. Without much reflection—presumably as a result of intuition—he found that a boundary was necessary to produce

colors, and "an instinct" induced him to say aloud
to himself that Newton's theory was false.

This among other things shows that instinct,
which at the beginning of the twentieth century has
again been praised so loudly and unreasonably as a
scientific guide, can become, even in the case of the
most excellent of men, a quite misleading power.
What Goethe saw, coincided entirely with Newton's
theory. Newton had never denied that colors seen
through a prism are visible only when and where
the light and the dark delimit each other; but he
had combatted the idea that this mutual delimiting
of the light and the dark produced colors; and he
had ascribed to the boundary line a value only as a
condition which brings it about that the picture of
the color becomes visible.

Every physicist of Newton's day had learned
from him that from the white wall, which Goethe
saw, there proceeded rays of just as many types of
light as there are degrees in the refraction. The
rays that are more strongly refracted at one point
are crossed by those that are less strongly refracted
at another point, and from their infringing upon
each other in this way white is produced. Only on
the edges did the partly less refracted partly more
refracted types of light become disclosed, and consequently the one edge had to appear yellow red,
the other blue violet, while the middle was and remained white.

Goethe, who believed that the truth had all of
a sudden been revealed to him, and that by virtue of
his talent as a seer he had made a discovery in the
science of optics just as he had formely made scientific discoveries in the fields of anatomy, geology,

and botany, requested Büttner to allow him to keep the prisms. In 1790 he began to make a serious study of optics and to carry on a number of optical experiments. He became more and more convinced that Newton's theories concerning light were false. That he could not persuade any of the physicists of his day to share his conviction deterred him in no way. He had become accustomed to having natural scientists completely underestimate at first every ingenious hypothesis he proposed.

It is here that we detect one of those misfortunes which arises from the fact that professional men are not infrequently irresponsive to and unappreciative of new finds. It not simply strengthens the pachydermic characteristics of the masses and gives food to their prejudices; it also fills him who has been the victim of such refractoriness with so great a contempt for men that he does not, even when he is on the wrong road, pay the slightest attention to the criticism of his colleagues. It makes the same impression on him that the shepherd boy's cry made in the fable: He was not believed when the wolf really came.

In his feeling for unity and belief in wholeness, Goethe felt himself blocked by the theory of Newton according to which white light is a composition and colors, consequently, take their origin from light. He was able only for a short while to adhere to the Wolfian conception of the *Iliad* and the *Odyssey* as consisting of individual rhapsodies; he soon returned to the belief that Homer was an individual. Of the *Xenien* we have this one against Newton:

Spaltet immer das Licht! Wie öfters strebt Ihr zu trennen,
Was, Euch Allen zum Trutz, Eins und ein Einziges ist.

And this one:

Welch erhabner Gedanke!   Uns lehrt der unsterbliche
    Meister,
Künstlich zu theilen den Strahl, den wir nur einfach gekannt.

There is an exact connection between these *Xenien*
and this epigramme against Wolf:

> Scharfsinnig habt Ihr, wie Ihr seid,
> Von aller Verehrung uns befreit,
> Und wir bekannten überfrei,
> Das Ilias nur ein Flickwerk sei.

> Mög unser Abfall Niemand kränken!
> Denn Jugend weiss und zu entzünden,
> Dass wir ihn lieber als Ganzes denken,
> Als ganzes freudig ihn empfinden,

Wolf, however, was no less right than Newton.
Goethe's point of departure was the circumstance
that for a painting light and shade are two equally
justifiable forces upon the correct distribution of
which rests the illusion which is to be evoked. It is
also on this distribution that the general color
scheme depends. Since the painter cannot possibly
reproduce sunlight with all its intensity, his task
consists in the reproduction of differences of light
and varying degrees of clarity. Since on the light
side yellow and yellow-red predominate, just as on
the dark side blue and blue-red, Goethe found that
to the contrast between light and shade the contrast
between warm and cold colors corresponded. Yellow
and blue became for him what he calls polar contrasts. It is to be presumed that he had observed
in Italy a kinship between blue and black, between
blue and shade. In this way he was prepared, as a
result of his studies in art, to proceed with the un-

scientific assumption that colors arose through the interaction of light and dark, of the light and the non-light. He saw of course that every color is darker than white, and he consequently called the colors for half light half shade, and ascribed to them all something of the characteristics of shade.

Johannes Müller, one of the greatest physicists of that time, indeed of all times, a physicist who owed an incalculable debt to Goethe even with regard to his work on optics, could not help but reject Goethe's views as to the origin of colors for the very simple reason that neither shade nor dark is anything positive. "Dark," he says in his manual on human physiology, "is physiologically only a part of the eye where the retina is perceived in a condition of rest."

While in Italy Goethe had made searching studies in aërial perspective, that is to say, in the artistic reproduction of air light, in so far as this, entirely according to the degree of opacity of the air, manifests various gradations and receives things to be revealed in finely shaded tones. "Aërial perspective, (says Goethe in his *Italienische Reise*) really rests on the important thesis that all transparent media are to a certain degree murky. The atmosphere is always more or less non-transparent, especially in the South with its high barometer, dry weather, and cloudless sky, since one can there observe a very perceptible gradation of objects that are but a slight distance from each other."

In this way Goethe approached the *Urphän-omen* upon which he rests his arguments in optics, just as he rested on the *Urpflanze* in morphology.

It was a question with him of finding the origin

of colors after he had rejected Newton's theory
which deduced them from light. Since he manoeu-
vred about with the concepts light and dark, white
and black, and since with the weakening of the light
and the darkening of the white, there can arise only
shades and gray, he found the especial cause that
produces colors in *the unclear media* (*die trüben
Mittel*).

He had observed that when the dark was seen
through an indistinct medium that was lighted by
having light fall on it, a blue color arose which became more and more light and pale the darker the
medium became; and it became darker and more
subdued the more transparent the dark medium became until the color finally passed over into the most
beautiful violet. He had noticed that if one looked
through an indistinct medium at a clear, colorless
light, this appeared yellow and with increasing indistinctness in the medium it went over to yellow-
red or ruby-red.

This revelation of colors through media that are
not entirely transparent, Goethe calls the *Urphänomen,* which neither necessitates nor permits further explanation. This *Urphänomen* is the corner-
stone of his doctrine.

Physicists could, however, at once prove that the
Urphänomen by no means encompassed all cases
that might arise. The sun, for example, often appears silver white, when it stands high in the heavens
and is seen through a stratum of clouds or through
a bit of colored glass or dark gauze. According
to Goethe's theory it should appear yellow. Likewise the color of the sky when seen from a high
mountain appears blue. When the air, however,

so high up becomes more and more pure and less opaque, it should, according to his theory, appear violet. All this, which was easily and fully explained according to Newton's theory, was inexplicable according to Goethe's.

Likewise with regard to the completing colors, Goethe, as an artist and a lover of art, allowed himself to be led, through his experiences, into a false theory. When the painter mixes blue and yellow, he gets green; there is no doubt about that; but not by a mixture of spectral colors. According to Goethe, green originates in the spectrum only when the yellow edge approaches the blue, a situation that was supposed to be brought about by removing the screen a sufficient distance from the prism. But those colors give in truth green only when they are themselves greenish. It is impossible to compound green from plain yellow and blue in the prism.

A fundamental question in Newton's optics was this: Can the individual colored parts of the spectrum be separated from each other? He found the solution of this question in the experiments in which he applied at once prisms and lenses. But in every case in which Newton in his experiments unites prisms and lenses, Goethe refers to the second, supplementary part of his *Farbenlehre* which, as is known, never appeared.

Goethe had ordered Newton's works as early as 1790; he gradually tried all of his experiments. They seemed to him, judged *à priori,* artificially done and complicated so as to conceal the real state of affairs. He wanted to perform for his own good the simple, basic experiments. His *Beiträge zur Optik* was published in 1791. *Erstes Stück* was ac-

companied with illustrations. *Zweites Stück,* with
new copper plates, came out in 1792. Later he
wrote his *Versuch, die Elemente der Farbenlehre
zu entdecken,* without publishing it. And on this
he worked year after year, heaped up and arranged
an enormous mass of material, the largest he ever
collected in his life, until finally, in 1810, he published his work entitled *Zur Farbenlehre,* in two
large volumes, with a number of appended drawings.
The first volume is in two parts, one of an argumentative, one of a polemic nature directed against
Newton's optics. Of the second volume only the
first and exceedingly valuable part, *Geschichte der
Farbenlehre,* came out. To this we will return subsequently. From this time on there followed a complete series of supplements to the theory of colors,
the most voluminous bit of writing that Goethe
ever produced.

No one will regret, if only for the sake of the
language, the reading of the contributions to optics
from the year 1791. The description is of classic
clarity, as beautiful as a beautiful poem. There is
in it the love of a great poet and a great naturalist
for nature, love for every rare phenomenon in nature and for its common occurrences as well, at least
for those he had observed. In the very introduction, however, we scent his opposition to Newton,
an opposition which amounted to a passion as the
years passed by and recognition was not forth-
coming.

In the *Xenien* of 1797, Goethe directs attack upon
attack against Newton, just as though he were some
mediocre poet or miserable magazine publisher of
that time and not the scientific genius upon the re-

sults of whose investigations all modern culture, down to Einstein, is constructed.

From the score of epigrammes against him we quote a few. They betray the severity and certainty of victory on the part of the misguided Goethe.

Liegt der Irrthum nur erst wie ein Grundstein unten im
    Boden,
  Immer baut man derauf, nimmermehr kömmt er an Tag.

Hundertmal werd ich's Euch sagen und tausendmal: Irrthum
    ist Irrthum
  Ob ihn der grösste Mann, ob ihn der kleinste beging.

"Newton hat sich geirrt?"—Ja, doppelt und dreifach.—
    "Und wie denn?"
  Lange steht es gedruckt; aber es liest es kein Mensch.

Leidlich hat Newton gesehen und falsch geschlossen; am
    Ende
  Blieb er ein Brite; verstockt schloss er, bewies es so fort.

Das ist ein pfäffischer Einfall! Denn lange spaltet die Kirche
  Ihren Gott sich in Drei, wie Ihr in sieben das Licht.

As we see, Goethe in his combative zeal goes so far as to see a parallel between Newton's theory concerning the refraction of light into colors and the dogma of the Trinity which he so detested.

Like all of his contemporaries, with the exception of Kant, Goethe speaks of colors as a phenomenon of nature which is independent of the sense of light. He came very near to the conception that light and color are only our impressions, but he never drew the logical conclusion therefrom.

When he appropriated Plotinus's mystic view in the above quoted verses,

  Wär nicht das Auge sonnenhaft,
  Die Sonne könnt' es nie erblicken,

he thought that there was, so to speak, a light dwelling in the eye. Since the various beings must be homogeneous in order for the one to be susceptible to the other, he avers that the eye is trained for the light by the light within it. What we term light perceptions were to him a relation between something tangible within us and something tangible without us, between something undivided within us and something undivided without us. Goethe, who had made such splendid progress in other domains through the use of his two open eyes, had a violent aversion to the *camera obscura*. He even accused Newton of falsification because the latter, in his experiments in the dark room, spoke of rays when in truth images appeared which were changed by the refraction of light. He would not even concede the significance of the Frauenhofer lines in the sun spectrum, because they showed only when the light was allowed to fall through a crevice. The decomposition of light, like the subdividing of Homer, was to him a species of vivisection, and filled him with the same repulsion which vivisection inspires in every layman.

One of his apothegms in prose (No. 864) reads:

Man in and of himself, insofar as and provided he uses his sound senses, is the greatest and most accurate physical apparatus there can be; and it is indeed the greatest misfortune of modern physics that it has, as it were, isolated experiments from man and shows a willingness to recognize nature only as it is manifested through artificial instruments.

He writes:

Freunde, flieht die dunkle Kammer,
Wo man Euch das Licht verzwickt
Und in kümmerlichem Jammer

Sich verschroben Bildern blickt.
Abergläubische Verehrer
Gab's die Jahre her genug.
In den Köpfen Eurer Lehrer
Lasst Gespenst und Wahn und Trug!

II

In the beautiful section entitled *Konfession des Verfassers,* with which the *Farbenlehre* closes, Goethe expresses his gratitude to those individuals who by their good-will and loyalty have assisted him in his investigations. There is the Duke of Weimar to whom he is indebted in general for the conditions that have made an active and satisfying life possible, and who gave him a place in which to work, and freedom so that he might work. Duke Ernst of Gotha opened to him his physical cabinet, whereby Goethe was enabled to repeat his experiments and carry them out on a large scale. Prince August of Gotha made him a present of some simple as well as some compound prisms, imported from England. Prince Primas of Dalberg gave his experiments unbroken attention; he even supplied some of his treatises with marginal notes in his own handwriting. Among the scholars, there are anatomists and men of letters and philosophers—but not one single physicist.

With Lichtenberg, the physicist and witty satirist, he corresponded for a while, but when Goethe became urgent and tried to secure Lichtenberg's agreement and "vehemently followed up the disgusting Newtonian white," Lichtenberg broke off the correspondence and left the letters unanswered. His friend Heinrich Meyer (the Swiss painter) on the contrary, to whom he was also indebted for instruction along other lines, collaborated with him and helped him in a goodly number of his experiments by making drawings in color. And at last Goethe mentions with effusive cordiality, among the men who have helped him spiritually, his "irreplaceable Schiller." He writes:

Owing to the great naturalness of his genius, Schiller not only grasped the main points with marked rapidity, the points upon which everything depended, but he also, owing to his reflective power, urged me to hasten on to the goal toward which I was striving.

It leaves a melancholy impression to see the *Farbenlehre* close with gratitude to a number of princely gentlemen who placed assistance of one sort and another at Goethe's disposal, and to a number of men who were laymen and laymen only, such as Meyer and Schiller, men who held up his courage by their friendship after he, through his stubbornness, had repelled all the real physicists of his age.

Meyer's participation was naturally concerned only with the artistic, just as Schiller's had to do with the cultural in general in Goethe's optical investigations. But it is to the sympathy of these two men, and of these two alone, to which Goethe clings while carrying out his work. On January 24, 1798, he writes to Schiller:

Not until I firmly determined to consult you and Meyer and no one else did I again feel joy and courage; for the repeated frustration of hope that others are going to help and coöperate always sets one back somewhat.

This unquestionably explains the fact that after Schiller's death his joy in the theory of colors for-

sook him. In a conversation with Eckermann he
said:

The delusions and errors of my opponents have been too
widespread during the past century for me to hope to find a
companion on my lonely way at this late day! I shall remain
alone! I seem like a shipwrecked individual who clings to a
board that is large enough for one and no more.

In the year 1798 he writes hardly a single letter
to Schiller in which he does not speak of his theory
of colors. In one dated February 14, he gives
Schiller for the first time his famous division of colors into three classes: the physiological, the physical,
and the chemical. The physiological are determined
by the condition and activity of our eye. The physical arise from the influence of the rays of light and
the waves of ether, and are therefore prismatic colors. The chemical are the colors of bodies, stones,
walls, clothes, and so on.

It was a great scientific achievement for those
days to place physiological colors first, and to char-
acterize them as the foundation of this teaching.
That part of Goethe's *Farbenlehre* which portrays
the physiological colors was, on this account, epoch-
making. He became one of the founders of physiological optics, just as he had been one of the orig-
inators of philosophic botany and osteology. Hence
we can say that his genius forsook him, in reality,
not even in this much contested domain.

His chief merit lies in the fact that he was one
of the very first to become attentive to and mindful
of the phenomena of sight in their scientific sequence,
and to elaborate these phenomena in a model fashion. The section on physiological colors is regarded
as a classic. Physicists of our own day ascribe also

to other parts real importance, because of the accuracy with which Goethe has told of his various experiments.

The phenomenon of colors, which had hitherto been regarded as accidental, delusive, or morbid, Goethe traced back to the healthy sight concerning the characteristics of which we never received anything reliable until color phenomena had been studied, and the real relation of the eye to them had been investigated. For Goethe, hallucinations, so-called sense deceptions, are optical truths. He says it is blasphemy to speak of an "optical delusion." He contends, as we all do nowadays, that we study the normal activity of the eye to the best advantage in those instances in which the phenomena of the world about us, the physical world, do not correspond to what is seen. That is precisely what Taine said, seventy years later, in his book entitled *De l'Intelligence*. In this treatise Taine formulated, and quite correctly so, this profound idea: *La perception extérieure est une hallucination vraie.*

Schiller, whom Goethe had convinced of Newton's supposed delusions, saw nevertheless with distress that his friend was losing himself in hypotheses over against which he, as a layman, stood in a shaky and skeptical frame of mind. He wrote, consequently, on November 30, 1798, to Goethe as follows:

This much, however, has become clear to me: A main objective in your method will be to separate from each other, and to keep separate, the purely factual and polemical part from the hypothetical, so that the evidence in the case, and the evidence bearing on Newton's *falsum* (!) will not become confused with the problematic part of the explanation.

The advice, to be sure, was good, but Goethe saw at once that he could not meet the demand; that he could not depict the actual altogether apart from the various conjectures that bore on its complete explanation. In his reply he took pains to emphasize the idea that "every lecture, indeed every method, is in itself hypothetical," that it rests, in other words, on an assumption.

He had the philosophers on his side, not simply Schelling, the philosopher of nature, but also the hostile brothers, Hegel and Schopenhauer who, at odds on everything else, were at one in their appreciation of Goethe's theory of colors. Among contemporary physicists, Seebeck and Schweigger were the only ones who, for a time at least, subscribed to Goethe's views. The renowned physiologist of the coming generation, Johannes Müller, who by 1826 had agreed, with reservations, with Goethe, came eventually to limit his sympathies to the section dealing with physiological optics. And it is this physiological part of Goethe's *Farbenlehre* which, according to the conception of modern scientists, retains its epochal significance. It had a decisive influence on Schopenhauer's monograph *Ueber das Sehen und die Farben* and it left its trace on such men as Himly, Troxler and especially Purkinje, with whom Goethe had associated personally from 1802 on.

It is, however, first and foremost the recognition from Johannes Müller on which posterity lays weight. As a student twenty-five years of age, he sent Goethe on February 5, 1826, his book entitled *Zur vergleichenden Physiologie des Gesichtssinnes des Menschen und der Thiere.* He declares that his work would hardly ever have been finished had he not spent several years studying Goethe's *Farbenlehre*. Along with the book he sent a letter in which he said, among other things and in substance, the following:

> I too appear as one among many who wishes to testify to you how I have understood the master's teachings. But what inspires me with greater confidence is the fact that in my case it is a question of a cause that lies close also to your heart, the theory of colors and the metamorphosis. After your investigations have been an inspiration to me for years, not only as to method but also as to the character of my efforts to penetrate the secrets of living nature, the good fortune has at last come to me to tell you publicly how the seed that has produced magnificent fruit in all branches of science among the older generation and that will bear no less important fruit in the generations to come, has also had a beneficent and fructifying influence on me. I owe everything to your sagacious teachings. And now I entrust to your kindly nature and forbearance this book, in the hope that you may feel a desire to examine more carefully the gift hereby dedicated to you from a disciple of yours, who, up to the present, has been unknown and reserved.

Though Johannes Müller, as was quite reasonable, later took objection to Goethe's opposition to Newton, this letter, coming as it does from the particular man who afterwards became the most prominent representative of the morphological tendency in zoölogy, as well as the originator of experimental physiology in Germany, is a full and fresh laurel wreath to Goethe as a naturalist, even in the sole domain in which he was partly mistaken.

CHAPTER XV

ESTABLISHMENT AND MANAGEMENT OF THE
THEATRE IN WEIMAR—GOETHE AND
CHRISTIANE NEUMANN: *Euphrosyne*

FROM early childhood on, the stage had had its attraction for the author of *Götz*. The puppet theatre described in *Wilhelm Meister* constitutes one of the greatest curiosities in the Goethe House at Frankfort to this very day. In 1775, when Goethe came to Weimar and brought life and enjoyment along with him, dramatic production was for him (as it was for Voltaire) the noblest of the major amusements.

Even before his day the Duchess Anna Amalie had been a zealous exponent of the theatre. First she called the Koch troupe from Leipzig; it had cultivated the operetta. It was succeeded in 1771 by Seyler's troupe which could boast of the two sole theatrical celebrities of pronounced fame in Germany at that time: Konrad Ekhof and Madame Hensel. It is of these that Lessing speaks at great length in his *Hamburgische Dramaturgie* (1767-68). From Hamburg, where it had been their intention to found a national theatre, they had come to Weimar and given performances at the castle. But the fire of 1774 left them homeless; they moved on to Gotha where the Duke took them into his service for a while.

195

On Goethe's arrival in Weimar there was neither
a fixed nor a wandering troupe; there was not even
a building in which performances could be given.
The standing of the actor and the business of acting
were on a low level. For this very reason the dilettant comedy and amateur theatre afforded great
amusement. And since there were no professionals,
society took it upon itself to play comedy. Goethe
naturally became the leader. Karl August and his
brother Konstantin, the men and women of the
court, Goethe, Knebel, Bertuch, Musäus, Korona
Schröter performed dramas with real passion, now
under the roof of a redoubt building in Weimar,
which the excellent theatrical master, Mieding, had
arranged, now out in the open, anywhere in fact
that they could find a suitable place:

> In engen Hütten und im reichen Saal,
> Auf Höhen Etterburgs, in Tiefurts Thal,
> Im leichten Zelt, auf Teppichen der Pracht
> Und unter dem Gewölb der hohen Nacht.

If Mieding, at whose death Goethe wrote one of
his most beautiful poems, (*Auf Miedings Tod*),
was an excellent machinist, Goethe was in one person the poet and the director and the regisseur and
the leading actor of this dilettant theatre. In the
capacity of actor he played the rôles of Wilhelm in
Die Geschwister and Orestes in *Iphigenie*. It was
not until the year 1783 that he withdrew from these
diversions.

In 1780 a new building was erected for the performance of masquerades and dramas. From 1784
a troupe under the direction of Joseph Bellomo gave
performances three times a week, at first mostly of

Italian operettas, and then of serious drama. But
at the beginning of the year 1791 Bellomo and his
company went to Grätz. The Duchess had decided
even a year before their departure to erect a court
theatre in Weimar and to place Goethe at the head
of it. In April, 1791, Germany's one really great
actor, Friedrich Ludwig Schröder, then director of
the theatre in Hamburg, stopped for some time in
Weimar and with him Goethe discussed in detail
the art of acting and the practical management of a
theatre.

Finally in May, 1791, the far famed court theatre
in Weimar was opened with a performance of
Iffland's *Die Jäger* preceded by a prologue by Goethe. The first lines of the prologue tell us that
the beginning is always difficult. It then shows that
should the artists take only themselves into consideration, they might cheerfully go ahead and hope to
make their talents, great or small, felt. But when
they remember that in a case like this it is a question
of making various powers harmonize, of working in
unison, they feel the difficulty of the undertaking:

> Von allen Enden Deutschlands kommen wir
> Erst jetzt zusammen, sind einander fremd
> Und fangen erst nach jenem schönen Ziel
> Vereint zu wandeln an, und Jeder wünscht
> Mit seinem Nebenmann es zu erreichen.
>
> Denn hier gilt nicht, dass Einer athemlos
> Den Andern heftig vorzueilen strebt,
> Um einen Kranz für sich hinwegzuhaschen.
> Wir treten vor Euch auf, und Jeder bringt
> Bescheiden seine Blume, dass nur bald
> Ein schöner Kranz der Kunst vollendet werde,
> Den wir zu Eurer Freude knüpfen möchten.

The enterprise was quite successful; but as Weimar was too small a town to be able to provide sufficient auditors for a large number of theatrical evenings, plays were given in summer in smaller towns in the vicinity, always in Lauchstädt which must be considered as a branch, most frequently, however, in Erfurt.

When the troupe returned from Lauchstädt in October, 1791, the theatre was opened with a new prologue by Goethe which is unfortunately nothing but sheer prose, clothed in iambics.   Of greater value is the epilogue which closed the year December 31, 1791.   Goethe had it recited by Christiane Neumann, then only thirteen years old, surrounded by a group of other children.   It is patriarchal:

> Liebt Euch,
> Vertragt Euch! Einer sorge für den Andern!
> Dies schöne Glück, es raubt es kein Tyrann,
> Der beste Fürst vermag es nicht zu geben.

After an attempt for a year and a half, Goethe disbanded the troupe, retained only its most superior members, and formed a new one, into which he introduced strict discipline.   He paid great attention to order and punctuality at rehearsals, demanded that all rôles be memorized thoroughly and accurately, and laid the greatest stress upon correct and distinct enunciation.   He instilled first and foremost into his actors the elements of correct pronunciation, punished carelessness and indistinctness, and challenged every ancient routine.

Already seriously engrossed, he assumed in addition the burdens and torments of a theatre director. An incessant secret opposition carried along with it the uninterrupted spreading, by discontented actors, of unfavorable reports among the people concerning new plays and their anticipated misfortune on the stage. By December, 1795, Goethe already had his share of discontent and wished to resign. But Karl August begged him not to let the reins slip from his hands; he submitted, but cast about in the meantime for a first class stage manager.

He believed that he had found the right man when, in the spring of 1796, August Wilhelm Iffland, Germany's greatest actor next to Schröder, came to Weimar, his association throughout sixteen years with Dalberg in Mannheim having become looser and cooler. Iffland was given a brilliant reception. He played thirteen rôles of the most variegated sort; his acting was looked upon as being beyond reproach. He appeared in many plays that are now hopelessly forgotten, though he also took the part of Egmont, despite the fact that he was ill adapted to tragedy for a number of reasons, including lack of compass and resonance in his voice. But in bourgeois comedies and dramas, he was a master who could touch any chord in the human soul with equal dexterity. He was sincere and simple, an enemy of bombast. He adapted himself to the ensemble of effects, or more correctly speaking, he formed a whole about him.

From the Duke's side as well as from Goethe's everything was done to make Iffland a fixture; but the scheme was not a success. The National Theatre in Berlin called him to its leadership, and Weimar was in no position to compete with the capital of a kingdom.

However eagerly Goethe tried to retain Iffland,

and however thoroughly he had discussed histrionics
with Schröder five years previously, neither of these
two men corresponded in reality to his ideal of an
actor; in truth they both strove toward a different
goal, Schröder as a genius and Iffland as a virtuoso.
At heart they were the antipodes of Goethe as theatre directors, just as they as dramatic authors were
poles removed from him.

Schröder was versatile. He could improvise
after the fashion of the actors in the *Commedia
dell' arte;* and he could play rôles from all the leading literatures with the utmost precision. He was
the man who had given German actors as a class a
feeling of self-respect; previous to his time they
were regarded as vagabonds and decadents. He
was closely akin to Goethe in so far as he wished
that every play should make a complete and collective impression, that every rôle should be totally lost
in the whole. His battle-cry was nature. Rhetoric
and plastic art did not thrive under him. But as a
result of this everything received a sort of work-a-
day stamp. In his hatred of declamation he robbed
the tragedy of its swing and splendor.

For Goethe on the other hand the classical theatre was the ideal. The time had long since passed
when he called himself a naturalist. He now regarded himself as an "Idealist." In matters of
rhetoric, plastic art, and mimicry everything should
be first and foremost in good style. Goethe's actors
should never forget that they were there simply for
the sake of the spectator; it should not be their business to create an illusion but to give examples of
noble dignity. They should never for a moment
turn their back upon the public; in case there were

several of them, they should stand on the stage in
a semi-circle. Since Goethe as the leader of a theatre would avoid above all things else the slurring of
words, the chief stress was laid not on natural accent
but on distinct pronunciation, especially upon a beautiful, almost singing style of recitation. Not nature
but beauty was for him the highest law.

It does not seem, however, that Goethe, the
"Idealist," felt personally that he was in any way
at odds with Schröder, the "Realist," for there is
no actor whom he honored more highly. He wrote
in Schröder's album, 1791:

Viele sahn dich mit Wonne, dich wünschen so viele zu sehen.
　Reise glücklich! Du bringst überall Freude mit hin.

And what is more, he later wrote in Schröder's
album Lessing's familiar lines:

> Kunst und Natur
> Sei auf der Bühne eines nur!
> Wenn Kunst sich in Natur verwandelt,
> Dann hat Natur mit Kunst gehandelt.

So far as Iffland is concerned, whom Goethe studied
quite carefully, it is entirely probable that he is the
model of the exceedingly interesting character Serlo
in *Wilhelm Meister*. Of Serlo it is said, with a pun
on *gebildet* and *bildlos* (just as Iffland, he came
from Mannheim to Weimar):

He came to that part of Germany where, in the cultivation of the good and the beautiful there was no lack of truth,
though there was frequently a lack of intellect. He could
no longer accomplish anything with his masks; he had to try
to influence the heart and the soul. The monotony which
then prevailed on the German stage, the vapid cadence and
ring of the Alexandrines, the perverted and vulgar dialogues,

the dryness and commonness of the spontaneous tone of the moralists, he had soon caught and noticed at once what pleased and moved.

By virtue of his excellent memory, it was possible for him to recite not merely an individual rôle with the precise accent of any favorite actor, he could even learn an entire play by heart, and could perform an entire play alone, quite regardless of the circumstances that surrounded him. His vehemence gave the impression of strength; his flattery passed for tenderness. He soon played better than the models he had at first imitated, and he learned what so few actors ever seem to learn—to exercise economy and discipline in the modulation of his voice and the use of gestures.

Of Serlo we read in *Wilhelm Meister*:

He was cold at heart; he really loved no one. With the remarkable clarity of his glance, he could not esteem anyone, for he saw in reality only the external characteristics of people, and these he introduced into his mimic collection. His self-consciousness was, moreover, deeply offended if the applause was not general. He made such a careful study of the devices that win applause that, not only on the stage but in real life as well, he was constantly ingratiating himself into the favor of his associates. His mental equipment, his talent, his manner of living worked together in a surprising way, so that, himself unaware of what was taking place, he developed into a really perfect actor. Indeed, with an apparently rare and quite natural coöperation of effects and counter-effects, his diction, art of speaking, and mimic gestures arose, as the result of unceasing practice and with an ever increasing knowledge, to a very high degree of truth, freedom and candor.

II

Among Goethe's poetical works there is an elegy entitled *Euphrosyne*. It preserves most cordial reminiscences of the most gifted actress at the Weimar Theatre, a young woman trained in her profession by the master himself and loved by him at the same time. She died in September, 1797, eighteen years and ten months old.

Her father, Johann Christian Neumann, belonged to the company that had come to Weimar with Bellomo. He had died in 1791, shortly before the company had been dissolved. His daughter, Christiane Neumann, was born December 15, 1778, and had made her debut on the Weimar stage when she was but eight years of age. She played the part of the page in Engel's *Der Edelknabe*. She revealed such pronounced talent that the Court, captivated by her, requested Korona Schröter to supervise her education. When thirteen years old, she had recited a prologue by Schiller with such perfect skill that the Duchess Anna Amalie had her painted in this situation—that of the Goddess of Justice.

But as early as 1791 Goethe had begun to study rôles with the child and the same year she made her artistic debut in Shakespeare's *King John* as the boy Arthur, who is to be blinded with a red hot iron. Goethe himself had put the play on the boards from the very first rehearsal and, astounded by the naturalness and genuineness of Christiane's acting, had made Arthur the real center of the drama and had brought all methods of procedure on the part of the other actors in harmony with Christiane Neumann's.

In *Euphrosyne* we are told how Goethe, at a general rehearsal, was so moved on seeing the young girl lying on the stage as the wounded Arthur that he picked her up in his arms and bore her away.

In the poem it is she who, like a shade after death, speaks to him:

Freundlich fasstest du mich, den Zerschmetterten, trugst
    mich von dannen
Und ich heuchelte lang', Dir an dem Busen, den Tod.
Endlich schlug die Augen ich auf, und sah Dich in ernste,
    Stille Betrachtung versenkt, über den Liebling geneigt.
Kindlich strebt' ich empor und küsste die Hände dir dankbar,
    Reichte zum reinen Kuss dir den gefälligen Mund,
Fragte: Warum, mein Vater, so ernst? Und hab' ich
    gefehlet
O so zeige mir an, wie mir das Bessre gelingt!
Keine Mühe verdriesst mich bei Dir, und Alles und Jedes
    Wiederhol' ich so gern, wenn Du mich leitest und lehrst.
Aber Du fasstest mich stark und drücktest mich fester im
    Arme,
Und es schauderte mir tief in dem Busen das Herz.
Nein, mein liebliches Kind! so riefst du, Alles und Jedes,
    Wie du es heute gezeigt, zeig' es auch morgen der Stadt!
Rühre sie alle, wie mich Du gerührst, und es fliessen zum
    Beifall
Dir von dem trocknesten Aug' herrlich Tränen herab.

She soon became not merely the idol of Goethe, but of the Court and the general public as well. Wieland said of her that if she made equal advancement for a few years to come, Germany would have but *one* actress. Unfortunately mad havoc was played with the talent that had matured so early and with the young character developed ahead of her years. It seems that Germany at that time had no law forbidding marriage with children. In the summer of 1793, Christiane, then fourteen years old, was married to Becker, the actor at Weimar, whose unconscientious heartlessness did not deter him from having her become the mother of two children before she was sixteen. Her health suffered a fatal shock. In her fourteenth year she played the rôles of Emilia Galotti and Minna von Barnhelm. When seventeen she undertook a variety of different rôles including several from Shakespeare, the page in *Don Carlos,* and a number of boys' and girls' parts in Iffland's *Reise nach der Stadt, Die Jäger, Der Herbsttag.* These last named plays, in which the lighter style did not call for unusual physical or vocal power, were admirably adapted to her talent and condition. Goethe wrote the niece's rôle in the *Grosskophta* for her. Of her Iffland said: "She can do everything. She will never sink to the plane of the artificial transport of sentimentality, which for our young actresses is and remains the most serious fault of all."

In the summer of 1797 she died at the age of eighteen. In her death the theatre of Weimar suffered an irreparable loss. She could never be replaced, not even by Amalie Malcolmi (married to Pius Alexander Wolff) nor by Caroline Jagemann, though the former achieved substantial renown while the latter won for herself a position of absolute power.

CHAPTER XVI

GOETHE'S COLLABORATION WITH SCHILLER ON
Wallenstein—GOETHE AND CAROLINE JAGE-
MANN; HIS STRUGGLES AS THEATRE DIRECTOR
—COÖPERATION OF GOETHE AND SCHILLER AT
THE WEIMAR THEATRE

AFTER the death of Christiane Becker, Goethe
turned to Schiller as the one individual from whom
a renewal of Weimar's theatrical existence might be
derived. Inspired by Goethe, Schiller resumed work
on his *Wallenstein*. He had begun it in prose, but
it took to wing and flight only with rhythmic treatment. The drama was destined to mark an era
against the naturalistic, bombastic prose of the
dramas of chivalry and the plebeian and emotional
elements in the plays of Kotzebue and Iffland which
then constituted the chief repertoire of the German
stage.

As a poet Iffland was the antipodes of Goethe.
But Goethe's admiration for Iffland, the actor, remained unweakened. In 1798, Iffland returned to
Weimar to play as a guest. At his arrival Schiller
lay sick in Jena. He found one single opportunity
to see Iffland in Rousseau's scene entitled *Pygmalion;*
Caroline Jagemann played the rôle of Galatea.
When the heroine came to life at the close of the
piece, Iffland was playing away without restraint in

monologue and pantomime. He lost himself entirely in declamation and all manner of violent outbursts; he assumed plastic attitudes and moved his hands about by way of depicting various feelings. To Schiller such acting was shocking; Goethe found that in comparison with it his own actors were mere "reporters."

Thereupon Goethe betook himself to Jena in order to discuss a number of things with Schiller, among others his *Wallenstein* and the affairs of the theatre in general. Schiller had the genius of associating with actors in a direct and friendly fashion; he treated them as his comrades. Goethe kept them at a distance; his attitude was cold. Nevertheless Eduard Genast's *Tagebücher* show that he could be paternal and benevolent if the spirit moved him. With an antique slant such as both Goethe and Schiller had, it was easy for them to come to a complete understanding with regard to the theory of the art of acting. For both of them, the typical, not the individual, was the chief aim to be sought after. The special function of the actor was not to depict the figure but to form a sort of ideal masque, and to render his part cleanly and with grace. Actors had long been accustomed to a flat, everyday prose. Now they were to learn verses by heart; and to recite them correctly and with force. And these verses Schiller was now striving to bring much nearer to daily speech than he had done in *Don Carlos*.

The real difficulty was to find an actor who could give life to Wallenstein. The greatest actor in all Germany would not be good enough. However, Schröder was celebrated for his natural treatment of verse.

Schröder's second directorship of the theatre in Hamburg came to an end in 1797, and though he was but fifty-three years of age, he withdrew to isolation in the country. It seems that Schiller, as early as the beginning of 1798, had turned to him for advice with regard to Wallenstein. Goethe's good stage manager Kirms had also been in touch with him. The preliminaries, carried on in the main by Weimar's factotum, Böttiger, extended to interminable length; Schröder said neither yes nor no. At Goethe's request Schiller then introduced into the beautiful and magnificent prologue to *Wallensteins Lager* these four lines which allude to Schröder, and which were recited at the first performance in the restored theatre.

> O! möge dieses Raumes neue Würde
> Die Würdigsten in unsre Mitte ziehn,
> Und eine Hoffnung, die wir lang gehegt,
> Sich uns in glänzender Erfüllung zeigen!

But despite the fact that Goethe himself sent the much admired copy of this prologue together with a friendly invitation, Schröder remained steadfast in his original determination to turn his back on the stage for good and all. They were now forced to be satisfied with lesser talents. Wallenstein was played by a local artist named Graff. Though not exactly brilliant, he at least satisfied the author and his great friend.

II

Caroline Jagemann who, as an actress and a singer, dominated the theatre in Weimar from 1797 to the death of Karl August in 1828, was born in

January 1777. She was the daughter of Anna Amalie's librarian. At the age of twenty, she appeared as a singer on the stage of her paternal city after having enjoyed a schooling of three years under Iffland in Mannheim. She was extremely beautiful, had an uncommon voice, pronounced ability as an actress, and became at once the all-powerful friend of Karl August,—became what he himself called "eine Gesellschafterin seiner Erholungsstunden."

By nature she was domineering, wily, enterprising, and ruthless. In her very first year as a member of the society in Weimar she demanded that Frau Weyrauch in Lauchstädt, an excellent singer, relinquish a certain rôle in her favor. The demand was met and Caroline Jagemann sang the part. The complaint from the offended artist was laid on the table and since her colleagues sided with her, great difficulties were in store for the board of directors. The Weyrauchs asked for their release but were bound for the time being by contract. The next year the same thing was repeated and the Weyrauchs left Weimar for good and all. During a rehearsal of Mozart's *Don Juan,* Caroline Jagemann demanded peremptorily that the director of the orchestra, Kranz by name, have the musicians play, not according to his own leadership, but in time and tune with her voice. At the performance Kranz carried out his own will in the matter and Fräulein Jagemann was unable to keep time. The result was so humiliating to Goethe that Kranz was temporarily removed as director of the orchestra and never again permitted to direct the operas in which Caroline Jagemann sang.

As a matter of course, she was always at odds

with the rest of the staff, including the stage manager and the director. She never lost sight of her
self-appointed goal: autocratic sway on the stage.
Here the creator and maintainer of the theatre,
Goethe, stood in her way and for twenty years in
succession she put countless intrigues into effect to
have Goethe's influence broken and to have him
removed. Chancellor F. v. Müller reproduces, 1808,
a conversation with Goethe in which the latter said
that if he had been minded to see Caroline Jagemann once a week and persuade her to be more
sober, everything would have gone smoothly. But
since she was utterly without logic, since she wished
to be the center and nothing less, since she wished
to live and have a good time, she demoralized every
situation and every home into which she was admitted, though she was not a really malicious person.

At the theatre she surrounded herself with obe-
dient slaves, one of whom was the actor Becker, another was the bass singer Stromeyer, her very intimate friend of many years who assisted her in
everything.

Originally she had been most effective as a singer;
but when Christiane Becker died she also took over
the leading dramatic rôles. She brought to grief
the principle that Goethe had so zealously defended,
that of having the individual disappear in the effect
as a whole. Her beauty as well as her double talent
made her the favorite of the public. She was the
Duke's favorite anyhow, and she knew that she
would always be protected by him. When she was
thirty-two, Karl August made her a member of the
nobility, invested her with the name of Freifrau
von Heygendorf, and enfeoffed her.

The opposition she led against Goethe gradually undermined the morale of the theatre. She never undertook, however, a decisive move against him until the close of the year 1808. Just a little before the performance of the opera *Sargino* the tenor Morhard sent in a doctor's certificate to the effect that hoarseness prevented him from singing. The prima donna became embittered and exclaimed: "If the dog can't sing, let him bark!" She referred the matter to the Duke who dutifully punished her with an arrest of one week in her private rooms and gave Goethe the brusque order to have Morhard removed without any payment of salary other than what was due him from the previous week. Moreover the director was to see to it that Morhard was beyond the boundaries of Weimar within a fortnight. All that Goethe could accomplish in this affair was to have the time extended to a month. But now he begged the Duke without ceasing to give him his release as director of the theatre. The Duke refused and tried to retain Goethe's services by giving him absolute sovereignty, Goethe having demanded this as the one condition on which he would stay. At last the entire matter was adjusted: Goethe was to have nothing whatsoever to do with the opera, and Fräulein Jagemann was always to have an under-study, so that the operas could be performed when she refused to play in Lauchstädt.

And so the storm subsided for a while. But in the next year the arrogant Stromeyer again caused trouble. On this occasion Goethe gave in at once and a number of important changes in the management of the theatre followed. They arranged an intendancy, an entire commission as a matter of fact, on which a certain Count Edling and Goethe's own son were given seats. But he himself remained of course, nominally at least, the actual leader. They were unwilling to accept his advice; but they were also unwilling to accept his resignation.

On the birthday of one of the princes, in February 1817, Kotzebue's *Schutzgeist* was announced as a gala performance contrary to Goethe's wish. He again asked for his release and was again refused. But in the spring of the same year, while he was over in Jena, they played, April 12, *Der Hund des Aubrey de Mont-Didier,* a farce in which a poodle was the hero. Goethe at once sent in his resignation and on the following day he received from Karl August a note granting his request. The expressions are humorous, since the Duke always addressed Goethe by *Du* in private correspondence:

My most dear Herr Geheimrath and Minister of State!
The observations that you have made to me convince me that the Herr Geheimrath and Staatsminister wishes to be relieved of his duties connected with the management of the Court Theatre, though I know that he will not on this account fail to support the artistic department of the theatre with advice and deeds. . . . Herr Geheimrath and Staatsminister receives herewith my profound gratitude for his excellent services of former days,—and I hope that he will use the greater freedom he will henceforth enjoy as a reason of this change to the very best advantage of the important and artistic institutions to which he has up to the present devoted himself with such marked zeal. . . .
KARL AUGUST, *Grand Duke of Saxony.*

When we recall that Frau von Heygendorf was forty years old at this time, that she had been the intimate friend of Karl August for twenty years, and the sympathetic companion of Stromeyer for eleven years, it is quite impossible to deny her the recognition that is due her.

III

During Schiller's lifetime he and Goethe worked together in a cordial and fraternal way for the welfare of the theatre at Weimar. Schiller's dramas constituted a most excellent repertoire. In addition to this he directed the rehearsals not merely of his own works but of Goethe's as well, including the latter's translations. He staged *Egmont*. He supervised the rehearsals of Voltaire's *Mahomet*. If this was not a success it was not Schiller's fault. The *Mahomet* that was played was not really a translation but a subdued revision in another metre. Numerous changes were made for the sake of greater clarity. Propagandistic issues were weakened, toned down, or omitted entirely. Additions were made with a view to the Weimar of that time. It was the same method that Goethe employed in his adaptation of Voltaire's *Tancred*.

Goethe had asked Schiller to revise *Macbeth*. Schiller acquiesced, of course. But his treatment of iambics, his long, eloquent periods, the emphasis he laid on the sonorous art of speech in general, were all directly contrary to the pithy spirit and other excellent features of Shakespearean verse. As for Shakespearean prose—Schiller and his English predecessor were the antipodes of each other. The author of *Kabale und Liebe* was a stranger to prose such as is spoken by the porter in Shakespeare. Truth to tell, Schiller, and Goethe as well, could not appreciate the effect of contrast in the works

of the great Britisher.   Just as Serlo in *Wilhelm
Meister* persuades the hero, in a production of *Hamlet,* to omit anything that might possibly impair the
unity of impression, just so did Goethe persuade
Schiller, who had formerly been influenced by the
Antique, to omit the vulgar but excellent monologue
in prose spoken by the porter.   He substituted for
it a pious song which is poles removed from Shakespeare both in tone and temperament.   The fact is
that both Goethe and Schiller, once the ardent devotees of Shakespeare, eventually came to the point
where they made a sharp distinction between the
comic and the tragic in art.   The French had under-
gone a similar reform.   Both adopted Napoleon's
slogan: *J'aime les genres tranchés.*

For this reason Goethe substituted, in his version
of *Romeo and Juliet,* for the sprightly introductory
scenes in which the men of the two hostile families
challenge each other to fight, a chorus during which
the servants of the Capulets decorated the palace
for a masquerade.   The humorous scenes among the
servants in the first act were discarded, also the jests
of the musicians before Juliet's burial.   Even the
nurse's drollness and loquaciousness and Mercutio's
whims and wit were deleted; she became a mere
matchmaker, he a mere jester.   And the entire story
of Queen Mab was omitted.

Of the two stage directors, Schiller was as a rule
the gentler, Goethe the sterner, though Schiller
could also become angry.   During a general rehearsal of Schiller's adaptation of *Macbeth,* Goethe, Schiller, and Heinrich Meyer were looking on.
The actor Vohs was quite uncertain as to his memory.   Goethe called the stage director, Anton

Genast, down to him and said very bitterly: "What in the world is the matter with this Herr Vohs? He doesn't know a word of his rôle; how can he play Macbeth! Are we to stultify ourselves before the dignitaries and the general public? The performance for tomorrow shall be canceled, and you need not bother about keeping the reasons for the cancelation from Herr Vohs and the rest of the staff." But in the meantime Schiller brought Goethe to reason, praised Voh's artistic composure and genius, which were to bring him safely over all rocky places, and the performance was given.

It met with great success. The applause increased from scene to scene. At the close of the second act Schiller came on the stage and said in his Swabian dialect: *Wo ischt der Vohs?* And when Vohs came forward embarrassed, with bowed head, Schiller said: *"Nein, Vohs! ich muss Ihne sage: meischterhaft, meischterhaft! Aber nun ziehe Sie sich zum dritte Akt um."* Then he said to the stage manager: *"Sehe Sie Genascht, wir habbe Recht gehabt! Er hat zwar ganz andere Vers gesproche, als ich sie geschriebe hab, aber er ischt trefflich."*

But however amiable and good-natured Schiller was as a director, it was nevertheless easily possible for him to lose his poise when he encountered irrational opposition. At a rehearsal of Goethe's translation of Voltaire's *Tancred*, Goethe had asked Schiller to keep a diligent eye on an actor by the name of Haide who played the leading part, and who began to fan about and fight with his hands and whistle with his voice so soon as he became excited. Schiller made some objections to this method of playing; but the good Haide paid no attention, indeed he even stopped and tried to explain to Schiller in detail why he played thus and so. Then it was all over with the dignified calm of Friedrich Schiller. He cried out in bitter anger: *"Ei was! mache Sie's, wie ich's Ihne sage und wie's der Goethe habbe will. Und er hat Recht; es ischt ä Graus, das ewige Vagire mit dene Händ und das Hinaufpfeife bei der Recitation.* The actor stood as if thunderstruck. No one had ever seen Schiller in this frame of mind.

He himself put his *Maria Stuart* on the stage and attended the rehearsals with untiring energy and genuine appreciation of theatrical effect. The scene in which the queen receives the sacrament gave rise to strong objections. Herder protested against the profanation that arose from acting the holy communion. The scene was given but once, since even the general public found it distasteful.

One consequence of the tendency to go back to antiquity on the part of the two great companions was the performance of Terence's *Die Brüder*. It was played not simply in Roman costume but also in accordance with the customs of Terence's day, in masks, masks however which did not cover the entire face, only the forehead, nose, and chin and in this way expressed the character of the rôle. The eyes, mouth, and cheeks were uncovered. The play amused and drew full houses. But the other dramas of Terence and Plautus were too far removed from the German public. And as is known, A. W. Schlegel's adaptation of Euripides's *Ion,* one of the antique dramas that Goethe's *Iphigenie* called forth, was a total failure. The wretched drama by his brother Friedrich Schlegel, entitled *Alarcos,* met with the same fate.

As an homage to Duchess Anna Amalie, Goethe himself wrote a little festival play in classical style that was performed with masks and in which he used for the first time in his life Greek trimeters, relieved every now and then by trochaic verses. It is the delightful little bagatelle with the forbidding name of *Palaeophron und Neoterpe*. It is an exceedingly clever allegory, introducing modern times as a beautiful young woman, accompanied, to be sure, by two naughty youngsters, Gelbschnabel and Naseweis, and ancient times as a dignified and sensible man, accompanied by two impatient old people, Griesgram and Haberecht. But so soon as Neoterpe and Palaeophron have given their companions a farewell, they are in a position to understand each other perfectly; they even make each other happy and give to each the wreath. Finally modern and ancient times jointly do honor to the lofty lady who long ago established the league between the two.

Two years later, Goethe wrote for the opening performance of the new theatre in Lauchstädt another prelude. This was somewhat more elaborate; it was another allegory entitled *Was wir bringen*. After a fashion which is not without charm, and in which verse and prose alternate, an old German couple and a number of symbolic figures with Greek names, *Nymphe, Phone, Pathos* (naturally ballet, opera, and drama) are united with the god Mercury who seems somewhat Latin-like in the midst of all this Greek and German. The *obligato* homage to the Princes is not lacking. In this case it is Karl August as the ruler of the country, Elector Friedrich of Saxony, the King of Poland as the benefactor who, after his consort had been restored to health

in Lauchstädt, had had the neighborhood adorned
with gardens and promenades. In order to effect
a more reasonable unity, an attempt is made in the
play to see in Märten and Mutter Martha Philemon
and Baucis themselves, of whom however the couple
never once in their lives have heard.

All of this is topical poetry written expressly for
the theatre. While director, Goethe wrote a great
deal more in the same vein. The most important
part of the piece is the sonnet, *Natur und Kunst, sie
scheinen sich zu fliehen.* It appears here for the
first time, spoken by Nymphe. The line, *Wer
Grosses will, muss sich zusammenraffen,* fitted quite
well into the work that interested Goethe from day
to day at this period of his life.

CHAPTER XVII

COMPLETION OF *Faust,* PART I

VIGOROUSLY challenged by Schiller, the author of *Faust. Ein Fragment* again went to work on his most fruitful theme in the year 1797, after having completed *Hermann und Dorothea.* He endeavored to elevate it, to saturate it with symbolism, and to give it a broad base from which it might rise without doing violence to spiritual logic. On the other hand, and quite unfortunately, he took it upon himself to weaken this very coherency that had been so slow in developing. He ruthlessly dissipated, if he did not destroy, the total effect by the insertion of whatever pleased him. It seems that there was a period in his life when he felt an ineluctable impulse to use *Faust* as a strong box into which drawers might be inserted to be filled as opportunity offered and inspiration came.

He had already written an admirable poem entitled *Die erste Walpurgisnacht,* depicting the embitterment of the old Druids at the triumphal march of Christianity. It is still another poem in which Goethe manifested his hatred of the religious negation of nature. In this cantata, arranged for several voices, we find a vigorous opposition on the part of old Germanic heathendom to the worship of the new God whose priests and confessors are accused of slaughtering heathen women and children. The following is a characteristic stanza:

> Diese dumpfen Pfaffenchristen,
> Lasst uns keck sie überlisten!
> Mit dem Teufel, den sie fabeln,
> Wollen wir sie selbst erschrecken.
> Kommt! Mit Zacken und mit Gabeln
> Und mit Gluth und Klapperstöcken
> Lärmen wir bei nächt'ger Weile
> Durch die engen Felsenstrecken.
> Kauz und Eule
> Heul' in unser Rundgeheule.

When Goethe wrote *Walpurgisnacht* in *Faust,* his poetic point of view was an altogether different one. Since he had had the devil himself appear in his poem, he could not logically protest against him as an imaginary or fabulous being. With fresh, vigorous, and teeming imagination he took up with the Blocksberg superstition, and had his Faust and Mephistopheles spend Walpurgis Night on the Brocken with will-o-the-wisps, wizards, and witches old and young. The picture of the landscape is marvelous; the verses, the serious as well as the humorous ones, have an extraordinary amount of color-depicting and sound-producing power. Here is a painting replete with mystery, though it is but two lines long:

> Wie traurig steigt die unvollkommne Scheibe
> Des rothen Monds mit später Gluth heran!

Here is a jovial stanza concerning two tall granite rocks at Schierke, the names of which are "The Snorers:"

Seh die Bäume hinter Bäumen,
Wie sie schnell vorüberrücken,
Und die Klippen, die sich bücken,
Und die langen Felsenmassen,
Wie sie schnarchen, wie sie blasen!

The hobgoblins in the spring night are delineated
with all the skill of which the poet was capable. In
the characterization of the witch-like creatures, the
portrayal is marked with coarse sensuality. Mephistopheles, and the witches as well, make constant use
of expressions which, in the various editions, have
been denoted only by dotted lines; their exact wording can be determined only by the rhyme. There
is a mixture of the generally uncomfortable and
disagreeable compounded of wild salacity, rank
smells and disgusting stenches with something of
Höllenbreughel's comic and grimaces. The impression made is tremendous when, in the midst of all
this run-away lechery, the vision of the decapitated
Gretchen suddenly appears before Faust. In the
Paralipomena, which were omitted, though they are
found after the tragedy in some editions, the obscen-
ity of the scene is much stronger.

From an artistic point of view, however, all of
this belonged to the picture of the world and the
picture of life that *Faust* was supposed to give. We
are repelled, however, when, in the midst of all this
witches' dance, Goethe's old and now otherwise
hopelessly forgotten opponent Nicolai is introduced
with vast scorn as a *Proktophantasmist,* that is, as
one who sees visions with his posterior parts. The
reference is to the fact, but little known to later
generations and quite without interest to any human
being, that Nicolai suffered from hemorrhoids and

in consequence of these, from delusions, and that he endeavored to cure himself by applying leeches to the more nearly designated section of his anatomy. Nor is this all. Four old gentlemen appear on the Brocken, a minister, a general, a parvenu, and an author, each of whom pecks and hacks away in his little stanza at the coming generation. The effect of this is null, quite so.

These however are all negligible matters; little specks. We are astounded and amazed, on the other hand, to see that Goethe, just before the strong closing scene with Gretchen in prison from the *Urfaust*—unhappily entitled *Oberons und Titanias goldene Hochzeit*—has had the heart to insert fifty strophes, *Xenien* in an abbreviated meter, each one with a blow to the left and a blow to the right against his contemporary opponents. Every vestige of the illusion is destroyed, and that on purpose. We have a reference to the deceased machinist Mieding; rationalists and artists who pay excessive attention to costumes are ridiculed. There is one Hennings, the editor of certain magazines. At the mention of his name, his two journalistic enterprises, *Der Musaget* and *Genius der Zeit,* are covered with derision. There is Lavater as a crane, with an illusion to the odd way he walked. And there is Nicolai as a persecutor of the Jesuits, snuffing about after those whom he hates.

This was done by the same Goethe who had had Schiller trim *Macbeth,* and who himself had deleted every phantastic expression or bit of exuberant jollity from *Romeo and Juliet* which did not appeal to him as being necessary to paint the moral and adorn the tale. Fortunately, his labors on the mas-

terpiece were not limited to such crimes against the
general spirit of the work. He wrote the touching
introductory poem entitled *Zueignung* in which he
tells how he feels on returning to his *magnum opus*.
His initial auditors were dead and departed:

> Sie hören nicht die folgenden Gesänge,
> Die Seelen, denen ich die ersten sang;
> Zerstoben ist das freundliche Gedränge,
> Verklungen, ach, der erste Wiederklang.
> Mein Leid ertönt der unbekannten Menge. . . .

There follows *Das Vorspiel auf dem Theater,*
consisting of a conversation carried on by the manager, the theatre poet, and the jester. The idea
he seems to have derived from Kalidasa's *Sakun-
tala.* It came out in English in 1789; Goethe had
read it and appreciated it. In the speeches of the
manager, he has assembled the sum total of experiences, bitter for the most part, to which he himself
had been subjected as director: contempt for the
public, insight into its taste for what is both bulky
and piecemeal, its utter inability to appreciate poetry, and so on and on. We have this reference to
the poet:

> Was träumtet Ihr auf Eurer Dichterhöhe?
> Was macht ein volles Haus Euch froh?
> Beseht die Gönner in der Nähe!
> Halb sind sie kalt, halb sind sie roh.

He requests the poet to adapt himself to the
public's undisciplined taste, so that he and the
theatre can go on. In the reply of the poet Goethe
has expressed his glorification of the profession of
poet, as did Shakespeare in the fifth act of *Mid-*

summer Night's Dream. The entire passage deserves study. Here is the main part of it. His intention is certainly serious, showing how, while time runs on without division or stopping, day after day, the poet interrupts the succession of days, and from one section forms a harmonious whole:

> Wenn die Natur des Fadens ew'ge Länge,
> Gleichgültig drehend, auf die Spindel zwingt,
> Wenn aller Wesen unharmon'sche Menge
> Verdriesslich durch einander klingt,
> Wer theilt die fliessend immer gleiche Reihe,
> Belebend ab, dass sie sich rhythmisch regt?
> Wer ruft das Einzelne zur allgemeinen Weihe,
> Wo es in herrlichen Akkorden schlägt? . . .
> Wer flicht die unbedeutend grünen Blätter
> Zum Ehrenkranz Verdiensten jeder Art?
> Wer sichert den Olymp, vereinet Götter?
> Des Menschen Kraft, im Dichter offenbart.

The *Vorspiel* is followed by the *Prolog im Himmel* motivated by the introduction to the *Book of Job.* More in accordance with the Old Testament than with the later development of the rôle of Mephistopheles in the work in which he directs so heinous a crime as the murder of Valentin in an unfair duel, the devil is conceived of as a sort of buffoon at the angels' court of the Lord, and one of the servants of the Lord among others. The Lord himself is inclined to tolerate him, gives him to man in attendance as a sting, as a stimulant, who shall prevent man from growing slack in his activity and sinking into torpid imbecility. To the angels, on the contrary, he delegates the spirit of progressiveness. While the devil is the power which steadily wills evil, but involuntarily produces good, the

angels are conceived with the love of everything on
earth. Their task is to secure by enduring thoughts
what they would otherwise let slip by as fugitive
phenomena. Goethe has put on their lips an antiphonal song, more beautiful than any psalm, in
which the sublime has received an expression of
exalted power. The first angel sings:

> Die Sonne tönt nach alter Weise
> In Bruder sphären Wettgesang,
> Und ihre vorgeschriebne Reise
> Vollendet sie mit Donnergang.
> Ihr Anblick giebt den Engeln Stärke,
> Wenn keiner sie ergründen mag.
> Die unbegreiflich hohen Werke
> Sind herrlich wie am ersten Tag.

At the beginning of the poem Faust's monologue
on suicide is added, which, with the beautiful, sublime flow of its iambics that strongly clashes with
the doggerel of the preceding dialogue, reminds of
the turn of the century. There is also a wonderful
Easter song of the angels, worked out on the basis
of an old Christian Easter psalm, with its *terza
rima* which tingles and rings like a silver bell, that
moves the despairing Faust, and calls him back to
life.

The elaborate scene *Vor dem Tor*, immortal in
its fresh beauty, one of the most youthful and vivacious parts of *Faust*, must, though not written until
now, certainly have been planned many years before. Since the burgher speaks of the Turkish War,
it is probable that the speech was written during this
war, so that, though omitted from the *Urfaust*, it
must have originated in 1774. For that was the
year in which peace was settled between Russia

and Turkey at Kystsjyk-Kainards-ji.   The passage
runs :

> Nichts Bessres weiss ich mir an Sonn—und Feiertagen
> Als ein Gespräch von Krieg und Kriegsgeschrei,
> Wenn hinten, weit in der Türkei
> Die Völker aufeinanderschlagen.

The peasant song under the linden tree, *Der
Schäfer putzte sich zum Tanz,* must likewise be of
earlier origin; for in Book II, Chapter 11, of *Wilhelm Meister,* which came out in 1795, Philine asks
the harpist whether he knows the melody to this
song.   He plays and she sings it; but Goethe adds
there that he cannot tell it to his readers for they
perhaps might find it dull or even improper.   Fortunately he has here thrown his scruples to the
winds.

It is impossible to read Faust's Easter Morning
monologue without admiration and enthusiasm.   It
is difficult to find anything more beautiful and picturesque than the speech beginning *Vom Eise befreit
sind Strom und Bäche.*   The landscape in the spring
with its hail storms and melting snow is depicted
with a freshness and assurance that enrapture.
Strikingly true in its benevolence is the application
of the idea of resurrection in the case of poor creatures who, on that morning, catch for the first time
in a long while the glimpse of a new sun and a breath
of fresh air:

> Denn sie sind selber auferstanden;
> Aus niedriger Häuser dumpfen Gemächern
> Aus Handwerks—und Gewerbebanden,
> Aus dem Druck von Giebeln und Dächern
> Aus der Strassen quetschender Enge
> Aus der Kirchen ehrwürdiger Nacht
> Sind sie Alle ans Licht gebracht.

The subsequent monologue between Faust and Wagner, of singular excellence, shows how much time must have elapsed since Goethe originally planned the leading figure. He has now forgotten a few individual touches that contradict each other. As is known, one of Faust's very first utterances is that he has never laid up honor for himself:

> Auch hab ich weder Gut noch Geld
> Noch Ehr und Herrlichkeit der Welt.

Here, a few pages later on, we see him honored and esteemed by the peasants as a benefactor. Every father points him out to his son. All question and rush up and hurry along in order to see him. The music and dance stop. The rows are opened. Hats are tossed in the air. But little more was needed, and they would have knelt before him as the common people do before the sacrament itself when it is carried along the streets of Catholic countries.

This does not harmonize especially well with the outbreak at the beginning. *Es möchte kein Hund so länger Leben!* The harmony is likewise tenuous between the determination on the part of Faust to go in for magic at the beginning of the work and his boundless contempt a few scenes later for his father's alchemystic attempts, the results of which were that the patients died like flies, so that his father and he himself were more of a plague to the neighborhood than the pest itself. But this is of very little importance where there is something to admire on every page; the point is that these frequent self-contradictions are disconcerting.

In the scene that immediately follows between

Faust and Mefisto as a wandering scholasticus, in which every other speech has become a standing phrase or apothegm, we are also conscious of the fact that considerable time has elapsed between the composition of the various scenes. When Mefisto has finished speaking, he wishes to go. Faust does not wish to let him go; he would like to hold on to the devil now that he has got him in his power. Mefisto begins with all his might to enchant; he calls up spirits who, singing in chorus, so stupefy Faust that he falls asleep. Mefisto even conjures up a rat that can gnaw through the pentagramme which prevents him from crossing the threshold; finally he disappears. Faust awakens a disappointed man. But quite soon Mefisto knocks at the door; he is back again. It was then really not necessary to go to all of this trouble in order to escape. The placing of the wager follows, the contract is agreed upon. Faust's outbreak against the conditions of life on this earth, the life that he himself has led, is a bit of unusual poetry; it expresses the pessimism of mature manhood:

> Verflucht voraus die hohe Meinung,
> Womit der Geist sich selbst umfängt!
> Verflucht das Blenden der Erscheinung,
> Die sich an unsre Sinne drängt!
> Verflucht, was uns in Träumen heuchelt,
> Des Ruhms, des Namendauers Trug!
> Verflucht was als Besitz uns schmeichelt
> Als Weib und Kind, als Knecht und Pflug. . . .

It was not until 1808 that the entire first part of *Faust* was accessible to the public; and there were even then not a few who comprehended the significance of the poem. Wieland admired this "barock-

ingenious tragedy which was dissimilar to any tragedy that had ever appeared, or that ever would
appear." He made the remark, too, that Goethe
had the same meaning for the poetic world that
Napoleon had for the political world. Jean Paul
forgot the injuries he had suffered from Goethe and
greeted in *Faust* a "posthumous Shakespeare." Rahel Varnhagen, one of the very first to appreciate
the general value of Goethe, had also a full understanding of *Faust*. Schelling said of the work that
it was "the greatest poem of the Germans, com-
parable only to itself." It was moreover the Romantic School that took it upon itself to glorify and
explain *Faust*, for it appealed to its members as a
romantische Tragödie. Friedrich Schlegel, like
many a man after him, compared Goethe, as the
author of *Faust*, with Dante Alighieri.

The work has indeed acquired a significance for
our day that is akin to the significance the *Divina
Commedia* had for the Middle Ages. All the forces
that ever moved Goethe come into their own in it;
they climb up and glide down and "reach to each
other the bright gilded vessels." The yearning of
the young man, the fate of the lover, the lonesome-
ness of the genius, the rich experience of the mature
man—all of these worked together and played their
part in its composition. And round about it and
through it the imperishable has been approached.

What difference does it make if the first part of
Faust is not a homogeneous work with an individual
harmony when it is so replete with independent
harmonies that are after all united! They are all
dominated by Faust's yearning for the infinite in
wisdom, in enjoyment, and in power.

The more developed the reader the less he will be offended by the heterogeneous nature of the individual scenes; and the undeveloped reader, who is simply and once for all accustomed to a wrong understanding, has now had more than a century to discover the heterogeneousness of the poem—and he has not yet succeeded: he does not feel it. He is satisfied with the many thoughts the work calls into play in his mind; he is rejoiced over the many better feelings it calls into play in his life. And he is right.

CHAPTER XVIII

Die natürliche Tochter—BREAK BETWEEN GOETHE
AND HERDER; SCHILLER'S DEATH

IT was in the year 1800 that Goethe, while suffering from frequent indisposition, wrote the matchless Easter Walk in *Faust*. The end of the century
was imminent. The time immediately preceding
midnight of December 31, 1800, he spent in serious
conversation with Schiller. The century to which
Schiller belonged heart and soul was over; the century to which the first fifty years of Goethe's life
belonged, with its ideals of humanity and cosmo-
politanism, was past and gone.

At the beginning of January he was seized with
a grave illness that affected him for a considerable
time. In the opinion of later physicians, it seems
to have been a case of violent influenza with symp-
toms of meningitis, and abscesses which, aside from
making him uncomfortable in general, closed his
eyelids. A long period of unconsciousness marked
the beginning of his discomfiture; a tumor on his
eye lasted until well on in March. Insomnia and
nervous restlessness continued until the summer,
when he sought relief in the baths of Pyrmont.

It has long been customary to contend that Goethe's sense for the secrets of art and nature dulled
his feelings for the social and political phases of
life. This is untrue. We have already seen how

profoundly the French Revolution interested him and how he tried, in his way, to set its ideas and events aright. In *Die natürliche Tochter* he puts some of the victims and coöperators on the boards incognito. He moved his source forward in point of time. The *Mémoires historiques de Stéphanie-Louise de Bourbon-Conti* had appeared in 1798. They told of the stern fate that had befallen a daughter born out of wedlock to the cousin of Louis XV, Prince Louis de Conti, by Countess Mazarin. The Prince had received permission from the King to give his illegitimate daughter the rank of a princess; but her legitimate brother ardently strove to prevent this by using force, falsehood, and deception.

The Princess was Goethe's contemporary, his junior by thirteen years. When, in 1801, he undertook to poetize her affair and her fate, he moves her up to his own time, since the King in the drama is evidently Louis XVI, and the Princess's father, the Duke, the King's disloyal and revolutionary kinsman, bears some similarity to Philippe Egalité. What we possess of this work is a single drama of a trilogy that had been originally planned. We have the same feeling here that we have everywhere: Goethe's mind was insusceptible to the great revolutionary emotion.

This drama that has been so unjustly depreciated, condemned for so long in an unreasonable way, makes its appeal to us on purely *human* grounds. Indeed, if we of today are to derive pleasure from Goethe's works at all, we must look for the human element in them; we must read them naïvely, personally, and try out what they say to *us*—wholly

regardless of what others have seen in them. How
can anyone attach importance to Huber's remark
that *Die natürlich Tochter* is "as smooth as marble
and as cold."

Goethe steeps himself in the tragic fate of an individual without being able, without wishing, to give
us an especially strong impression of the general
spirit and public life. In the domain in which Schiller moved about naturally and freely, Goethe could
scarcely breathe. But the entire age is reflected
in the tragic fate of this individual.

We learn that the King is too mild; that he
thereby makes enemies for himself; that the Duke
belongs among those whom he fears. The enthusiasm the Duke's daughter cherishes toward the King
is beautiful, just as the King himself is a high-minded
man. He is informed that the Duke, out of a whim,
has concealed his relation of father to Eugenie,
though this is an open secret. The King replies:
There is something noble in this action. It is natural that one conceal a great deal that everybody
knows:

> O lass dem Menschen diesen edlen Stolz!
> Gar Vieles kann, gar Vieles muss geschehen,
> Was man mit Worten nicht bekennen darf.

In this excited and disturbed time the young Princess Eugenie puts unalloyed faith in the people.
The King solemnly reminds her that democracy is
not the sole force deserving of sincere consideration:

> Wenn Dir die Menge, gutes, edles, Kind,
> Bedeutend scheinen mag, so tadl' ich's nicht,
> Sie *ist* bedeutend. Mehr aber noch sind's
> Die Wenigen, geschaffen, dieser Menge
> Durch Wirken, Bilden, Herrschen vorzustehn.

The most beautiful part of the drama as an individual element is this purely human factor: The father's boundless joy when his daughter, whom he thought a misfortune had befallen while on a daring riding tour, stands liberated and safe before his eyes; and the father's despair when he really loses his daughter.

But no less profound is the *political* teaching of the drama. We see from it how the most rebellious act can be carried out by a well meaning man when he tries, for example, to prevent an even greater misfortune, a murder. We see how political actions are executed without a shimmer of regard for the permissible, how a subordinate—somewhat as happened a century later in the Dreyfus case—calmly practices every sort of baseness that his superior officers demand of him. Goethe has studied and appreciated what has been called political Jesuitism —without the Jesuits being held responsible for the expression; they are, as a rule, personally excellent people.

In the drama, the lay brother, who causes a misfortune by his false testimony to the effect that the Princess is dead, is no longer willing, when seized with ambition, to be the mere tool of the timid, but wishes also to have a seat from now on in the council.

In the development of the action there are two features of supreme importance. The first is the marriage proposal made by the lawyer. He offers her his hand as the best means of making it possible for her to remain in the country; and he makes her the offer in a dignified and attractive way in that he emphasizes the significance of the protection that comes from having a private home:

Eugenie: Bist Du in Deinem Hause Fürst?
Gerichtsrath: Ich bin's
Und Jeder ist's, der Gute wie der Böse. . . .
Nicht Heldenfaust, nicht Heldenstamm, geliebte,
Verehrte Fremde, weiss ich dir zu bieten,
Allein des Bürgers hohen Sicherstand.
Und bist du mein, was kann Dich mehr berühren?
Auf ewig bist du mein, versorgt, beschützt.
Der König fordre Dich von mir zurück—
Als Gatte kann ich mit dem König rechten.

The second feature is the originality in Eugenie's development. At first she refuses the lawyer's proposal. Then a great change takes place within her. She forces the private cares of her life into the background under the impression of the general distress of the situation. She no longer wishes to leave her country; she will share the danger and the possible victory with her countrymen:

Nun bist du, Boden meines Vaterlands,
Mir erst ein Heiligthum; nun fühl ich erst
Den dringenden Beruf, mich anzuklammern.

And she offers her hand, with refinement of soul and queenly bearing, to the rejected suitor on the condition that she retain the control of her own person:

Nun sei's gefragt: Vermagst du hohen Muths
Entsagung der Entsagenden zu weihen?
Vermagst du zu versprechen, mich als Bruder
Mit reiner Neigung zu empfangen, mir,
Der liebevollen Schwester, Schutz und Rath
Und stille Lebensfreude zu gewähren?

Since he would rather do anything than lose her he agrees to this arrangement. Unfortunately,

Goethe let also this plan lie. There is only a brief outline instructive in itself, of the drama that was to follow.

The peculiarity of *Die natürlich Tochter* that especially attracts the attention of the reader is the method of treatment, the change that has taken place in Goethe's dramatic style during his continued flight from the individual, and his continued tendency toward the typical. In this drama with its eleven characters, Eugenie is the only one that has a proper name. The others have only rank, position. They are evidently meant to correspond to norms, just as Goethe believed in a rule for male and female proportions in ancient statues.

Corresponding to this is the fact that the style is somewhat affected. In the conversation between Eugenie and the lawyer, or between Eugenie and the governess in the fourth act, Goethe has adopted the stichomythy of the ancient tragedy. In the second act one reads with astonishment the sonnet that Eugenie writes and declaims. It is at once stiff and gloomy, written in a senile style. But worst of all is Goethe's dread of the designations for the things of everyday life. He reminds us of the old French poet Delille with his circumlocutions, all of which is poles removed from the bluntness of style in the works of Goethe's youth. One hardly believes one's own eyes when one reads from the author of *Götz* this circumlocution of the word for *uniform:*

> Was reizt das Auge mehr als jenes Kleid,
> Das kriegerische lange Reihen zeichnet!

Significant indeed is also the fact that in the first scene of the fifth act we are *told* of a situation which reminds us in its essential points of Clärchen when she seeks in vain to call the citizens to arms to liberate Egmont. The difference lies in the fact that Eugenie herself is to be helped and freed. But whereas in Goethe's young days the scene was depicted before our eyes so that we ourselves experience it, here it is narrated in a report just as in a French tragedy from the seventeenth century:

Hofmeisterin: Und riefst Du nicht das Volk zur Hilfe schon?
Es staunte nur Dich an und schwieg und ging.

The immediate life that pulsates and throbs has disappeared from Goethe's dramatic art, however moved by emotion and rich in thought it had continued to be.

II

The drama, stupidly and crudely parodied by G. Merkel in his *Kakogenia,* was performed in 1803 in Weimar, Lauchstädt, and Berlin. Schiller, Karl August and Fichte found it pleasing; Knebel and Friedrich Schlegel condemned it.

Herder died in the same year. Though he had had a pronounced influence on Goethe as a young man, the mature Goethe turned to other sources of human inspiration. Goethe himself has told us in his *Biographische Einzelheiten* of his last conversation with the friend of his youth. It took place at the castle in Jena where the two men stopped shortly after the performance of *Die natürliche Tochter.* Goethe had already heard of Herder's most favorable remarks concerning the play. These were all the more pleasing to the poet since they led him to believe that a renewal of their former friendly relation was possible.

One evening Herder came to see Goethe; they were living under the same roof. He discussed the drama with the unaffected air of a connoisseur, praised it in an intelligent way, and shed so much light on its real meaning that Goethe felt he had really not understood his own creation. But then, to Goethe's great surprise, he ended with such an outbreak against him that Goethe felt the offences he suffered were irreparable. "I looked at him," Goethe writes, "and replied that the long years of our association terrified me to the point of actual consternation. We separated; I never saw him again."

Goethe docs not tell us what Herder said; he expresses himself quite impersonally:

How easy it is to offend or distress one by reminding him, in free and easy moments, of his own defects or the faults of his wife or his children or his home or general status as a citizen, particularly if one does this in cutting, trenchant and epigrammatic language. This was one of Herder's earlier shortcomings, one from which he never completely freed himself and which at last estranged everyone who might otherwise have been his friend. We can overlook the mistakes of youth and regard them somewhat as we regard the transitory sourness of fruit that has not entirely ripened. But let faults of this kind be continued until late in life and they bring us to despair.

And thus the relation, at one time fatherly and later fraternal, which Herder bore to Goethe came to a close with a sharp dissonance.

Among the spectators at the performance of Goethe's drama was a woman who did not understand German. This woman was Madame de Staël.

She was staying at the time in Weimar and collecting, there more than anywhere else, material for her book entitled *Ueber Deutschland*. It was a book that was destined to draw the attention of Europe to modern German literature as it was then beginning to manifest itself. In his notes Goethe has done justice to Madame de Staël, though it is obvious that she irritated him with her incessant questions and by her pronounced inclination to jump from one topic to another. She is treated in another place (in my "Main Currents") so exhaustively that further discussion of her at this point may be omitted.

During this same year, Schiller's most renowned dramas were performed on the Weimar stage. *Die Braut von Messina* and *Die Jungfrau von Orleans* were both produced in 1803, also Schiller's translation of Racine's *Phaedre*. In March, 1804, there was a performance of *Wilhelm Tell*. Schiller, who was soon to dominate the stage in Germany, already dominated that of Weimar. But his health was undermined. Death carried him off in May, 1805, then only forty-five years of age.

This loss made Goethe a lonely man. The friends who in the future were to offer him a species of substitute, the frequently mentioned Heinrich Meyer, who lived for a long time in his house, Dr. Riemer who from the very beginning became attached to him, first as the tutor to his son and then as his own private secretary, and his Berlin correspondent, the musician Zelter, were in no case his mental equals, nor did they stand in general on his level. And the loneliness increased. The Duchess Anna Amalie died in 1807, and in September, 1808, Frau Aja, his mother, passed away. The last years of her life had been sweetened by a long visit from Christiane and her grand-son, "Augst," as she called him.

But let us turn back to the years 1804-1805. As an epilogue to a dramatic performance of Schiller's *Glocke,* Goethe wrote his *Epilog* which contains the profound portrayal of the friend he had lost, and in which the repeated refrain, *Denn er war unser,* rings so true and so strong! In these stanzas Goethe has portrayed Schiller for all time. There is room for but two of them:

> *Denn er war unser!* Mag das stolze Wort
> Den lauten Schmerz gewaltig übertönen!
> Er mochte sich bei uns im sichern Port
> Nach wildem Sturm zum Dauernden gewöhnen.
> Indessen schritt sein Geist gewaltig fort
> Ins Ewige des Wahren, Guten, Schönen,
> *Und hinter ihm in wesenlosem Scheine*
> *Lag was uns Alle bändigt, das Gemeine.*
>
> Nun glühte seine Wange roth und röther
> Von jener Jugend, die uns nie entfliegt,
> Von jenem Muth, der früher oder später
> Den Widerstand der stumpfen Welt besiegt,
> Von jenem Glauben, der sich stets erhöhter
> Bald kühn hervordrängt, bald geduldig schmiegt,
> Damit das Gute wirke, wachse, fromme,
> Damit der Tag dem Edlen endlich komme.

This *Epilog* contains the whole of Schiller, clarified, with his ideal striving, his hectic zeal, his invincible youth, and his fighting spirit which brought him victory on victory—after his death.

CHAPTER XIX

GOETHE's *Propyläen;* THE BIOGRAPHY OF WINCK-
ELMANN—GOETHE AND DIDEROT; RAMEAU'S
Neffe—BATTLE OF JENA, 1806

GOETHE had learned from Schiller the art of
founding short-lived magazines that no one wished
to support. He established as early as 1798, in
order to spread his views concerning plastic art, the
periodical entitled *Die Propyläen.* Its aim was to
develop the artist, to interest him in thorough and
scientific study of the human body, to make clear
the relation between the artist and the public, and
especially to liberate the artist from the taste of
the public. It demanded that the highest standard
be set in the discussion and criticism of a work of
art. It was in this journal that Goethe published
a series of his treatises on the science of art, such
as *Ueber Laokoon, Der Sammler und die Seinigen,
Ueber Wahrheit und Wahrscheinlichkeit der Kunst-
werke, Ueber den Dilettantismus,* and other themes.
Schiller assisted in the elaboration of the last named
treatise. In all of them Goethe combats the idea of
merely imitating and copying nature.

Goethe and Heinrich Meyer alone constituted
the firm W. K. F. (Weimarer Kunstfreunde) which,
after *Die Propyläen* had been discontinued, kept on
committing itself on all manner of questions pertaining to art, and to propose prize tasks. It is to

241

this series of efforts that Goethe's most important work of this kind belongs, his book on *Winckelmann,* written in the years 1804 and 1805. This book is a part of an elaborate work on the great art student. It contains both his letters to a friend, Berendis, and treatises on him by Heinrich Meyer and F. A. Wolf.

Goethe's work is grounded first of all in the love he naturally cherished for Winckelmann; for Goethe was the poetic representative of that very conception of the Antique which, through Winckelmann, had become the Germanic, and which from an artistic point of view, was soon represented— through the influence of Zoëga—by Thorvaldsen, while from the point of view of architecture, it was taken up by the Bavarian King Ludwig, who surrounded his beer-drinking Munich with an Old Greek shell. Winckelmann was of course the true author of Neo-Classicism in Germany, and Goethe could not help but feel deeply indebted to him. To this was added the fact that for a long time he was vehemently aroused by the reverential whining, the saccharine pining, the lay-brother sanctimoniousness, the systematic hero-worship which the German Romanticists had just then made fashionable. Wackenroder's *Herzensergiessungen eines kunstliebenden Klosterbruders* and Tieck's *Franz Sternbalds Wanderungen* were both fundamentally opposed to Goethe's method of thinking and feeling. And, it sounds amusing at present, the Romanticists had begun to compare Tieck favorably with Goethe. In a little country like Denmark, to which the movements from Germany are always somewhat belated in arriving, it was felt as late as 1860 in romantic,

that is literary, circles that it was quite correct to
refer to Tieck and Goethe as poets of equal merit.
The paintings of the New German school, corresponding as they did to *Sternbalds Wanderungen,*
could only be an abomination to Goethe.   His monograph on Winckelmann was accordingly aimed at
the Romanticists.   It became his pagan confession
of faith.

What he wrote is in no sense of the word a biography.   It does not concern itself with chronology;
it characterises Winckelmann under such short rubrics as paganism, friendship, beauty, Catholicism,
Greek art, and so on.   Here is a sample, not written in Goethe's most lucid prose:

> The delineation of the antique temper with its eye fixed
> on this world and the goods thereof, leads at once to the
> observation that such superiority can be the product only of a
> pagan mind. That self-confidence, working on what is near
> at hand, reverence for the gods as progenitors, admiration
> for them almost only as works of art, resignation to an all-
> powerful fate, and the purely earthly faith in posthumous
> renown—all this belongs so necessarily together, forms such
> an inseparable whole, is united into a human existence prom-
> ised by nature itself that in the case of the heathen an im-
> perturbable soundness dominates in the enjoyment of the
> highest moment as well as in sacrificing, indeed even in the
> painful hour of self immolation.

After having established Winckelmann's paganism in this way, Goethe is obliged to explain, and to
explain away, his conversion to Catholicism, and
to show that it was utterly unlike the conversion to
Roman Catholicism which Friedrich Schlegel and
his wife were then on the point of undergoing, and
the conversion to Catholicism which Tieck's wife
and daughter did undergo in Rome.

Goethe writes:

The pagan temper radiates from all of Winckelmann's actions and writings. . . . His remoteness from every sort of Christian way of thinking, indeed his very aversion to this sort of thinking, must be kept in mind when we attempt to pass judgment on his so-called change of religion. The parties into which the Christian religion is divided were to him a matter of utter indifference, since he, according to his own nature, never belonged to any of the churches that adapt themselves to these various divisions.

We are also shown how the impecunious Winckelmann looked about long and in vain for assistance. Help could be expected only from the court in Dresden; but this court confessed the Catholic religion, so that there was no other way for him to receive favor and mercy than that which was directed by the father confessors and other clerical persons:

He felt that in order to be a Roman in Rome, in order really to grow into the life there, it was absolutely necessary to belong to the Catholic Church, to accept its faith and adapt himself to its usages. The result showed, too, that without this resolution he would not have reached his goal; and it was made easy for him because the Protestant baptism had not been able to make him a Christian, he having been born a genuine pagan.

Goethe continues with the admission that it besmirches one to change his religion, since people value enduring will above everything else, and the less important they are, the more zealously they demand that one shall hold out in that place where one has been set. But he explains that the matter has, in addition to this serious phase, another which is lighter and easier, since there are certain conditions of which we by no means approve though they have a sort of attraction for us. By way of making his point clear, he uses expressions that were especially calculated to annoy the German Romanticists. Dorothea Mendelssohn had become separated from Veit in order to marry Friedrich Schlegel; Caroline Michaelis had become separated from A. W. Schlegel in order to marry Schelling. Goethe writes:

> If I may be permitted to use a simile, I should like to say that the present situation is similar to that we have in the case of wild game which tastes far better to the fine palate when it has a slight tang than when it is fresh cooked.   A divorcee and a renegade make a pleasing impression upon us. . . . But for Winckelmann there was nothing attractive about the Catholic religion; he saw in it merely a mask in which he eneveloped himself; he expressed himself in harsh terms regarding it.

It is no wonder that Friedrich Schlegel sought relief by pouring out his boundless contempt for Goethe's *Winckelmann*. It is no wonder that the most cynical and best paid man among the men belonging to the political-religious reaction, Friedrich Gentz, wrote (1805) to Adam Müller in the following words:

> The treatise on Winckelmann is godless. I would not have expected such a bitter, treacherous hatred for Christianity from Goethe, though truth to tell I have been looking for something malicious from him on this subject for quite a while. What indecorous, faun-like joy he seems to have felt on discovering that Winckelmann was a born heathen!

Posterity has judged the work otherwise: Gervinus called it "the best German biography."

II

Though Voltaire published nearly everything he wrote, some of it, to be sure, anonymously—caution dictated his action—Diderot never collected his works; he never bothered about publishing them; nor did anyone else concern himself with them, or see to it that they were given out to the public. He died in 1784, and works of the rank of *La Religieuse, Supplément au Voyage de Bourgainville, Jacque le Fataliste* never came out until 1796. *Ceci n'est pas un Conte* was published in 1798, *Paradoxe sur le Comédien, Promenade du Sceptique, Le Rêve d'Alembert* in 1830. The masterpiece of all, *Le Neveu de Rameau,* was not published until the Restoration.

This last work, however, as well as several others, existed in various manuscripts which passed from hand to hand. Schiller got hold of one of them from France and sent it to Goethe with the request that he translate it. Goethe, who was wise enough to appreciate the uncommon value of the dialogue, undertook the work with pleasure. His translation appeared in 1805, an excellent bit of work which (with the necessary toning down of individual expressions and phrases for the German public) reproduces the tone and style of the original—in so far as this can be done. For it is impossible to deny that the prose from 1762, overflowing with life and inspirited ingeniousness, stood above all the German prose that was written forty years later; nor can it be affirmed that Goethe's own prose style attained at any time the high level of that on which the prose of the original dialogue moves.

The depiction of the endowed and brilliant slug-
gard and cynic, Rameau's nephew, is a work of art
of first rank. Through its slipshod superiority and
branding contempt Diderot had used the figure as
a means—just as Goethe and Schiller did, too point-
edly and directly, in the *Xenien*—of mowing down,
through his casual remarks, his own and his fellows'
malicious and hateful opponents, a Palissot, a
Fréron and others, though he praises, indirectly and
with brave loyalty, all that is valuable in his French
contemporaries, such as Voltaire, Buffon, d'Alembert, and Helvetius. Salutary indeed is this de-
praved Rameau's thorough knowledge of men and
his contempt for men; salutary also is his extraordinary musical insight and finesse.

As a bit of description the scene in the Café *de la
Regence* is especially admirable. He walks up and
down the floor, begins to sing Italian, French, tragic,
comic melodies, some thirty different pieces one after
another, transforms himself, becomes mad, becomes
gentle, now imperious, now grinning, imitates a
young girl in distress, a priest, a king, a tyrant, gives
commands or is submissive, sobs, complains, laughs
without ever once departing from the tone or the
tact or the character, so that all rise from the chess
tables and gather around him in a merry jubilee.
But he does not notice it; he is so taken up with his
own business, so inspired that he resembles a mad-
man. He sings a recitative in which a prophet
paints the destruction of Jerusalem and there is not
a dry eye in the house. He imitates all the instruments, a horn, a fagott, a oboe, small flutes and
strings; at last he becomes a complete theatre, dancing men and dancing women, women who sing and

men who sing, an orchestra all to himself. In other
words, he anticipates possibly the greatest work
Victor Hugo ever wrote, *Le Satyre,* in which the
Faun little by little becomes Pan and, singing, reproduces the universe while all the tame and all the wild
animals, all the gods and all the goddesses, listen.

In the notes Goethe praises Voltaire in the most
earnest, though in the most droll fashion, by ascrib-
ing to him forty-five great characteristics. But he
grasps this opportunity to tell the public and his
opponents some sharp truths. He makes the point
that, taken as a whole, the public is incapable of
passing judgment on any talent whatsoever; to do
this practice and study are necessary. And with
regard to Palissot he says:

In Germany we have also instances in which evil minded
people, partly in flying sheets, partly on the stage, try to
harm others. But he who does not allow himself to become
exasperated at the moment, can calmly await the result; in
a short time it is as if nothing had happened. It is only
presumption and sham merits that need to fear personal
satire.

III

The battle of Jena was fought on October 14,
1806; Prussia collapsed. The beaten regiments
scurried through the streets of Weimar in the wild-
est sort of flight. All the wagons were overloaded
with fugitives. The French had taken Altenburg
near Weimar, and were firing over the town at the
Prussians posted in the rear. The bullets passed
over the houses without doing any harm to them.

The city, by force of circumstances, became a
prey for plundering. The officers and the cavalry
did what lay in their power to protect the citizens

and the property and to help out in other ways. But they were nearly powerless against the fifty thousand uncaged soldiers who, after having broken into the stores and emptied them, took such food and drink as they found, seized linen, money and silverware, smashed furniture, and lighted watch-fires in the squares and parks. Murat and the other generals endeavored to restore order; but not a few places were burned.

By the fifteenth the suffering was extreme: There was no bread to be had in the town. The Duchess was in the castle in which most of the women of Weimar had found an asylum. Towards evening Napoleon arrived. The Duchess went out to meet him; she spoke a few words to him regarding the excessively hot weather, and the hardships they had to endure. He replied abruptly: *Ce sont les suites de la guerre.* Thereupon he asked to be shown to his rooms.

On the following day Duchess Luise was formally announced to him. He received her standing, and allowed her to remain standing. He reproached her because the Duke was an officer in the Prussian army and had led his soldiers against him. The Duchess did not permit herself to be disheartened: She asked Napoleon what would have been his judgment if one of his family, as closely related to him as the Duke was to the King of Prussia, had, at the outbreak of the war, taken leave of the army to which he had for so many years belonged, Napoleon was impressed: He informed her that for her sake he would spare the country—on the condition that the Duke withdraw from Prussian service immediately.

Goethe's house was spared from fire and plundering. A few brutal soldiers did, to be sure, rush in upon him with their swords and would perhaps have wounded him had not Christiane thrown herself between him and them and in this way protected him; and with a great deal of presence of mind, she offered them a few silver candle sticks with which they went their way. Later on the highest of French officers were billeted in the house. Among others Marshalls Augereau, Lannes, and Ney, but only for a short time. Riemer relates, as an eye-witness, that after the French soldiers had secured admission to the house Goethe quietly went up to them and asked them what they wanted and whether they had not already received everything that they could reasonably expect: They had already been quartered in his house. The dignity of his very figure seems to have instilled a certain amount of respect in them. They became all of a sudden exceedingly polite. They simply appropriated a glass of wine and asked him to clink glasses with them, which he did. And then they went away, decently and in order.

In a letter of warning which General Victor issued soldiers were forbidden to disturb "the distinguished scholar," Goethe. In a similar letter, issued by Augereau, he was called "a man who is commendable in every way." And in the letter of the French Commandant of the city the wording is even stronger: "With regard to the great Goethe, Weimar's Commandant will take all measures to protect him and his home."

A few days after the battle, and undeniably under the feeling of gratitude to Christiane for her courageous and expedient conduct, Goethe wrote the Superintendent of Weimar: "During the last days and nights an old purpose of mine has come to maturity. I wish to recognize, fully and civilly, as *mine* my little friend who has done me so much good and who has now lived through also these trying times." And in perfect quietness he was married to Christiane.

The storm that had swept over Weimar never once shook his admiration for Napoleon. He had seen him rise and win victories wherever he went. In vain had he used his powers of persuasion to prevent Karl August from becoming a general in the Prussian army. And he had looked on with perfect equanimity when, during the battle, Napoleon formed the *Rheinbund* consisting of German Princes though under French supremacy. He felt somewhat as did Hegel who, on Napoleon's entrance into Jena, wrote as follows: "It is a peculiar feeling to lay eyes on an individual man who from this time on will rule the world." Goethe himself had written in his diary of August 7, 1806, these words: "The squabble between the servant and the coachman on the box excites us more than the dissolution of the Roman Empire." He meant the downfall of the German Empire that had been established at Verdun in 843.

CHAPTER XX

GOETHE AND BETTINA; GOETHE AND MINNA
HERZLIEB—*Pandora*: A DRAMA—GOETHE AND
NAPOLEON—NAPOLEON AND WIELAND

ON April 23, 1807, Bettina Brentano, then twenty-three years of age, entered Goethe's home. She came from his mother, whose favorite she had been, and whom she questioned on all the details of Goethe's childhood and early youth. She wished to make use of these data in the book she was then planning to write on his life. Bettina was the granddaughter of Sophie von la Roche, Wieland's old friend, the daughter of Maxe Brentano, who had felt a passion for Goethe, and who is one of the two models of Lotte in *Werthers Leiden*.

Immediately after her arrival in Weimar she had gone to Wieland, whom she had never once seen before, in order to beg him for a letter of introduction to Goethe. She received this card written in this German:

Bettina Brentano, Sophiens Schwester, Maximilianens Tochter, Sophie la Rochens Enkelin, wünscht Dich zu sehen, lieber Bruder, und giebt vor, sie fürchte sich vor Dir, und ein Zettelchen, das ich ihr mitgebe, würde ein Talisman seyn, der ihr Muth gäbe. Wiewohl ich ziemlich gewiss bin, dass sie nur ihren Spass mit mir treibt, so muss ich doch thun, was sie haben will, und es soll mich wundern, wenn Dir's nicht so wie mir geht.

She had loved and adored Goethe from her childhood, not after the fashion of Rahel in purely spiri-

252

tual idolization and reasoned reverence, but with an admiration which, half sensual, half mental and altogether fiery, would ingratiate itself as importunate amiability, make itself indispensable through a burr-like, hanging-on, and vehemently insinuate itself into good graces through enthusiasm's highest flight up and above all mountains.

In Goethe's room she stretched out both hands toward him and became at once utterly unconscious of herself. He pressed her to his heart: "Poor child, did I frighten you?" Those were his first words. He placed her on the sofa opposite himself. And thus the two sat for some time in silence. He broke the silence: I presume that you have read in the newspaper of the great loss that we recently suffered through the death of Duchess Amalie.—No, she said; I never read the newspapers.—Is that so, I thought you were interested in everything that takes place in Weimar?—No, I am interested only in you, and I am far too impatient to go leafing around in newspapers.—You are a friendly child.—Long pause.—Then she leaped from the sofa and threw herself on his neck.

From childhood on she had had this youthful boldness. In Marburg there is shown to this day a tower up which she used to creep and crawl and then draw the ladder up after her in order to be alone. She had the suppleness of a juggler in her limbs and in addition something of the childlike *Schwärmerei* of Mignon. She was a Mignon transferred to actual life, with the same charm and much less seriousness.

In the book entitled *Goethes Briefwechsel mit einem Kinde,* which she published after his death, in 1835, she has treated her own letters freely, inserted many things and much which seemed to her might have been felt; and she gave the entire affair a more passionate coloring. She wished to make it appear that Goethe was quite taken up with her in 1807-1808. She really thought so at that time, for he was accustomed to send the poems that he had just written along with the letters. It was excusable that she should think that these sonnets were addressed to her. It was inexcusable for her to turn them into prose and then introduce the prose into her letters so as to make it appear that Goethe had simply set her thoughts and feelings to rhyme. She is punished by the comic element that arises from the fact that the most of these poems were addressed to Wilhelmine (Minna) Herzlieb.

From May to September of this year, Goethe was living in Karlsbad in intimate association with the famous Prince of Ligne, the German-born French Minister Reinhard, the geologist Werner, and Metternich's literary mouth-piece, Friedrich Gentz. In November Bettina returned to Weimar. Goethe now had enough of her and her passion. He had, though he himself was unaware of it, fallen deeply in love with a young girl as unlike her as possible, a quiet girl of the instinctive sort, beautiful with her charming figure and fascinating, small oval face, innocent and shy, the foster-daughter of the bookseller Frommann in Jena, to whom Goethe paid daily visits during that autumn. We have one single declaration by Wilhelmine concerning him:

Goethe had come over from Weimar so that he might work out his beautiful thoughts for humanity in peace and quiet. To our great joy he lived in the castle, for had we not been so near to his residence, who knows whether we would have seen him every evening. He has to look out for his health a little bit now too. Otherwise he seems well. He was always so cheerful and social that one felt indescribably happy and yet painfully moved withal in his presence.

She writes to a friend that, after listening to the golden words that flowed from his lips, she would retire to her room in the evening and then the tears would gush forth and there was but one thought that could console her:

We mortals are not all born for the same degree of excellence; each of us must strive and work according to his talents in that place where fate has placed him, and that is the end of it.

Goethe's love for her was deep. Those sonnets are of course addressed to her which play with her name, and which Bettina had the naïveté to believe were meant for her; she even insisted in so many words that she was the originator of them. And what is more, Goethe constantly dreamt of Wilhelmine while he was working on his *Pandora*. She is also the model of Ottilie in *Die Wahlverwandtschaften*. She did not marry until fourteen years later, in 1821. The marriage was soon dissolved; she became insane and died in 1865.

It was in Frommann's house that Goethe came into constant association with Zacharias Werner, one of the most disagreeable of the German Romanticists. Like all of the Romanticists he wrote sonnets. The year before, Frommann had published a translation of Petrach's sonnets that made a distinct impression on Goethe; and he now began to com-

pete with Zacharias Werner in the writing of sonnets.

The form was contrary to Goethe's nature,
though he mastered it as he did every other verse
form. He had in earlier days so frequently expressed his aversion to the restraint imposed by
the fourteen liners that, now that he was writing
sonnets, he treated this aversion in his lines. But
it is not amusing for a modern reader to read the
sonnets that treat the sonnet itself, such as numbers
11, 14, and 15, though some of them possess great
charm. There is, by way of illustration, *Freund-
liches Begegnen,* which tells how the lover, wrapped
up in a mantle, meets the young girl, attempts to
pass by her without slipping the mantle to one side,
stops, involuntarily throws the mantle off, and—
she lies in his arms.

As is usually the case, Goethe's skill is more certain when he allows his women to commit themselves
than when he relegates this function to his men. A
few of his sonnets reproduce letters by women; one
from Bettina and one from Minna Herzlieb. The
close of the sonnet in which (in my judgment) it is
Bettina who writes, has a high degree of perfection:

> Ich mag heut'gen Tag Dir nichts vertrauen,
> Wie sich im Sinnen, Wünschen, Wähnen, Wollen
> Mein treues Herz zu Dir hinüber wendet:
>
> So stand ich einst vor Dir, Dich anzuschauen,
> Und sagte nichts.   Was hätt ich sagen sollen?
> Mein ganzes Wesen war in sich vollendet.

The sonnet in which the infatuated woman remarks that she would greatly prefer to post the

white, untouched paper than to write upon it herself, since *he* would then probably cover it with
words of love, contains without the slightest doubt
a play on her name: *Lieb Kind! Mein artig Herz!*
Mein einzig Wesen! It is even more certain that
the seventeenth and last sonnet, entitled *Charade*,
refers to Wilhelmine. In it there is a riddle, the
solution of which is *Herzlieb*.

II

Pandora is a mythological drama which Goethe
planned—but never finished—while he was stirred
with passion for a young girl who was removed from
him by forty years, and by his own marriage of
some time previous to the present affair. It is one
of the most unpopular works he ever wrote, at once
artificial and affected, written in ancient Greek style,
and confined to the circle of Hellenic myths. Chem-
ically devoid of naïveté, it is done in the tone of
tiresome virtuosity, and is weighed down with complicated and solemn metrical forms. The fragment
is cryptic and allegoric, a work of art created for
philologists and professors. The language is unusually abstract, the substantives rarely have articles. And yet, there is much rhythmical resonance
in the work—such as we find in scholarly, technical,
absolute music.

Prometheus and his brother Epimetheus are the
two leading male characters. Prometheus, having
completely abandoned the idea of further fighting against Zeus, is engaged in an active life on
earth. He is the originator of fire, and for this
reason also the creator of industry. He has like-

wise done much for art, especially the art of the smith. As a maker of weapons on a large scale, he has all manner of people in his employ, and equips them for the business of war. He is the prehistoric Krupp. In contrast to him, Epimetheus is the dreamer and the brooder. His whole mind is taken up with the charming Pandora, who once was his but who was forced to leave him. His entire life is filled with longing for her return. He has by her a daughter, Elpore, an airy creature with the morning star upon her head; she disappeared with her mother, but now she reveals herself to Epimetheus, and in a beautiful song characterises herself as something that can perhaps be called the erotic hope and the dreamed of petition. In addition to her, Epimetheus has a daughter Epimeleia, who lives with her father. She is a young being whom Prometheus's son, Phileros, loves. But out of foolish jealousy he wishes to murder her; he does wound her before the eyes of her father—all of which makes a rather disagreeable impression. The whole of her culpability lies in the fact that just as she left her door ajar in order to receive Phileros, a young shepherd, who forestalled him, pushed the door open and was in the act of doing her violence. After this her lover no longer believes in her innocence—which is rather fatuous.

The best part of this drama is Epimetheus's expression of his love for the beautiful, and his loss of the charming one in whom he is infatuated:

> Wer von der Schönen zu scheiden verdammt ist,
> Fliehe mit abgewendetem Blick!
> Wie er, sie schauend, im tiefsten entflammt ist,
> Zieht sie, ach, reisst ihn ewig zurück.

Or as he says in another place:

> Der Seligkeit Fülle, die hab ich empfunden,
> Die Schönheit besass ich, sie hat mich gebunden,
> Im Frühlingsgefolge trat herrlich sie an.

The rhythm in this drama is altogether deserving of study. Goethe has tried, with success, the effect of meters hitherto unused by him. He has given, in singularly felicitous fashion, expression to the primitive bluntness of seasoned soldiers. They sing:

> Wir ziehn, wir ziehn   So geht es kühn
> Und sagen's nicht.   Zur Welt hinein,
> Wohin? Wohin?   Was wir beziehn,
> Wir fragen's nicht   Wird unser sein.
> Und Schwert und Spiess   Will Einer das,
> Wir tragen's gern.   Verwehren wir's;
> Und Jen's und Dies   Hat Einer was,
> Wir wagen's gern.   Verzehren wir's.

The drama was built on a large scale. The continuation that was planned indicates that Goethe wished to depict by symbols of a serious nature the entire development of human culture from prehistoric times to the domination of art and science. He was occupied with the work from 1807 to 1809. Then it was put aside forever.

III

Napoleon, after the battle of Jena, was moved only by the dignified deportment of the Duchess Luise not to vent his wrath so thoroughly upon Weimar. Something happened also after the conclusion of peace which was objected to on the part of Karl August and which could not help but arouse Napoleon and show him that the people of Weimar

were unfriendly to him: donations of money to
Blücher and the reception of dismissed Prussian
officers into the court service of Weimar. But since
the Emperor of Russia, at that time Napoleon's
ally, was the brother to the hereditary Princess, the
Duke could appear without causing too much unrest
at the Congress of Erfurt in 1808, where four kings
and thirty-four princes, in addition to the two emperors, met by appointment.

Goethe did not wish to be present but was expressly requested by the Duke to appear. He was
far from seeing in Napoleon the destroyer of the
fatherland. He had never known any German
fatherland. He wrote on July 27, 1807: "When
people complain about a whole which is supposed
to have been lost and which, however, no human
being in his lifetime ever saw in Germany, much
less bothered about, it is impossible for me to conceal my impatience." He did not look upon foreign
supremacy as a disgrace and nourished no particular
animosity towards it. Quite the contrary. In place
of a countless number of badly governed little prin-
cipalities there had come to be a smaller number
ruled in a relatively modern spirit, in harmony with
the principles of the French Revolution. They
made their impression upon him only now that they
were embodied in a great personality. No one
wanted to pick a quarrel with Germanism; none of
the German princes under Napoleon, least of all
Jerome in Westphalia, upon whom Napoleon had
depended to win his subordinates' affection, and who
had Goethe's friend, Count Carl Reinhard at his
side, Jacob Grimm as librarian, and the historian
Johannes von Müller as minister of instruction.

By force of good politics, Napoleon together
with his marshals and envoys, brought German
science and literature into real repute. Hence Goethe's disinterestedness, mortifying to the nation,
toward the German's so-called struggle for liberty
against Napoleon, a struggle for national independence, but which merely tended to call back into
existence all the reaction of the past. Hence his
words: "It will do them no good; the man is too
big for them." Hence as late as July, 1812, his
poem of homage to Marie Louise and Napoleon
when the Empress came to Karlsbad. The hope
which the poem expresses was not well founded in
1812: *Der Alles wollen kann, will auch den Frie-
den.* It expresses, however, joy over the birth of
the King of Rome:

> Und wenn dem Helden Alles zwar gelungen,
> Den das Geschick zum Günstling auserwählt,
> Und Ihm vor allem alles aufgedrungen,
> Was die Geschichte jemals aufgezählt,
> Ja reichlicher als Dichter je gesungen—
> Ihm hat bis jetzt das Höchste noch gefehlt;
> Nun steht das Reich gesichert wie geründet,
> Nun fühlt er froh in Sohne sich gegründet.

When Napoleon, in October, 1808, learned from
his Minister Maret that Goethe was in Erfurt, he
made an appointment with him for the following
day. He had read *Werther* seven times during his
youth and had followed Goethe's career with interest and attention.

As Goethe appeared in the doorway, Napoleon
raised his head from the dinner table, motioned to
him to come in, cast one glance at him, and made
the historic remark: *Vous êtes un homme!* That

is the best comment that has ever been made on
Goethe. While Napoleon was giving various orders
to Daru and his lieutenants who came in to make
their reports, he plied Goethe with questions about
his dramas. Daru told the Emperor that Goethe
had translated Voltaire's *Mahomet*. "That is not
a good drama," said Napoleon, and then proceeded
to show how absurd it was for Mahomet to give
such a disparaging picture of himself. He himself
wrote a derogatory critique of *Mahomet* while at
St. Helena. He then brought the conversation
around to *Werther,* and with the insight of the
tactician drew Goethe's attention to the fact that
he had not adhered to the theme of unrequited love
as the basis of suicide, but had fused this motif with
the irrelevant one of an offended sense of honor.
He then quoted another passage from *Werther*—
a passage Goethe could never be persuaded to mention—and said: "Why did you write it? It is not
natural." He then proceeded to justify his objection in detail. Goethe writes: "The observation is
quite correct." He conceded, and apologized for,
the unnaturalness of the passage in question; he
had made use of an artistic trick in order to produce
certain effects. The Emperor was satisfied, turned
again to the drama and made, according to Goethe
himself, "some very significant comment, such as we
would expect from one who had studied the tragic
stage of France with the greatest attention, and had
felt deeply the deviation of it from nature and
truth."

After closing a series of remarks, he usually said:
"Qu'en dit Monsieur Goethe." He discussed likewise the Fate Tragedy that was just then coming

into vogue and made use of an expression that
strikes us with surprise coming as it did from a fa-
talist; "What do people mean anyhow in our day by
Fate? Politics, that is Fate."

He interrupted himself then and spoke with Daru
and Soult on political affairs. Then he questioned
Goethe as to his personal position and the Court
of Weimar: "I answered him naturally. He
seemed satisfied and translated my expression into
his language so that it became clearer than I could
have expressed it myself." The Emperor showed
his approval again and again, when Goethe said anything, and made him laugh so heartily by his jovial
comments that Goethe believed he would have to
beg his pardon.

Several days later Goethe was made a member
of the Legion of Honor. In a letter to Maret in
which he thanks him for it, we read: *Votre Excellence voudra se faire interprète vis-à-vis de sa Ma-
jesté des sentiments que je suis incapable d'articu-
ler, et que je voudrais pouvoir témoigner par un
devouement parfait.*

On the sixth of October Napoleon announced
himself as guest at the home of the Duke of Weimar. He took his actors with him and now, on
Goethe's stage, Napoleon's company—among whom
were Talma and Mlle. Georges — played "The
Death of Caesar" by Voltaire.

When Caesar said:

Je sais combattre, vaincre et ne sais point punir.
Allons, n' écoutons point ni soupçons ni vengeance,
Sur l'univers soumis regnons sans violence!

all eyes turned toward Napoleon.

After the performance there was a ball. Napoleon took Goethe aside and said with reference to the dramatic production: "The serious drama could very well be a school for princes as well as for the people; for in certain ways it is quite above history. . . . *You* ought to portray the death of Caesar, more magnificently than Voltaire has done, and show how happy Caesar would have made the world if the people had only granted him time in which to carry out his lofty plans."

A little later: "You must come to Paris! I make this definite request of you! You will obtain a larger view of the world there, and you will find a wealth of themes for your poetry."

The strength of the impression that Goethe made on Napoleon is best shown by the fact that when the Emperor, after his fearful defeat in Russia and his mad sled-ride through Europe, arrived at Weimar he asked, while they were exchanging horses, about Goethe and requested the French Ambassador to extend him his greetings.

But the impression that Napoleon made on Goethe was deeper: "The greatest mind the world has ever seen," exclaimed Goethe to Boisserée. His admiration went so far that he at that time in the house of the Wolzogens found it absolutely right that anything which stood in the way of such a justified genius should be removed. He defended Napoleon's conduct when he had a pretender like Enghien and a demagogue like Palm shot so as to give the public, once for all, a conspicuous example that would prevent it from constantly interfering with the plans of the genius.

Goethe was deceived by Napoleon's straightforwardness and amiability toward him. However frequently the King and Queen of Prussia might come to Weimar, they never took any notice of him. Frederick the Great, his senior by thirty-seven years, scorned, as an old man, his *Götz* and had not the slightest appreciation of his personality. Napoleon, his junior by twenty years, understood him thoroughly.

It *did* seem to him that Napoleon had crowned his career, "had put the dot over the 'i' of his life," as he expressed himself. He wrote to Cotta: "Never has another individual of higher rank conducted himself in this way toward me; with an especial degree of confidence he gave me a place in the world (alongside of himself) and did not remark in some dubious tone that my personality was agreeable to him." In other words, for the first time in Goethe's life, he had stood face to face with his equal. Neither Herder nor Schiller, nor anyone of the other many friends who associated with him, had ever been his peer. In October, 1808, the two greatest men on this earth at that time met in mutual understanding.

When Napoleon so forcefully asked Goethe to come to him, live near him, and exchange Weimar for Paris, he was in a serious frame of mind, and for one moment both indeed caught a glimpse of the phantasmagoria of the Maecenas that Frederick had tried to be for Voltaire—but did not become—and which now, though with reversed rôles, Napoleon should be for Goethe. Paris could have been the best point of departure for his influence on world literature. It did not come to pass. This one meeting alone was written in their stars. But for the first time in his life Goethe met his equal in genius.

IV

There was another of Weimar's celebrities whose acquaintance Napoleon wished to make, and to whom he showed genuine good will: It was Wieland, then seventy-five years old. The especial reason why he was pointed out is quite noteworthy by way of proving that in a highly gifted man there is at times material for a prophet.

In the March number of Wieland's magazine *Der neue teutsche Merkur,* 1798, a prose conversation is carried on between two fictitious persons, the German Wilibald and the Frenchman Heribert. The German expresses himself on the condition existing in France, then racked by party schisms, makes it clear to the Frenchman that such a republic can survive only with difficulty. The antipathy toward royal power could easily slip over into the opposite. The Frenchman expresses the hope that France's good genius will save it from such retrogression, while the aversion to new revolutions will lend approval thereto. The German maintains that the various parties are so zealously militating against the good spirit of the French nation that one can assuredly count upon the desire for peace. But he has a bit of advice to give the French, and unless he is very much mistaken, his method is the sole way of saving French society from the destruction that is becoming more imminent every day despite its material victories and conquests.

Herbert asks what this sole means of salvation is. Wilibald replies that since the French no longer wish a king, and since they can as a matter of fact

not have a king so long as there are members of
the House of Bourbon living, there is only one thing
left for them to do, and that is to chose a dictator.

Heribert: A Dictator?

Wilibald: Or a *Lord Protector* or a *Protarchon*. The
name makes precious little difference, just so it is a man
in whom you can safely vest unlimited power, just as one
appointed in dangerous times a Dictator in Ancient Rome.
. . . He would have to be an amiable young man with
great, high-minded endowments, with the most excellent
talents for war and peace, with untiring activity, with as
much shrewdness as courage, with the firmest character, clean
morals, simple and unpretentious in his manner of living,
always in control of himelf, . . . at once open and resolute, flexible and hard, mild and inexorable, everything in
its time. In short, a man such as is found but once in a
century, and whose genius could hold the respect of all the
others and overpower them. . . . But for a number of
reasons he should not be a real Frenchman; and if he after
all had a foreign name, so much the better. He must have
already given many proofs of the fact that he really possesses the powers I find necessary to make your Dictator a
success; and of the talents mentioned, I cannot omit a single
one. If he had already acquired a great name for himself
in the world and enjoyed general esteem, I do not see what
he would lack that would prevent him from becoming the
rescuer of you yourself, indeed of the whole world. And
the extraordinary feature of it all is, you do not need to
go out first and search for this man, for, owing to a happy
coincidence, a coincidence which could be called unique,
he has already been found.

Heribert: I presume you mean Buonaparte.

Wilibald: Of course I do.

Heribert: For how long a time should he be appointed?

Wilibald: For as long as he holds out. I fear you will
lose him all too soon. The longer the better therefore.

The results of this vaticination were most remarkable. Two years later an English magazine,

St. James Chronicle, which was always detecting the
influence of the Jacobins and of the secret society
called the Illuminati, contained (January 25, 1800),
a bitter article against Wieland as the tool of this
society. The sagacious sheet had found out that
Wieland, whom it persistently called Weiland, was
an accomplice of the Illuminati, had advised the
French what to do with regard to Bonaparte, and
the French had followed his advice. The article
reads (in translation):

> However strange it may seem, a German writer has had
> the temerity to give, in one of his magazines, the French
> some advice concerning Bonaparte, who was then far away
> in Egypt and totally forgotten by the French, and they have
> followed his advice literally. . . . It is impossible not to
> detect the secret motives and means of this abominable sect,
> with its untiring efforts it is accustomed to employ to reach
> the most culpable goal. The dialogue between Wilibald and
> Heribert is nothing in the world but a suggestion from
> Weiland's pen, inspired most likely by the Illuminati, who
> have been endeavoring to familiarize Europe with their
> plans and to make their hero acceptable to the French peo-
> ple. Conspicuous indeed is the corruption in that they in-
> sist that there can no longer be any thought of a king, so
> long as the legally justified but unsuccessful Bourbons exist.
> Notice, too, the exaggerated description of the virtues that
> the dictator must necessarily have and the contention that
> the description fits Bonaparte, who is after all only a suc-
> cessful adventurer who, in his brief and gigantic career,
> has been the incarnation of all the crimes that are found in
> the most gruesome of tyrants without a single one of their
> good traits. All of this cannot leave the slightest doubt in
> anyone's mind but that this large and loathsome gang is
> working effectively and in secret.

A few words concerning the prophecy and the
embitterment it awakened in England must have
called Napoleon's attention, ten years later, to the

old German writer. He talked with him for some time at the court ball, October 6, and took delight in his spiritual good humor. The conversation revolved at first about Tacitus, from whom Napoleon insisted that he had never learned the slightest thing. He expressed vehement opposition to the admiration for him, and called him an unjust libeller of men. Tacitus hated tyrants, but he, Napoleon pronounced his name without fear. Tacitus found criminal motives for the very simplest actions, made all Emperors criminals together, so that one could admire his genius in having seen through them. He had not written a history of an empire, but had given excerpts of law-suits. His work treated of complaints, complainants, and of people who had their arteries opened. And what a style. I am not an expert Latinist; but the murkiness of his writing is undeniable if I may depend at all on the ten or twelve translations, in French and Italian, that I have read. Am I not right, Monsieur Wieland? But I am boring you. We did not come here to discuss Tacitus. Just look how well Emperor Alexander dances.

He continued to discuss the affairs of the Greek and Roman republics, and the benefits mankind had received from the Christian religion in olden times. When Wieland had an audience with Napoleon in Erfurt, the latter talked with the former in a most intimate tone, and plied him with questions concerning his domestic affairs.

CHAPTER XXI

Die Wahlverwandtschaften

IT had long been Goethe's plan to insert a series of novelettes in the continuation of *Wilhelm Meisters Lehrjahre* which would throw light on what he considered the most basic element in human life: renunciation and resignation. He was now nearly sixty years old. He compared, as he had done in *Werther,* man's yearnings and longings with the obtainable. Now, as then, he saw the innate power of the passions beating away against the rock of social order. Now, as then, he followed the swell with a sympathy such as is found in those people who know precisely what they are talking about. But the impression as a whole was no longer one of youthful despair; it was rather a melancholy assurance of the inevitableness of renunciation. Had he not recently been obliged to renounce Minna Herzlieb?

It soon became evident, however, that the novelette, as it grew in his mind, was going to be far too elaborate for *Wilhelm Meisters Wanderjahre*: it grew into a work that was complete in itself. It was finished many years before the *Wanderjahre*— to which it proved to be vastly superior.

Various experiences in Goethe's past life were utilized as elements of the work at present taking shape in his mind. In 1771, thirty-eight years, in other words, before the appearance of the novel, he had gone on a journey through Alsace and had visited the Alsatian Ottilieberg where, according to a legend, a beautiful and pious countess had sought refuge from the world, and where a chapel still bore her name. From this we have the name of the heroine, the motif of the chapel itself, and the miracles of the dead body. Moreover, Goethe's fifty-eight years did not prevent him from being passionately loved by two young women, Bettina Brentano and Minna Herzlieb. This was in 1807. For the latter of the two he cherished an ardent affection. It is however impossible to see from the sonnets addressed to her—they are playful and rather flirtatious in tone—just how warmly Goethe had loved in these years, and what a thorough-going study of passions he planned and carried out.

For him the attraction that one person has for another, mutual attraction, seemed in his present state to be a physical necessity, a demoniac power which works with law-abiding magic. Since he found this force at work even in the lower stages of nature, such as the chemical attraction and repulsion of bits of matter for each other, he took up with the expression *Wahlverwandtschaft,* or "elective affinity," which the Swedish physicist Bergman[5] had introduced some twenty years previously.

[5] Torbern Olof Bergman (1735-1784) entered the University of Upsala in 1752. His father wished him to study theology; he wished to study science. In order to please both himself and his father he studied both and injured his health. While convalescing he made some important discoveries in botany. In 1768 he was appointed professor of chemistry at Upsala, though it was a phase of science of which his knowledge was not profound. He began to study it in a quite serious fashion and wrote a number of articles on it. Of these the most important is his "Elective Affinities" (1775).   —TRANSLATOR.

The local descriptions that consume so much space
in the novel and constitute so important a part of
it were based on the environs of the castle at Wil-
helmsthal near Eisenach. It had been founded by
Karl August. The splendid garden, the three fish
ponds, and Ottilie's favorite spot, all so vividly portrayed in the novel, have their counterpart at the
castle. He availed himself right lavishly of the
opportunity to describe the natural surroundings,
but not as is done to-day, in order to emphasize the
influence of nature on the souls of men. His purpose was rather the reverse: He wished to visualize
the contrast between man's supremacy over such
nature as surrounds him from without, and man's
subjection to the nature that is within him. Hence
the part played by horticulture, architecture and en-
gineering on the one hand, and the "elective affinities" on the other.

None of Goethe's more pretentious works is constructed as is this one. And none, absolutely none,
has such a profound and coherent, though schematic,
composition. Epic writing comes as far from being
Goethe's strong point as does dramatic. Neither
in *Wilhelm Meister* nor in *Faust* is there much
coherency; both works lack unity. As if in the anticipation of an unusually long life, Goethe was
never in a hurry to finish anything. He let his works
lie, took them up again and again, inserted other
works in between those that had previously been
written, and completed the entire product at a late
period and frequently in a distinctly careless fashion.
He reminds us, in this connection, of one of the
greatest minds this earth has ever known—a mind
that his resembled in no other way—that of Michael

Angelo. As the result of a hardy and heroic self-criticism, Michael Angelo left the majority of his works unfinished.

Die Wahlverwandtschaften consists of two equal parts, each divided into eighteen chapters, and each containing a mass of parallel features of a symbolic or allegoric nature. They call to mind Dante's method of procedure in the *Divine Comedy*. The work has moreover a strict, almost rigorous motivation, with precise and quite conscientious attention to details. For Goethe this is an innovation; it is a spiritual novelty. There is hardly anything that he disdained in his earlier days as he did logical motivation. Take such a fundamental question as the following: Why does Faust forsake Gretchen? Goethe never answers this question. Here however we have, so to speak, an unbroken net in which each mesh fits exactly into the next following.

It would be unfair however and uncritical not to remark that the work contains an enclave. Let us call it by its right name, a digression. Goethe's inescapable inclination to retard the decision has prompted him to make the first larger half of the second part—almost a third of the entire work—of unnecessary and excessive breadth. Had this been condensed into about twenty pages, the work would still be what it is, a masterpiece, but then it would also be a highly diverting, even thrilling book for the great majority.

In accordance with the tendency of his later years, Goethe has sought the typical. This hovered before him constantly, not only in his scientific investigations but also in his poetic activity. By this we are not to understand that he took either a supercilious or an entirely neglectful attitude toward the individual. The opposite assumption would be more nearly correct. But what he wished to do here was to portray a permanent, fundamental relation, and by steeping himself in the individual instance so passionately, as though it were the only one of its kind, he came upon peculiarities that are not unique but seem to belong to certain forms common to human development. He ventures to assume the existence of natural laws.

In *Werther,* Goethe himself had, so to speak, gone through an assault of the passions. Here he looks down upon them from above somewhat as one watches the materials in a laboratory. Though this novel, the only one that Goethe ever wrote with a single guiding idea, revolves about marriage, it treats marriage primarily because the conflicts in private life were the ones that Goethe best understood. The real basic theme and subject of the novel however is more comprehensive than this statement would seem to indicate. *Die Wahlverwandtschaften* treats every single conflict that arises between the natural powers in man and existing human relations.

Goethe does not judge; he merely thinks. He never thinks in a Christian or moral way, but in unqualified harmony with a cryptic pantheism of nature.

At the beginning of the novel, the situation is as favorable as possible. We see a married couple of high rank, opulent in material goods and in the enjoyment of a wholesome life. He and she had early felt drawn to each other; but they had been separated by external forces. Both had been married before: He to a woman much older than him-

self, she to a man who was indifferent to her. They
both became free. Eduard urges Charlotte to give
her consent to marriage. She hesitates for a long
while. When she finally yields, the goal of their
life seems to have been reached.

It is now her wish that they shall live wholly for
each other. She sends her only daughter away, and
removes her niece Ottilie. They plan a life of mutual entertainment. For the moment their scheme
is to take up the scattered, confused leaves from
his diary and make something coherent and attractive out of them. They are both fond of music;
they play together. Eduard plays the flute irregularly: his art is like his life. First he plays too fast;
then too slow. Charlotte, more gifted than he,
accompanies him in such a way that the tempo of
the whole becomes just right, however much individual passages may be out of time. Then Eduard
conceives a fancy for reading aloud; but he has
this trifling oddity: He finds it quite intolerable to
have someone looking on his book while he is
reading.

Eduard wishes to have the friend of his younger
days, the Captain, visit him. Charlotte opposes the
idea; she has a presentiment that some misfortune
will arise therefrom. Eduard pleads their development; he insists that they have learned reason
through experience. He emphasizes their consciousness. Charlotte replies: "Consciousness is an inadequate weapon."

These are the characters: Charlotte, dignified and
cultured. We picture her to ourselves as being tall
but rounded out, the *grande Dame* in every sense
of the word. She is susceptible to strong impres-

sions, but abounds in self-control and good sense.
Eduard is restless, passionate, an artistic nature,
spoiled by his first marriage with a woman older
than himself, quite unaccustomed to self-denial, incapable of resignation, and with a tender spot in
his soul, a spot that always bleeds, figuratively
speaking.

Eduard entreats; he implores her to accede to
his wish regarding the Captain. She finally does
so, with no little display of reluctance. It is at this
point that Mittler is introduced. He is a character
necessitated by the basic thought of the novel. It
would always be easy to identify him with living
models. But as Goethe has arranged his rôle, he
is quite removed from the sphere of such circumstances as go to make up reality. He is a marriage
fanatic as such. First he was a priest, then a law
student. At the present stage of his life he tarries
only where there is something to be straightened
out, something to be fixed up between married
people. Everything is in excellent condition in the
case before him, so he leaves immediately.

The Captain comes. Charlotte tries quietly to
get him away by securing him a position. He proves
to be all tact and consideration, a practical man,
efficient, wise as to the things of this world, a man
of integrity. Eduard tries to make use of his
talents; he will employ him in the carrying out of
the improvements he is planning to make on the
estate. The Captain takes up with the idea, determined though he is not to offend Charlotte's wishes
concerning the arrangement of the garden.

The very first consequence of his coming however
is that Charlotte becomes more and more lonely;

for the two men are constantly together. He involuntarily keeps Eduard away from her.

The fourth leading character, Ottilie, is now introduced, at first by remarks made about her. We are prepared for her introduction by a letter from her inspired teacher at the educational institution she has been attending. In this way we become acquainted with her gentle disposition, her temperance in food and drink, and her rather frail health: She suffers frequently from pains in the left side of her head. Through a number of small, portrait-like features her personality is thrown into quite distinct relief. She writes slowly and stiffly; she writes a child's hand. She is unable to understand anything that does not follow from the immediately preceding, but give her all the intervening steps and she will grasp the most difficult situation. She wins no prizes in school; she has talents; special skill she does not have. Her charm is revealed indirectly through the cordial interest her teacher takes in her. We note that he pays attention to the very smallest features of her character and her personality, not omitting the habit she has of making a kind of warding-off gesture every now and then with her hand.

Eduard is quite devoid of any sense of order; the Captain on the contrary, who always works with a definite goal in mind, is order personified. It is under his leadership that the archives are arranged in the castle; the papers are all carefully classified. They likewise establish a first-aid society, and set up a domestic apothecary shop. This latter gives rise to extended conversations bearing on fundamental principles in physics and chemistry.

This, in substance, is what is said: We call those
natures and materials related which, when they
meet, quickly influence, indeed mutually determine
the fate of each other.   Such are nature-relation-
ships, mind-relationships.   They do not become
interesting, however, until they cause dissolutions,
separations.   The chemist is the artist of separations.   The term *elective affinity* has been formed,
for it looks as though some relations were preferred
to others.   When limestone, for example, is placed
in diluted sulphuric acid, the latter reacts on the
lime and forms gypsum.   The airy acid is disen-
gaged, separated.   "Poor acid," exclaims Charlotte.

It then becomes the privilege of the acid, we are
told, to unite with water, form mineral water and,
as a mineral spring, bring the diseased back to a
state of reconvalescence and complete health.   From
her moral point of view, Charlotte has an objection
to raise.   She insists that we do not have to do here
with choice, hardly indeed with natural necessity,
but with an occasion or an opportunity which creates
relations just as it makes thieves.   She forgets that
natural necessity creates the occasion, gives rise to
the opportunity.

The result of this conversation for the reader
is as follows: We see human life portrayed in the
lower stadia of nature.   In the depths of nature we
see these materials and beings which are really not
living, and which seem quite lifeless, entering after
all on the point of actual activity.

Ottilie's arrival necessitates a change in the distribution of the living quarters.   Eduard and the
Captain occupy one wing of the castle, Charlotte
and Ottilie the other.   Ottilie is not excessively com-

municative; Eduard finds her entertaining. Just as when she was in school, she eats and drinks too little, and yet she looks so well that she is a feast and a consolation for men's eyes. They compare her to an emerald: She is as beneficial to the eyes as it is. A characteristic feature is her complaisant obligingness which, if not hindered, rises to actual servility. If anything falls on the floor, she picks it up; she does this even for the men.

Eduard and the Captain lay new plans and introduce new improvements. A Swiss-like cleanliness is made a feature of the town. In order to prevent its being filled with the numerous roaming beggars, they institute this bizarre custom: They place small sums of money in the outmost house of the town so that these indigent wayfarers will not receive support until they come to the end of the town.

Fine little traits, such as the fact that the Captain forgets to wind his watch, prove the general absorption and distraction. Time is forgotten out of a feeling of mutual good will and rare happiness. Charlotte had had the moss hut made quite narrow; really only for two. Mention is made of this at the very opening of the story, though we are told that it can hold three, even four. And now for the first time there are four in it.

Eduard begins to admire Ottilie, to love her. He expresses a tender affection for her. He begs her, by way of illustration, to take off the medallion she wears so that there may be no danger of her pressing it against her breast and thereby causing a dangerous sickness. (We see that the portrayal of this idea interested Goethe in a quite real and living way; it is the same motif that is given a tragic turn in *Wilhelm Meister*.)　Ottilie's and Eduard's hands meet, "the two most beautiful hands that were ever clasped."　He asks her to decide where the new house he is planning to build is to be located.　The corner-stone is to be laid on Charlotte's birthday, which Eduard wishes to celebrate so that he can later pay due and becoming homage to Ottilie apropos of the same event in her life.

The two grow more and more closely together as time goes on, though their habits are so totally different.　She likes to remain in the house; he is never satisfied unless he is outdoors.　But their inner agreement is proved by their constant association with each other.　If he reads aloud, she looks over his shoulder and it does not annoy him at all.　They play selected music together and never out of time, though he plays irregularly.　The others look upon all this as upon the harmless diversion of two good children who love each other.　And the other two likewise make music in ensemble.

The corner-stone is laid.　The address which the young mason makes has a direct bearing on the teachings of the novel.　The corner-stone, he remarks, might be laid without ceremony or ado, for it rests in its position by reason of its own weight and without the mortar:

But the mortar will not be omitted; cement there must be.　For just as in the case of human beings who are bound to each other by nature, but who are bound even more firmly together when cemented by the law, just so it is with the stones whose forms fit together, but which are held even more firmly when held by this binding matter.

This is the basic problem in the book: If two

people have a natural affection for each other, are
they held together even more firmly by the binding
influence of the law?

The mason empties his glass with a toast to the
health of those present, and then tosses it high in
the air so that it may be broken to pieces on falling
to the ground. But it is caught up by one of the
bystanders. We are inclined to interpret the incident as a dubious omen: This glass on which is
engraved the monogram of the master of the house,
E-O (Eduard Otto), remains intact.

Mittler arrives and delivers an enthusiastic speech
in praise of marriage. To him it is the keystone
and corner-stone of all civilization; to attack it is
to attack the very foundation of social order. It
must be inviolable, for it brings so much happiness
that the isolated unhappiness caused by it is as
nothing in comparison. Why indeed speak of unhappiness at all when the real root of the trouble
is impatience? That marriage is at times uncomfortable and inconvenient is also good, and constitutes an additional reason for preserving the tie.
Some are married who would like to be free; and
some would like to be rid of their consciences, to
which and with which we are likewise married.

Mittler is driven off by the arrival of a Count
and a Baroness whom he does not wish to meet;
for they are his opposites, spiritually speaking.
They are also the opposite of economy in the epic
construction of the work. They have long been in
love with each other, but they are both married.
The Baroness has succeeded in obtaining a divorce.
The Count's wife however has refused to give her
consent to the complete annulment of her marriage.

On this account the two lovers can spend only the summers together. They come every year on the stroke of the clock, each on a different road, up to the castle or the manorial yard, where they have established a rendezvous. They have been meeting here for years; they are quite welcome because of their naturalness, their refinement of manner, their dignity, and their complete lack of affectation.

The Count contends that we are as a rule surprised when our hearts cease beating in unison. The conventional close of the comedy, marriage as the end of all things, he avers, has confused our ideas on this subject. At first we act quite involuntarily, as though the relations established on this earth were much more enduring and durable than reality shows them to be. In the end we are surprised at their evanescence and mutability. The Count suggests that marriages be entered into for a period of five years, with the privilege of renewal. Marriage should be indissoluble, if at all, in the case of a third marriage, in which state of affairs both parties could be supposed to have had a double antecedent experience. The institution, he asserts, has a loutish element in it; it destroys the most refined and tenderest of feelings; its blunt certainty is grim and demoralising. His idea is that marriage as an institution is either useless, as in the case of the mortar between the foundation stones, or distinctly nefarious, as when two substances or powers are joined together which exercise a mutually repellent influence over each other.

That same evening Charlotte is made to see that in all probability the Captain will receive an appointment that will take him away from them. To her this is a peal of thunder from a cloudless sky; she is obliged to conceal her passion and despair under the cloak of external or visible calm.

In the meantime the Baroness observes, quite to her displeasure, the mutual attraction of Eduard and Ottilie for each other. She takes the side of Charlotte, silently and by virtue of that unconscious alliance in which married women stand with regard to those who are unmarried.

The story has now reached the point where each of the two consorts is taken up with a woman who is not his spouse, and the other way about. And from this point on the course of events is cared for with the familiar refinement, and occasional boldness, of mental, spiritual and psychical motivation.

Late that evening Eduard and the Count have a long talk with each other. The newly arrived Count praises Charlotte's beauty; he finds her feet especially charming because of their smallness. He recalls with enthusiasm how she formerly shone at court. He asks Eduard to take him to the apartment of the Baroness: He has thus far had no opportunity to see her alone, and, having been separated from her for so long, he has a great deal to say to her.

Having accompanied the infatuated Count, Eduard stands for a while by Charlotte's door; he is tempted to knock. She has been weeping, and has sent her maid away. She lets him in. A mutual transposition of identities ensues: The unsatisfied yearning for an absent person conjures up before each of them the picture of another.

The following day, Eduard receives the copy of a manuscript from Ottilie; it is for him. On the last pages he recognizes, with unfeigned amazement, his own handwriting; this she has assumed. A declaration and first embrace follow. From this moment on Eduard scarcely has enough self-control to conceal his passion during an ordinary conversation.

At the same time however that the first real meeting took place between Eduard and Ottilie, the Captain and Charlotte feel irresistibly drawn to each other. The motif is executed parallel and symmetrically, just as in an old-fashioned drama. The yawl in which they are sitting has run aground. He carries her in his arms from the boat to the land, and they exchange the first and the—last kiss.

Different people act differently when in love. Eduard is undisciplined; Charlotte controls herself perfectly. She observes Ottilie, keeps close watch on her. The situation however is growing worse and worse; it is becoming envenomed. Eduard begins to complain to Ottilie about the other two. She replies, rather flippantly, by disclosing to him a derogatory remark the Captain made to Charlotte concerning his flute-playing. This offends him; it wounds his very heart. He now feels relieved of all duties; considerate he need no longer be. He is of the distinct conviction that Charlotte herself merely wishes to get rid of him.

Everything now has a special meaning for Eduard. He detects an omen in everything that happens. Ottilie's birthday is to be celebrated. It suddenly occurs to him that he planted the most beautiful trees in the garden in the year of her birth. A little research shows him that he planted the trees on her very birthday. From this coincidence he deduces a mystic connection between her and himself. He buys a whole trunk full of beautiful and costly things for her.

One day, when Eduard is about to have the fireworks set off from the central dam in the large fish pond, the explosives that had been collected into one place are discharged. One of the dams, just then crowded with spectators, breaks. A boy is on the point of being drowned when the Captain rescues him and hastens away from the festivities. Charlotte follows him. In course of time all those present join them. Eduard then has fireworks just for Ottilie and himself all alone.

The Captain departs that same night, and quietly. Charlotte's resignation is complete. She is composed to the extent that she looks forward to a future that is to be serious but not necessarily unhappy. Eduard however is transported to another world; he is captivated by his love as by an intoxication of good fortune.

Charlotte now holds the centre of the stage. She addresses some vehement reproaches to Eduard for his passion but can, as was to be expected, make no impression upon him in this way. Since neither of the husbands is able to overcome the resistance of the other, Eduard elects the rather passive means of solving the difficulty by simply leaving and going on his way. He does so however with the express threat that he will somehow get possession of Ottilie in case Charlotte sends her away.

He settles down quietly in a lonely place. Where Charlotte, with her naturally active temperament, finds occupation for herself and Ottilie by interesting herself in the education of the children of the neighborhood, Eduard has nothing to do but to brood in an idle and ineffectual way over his anguish.

The section of the novel that follows is treated with a sentimentality that is quite foreign to the modern mind. We can even assert that a sentimentality such as this is totally affected in its presentation. When Mittler, who soon becomes intolerable to the reader, looks up Eduard in order to persuade him to return to the right way, the latter portrays his fanciful life in the loneliness: "I write sweet, confidential notes in her name to myself and answer them and then keep both the letters and the replies." His one joy is in drinking from the glass with the monogram. As this has proved to be unbreakable, so are all the circumstances, all the relations, that fate determines. For it seems that everything in his previous life has been merely "a prelude, a retardation, a pastime, a killtime, until he became acquainted with her."

And so Mittler goes away from him and to Charlotte. She hopes that everything will come to a happy end, and that Eduard will return to her: "How can it be otherwise, since you find me in the condition in which I am?" Mittler exclaims: "Do I understand you correctly?" She begs him to take the message to Eduard; he declines, remarking that for such any messenger is good enough. He regards the entire affair as settled, so he must be off to other places where his presence is more needed. Goethe has experienced no doubt regarding the plausibility of his plan. He asks us to think of Mittler as spending his entire time, day in and day out, going from place to place, trying to keep married people married and together.

This is, incidentally, the turning point of the book. Eduard's nocturnal visit to Charlotte has borne fruit, and from now on the whole situation is fundamentally changed. Eduard is in despair; he draws up his last will and testament, and goes to war to fight "under a general with whom death is probable and victory certain." It is all so unhistorical that it is quite impossible to determine whom Goethe had in mind.

There follow, during Eduard's campaign and the Captain's absence, the above mentioned multitude of subordinate events and accessory figures that delay the coming of the catastrophe. There is a lawsuit, a discussion of memorials to the dead, building enterprises, and the introduction of the young and amiable architect who interests himself in the castle church. He falls in love with Ottilie. He paints the ceiling of the chapel with the figures of angels that resemble Ottilie. There follow the arrival and stay of Ottilie's former teacher, and the visit of two travelling Englishmen one of whom relates a story bearing on the Captain's youth. And, interwoven among the other events and episodes, we have laid before us a series of extracts from Ottilie's diary. These are in truth only partly in keeping with Ottilie's mind; they serve rather as a spiritual emporium for Goethe's own reflections, being merely sprinkled here and there with observations that might come from Ottilie.

Here we have for the first time the comparison that has since become so trite about the red thread that runs through the cordage of the British navy. Just like this noted thread does Ottilie's passion for Eduard run through all her thoughts.

The following is a specimen of an aphorism that
is really conceived after Ottilie's own heart: "Voluntary dependence is the most beautiful condition
imaginable, and how would it be possible without
love." Such desultory thoughts as the following
however point plainly to the elder Goethe as their
author:

> There is no external sign of courtesy that does not have a
> deep moral basis. The right sort of training would be the
> one that would give at once the sign and the basis.

This aphorism would make a suitable motto for
Herbert Spencer's *Ceremonial Government*. It discloses the mind of a venerable thinker.

The following came from the experience of a
man of the world: "Fools and sages are equally
harmless. Half fools and half sages are the really
dangerous members of the human family."

We feel, too, the experience of a great poet and
a profound observer back of such an expression as
this: "Mediocrity has no greater consolation than
this. Genius is not immortal." The same applies
to this thought. "The greatest men are always connected with this or that weakness of their century."

The parallel figures and features that are introduced into this lengthy *entre-acte* help to emphasize
the peculiarities or the position of the leading personages. The crude and secular, though externally
radiant Luciane, Charlotte's daughter by her first
marriage, is the exact opposite of Ottilie. Likewise
the Count and the Baroness, who now appear as
united and happy, are contrasted with the separated
lovers. The teacher and the architect are the opposites that complement each other. The architect,
with an enthusiasm for art that reminds of Goethe's

own, has the appreciation of a real artist for plastic and picturesque beauty. At Christmas time he arranges living pictures; Ottilie has to represent the Madonna. Goethe writes in rapture concerning her: "In this figure she surpasses everything that any painter has ever portrayed." His enthusiasm could hardly be expressed in more visionary terms. He refers to her as "the heavenly child." His style even rises to this lyric height: "The trees should have been given life, and eyes to see, in order to rejoice in her." One feels that Ottilie is Goethe's conception of the Madonna.

Where the architect has an appreciative insight into the combined grandeur to which the physical world gives expression, the teacher, who cordially disapproves of the blending of the divine and the physical in the realm of sacred art, regards the formless as the most sublime. He has the inborn fear of an Israelite or a Mohammedan of seeing the celestial made idolatrous by being put into corporeal form. His interests are confined to a single issue: the training and development of the mind. In his own field he makes some discriminating, indeed quite surprising observations. He calls "change without distraction," for example, the right and ultimate solution of the teacher's problem. He hurls out into the world this striking paradox: "Women are created to stand alone." He explains his meaning in the following terms:

A man longs to be with a man. He certainly would have created one had he found none on the earth. A woman, however, could live for all eternity and never once think of creating another woman.

That is, if she had a husband of her own.

With his old and passionate interest for Ottilie,
the teacher would like to take her back to the boarding school; for she has been torn away from regular and coherent instruction. Goethe makes the
admirable observation that Ottilie, though obliged
to confess this much, did not after all understand
her teacher; for she no longer found anything that
was incoherent when she thought of her beloved,
and she did not see how there could be anything
coherent without him.

As soon as she learns that Eduard was exposed
to all the dangers of war, she suffered profound
distress. Later on, this anxiety became duller and
less acute until it amounted to nothing more than
apathy. Goethe then makes the genuine observation that fear can be strained and brought up to a
certain point, but not beyond this point. The law
is applicable to Ottilie.

Charlotte gives birth to a boy. It has been named
Otto after its father; but Otto is also the baptismal
name of the Captain. Nor is it wholly a matter of
accident that the feminine form of Otto is Ottilie.

Mittler appears and makes one of his vigorous
speeches at the baptism. His remarks are so copious that they have a fatal effect. The decrepit old
priest would have liked to sit down. As it was he
was obliged to listen to Mittler while standing.
The embarrassment due to this predicament entirely
escapes the attention of the eloquent speaker. He
finally talks the venerable priest to death. In this
indirect way, Goethe pours out a measure of harmless ridicule on the head of the doughty matrimonial
negociator.

In this way, birth and death are brought into

immediate juxtaposition. The taking off of the old priest seems like an ill omen for the existence of the infant. It is given over to the care of Ottilie. But, wonder of wonders, its facial expressions, its bodily features, are those of the Captain. Its eyes, large and black, are Ottilie's.

At this juncture Eduard returns from war covered with badges of distinction. He longs to go home. Out in the park he catches sight of Ottilie with the child. He makes himself known; he sees the child; he notes the similarities. The child spells the doom of his marriage: It was, he says, begotten in dual adultery. In other words, this child is Goethe's mute criticism of Eduard's and Charlotte's marriage.

Eduard and Ottilie now resign to the belief that they can belong to each other. It is the ephemeral culmination of the mood just before the tragedy. The child falls from Ottilie's boat into the water and dies. Fate exercises its gruesomeness here as in *Wilhelm Meister,* where Wilhelm's ungrounded suspicions become responsible for Marianne's desertion and lamentable death.

The news is brought to Charlotte. Thereupon she consents to the separation, for fate has willed it. But now Eduard is confronted by definite resignation with regard to him himself, on the part of Ottilie. She fancies that only by renunciation will she be able to expiate her guilt. She undergoes a complete change in the depths of her heart; she is freed from her intense desire to serve, freed also from contrition, and is to this extent at rest. But she slowly wastes away, for she eats almost nothing.

The daily life begins again between the two

couples, apparently just as in days of old. They
talk together, play their musical instruments in ensemble, and Eduard reads aloud while Ottilie looks
over his shoulder. But it is nothing more than a
faint reflection of their former life.

The attraction of Eduard and Ottilie for each
other now becomes almost magical. There is no
longer need of actual contact; it is enough simply to
be together. If anyone had kept either of them at
one end of the building, the other would voluntarily
have reached that same end. It seems as though
they are only one human being, so completely are
they occupied with the unconscious and perfect love
that arises from their common existence.

Eduard's birthday draws near. Ottilie accordingly unpacks the trunk he gave her a long while
ago so that she may adorn herself for the first, last
and only time with the gifts he lavished upon her.
Some well meant, and in themselves by no means
unreasonable, expressions of zealousness on the
part of Mittler evoke the ultimate dissolution.
He contends that nothing is more barbaric than acts
of interdiction and suppression. Positive commands
alone, he insists, are good and beautiful. He criti-
cises vehemently the Ten Commandments. Honor
thy father and thy mother is the sole exhortation
that has sound meaning for him. The fifth commandment he finds decidedly imbecile; it sounds as
though people would take special pleasure in going
out and killing some one—as though such an act
would be agreeable to any mortal man! Instead
of forbidding children to kill people they should
have instilled in them the desire to help people, to
do them good. As to the sixth commandment he

becomes infuriated at the mere mention of it; it intrigues the curiosity of the young out on to quite dubious paths; it is coarse; it is indecent. Instead of this each one should have it brought close to his heart that the path to pursue is the one that will promote the happiness of married people, and will teach them to overcome the obstacles that stand in their way.

At this moment Ottilie enters; but she withdraws immediately and in silence when she hears the subject that is being discussed. This incident she does not survive. The encounter with the remarks that are being made about the sixth commandment, and the reminder that she has transgressed it in spirit, gives her the death-blow. She dies, having been previously consumed by hunger.

She is buried in the chapel. The miracles at the grave recall in a remarkably subtle manner the miracles at the Ottilieberg, which had been the poet's point of departure. On her deathbed Ottilie has made Eduard promise that he will not do violence to his own life. He refuses however almost consistently to eat and when, as a result of carelessness on the part of a servant, the precious glass is broken, he likewise refuses to take almost any nourishment in liquid form. He dies, and Goethe closes the sentence in which he says that this heart, so moved but a little while ago, has at last found perfect peace, with the rationalistic application of religious terminology: "And since he passed away with his thoughts directed to the Saint, we may well call him blessed."

Such is the course of events, such is the basic thought in this renowned novel, Goethe's most perfect production from his older days, the model of all later novels of a tragic character that are based on married life. It is the melancholy book of a student of nature. Its art is somewhat antiquated as viewed by the modern mind; it belongs to an age that is gone. The personages do not stand out especially sharp before us; it is rare that we hear them speak with their own voice. We have to do with the author; he explains the characters to us. We do not hear their conversations in their entirety, or with the animating force that accompanies the spoken word. We hear instead Ottilie's monologues, and of these freshness is not a consistent attribute. But the features of the novel that gave it its initial renown, and that have retained its interest to the very present, are not to be sought in the art of execution; these are to be found in the cleverness, the genius of construction, and the originality and profundity of the underlying idea.

Man is not seen here struggling with men, or seized by a passion, or developing innate talents. This book is neither a novel of adventure, nor of love, nor of crime, nor of education. Man is not seen here as the new beginning which takes up where nature leaves off; he is seen rather as a part of nature, in the grip of nature, and subjected to its laws which, totally indifferent to the individual's welfare, unite, dissolve, join, and separate.

We see a man and a woman joined together in such a way that there is apparently every reason to believe in the seriousness and permanency of the union. Those are not young, flippant persons that make up the characters of this book. It is the second marriage in the case of both parties, and both parties have been yearning for this second marriage for quite a while. The relation bursts however with a centrifugal force, though it bursts without an external break. Neither he nor she breaks the marriage in the vulgar connotation of the term. It breaks in truth for the very reason that it has been preserved. The child that is born and which, by a freak of nature, destroys both is the child of both. But this new life, born of custom, the life under which newly awakened passions flourish, opens the abyss beneath their feet.

With his wonted originality, Goethe has chosen an instance in which the child, as is so frequently the case, holds two people together who really do not harmonize at all. At the beginning of the novel, Eduard and Charlotte have no children. They do not become parents until the discord has begun; and their child which, under other circumstances, would bring the mother and father more closely together than ever and cause each the joy that attaches to parenthood, merely binds them externally. It doubles their anguish in truth instead of reënforcing their happiness. And its death does no more than make a bad situation worse.

In *Hermann und Dorothea* Goethe had depicted the happy finding of each other on the part of a young man and a young woman; their union was idyllic. In *Die Wahlverwandtschaften* he visualized the seamy side of domestic life, portrayed the passions as dark powers, and set forth marriage as an institution which constitutes for some an easy and useful cloak for their feelings, for others a straitjacket.

CHAPTER XXII

GOETHE AND SOCIAL POLITICS; GOETHE AND AMERICA

THAT social politics and social ethics lay beyond Goethe's interests, if not beyond his reach, has become an almost proverbial belief. It is a belief that is poles removed from the truth. Even in the eighteenth century he took a cordial interest in social questions, as can be seen by the immense space taken up in his consciousness by the affairs of the North American Colonies, and the emigrations from Europe to them. Lothario, in *Wilhelm Meister,* emigrates to America in order to find virgin soil for his enterprises. Jarno follows him across the Atlantic to the end that he may avail himself of the advantageous situation his predecessor has created there. It is in the *Lehrjahre* however that Lothario, like Goethe himself, expresses the belief that every man has an opportunity, also in Europe, to work and to improve things in many ways. He exclaims: "Here or nowhere is America!" That is to say, one finds his America everywhere.

But at the beginning of the nineteenth century, Goethe studies the prominent French socialists, Saint-Simon and Fourier, the Englishman Owen and also the English utilitarian philosopher Jeremy Bentham. He loses himself in plans for the refor-

mation of society. He ascribes this duty to the
person who in the *Wanderjahre* is called the Uncle.
There had also been an Uncle in the *Lehrjahre;* he
had transformed his castle into a temple for artists.
It is the castle where Mignon's burial takes place.
But the Uncle in the *Wanderjahre* is an American
who is now living in Europe. Though permeated
with the old civilization, he is a practical man. His
grandfather emigrated. He has now returned to
his estate in Germany, supervises it as a free vassal
and also as the most conscientious worker. On his
belongings we read: *Possession and Joint Property.*
He exploits them for others; he is as economical as
a parsimonious individual can be—for others. He
is not simply a giver, but also a promoter. For
example, he presents industrious farmers with young
shoots from his plantations, is inexorable to slipshod and dilatory tenants who let the place run
down. With him everything is useful. It is indeed
from the useful that he wishes to rise and to mount
up to the beautiful.

In the oldest edition of the *Wanderjahre* Goethe
still (1821) looks upon emigration as an oddity, as
an absurdity. But by 1827 he has changed his mind.
No one is a more radical state economist than the
old Goethe, the Goethe approaching his eightieth
year. He does homage to America:

> Du hast es besser
> Als unser Kontinent, der alte,
> Hast keine verfallene Schlösser
> Und keine Basalte.
> Dich stört nicht im Innern
> Zu lebendiger Zeit
> Unnützes Erinnern
> Und vergeblicher Streit.

We notice the mineralogist in the remark concerning the basalt rocks, though they have since
been found in various parts of America, and the
mind that always looks ahead and forward in the
remarks concerning useless memories.   Goethe is
still the same he was nearly fifty years previous to
this time, when he wrote:

> Es erben sich Gesetz' und Rechte
> Wie eine ew'ge Krankheit fort,
> Sie schleppen von Geschlecht sich zu Geschlechte.

Goethe turns in this case with aversion away from
the Old Europe.   In his new edition he has Wilhelm
exclaim: "In the Old World everything goes along
in a blundering jogtrot.   In the Old World the new
is treated in an antiquated fashion and that which
is growing according to cramped rules."
The singular Uncle has had his watchword, *Be-
sitz und Gemeingut,* attached as an inscription round
about on his various buildings, somewhat as the
Oriental peoples adorn the walls of their houses
with excerpts from the Koran.   In this connection
Goethe develops, by means of a dialogue, his ideas
concerning the ownership of capital and the enjoyment of life.   He is of the opinion that every man
has a right to preserve and augment whatever possessions fate has given him.   But the individual
owner in question must always involuntarily be
thinking how he is to arrange things so that others
may have part and share in his goods.   He himself
is appreciated only in so far as others enjoy his
possessions along with him.   A prince is also honored because he imparts his power to others and
gives other people employment.   A rich man is hon-

ored because he gives of his superabundance to others. A musician or a poet is envied because his very nature is communicativeness itself.

Man should hold fast to any sort of possession that he may rightly call his own; he must make it a central point from which common property proceeds. Nothing is more absurd, nothing is more foolish, than to follow out the injunction of Holy Writ and give one's goods to the poor. It is much more praiseworthy to take good care of them, to leave the capital intact, but to let the interest, as time goes on, accrue to the benefit and joy of everyone.

The bizarre Uncle has studied the great Italian jurists Beccaria and Filangieri (Goethe's acquaintances from Naples) who jointly embody the breaking-through of the humanity of the eighteenth century as contrasted with the barbarous practice of law in previous times. Beccaria's goal was this: The greatest good to the greatest number (*la massima felicitá, divisa nel maggior numero*), which Goethe reproduces in abbreviated form in German as follows: *Den Meisten das Beste!*

The Uncle revamps this motto into the following: *Vielen das Erwünschte!* For, we read, one can neither find nor know "the most," and much more difficult is it to determine what is "best." But there are always many round about us. We become acquainted with their wishes. We can take into consideration what they should wish. And therefore this nameless Uncle plants, builds, equips incessantly and with a goal immediately in sight: No child shall want for a cherry or an apple; no mother shall be without cabbage or turnips.

Of salt and spices he has a whole storehouse. He lets others look after tobacco and brandy; according to his way of viewing things these are not necessities. Significant for Goethe's love of liberty with regard to small things is this touch: The Uncle cordially dislikes having his meals served at the stroke of the clock. The *à la carte* meal, ready at any hour, is to him the acme of modern civilization.

CHAPTER XXIII

Wilhelm Meisters Wanderjahre

Wilhelm Meisters Wanderjahre, originally intended as a continuation of *Wilhelm Meisters Lehrjahre,* never became this in any sense of word. It would have been much better if Goethe had not given the leading character the name of Wilhelm, and had not made Wilhelm's son Felix and his education and training the center of the work, for he thereby nourished a delusive idea and strengthened it by re-introducing the names of a few of the persons of the older novel. But these appear completely changed. There is Jarno, for example, now wholly taken up with mining, and known to those about him as Montan.

The work on this detailed book, which is really a collection within a frame of a number of short stories that do not concern Wilhelm, stretches out over an appalling number of years. One of the stories, *Die neue Melusine,* is supposed to have been told in Sesenheim as early as 1772 and written down shortly thereafter. The embryo of other stories such as *St. Joseph der Zweite,* and *Der Mann von fünfzig Jahren,* seem to belong to the year 1797, though the latter was not really designed until 1807. The story entitled *Die pilgernde Thörin* and the first two chapters of the novel were published separately in a *Taschenbuch für Damen* in 1808 and

1809. There was published in the same place in 1815 *Das nussbraune Mädchen,* though not in its entirety, and in the same place in 1816-1818 *Die neue Melusine* which, as we have seen, is supposed to have been written forty years previously. And finally the fragment *Der Mann von fünfzig Jahren,* which had been in process of completion for twenty-one years—apparently not a long time. In 1820 Goethe wrote *Wo steckt der Verräther?* and at the close of the year he has progressed so well with his work on the novel that he can afford to have the printing begun.

As has been pointed out, he rests the frame of the work as a connecting idea as much as possible on the development of the individual for the public and society in contrast to the ideal of a purely personal training and development such as that around which the *Lehrjahre* had revolved. The social dominates here, or according to the intention of the poet, should dominate. It has two especial organs which remind us more of Plato's *State* than the beginning of the nineteenth century: *Der pädagogische Provinz,* in which the peculiarities of the individual were to be developed as rapidly as possible, and *Der Wanderbund* which works in opposition to emigration. In return, Wilhelm, who loves and worships his wife Natalie, pledges himself to her to something so bizarre and epically impossible as this: He is to spend not more than three days at a time under the same roof and not to leave an inn without going at least a mile away from it. This alliance, which goes under the name of *Die Entsagenden* (the subtitle of the novel), imposes upon its members this no less bizarre and romantic obligation: When they meet they are never to discuss the past or the future; they are to confine their attention to the present. By this arrangement Goethe in all probability wished to bring it about that Wilhelm and Jarno would not need to go back to reminiscences from the *Lehrjahre* when they see each other, the contents of which no longer stood out clearly in his mind.

In 1821, as the outcome of severe diligence, Goethe succeeded in forging together a sufficient amount of successful and unsuccessful material to make the appearance of the first part of the *Wanderjahre* a possibility. For the second part a provisional plan had been laid. The book was well received and the shameless forgery from the Preacher Pustkuchen, which came out at the same time under the same name, did it no great harm. But Goethe did not feel like going to work on this odd creation again; it was not until 1827, the year in which he completed the *Helena* act of the second part of *Faust,* the act parts of which he had read to Schiller as early as September, 1800, that he resumed work on the *Wanderjahre.* He remodelled the first part, which had to be revised for the sake of continuity, and was going ahead with the second and third parts when he was grievously depressed by the sudden death of Karl August in the summer of 1828; the work did not appear until 1829. It was unfavorably received.

In actuality the *Wanderjahre* falls into two parts; one is poetic and contains the novelettes; the other is didactic and contains the narrative with its Utopias. If we read these novelettes attentively, we cannot help but be struck by the personal element ın a number of them. When Goethe was between fifty and six years old, his age apparently gave him a great deal of concern. He was especially interested in the question as to whether a man of that age could win the love of a young woman and retain her love against a younger rival, especially if this younger rival happened to be his own son. Just as the relation between father and son (Wilhelm and Felix) is of the greatest significance for the frame, just so is the relation between a father and a son who fall in love with the same girl touched upon frequently in the novelettes. One is tempted to believe that Goethe and his son August now and then felt an attraction for the same girl, or she for both of them. This is not at all incredible when we recall that, when August in 1817 became engaged to, and married, Ottilie von Pogwisch the young, sprightly, clever woman was much later somewhat taken up with her father-in-law, perhaps as much as with her husband.

He was presumably thinking of himself when he wrote this humorous little verse:

> Aspasia, wie das Sonnenlicht,
> Begünstigt zwar so manchen Wicht,
> Doch mag ich gern bei ihr verweilen,
> Eine Kartoffel theilt man nicht,
> Doch lässt die Ananas sich theilen.

In *Die pilgernde Thörin* (a revision of a French story entitled *La folle en pélérinage*), the gadabout and mysterious but refined and, to her lover, steadfast beauty comes to a castle where she is hospitably received by the father, who, in course of time, feels so strongly attracted to her that he offers her his hand and his heart. But right at this very moment his own son also falls hopelessly in love with the fascinating guest and competes for her in such vehement fashion that she finds the situation unendurable and disappears.

The same chord is struck, gently, in *Wer ist der Verräther?* The young Lucidor is selected by his father, a professor, and his father's intimate friend, an official, for the younger and livelier of the latter's two daughters, Julie by name. Julie finds inexhaustible entertainment in the professor's house when he instructs her in geography and topography; she knows all the harbors and the towns with their towers, cupolas, and minarets. She is in truth just as much interested in the professor (he has no name) as she is in his son.

But Lucidor, when he comes as a wooer to the official, feels much more strongly drawn to the older, quieter, more sedate sister Lucinde than to the younger and jollier Julie. On account of this he feels a certain amount of anguish which, as his stay in the house is prolonged, goes over into despair. His father desires, and expects, his union with the younger sister who makes advances to Lucidor in a straightforward and unsuspecting way. The older sister seems bound to Antoni, the much travelled and experienced friend of the family. When the young man is alone in his room in the evening, he gives vent to his torture in passionate monologues.

At last all the obstacles disappear as if by the waving of a magic wand. The professor who arrives on the scene because the engagement is to be announced seems to know all about his son's coolness toward Julie; nor does he blame him for his indifference. Since Lucidor does not dare to go to

Lucinde, she herself declares to him frankly and openly that she knows of his—presumably concealed —love for her and she assures him that his love is not unrequited. He shall, she says, not be afraid of causing Julie distress, nor must he fear Antoni as a competitor, for everything has been straightened out between these two. And when he, in blank astonishment, asks how it comes that everybody in the house and out of it knows all about his secret, the explanation is given, an explanation which undeniably makes the entire novelette quite juvenile, that he has the bad habit of talking to himself and that the entire family, the acoustics of the house being matchless, have from the very start been well informed as to his disappointment in Julie and his ardent admiration for Lucinde. Moreover, they have informed his father of the true state of affairs long ago.

In *Der Mann von fünfzig Jahren* the question is raised whether a man who is fifty years old can still be regarded as young, and whether he can seriously fall in love with a really young woman. The Major—he has no name—has for sometime looked upon himself as an old man. He meets a friend who is an actor. This actor not only knows the principles of reasonable hygiene, but also the use of paints and all manner of cosmetic remedies and aids which bestow upon the user an artificial youth. He is ten years older than the Major and looks much younger. The Major applies the cosmetics and is rejuvenated after having learned to his astonishment the day before from his sister, the Baroness, that if her daughter Hilarie's heart is no longer free, it is not owing to the fact that she loves the

Major's son, for whom the father intended to compete, but the father himself, her uncle, in whose head she never seems to have found any gray hairs, on whose face she never seems to have detected any wrinkles, these, too, having been removed by artificial means.

Hilarie, deeply in love with her uncle, wants to be his forever; they become engaged. At this point the son arrives, the young lieutenant, and tells his father that he has no desire whatsoever for the hand of Hilarie, nor does he wish to be united to her; a young widow has aroused his passion and captivated him body and soul. The father is to meet her and approve of his choice. But he suspects from the son's description that the beautiful widow will pay as little attention to the young man as she pays to her other wooers.

The Major finds in her one of those amiable feminine beings who try to catch all men. With extraordinary skill she at once makes him the chief and central point of her society. To the young lieutenant she praises the father at the son's expense. To the father she never once mentions the son. But the son, who imagines that he is being loved, is in the seventh heaven.

The beautiful widow does not give the Major an opportunity to woo for his son. She herself coquettes bravely with him, finds his poems better than those of the son though he himself insists that he is a mere dilettant. When the man of fifty years is so indiscreet as to tell his sister of the strong impression that the young widow has made on him, the sister becomes peevish. Goethe remarks, and rightly so, that one must never talk to one woman with enthusiasm about another. Women regard men as buyers in a market; the men allow themselves to be deluded by the wares that are placed in the best light, whereas women, with their keen eyes, appreciate at once that these very same wares have precious little value. She finds moreover deep down in her heart that Hilarie is too young for her brother, and that the widow is not young enough for her nephew.

Weary, weather-beaten and wet-through, the young lieutenant arrives one evening at the house of the Baroness. It is to be presumed that he has been jilted by the beautiful widow. He has to be put to bed and is nursed and consoled by his cousin. When, on the next day, he appears in his father's clothes, a transformation takes place in Hilarie's soul. In her heart Flavio gets the advantage of his father.

One evening as Flavio and Hilarie are skating together they discover a third party on the ice. Hilarie wishes to avoid a stranger, but when he encircles the young girl they discover that it is the Major. Hilarie is so dismayed that she loses her balance and falls. This situation is portrayed vividly and compactly, though the rest is rendered, in places at least, in *Kanzleistil*.

We come to the explanation. The Major understands that he has been demoted from first lover to father-in-law, and since at the same time the chamberlain, who rejuvenated him with cosmetics, has taken his final leave, the Major renounces, under force of circumstances, after the fashion of all others who renounce, the idea of fighting against old age which has at last really appeared.

There is a great deal of actual experience and perhaps one or two personal confessions in this story, about the best novelette in the entire work. But it is written with constant reference to the reader, so that the real course of events is sprinkled with an old man's chatter. How much better Goethe wrote when he *wrote* than now when he *dictates!*

The next story, *Die neue Melusine,* is more briskly and coherently executed. *Melusine* is a fairy tale, though not like H. C. Andersen's fairy tales for children, nor is it easily understood and transparent as are the Danish fairy tales. Goethe's story is totally devoid of childlike simplicity, though it gives evidence of an unusual inventive power. A young man on a journey meets in an inn a beautiful young woman who shows him kindness, though no favor, and who entrusts to him a box that she owns. He is requested to take it with him for her from town to town. He must always rent an especial room for the box adjoining his own. For his trouble he receives a purse of gold with which he is expected to proceed economically. Since he however spends the money in riots and revels, his fair one comes to him one evening from the side room and supplies him anew with apparently inexhaustible riches. At times they travel together on the journey; at times he travels entirely alone with the box. The beautiful young lady becomes more affectionate toward him, their relation becomes quite intimate; the consequences are soon noticeable. The beautiful body no longer has the same bearing. One night, as the young man is travelling all alone in his carriage, he sees to his astonishment a light through a crack in the box and discovers that his sweetheart is on the inside, in miniature; she sits reading in a doll's room.

In course of time she tells him that she is really a little dwarf, that she has received permission from the king of the dwarfs to transform herself into a human being, to love a man, and from him to have the dwarf's blood, which naturally grows thinner and thinner, renewed and strengthened. However precious she has been to the young man up to this point, he no longer loves her with the same warmth and vehemence. One evening they are invited to a large party; Melusine entertains by singing and playing; her companion is not at all musical and in one of his tantrums he abuses her by calling her a *dwarf*. He regrets his rude conduct and begs her pardon. She is not exactly angry at him, but she is firmly determined to desert him. He begs and beseeches. She says that they can remain together on just one condition: He must become just as small as she. This takes place; they live for some time right happy together in a doll's palace and associate only with dwarfs, her relatives, her friends.

The good relation is broken when her parents demand that they become really married. A gold ring is placed on his finger. He hates, he loathes this gold ring, succeeds at last in having it filed off, grows up again to the height of a normal man and again finds himself in the inn where he had originally made the acquaintance of the lovely Melusine.

The teaching that may be deduced from this is rather uncertain, and rather manifold. It may mean to the woman one loves. It may mean that a man that one should never speak a mortally painful word

cannot feel happy in the long run while living with
a woman who drags him down, debases him, de-
grades him. It may mean that the most cordial
sort of relation can be broken off when it is to receive the stamp of the marriage vow. And it may
mean a number of other things.

Though not written for children, this fairy tale
could, if slightly modified, amuse them also.

A quite unimportant but frolicsome jest is the
little story entitled *Die gefährliche Wette* which revolves around nothing else than just this: A band
of young fellows are sitting at a hotel window. They
see a distinguished and stately man, well on in years,
get out of his carriage and enter the hotel. Since
he seems accustomed to being treated with profound
respect, one of the young madcaps bets the others
that he can take this fine and mighty gentleman by
the nose and move that self same nose back and forward without being molested therefor. Each of
them promises him a gold piece if he can carry out
his undertaking. The young man announces himself to the aristocratic old man as an especially deft
barber, and before the open hotel window he takes
him by the nose and shaves his upper lip.

He returns to the group; they break out in such a
howl of jubilee that everybody in the hotel learns
of the wager; and the dignified old gentleman—so
that the story may contain a moral—sends his servants to give the party of youngsters a sound thrash-
ing. They depart in great haste, while his son, who
has discovered the ringleader, gives him in a duel
a wound that cripples him for life. The moral
solemnity of the close grates on the innocence of this
unimportant students' prank.

In *Nicht zu Weit*, ingeniously planned but poorly written as it is, the contents of an entire novel are compressed into just a few pages. It depicts a case of marital misfortune and unhappiness on the part of two people each of whom is an excellent individual. By reason of her frivolity the wife brings the husband to the point of despair, so that both are tempted to enter into a new union where new disappointments await them.

It is plain that these various and variegated stories do not stand on the usual lofty level of Goethe's art. They are interesting simply because they were written by a great personality whose heterogeneous forms of expression all belong to the picture of the man as a whole. But had these stories been written by a lesser hand, they would not fascinate.

And there is even less artistic value, though decidedly greater psychological interest, to be attached to that part of the *Wanderjahre* which is purely didactic. In the first place there is the section called *Lenardos Tagebuch*, unhappily divided into parts that lie far removed from each other. It is distinctly touching to see in this section how thoroughly Goethe studied the spinning and weaving of cotton in Switzerland, and his intensely spiritual conception of a practical trade as *eine strenge Kunst* from which all frivolity is banished in contrast to the *freie Künste* in which there is so much talentless dabbling. There is a portrayal in this story, with the foresight of one who knows, of the danger that threatened the tradesman at that time when the introduction of machinery was imminent; they are told that there are just two courses open to them: to emigrate, or to set up machines of their own. The amiable story is collected around the charming description of *Frau Susanne,* called the Beautiful-Good (apparently from the Greek *Kalé-k'agathé*) in which Goethe has finally succeeded in sketching an exceedingly fascinating woman who is just as sensible and just as mentally independent as she is captivating when she stands in the presence of the other sex.

One sees from the efficiency with which the author allows her to defend the freedom of her thoughts, placed as she is in a pietistic society, that the fine, poetic conception of the Christian legend, which is discussed in the attractive idyl entitled *St. Joseph der Zweite,* does not carry with it any noticeable concession to belief in dogma.

The way in which Goethe at this stage of his life will have religion understood and practised is best seen in the pedagogical province from the *Wanderjahre,* where all religion that is based on fear is rejected, but where the religious life is based wholly and entirely on a worthy feeling such as reverence, *Ehrfurcht.*

There is no reason why we should dwell on the romantic frame out from which the threads stretch into the various narratives. It is far too clumsily worked out and far too muddled. The leading characters are Wilhelm himself, who ends his career as a surgeon, the half supernatural character called Makarie, the sun-woman, a higher unity of Natalie and "the fair soul," Wilhelm's son, Felix, who loves and eventually marries Hersilie, the daughter of an art-loving collector. In contrast to his father, Felix loves just one woman his whole life long. And then at last a number of individual characters from the *Lehrjahre* are re-introduced, the most of whom are no longer recognizable. There is Philine, for example, now a quiet woman who spends her time at a useful and practical occupation: she cuts out dresses.

The entire affair revolves around such an impossible epic hinge as a jewel box into the possession of which Felix has come at the beginning of the novel, but to which the key is missing. Then, in the third book, Hersilie writes to Wilhelm telling him that Friedrich (from the *Lehrjahre*) has found the right key to the box. The remarkable key is even described in the text. It is said that this is the usual way of things in life. One had, for example, a very precious wooden cross, the arms of which, unfortunately, turned out to be spurious; they had been arbitrarily attached by an artist far inferior to the artist who had made the original cross. But years later the man comes, through a remarkable coincidence, into the possession of the genuine arms. The coincidence is certainly untypical. The great majority of us never find jewel boxes, nor do we have fitting keys sent us at the opportune moment.

The *Wanderjahre* marks a receding wave in Goethe's spiritual life. There is much in it that is beautiful and profound, but it would have been quite impossible for so recognized a master to write a book of such breadth and disorder had he not been fully acquainted with the ability of the German people to tire itself out in patient admiration, and never to find any of the works of its favorites of excessive murkiness or prolixity. But on this occasion it was shown that even that ability had its limitations beyond which it was impossible to go with impunity.

CHAPTER XXIV

PUSTKUCHEN's *Falsche Wanderjahre*

THERE lived at this time a little Protestant preacher, as stupid as he was conceited, in the forsaken hole called Wiebelskirchen near Ottweiler. His lofty name in full was Johann Friedrich Wilhelm Pustkuchen. He was born in 1793 and was consequently no less than forty-four years younger than the Goethe whom he honored with his sincere hatred and in whom he saw a danger to, if not the actual destruction of, German literature and German spiritual life. Even before Goethe had published his *Wanderjahre*, Pustkuchen had finished his continuation of the *Lehrjahre*. He published, without betraying his exalted name, his *Wilhelm Meisters Wanderjahre* in Quedlinburg, in four volumes. It is a glorious work in which to receive enlightenment. Not that it has the slightest value. It is soft, sweet, empty and pharasaical. But it gives one an insight into the way Goethe's pious contemporaries regarded his character and activity. It is a pity that its stupidity is not so condensed as it is in Wolfgang Menzel's criticism of Germany's greatest man. And yet, it is stupidity pure and undiluted and doubly diverting because of its conventionality: It is masterful morality, perfect piety. And it is always "sweet to listen" to his sort of mindless matter, as Welhaven [6] well says. Goethe, however, was not gifted with the talent of deriving pleasure from this spiritual *genre*. Among other epigrammes which the *Wanderjahre* induced him to write, there is this one. Flatter Pustkuchen it does not:

> "Was will von Quedlinburg heraus
> Ein zweiter Wandrer traben!"
> Hat doch der Wallfisch seine Laus,
> Muss ich auch meine haben.

In his *Wanderjahre,* Pustkuchen has Wilhelm come to a castle where he is hospitably received by a captain and his fair daughter. Through the former, the author expresses his settled convictions regarding literature. They are not, however, meant as mere personal opinions; they are decisions handed down by the highest court. They effect in time a conversion to more wholesome views on the part of the hitherto deluded Wilhelm.

After making clear, and strongly emphasizing, the fact that the hero has led a planless and dissipated life up to this point, the Captain inveigles

---

[6] Johann Sebastian Cammermeyer Welhaven (1807-1873) had abundant opportunity to listen to the arrows of attack as they flew by. In the firm belief that the culture and civilization of Norway should be brought in line and put on a level with the rest of Europe, he assailed Wergeland's efforts to make Norway stand out as a separate, distinct, and intensified entity. The aims of the two men were in reality more or less similar. Welhaven did all in his power to restore and reinvigorate Norway's past. He had a patriotic enthusiasm for old Norse poems and sagas. His sonnet cycle entitled *Norges Daemring* (1834) brought him lasting fame. He wrote critical studies of Ewald and Holberg. But none of this prevented him from becoming a storm-centre of attack. The poem to which Brandes refers runs as follows:

> Det var ham sôdt at lytte
> Mens Pilene flôj paa Bytte
> Til Buesnorens Klang.   —TRANSLATOR.

him into a discussion of German books. It is during this discussion that Wilhelm admits that Goethe is his favorite author.

The writer explains this as follows: Because of his distracted method of living, Wilhelm has always been a few decades behind the actual state of literature at any given time. And since he has appeared, in his capacity as an actor, in various dramas by Goethe, this poet rather than another made an impression on him for the very reason that he found in Goethe's works the formal training after which he had been striving. There never was any distinct belief or well founded enthusiasm in Goethe's books such as is to be found in those of Herder, Klopstock, and Schiller. Goethe's books make very slight demands on the reader, since they view all human relations from the point of view of social custom.

The first thing the Captain does is to attack *Die Wahlverwandtschaften*. In it love is degraded to a mere physical necessity, even to a force that works in opposition to the plan of the universe as elaborated on the basis of moral beauty. All of the characters of the book are mediocre individuals, totally devoid of inner clarity and trustworthy strength. And so on. In other words, Pustkuchen, by virtue of his inner clarity, is fully acquainted with all things, including the plan of the universe.

The Captain's sister makes the point that all of Goethe's men are devoid of real manliness. They have no regard for the sacred relations in life, nor do they have that faith which binds us all together and makes us safe. No girl could ever find a friend in any of them.

The Captain drives the point home that Goethe, in his poetry, is a materialist: He does not worship the invisible God but visible beauty. Nothing that is worshipped and admired by mankind is considered sacred in Goethe's works. He never portrays the ideals of faith, nor the most sublime thoughts, nor the eternal destiny of man, nor piety, nor truth, nor justice, nor pure love, nor steadfast courage. All this has become a chaos in which, under delusions and dirt, individual remains of the divine go idling about. And especially is it to be noted that Goethe never understood the nature of the clergy as a class, nor the poetic side of them as clergymen.

As a result of this eloquence the Captain succeeds in converting Wilhelm, until he too exclaims:

This, then, is that admired Goethe, the poet I placed above all others, and through whose art I was trying to educate myself for the very reason that I thought that all humanity was reflected in it. And it just happens that the greatest characters, the heroes of liberty and patriotism and moral strictness and faith and love and friendship, all of these are absolutely lacking in his works. For us there is then a world without heroes, a world in which shrewdness, sensuality, the passions of the weak, aristocratic education and good will are the only principles and concepts that are given recognition, and in which the purity of just one woman (he means "the fair soul") is conceived of as a sort of miracle; and the attempt is made to explain even this as the result of her physical temperament. Is *that* humanity?

And Faust, this heroic spirit who even outdid the Devil in wild power, becomes in Goethe a hero just like all his other heroes. The events go on their marrowless course just as they do in a *bourgeois* drama. What an Aeschylus or a Dante or a

Shakespeare would have made out of this German
Prometheus!

The time when Goethe knew how to strike the
fundamental note of the age seems to the Captain
to be past. Even the Schlegel brothers have begun
to have a kind of premonition of a higher type of
poetry than Goethe's. More and more frequently
does this once so highly praised poet come to hear
that he lacks poise, measure and balance. The ease
and comfort which he tries to substitute for inspiration can never possibly be looked upon by others as
a life principle.

In the third book the Captain compresses his
charges into these words. Goethe's chief fault lies
in the fact that he misunderstands the real nature
of the Germans; he is a representative only of the
miserable, formless, licentious, modern times, not
of the original German disposition. He never understood the meaning of loyalty. But loyalty is
German. There is only one sort of life that he can
portray: the faithless, honorless, hybrid life such
as the Gipsies lead. This he can depict in bright
colors.

The town clerk has lent the Captain's daughter
some of Goethe's books: "You must not read
them," her father says, "I have looked at them and
locked them up in the cupboard. When the clerk
comes you can give them back to him." It was
the judgment of the Protestant parsonage on the
destroyer of German taste and underminer of German morality. Professor Schütz in Halle published
a book of 400 pages in which he compared Goethe's
Wanderjahre with that of Pustkuchen, conceded to
each of them its advantages, but the greater num-

ber of advantages to Pustkuchen's. On this occasion Goethe wrote some verses in which he treated Schütz as a kitchen police:

> *Pusten,* grobes deutsches Wort!
> Niemand, wohlerzogen,
> Wird am rein anstand'gen Ort
> Solchem Wort gewogen.
>
> *Pusterich,* ein Götzenbild,
> Grässlich anzuschauen,
> Pustet über klar Gefild
> Wust, Gestank und Grauen.
>
> Will der Pusterich nun gar
> Pfaffenkuchen pusten,
> Teufelsjungen-Küchenschaar
> Wird den Teig behusten.

Neither moralizing nationalism nor ebullient clericalism was routed from the field by this play on an ill sounding name.

CHAPTER XXV

GOETHE'S *Tafellieder; Gesellige Lieder*

THE Goethe with whom we have thus far been concerned was the solitary, the poetising, the effecting, the investigating, the struggling Goethe. Then we saw him not rarely face to face with another, either loving and loved, or like unto Castor in his relation to Pollux in Heaven, in constellation with a twin star, Herder, or Schiller, or Napoleon.

But there is still another Goethe, the social. The solitary man as a worker was also a social nature to a high degree who, with his brilliant mentality in control, never sank irretrievably into bitterness and aversion. He could curse the entire human race one day and speak cordially with a visitor the next:

> Der Teufel hol' das Menschengeschlecht!
> Man möchte rasend werden!
> Da nehm' ich mir so eifrig vor:
> Will Niemand weiter sehen.
>
> Will all das Volk Gott und sich selbst
> Und dem Teufel überlassen!
> Und kaum seh' ich ein Menschengesicht,
> So hab' ich's wieder lieb.

In Weimar, at the Court as well as in his home, he was constantly organising social circles. One time it was a *Cour d'amour* after the fashion of the Minnesingers, another it was merely a table company. He saw to it that no false note should arise

through the entrance of some disinterested individual who was not congenial to the circle. How
harshly he acted toward Kotzebue, for example, I
have already discussed in the fourth volume of my
collected works. It was for these circles that Goethe wrote during the first two decades of the nineteenth century his *Gesellige Lieder*, songs for which
there is certainly even now no equal.

Some of them, such as *Stiftungslied*, *Frühlings-
orakel* and *Die glücklichen Gatten*, possess the
naïveté of the folksong and yet are free of the heavi-
ness that characterizes after all so many folksongs.
Goethe's *Lieder* are borne aloft as it were by a
joyousness and a manifestation of good spirits.
Through nearly all of them there runs the susceptibility, on the part of the poet, to the joys of the
table. This is in keeping with his unfailing optimism
and acts as a logical protest against hangdoggedness,
woebegoneness and general repudiation of human
nature. Two of the *Lieder* are parodies on pious
and religious songs. One renunciatory song of the
time began with the line, *Ich habe geliebet, nun
lieb' ich nicht mehr.* Goethe wrote, in protest, as
late as April, 1803, though nigh on to sixty-four
years old:

> Ich habe geliebet, nun lieb' ich *erst recht!*
> Erst war ich der Diener, nun bin ich der Knecht.
> Erst war ich der Diener von Allen;
> Nun fesselt mich diese charmante Person,
> Sie that mir auch Alles zur Liebe, zum Lohn,
> Sie kann nur allein mir gefallen.

As a witness to Goethe's enjoyment of a well-
prepared dish and to his deep-set fondness for a
glass of good wine, two of the following stanzas

begin, *Ich habe gespeiset, nun speis' ich erst gut!*
and *Ich habe getrunken, nun trink' ich erst gern.*
The final stanza runs:

> Drum frisch nur aufs Neue! Bedenke Dich nicht!
> Denn wer sich die Rosen, die blühenden, bricht,
> Den kitzeln fürwahr nur die Dornen.
> So heute wie gestern, es flimmert der Stern,
> Nur halte von hängenden Köpfen Dich fern
> Und lebe Dir immer von vornen!

Goethe's preference for good wine is prolonged
throughout his entire life. In every record of a
person who sat at his table as guest there appears
a statement as to how frequently red wine, or a
rare old Rhine wine, was offered him; and if anyone at the table mixed water with his wine, he was
accustomed to exclaim: Who taught you that horrible habit?—Ladies at whose house he visited frequently expressed their wonder as to how much he
could stand. Many emphasized the finesse of his
senses of taste and of smell which made him an unusual connoisseur of wines. A courtier of Weimar
by the name of Schwabe proves this for posterity
by relating an anecdote concerning a certain test of
this sort that Goethe stood one day.

Karl August had gathered a small circle about
him. At dessert various kinds of good wines were
tried, when the Court Marshall von Spiegel asked
permission to have a wine without a name brought.
Several of the men declared that the wine was Bourgogne though they could not define it more closely.
When the Duke himself, who was a connoisseur, had
also said "Bourgogne," the affair was looked upon as
settled. Goethe tasted it and tasted it again, shook
his head and put the glass down.—"Your Excellency

seems to be of a different opinion," said the Court Marshall. "May I ask what name you would give the wine?"—"I don't know it," answered Goethe, "I should think it is a choice wine from Jena which has been lying for some time in a Madeira cask."— "That's just what it actually is," said the Court Marshall.

The song *Vanitas Vanitatum vanitas!* is, as the last mentioned poem, also meant as a parody. There was a spiritual song, which began: *Ich hab' mein Sach Gott heimgestellt.* Goethe wrote:

> Ich hab' mein Sach auf Nichts gestellt,
>   Juchhe!
> Drum ist's so wohl mir in der Welt,
>   Juchhe!
> Und wer will mein Kamerade sein,
> Der stosse mit an, der stimme mit ein,
> Bei dieser Neige Wein.

In seven stanzas it runs through all the circles of life precisely in the same spirit and with the same refrain. The strophe on women is especially neat in its form:

> Auf Weiber stellt' ich nun mein Sach
>   Juchhe!
> Daher mir kam viel Ungemach;
>   O weh!
> Die Falsche sucht' sich ein ander Theil,
> Die Treue macht' mir Langeweil',
> Die Beste war nicht feil.

The song entitled *Dauer im Wechsel* is beautiful without being flippant. Its lightly flowing verse depicts the fleetness of life, the impossibility of rejoicing for any length of time over the florescence of the fruit tree since the west wind shakes down a flowery rain, and the impossibility of twice swimming in the same stream. Art alone gives something that is lasting:

> Danke, dass die Gunst der Musen
> Unvergängliches verheisst:
> Den Gehalt in Deinem Busen
> Und die Form in Deinem Geist.

The *Tischlied* is the expression for a charming healthfulness. It is one of many among these beautiful poems that seems produced in that state of incipient intoxication which makes an excellent head clear-sighted, imparts to a fully developed nervous system the bliss of the moment, and makes the imagination, deluded in satiation, spread forth its wings and rise up from the earth empowered to soar:

> Mich ergreift, ich weiss nicht wie,
> Himmlisches Behagen,
> Will mich's etwa gar hinauf
> Zu den Sternen tragen?

It is the true song of society. We hear the clinking of the glasses while the stream of life grows broader and the good feeling increases until it finally embraces the entire human race, and the group at the table, grown merry to excess, end by drinking its health.

Even more dithyrambic is the poem *Weltseele,* with all of its metaphysical profundity which, though not formally belonging to the table songs, must be classed with them because it was written in 1804, and because of its spirit:

> Vertheilet Euch nach allen Regionen
> Von diesem heilgen Schmaus!
> Begeistert reisst Euch durch die nächsten Zonen
> In's All und füllt es aus!

Friends are to fill the universe, hover through the expanse, encircle the limits of the sun and the planets, and influence vigorously by the act of creation which has not yet been wholly consummated. Immediately preceding this poem, and intended as an introduction to it, there is an epigrammatic stanza on the universe and its God. It is dry and sharp in its effect:

> Im innern ist ein Universum auch!
> Daher der Völker löblicher Gebrauch,
> Dass Jeglicher das Beste, was er kennt,
> Er Gott, ja seinen Gott, benennt,
> Ihm Himmel und Erden übergiebt
> Ihn fürchtet und womöglich liebt.

Extremely exuberant and permeated with spirit is, finally, the magnificent table song, *Generalbeichte.* It is in the form of a general confession of sins of omission for which friends, both men and women, have to reproach themselves. They have on their conscience the neglect of the good things which life has offered them, and which through ignorance they have let slip. This song corresponds to Bettina's remark in a letter: "I have forgotten the strawberries I ate in the garden: those that I left still burn in my soul."

> Ja, wir haben, sei's bekannt,
> Wachend oft geträumt,
> Nicht geleert das frische Glas,
> Wenn der Wein geschäumet,
> Manche rasche Schäferstunde
> Flücht'gen Kuss vom lieben Munde
> Haben wir versäumet.

Some of these poems belong to the year 1804, others, the last one quoted for example, to 1807,

Gewohnt, gethan to 1813, *Kriegsglück* to 1814, and
the extremely graceful *Offne Tafel,* the revision of
a French table song, to October, 1813. The uproari-
ously jolly *Ergo bibamus* was written in 1810.
Goethe, then, was about sixty years old when these
lyrics came from his pen. It is obvious that so soon
as he expresses himself in verse he is in full possession of his youthful powers, though at this period
of his life as an author his prose had already begun
to lose its freshness.

Zelter was, as a rule, the original composer of
these songs. A great artist he was not. But he was
willing, docile and enthusiastic. He adapted himself to the poet's plans in every way and without
question.

CHAPTER XXVI

Geschichte der Farbenlehre

BETWEEN April 1805 and April 1810, Goethe completed the elaborate work which he modestly called *Materialien zur Geschichte der Farbenlehre.* In very truth, this treatise is exactly what Johannes Müller called it: a spiritually historic portrayal of natural observations. Though the material is far from being well moulded, and though Goethe is frequently content with excerpts and translations from the countless scientists who, from the earliest times to his own, had interested themselves in the problem of colors, he nevertheless set the mark of his own personality on the entire production and permeated it with his own reason. It is only when he approaches Newton that we find traces of the controversialist. And even Newton, as a man, is delineated with intelligence and relative sympathy.

Permission must be granted a layman to limit the discussion to individual sections which for one reason or another are especially instructive and in which the personality of the author is conspicuously brought to light.

The section entitled *Zur Geschichte der Urzeit* is written with Goethe's established genius. He begins with the rainbow and with the impression it has made upon primitive people among the various tribes. It revealed all at once the entire color scale. To a character-forming people such as the Greeks,

328

it became an amiable girl, Iris, a bringer of peace, and generally speaking a messenger of the gods. To other tribes it was the impersonal sign of peace. The remaining color phenomena in the air were, in ancient times, less taken into consideration; the morning glow alone was personified as Eos or as Aurora, or among the Hindoos as the goddess of the dawn.

Though not much attention was paid to the colors *above* one, people made so much the more of colors *about* one, of dyeing materials which were found everywhere. The pleasing in colors, in that which is motlied, was immediately felt, and since finery is a necessity to man almost more than the actual needs of life, the application of color to the nude body or to clothing soon came into use. Fruit juice, blood, metallic oxide, decayed plants, the mud from the fords of large rivers, everything in fact that left spots, was material for coloring. Tattooing arose with the inunction of color. A color varied in value according to its permanency. The juice from the purple mussel grew into high repute. The art of dyeing could quickly be perfected, since mixing, rummaging, and dabbling has a great attraction for primitive beings. They made new tests as they went along. For a race of people as conservative as the Egyptians, Hindoos, and Chinese, who quickly approached a high degree of perfection in coloring, their technique became religion; they proceeded from a certain pious conception. More advanced peoples longed for a momentary influence; they wished to gain approval and earn money.

The oldest peoples were acquainted only with the practical side of colors. The study of the theory

began with the Greeks. Goethe has given a lucid
résumé of the various and variegated opinions that
have been handed down from the Hellenic thinkers,
from Pythagoras and his followers, who explained
the differences in colors from the different blending
of the elements. The colors of animals were supposed to be due to the food they ate. He sets forth
the views of Empedocles, Democritus, Epicurus,
Zeno, Plato and Aristotle. It is almost pathetic to
observe the thoughtfulness and zeal with which the
philosophers of antiquity, who lacked all the apparatus for scientific study known to modern times,
tried to explain to themselves and others the mystery
of the genesis of colors. Plato believed that a flame
emanated from every body and that its parts were
perceived in the sense of sight. The eye itself was
considered in *Timaeos* as a fire which causes the
light to flow forth from the eye as from a lamp.

Aristotle regarded this as wholly erroneous: the
eye is aqueous, not igneous; else why does it not see
in the dark. The eye is not, as Democritus believed,
reflected in objects; the objects, on the contrary, are
reflected in the polished surface of the eye. Otherwise the thing in which any object is reflected, water,
for example, would see just as well as the eye. But
the eye sees nothing. Light is, so to speak, the
color of that which is transparent. The presence
of something igneous in something transparent gives
light, the absence thereof darkness. In this way the
oldest thinkers groped about and felt their way
around looking for the solution of the enigma.

Goethe runs through all the Greek names for
colors in order to derive an idea as to how many
shades the Greeks knew and what impression they

made upon them. Then he goes on to the Romans
and gives, in good hexameters (most likely Knebel's), the section from Lucretius's *De rerum na-*
tura, in which the latter explains the origin of colors.
He denies that when something appears to us as
white that it is white in the material itself. He
holds that matter is colorless.

The individual who is blind from birth knows all
materials though he has never seen a color. Each
color easily changes before our eyes into another;
which is adequate proof that it is not a fundamental
element. If the waves of the ocean were in themselves dark, they would not whiten into foam; if
the throat of the dove had a different color in itself,
it would not, when looked upon in the sunshine as it
turns its neck, seem now red, now emerald green,
now cast a gleam like the blending of copper and
gold, called in ancient times *pyropus.*

Goethe interweaves at this juncture a hypothetical
history of colors in the works of the Greek painters.
Though sketched, it is to be presumed, by Heinrich
Meyer, Goethe himself placed his own construction
upon it in the essay, that immediately succeeded, and
which has to do with color and the treatment of
color in times long since passed. This essay emphasizes the fact that among the Greeks science was
an art; human powers and forces were in no way
excluded from their scientific activities. With their
abysmal presentiment, their keen and certain eye for
the present, their mathematical insight, their physical preciseness, lofty instinct, clear understanding,
agile imagination, amiable delight in the sensuous,
nothing was wanting to them. Goethe remarks in
this connection—he was rarely without his unpre-

meditated efforts in the realm of surprises—that
no race, perhaps, has ever possessed these elements
to such a degree as the German of his day. The
Germans lack, he avers, neither depth nor diligence.

Under the rubric of *Lücke*, Goethe next proceeds
to fill out the vacant space, the gap, between antiquity and such science as emerged with the coming
of Roger Bacon in the thirteenth century. His
observations, though general, are well reasoned.
He surveys the various authors from century to century; his knowledge is sound. In olden times, all
wrote in Mediæval Latin. Where Scaliger (1484-
1558) is referred to, Goethe expresses the opinion
that science would have gained much in freedom
and in gaiety had the plain, flexible Greek language
been used instead of the harsh and commanding
Latin. Paracelsus and the alchymists are treated
cursorily; Bacon of Verulam is discussed in detail
and comprehensively, but not with an excess of sympathy.

Goethe emphasizes the thoroughness and con-
scientiousness with which they proceeded, in the first
half of the sixteenth century, at the expense of the
impulse toward freedom with which individuals of
the second half of the century rebelled against au-
thority. Then came Lord Bacon. He wiped away,
as with a sponge, everything which up to that time
had been written on the tablets of humanity. Ga-
lileo, Kepler, Vossius and other scientists are discussed and compared with each other in this portrayal of science in the seventeenth century.

Goethe inserts at this juncture, with amusing ir-
regularity, a history of color in the pictorial art of
the Renaissance. He begins with Cimabue, discusses

the Florentines and Venetians, dwells on Masolino
and Massaccio, on Titian and Giorgione, characterizes briefly Leonardo, Raphael, Dürer, Holbein,
becomes enamored of Correggio, singles out Cara-
vaggio, displays a vigorous interest in Guido Reni,
passes over the French quite hurriedly, and ends by
stressing the services which Oeser, Raphael, Mengs
and Angelica Kauffmann rendered in Germany. Nor
does he omit Reynolds in England; nor David in
France, whom he holds up as the conqueror of
Boucher's "vapid, salacious mannerism." He also
expresses his opinion of Greuze's sentimentality.

Then we come to Isaac Newton, whom he compares to Tycho Brahe[7] as the one who misconceived
a basic principle and stubbornly asserted the accuracy of his mistaken ideas. He comments, of course,
on Newton's great powers. He was one of those
investigators who produce from themselves a complete world without taking the trouble to ascertain
whether it harmonises with the real world. In this
section, dedicated to Newton as a personality,
Goethe speaks still better of him. He calls him a
"systematic, sound, well-tempered man, devoid of
passion and knowing not envy." He admits that
Newton's mathematical talent lies beyond his own
horizon—which was indubitably a pity and the
source of very great and lasting harm.

[7] In a sense, Tycho Brahe (1546-1601) was the most famous
Dane that ever lived. He studied at Copenhagen, Leipzig and
Augsburg and became the most advanced astronomist of his time.
His protector, King Frederick II, fitted out an observatory for
him on the island of Hveen, now Swedish territory, in the Oere-
sund. When his patron died, in 1588, Tycho Brahe went to
Prague in response to a call from Emperor Rudolph II, where he
himself died. It was his teachings that enabled Kepler to build
up the Copernican system. Brahe himself regarded the Earth as
the centre of the cosmos.   —TRANSLATOR.

CHAPTER XXVII

Goethe and Voltaire

THE greatness of Voltaire's personality makes discussion of it at this point imperative. Goethe's opinion cannot be passed over in silence; nor can it be studied without interest.

In the superciliousness of youth, and with youth's lack of critical acumen, Goethe had held Voltaire up to ridicule. But so soon as he came to years of mental and spiritual maturity he translated a number of Voltaire's works, and in the notes to his translation of "Rameau's Nephew" he showered lavish praise upon his great predecessor in the world of letters. If this homage could not be sustained, it was due to a genuinely scientific reason.

While a fugitive in England, Voltaire had been initiated into the teachings of Newton; on his return to France he came out as Newton's enthusiastic apostle. Through the influence of "the divine Emilie" (the Marquise of Châtelet), Voltaire had kept up his studies in mathematics and physics. This had enabled him to explain Newton's theories to the French people, indeed to all Europe. In 1738 he had published at Amsterdam his book entitled *Elémens de la philosophie de Newton mis à la portée de tout le monde*. And in his letter to the Marquise he had made himself the special interpreter and

334

mouthpiece of Newton's teachings with regard to
color.

Il déploie à mes yeux par une main savante
De l'astre des saisons la robe étincelante.
L'émeraude, l'azur, le pourpre, le rubis
Sont l' immortel tissu dont brillent ses habits.
Chacun de ses rayons dans sa substance pure
Porte en soi les couleurs dont se peint la nature.
Et confondus ensemble, ils éclairent nos yeux.
Ils animent le monde, ils emplissent les cieux.

Goethe shows why Voltaire felt impelled to lay
before good society in France anything and everything that was calculated to entertain, instruct, ex-
cite—and shake it. Voltaire left nothing undone.
He portrayed feelings and tendencies, past and present, far and near, spiritual as well as natural phenomena. His talent and his genius were equally
great, and both made themselves felt, no matter
what form they assumed. He soon became the un-
disputed master of his race. Goethe was sincere
though somewhat misguided, when he found fault
with the method by which Voltaire had blindly
joined the school of Newton. There is point only
in the way he attacks the inadequate drawings with
which Voltaire had had his work illustrated.

The occasion arises, and calls for settlement at
this point, to draw a comparison between the two
great minds who, by virtue of their positions as in-
contestable centres of literary and intellectual life
in Europe, were destined to relieve each other.

Goethe and Voltaire resemble each other very
little in mental construction; they are akin in that
intensity and universality that gave them dominion

in the spiritual world. Voltaire covers an even
broader field than Goethe. Even granting that in
natural science he was merely a disseminator, and
not a creator, of ideas, he had after all a grounding
in mathematics which Goethe lacked. As a physicist, he was without Goethe's independence and yet,
in contrast to his gifted successor on the throne of
literature, he abounded in that hard, sound sense
which enabled him to grasp the fundamental meaning and value of Newton's investigations. Human
understanding was in fact in his case developed to
such a marked degree of clarity, conciseness, and
brilliancy that it became the exact equivalent of
genius.

In the writing of history he anticipated Goethe,
and was in general his superior. His *Histoire de
Charles XII* and his *Essais sur les Mœurs* were
both influential works.

If Goethe did not attain during his own life to
such world sway as did Voltaire, it was due solely
and exclusively to the language in which each wrote.
Voltaire took over a language which constituted
even then the court tongue of all Europe. It was
the language of diplomacy; it was the most adapta-
ble, flexible, and elegant of all; it was a language
created, as it were, for concealed thoughts and allu-
sions, alike adapted to derision and pathos, to the
obscuring or the revelation of ideas. He developed
it in verse, in the species of poetry of which he was
the complete master—the epigramme—and made
it the organ for the most subtle wit and brilliant
reasoning. This is best discerned in his *Poésies
fugitives*. And in prose, in which it already excelled,
he developed it in the direction of firmness, solid-

ity, force, and illuminating clarity. Voltaire never wrote a nerveless or marrowless paragraph.

Poet in the sense that Goethe was a poet Voltaire never succeeded in becoming. He was a dramatist who, like Euripides of old, made the tragedy the organ for new ideas. He was a pamphleteer who could arouse a whirlwind of laughter and was therefore to be feared. He was the author of short, philosophic novels that penetrated everywhere and won the minds of men through an appeal to reason. And he was, what Goethe never could be, a fighter. He was the champion of tolerance, the lover of freedom, the spokesman of justice. He made the mighty tremble through the power that lay in his pen.

Voltairean audacity was not in Goethe; he had his own brand; it was spiritual in both form and substance. In comparison with Goethe's pantheism, Voltaire's deism is local, limited and old-fashioned. Compare both of them to Spinoza and note Voltaire's inane condemnation of the great Jewish-Spanish-Dutch liberator as an atheist. Goethe, on the other hand, not merely understood Spinoza; he allowed himself to be filled with his spirit; and he wrote in his spirit.

With the exception of the epigramme and the satire, Goethe is far superior to Voltaire. That his German prose is inferior is quite easy to understand. The prose to which Goethe fell heir was not much more than the embryo of a real medium of written expression; it merely had in it the makings of a real prose; it was either *burschikos-sentimental* or it was stilted, wooden and affected, after the manner of eighteenth century style in Germany. In the

works of Wieland and Lessing it had only to receive
form in order to become French. Under the management of Goethe it became full and emotional,
rich in thought, but all too often formless and rick-
ety. As a great author, though not a great lyric
writer, Voltaire had said: "Every species is good
except the tiresome." German prose tended to become tiresome—even in Goethe's works.

Goethe was superior to Voltaire as a poet for
one reason that lay beyond the control of either:
Voltaire was all mind (in the sense of *esprit*); he
was a prodigious talent, a darting, unquenchable
flame. Goethe was all nature; he was an expression
of All-Nature's very being. Viewed from this angle,
his equal has possibly never lived on this earth.
Then there is another reason for Goethe's lyric emi-
nence: The German language, so long spurned and
maltreated, became, what the French had been for
ages, a world language. And happily enough, and
not without significance, this is one case where the
cause and the result were coeval and coöperative.

We are forced to concede one small personal superiority to Voltaire; his position in and attitude
toward the society of royalty was commendable.
From his very youth he had been wont to associate
with lords and ladies of high degree. Fully aware
of his intellectual endowments and acquirements,
he considered himself their equal. That gave his
position a saving grace. He moved about among
them with complete ease; he never appeared subservient other than in a purely formal way demanded by the etiquette of the age. It is true that
his letters to kings, empresses and other lofty personages rarely failed to flatter. But they flattered

him first. And his flattery is so elegant and witty
that to read it is a distinct pleasure. Think of his
numerous epistles to Frederick the Great! They
flatter, but back of them lie self-assertion and criticism, sharp, caustic and corrective.

Goethe, on the other hand, as the son of a middle
class father and the comrade of an unimportant
duke, had the German's innate respect for the social
hierarchy developed to such a high degree that it
gave him unequivocal pleasure to envelop himself
with all the formulæ of subserviency prescribed by
the court. His flattery is devoid of mental reserva-
tion or betrayal of his mental superiority. Without
moving an eyelash or permitting a smile, he can tell
how a certain Prince of Reuss with a number running up into the thirties had always been a gracious
lord. He can write about a Russian Grand Duchess,
something that Börne in his time abused him for:
"Her Royal Highness, the Grand Duchess, was so
benevolent as to grant me the gracious privilege of
inscribing some poetic lines in her elegant and magnificent album." In 1810 the young Italian-born
Empress, Maria Ludovica of Austria, came to Karlsbad. She treated Goethe decently, even kindly;
he raved about her, though she was quite tenuously
gifted. With German literature she had at most a
distant familiarity. Ludwig Geiger has shown how,
in 1809, she confused Schill (the courageous Prussian officer) with Schiller. Of the latter the extent
of her criticism was confined to the safe observation:
"He is known for his writings." And indeed the
only remark that she is known to have made concerning Goethe himself is the following in German
that puzzles and in orthography that needs repair:

*Der berühmte Verfasser machte darüber eine an-
spielende Poesi.*   But Goethe was all taken up with
her; she was an Empress, and she had paid him
some attention.

He sang of her arrival in Karlsbad, her chalice,
the position she occupied, her departure, and even
her non-committal consort in the following meek and
mirth-provoking stanza:

> Von seines Auges mildem Blick entbrennet
> Ein heilig Feuer, das uns nie entweicht;
> Und wie man erst des Sommers Kräfte kennet,
> Wenn sich im Herbst der Traube Fülle zeigt,
> So zeige sich, wenn er von uns getrennet
> Der Segen wirksam, den er uns gereicht,
> Und werde so, beim glücklichsten Ereignis
> Die kleine Stadt des grossen Reiches Gleichnis.

Karl August was awarded the title of Grand Duke
at the Congress of Vienna in 1815, though the girth
of his dominions was not noticeably increased.
Goethe immediately sent in his felicitations in the
following swollen words:

Ereignet sich's nun, dass Höchstdenenselben für so viel-
faches, redliches, inneres Bemühen auch von aussen ein
gebührendes Beiwort ertheilt wird, so benutzen wir es mit
Freude, wenn die Hof-und Kanzleisprache uns nunmehr
erlaubt, dasjenige als ein Anerkanntes auszusprechen, was
sonst bei aller Wahrheit als Schmeichelei hätte erscheinen
können.   Eurer Königliche Hoheit haben bisher den kleinen
Kreis bis ins Unendliche erweitert, indem Sie in einen jeden
einzelnen der Ihrigen ein gemässe Thätigkeit zu erregen
und zu begünstigen gewusst.   Möge Höchstdenenselben
eine lange Reihe von Jahren gegönnt sein, um in eimem aus-
gebreiterten Wirkungskreise eben diese Wohlthat fortzu-
setzen.

When we read this kind of verbiage we are inclined to allow Voltaire full indulgence for all the

frolicsome tricks he played against his contemporaries in Germany—those tricks which German snobbishness has found so irritating to its sensitive morals. Voltaire did not spare Maupertuis right before the eyes of his harsh benefactor, Frederick the Great. Nor did he forget Frederick himself.

It is sometimes a relief not to be weighed down with a huge amount of respect for those in momentary possession of great power. This has, however, nothing to do with the deeper ego of the two great men. If we would derive a sharp and definite idea of the contrast between the nature of Voltaire and that of Goethe, it is only necessary to study Goethe's poem entitled *Gross ist die Diana der Epheser*. It had been called forth by Fritz Jacobi's book entitled *Von den göttlichen Dingen und ihrer Offerbarung*. Remember how Voltaire reacted toward writers of this kind. And think what he would have done in this case. He would have approached it with the sharpest ridicule. He would have shown up the illogical phases of it. He would have appealed to reason. He would have demonstrated all that is contrary to reason in revelation as championed by Jacobi. He would have waged war high up in the air—where Kaulbach's "Battle of the Huns" is continued.

But Goethe—he never once appeals to *raisonnement;* he goes in for nature. He merely contrasts the cultivation of nature with mental chimeras. He portrays the goldsmith in Ephesus as he steadfastly works in his shop for the honor of the Ephesian Artemis, the goddess with the many breasts, the worthy symbol of nature. Even as a child the goldsmith had knelt at her throne and begun to mould

with religious zeal the girdle under her breasts which
is adorned with so many beasts of the field—the
stag and the hind and other wild animals. Suddenly he hears from the street that a god who dwells
in the brain back of man's stupid forehead is supposed to be far more powerful and far more worthy
of worship than the goddess who rules All-Nature.
He works along quietly. The relevant verses run
as follows:

> Als gäb's einen Gott so im Gehirn
> Da hinter des Menschen alberner Stirn,
> Der sei viel herrlicher als das Wesen,
> An den wir *die Breite der Gottheit* lesen.

> Der alte Künstler horcht nur auf,
> Lässt seinen Knaben auf den Markt den Lauf,
> Feilt immer fort an Hirschen and Thieren
> Die seiner Gottheit Kniee zieren,
> Und hofft, es könnte das Glück ihm walten
> Ihr Angesicht würdig zu gestalten.

That is Goethe's position expressed in a masterful simile. Where Voltaire, through the power of
his position and his pugnacious temperament, was
forced into incessant attack, either straight ahead
or by detour, upon the forces of the past which
limited his freedom and which he therefore wished
to destroy, Goethe moved along in calm and quiet.
He felt that the negative soon became antiquated.
Unperturbed as he always was, he influenced the
world about him in a positive way and because of
his persistence. Over against the so-called supernatural he set up his deeply emotional cultivation
and reproduction of nature. He made poetry out
of his harmony with and penetrating insight into
nature. Voltaire was all mind; Goethe was all nature.

CHAPTER XXVIII

GOETHE's LIFE: *Dichtung und Wahrheit*

IN 1808 Cotta brought out a new edition of
Goethe's collective works. He was enabled to survey his complete body of letters for the first time.
He had never wished to have his works published in chronological order. As he looked at
the new edition it occurred to him that they had
been published strictly in accord with his wishes.
There was no order. Fiction and criticism stood
out in wild topsy-turvydom. There were sections
and headings and rubrics, everything but clear arrangement. He saw what a disconcerting effect this
would have on the general public. He was seized
with a desire to relate those incidents of his life
which would clarify the genesis of his works and
put them in their proper light.

At first he hardly thought of more than a *bio-
graphia litteraria*. But the task grew as he worked
on it and thought about it. He saw that his explanation must be laid out on a broad basis if it was
to be at all satisfactory; that the places where the
events occur must be described; that the conditions
of the time must be visualized; that personal influences, historic relations and the state, or states, of
spiritual life accurately delineated. As a critic of
others he had seen how most historians make the
mistake of assuming too much on the part of their

readers. He himself had said in his review of
Johannes von Müller's biography that there was
one thing an autobiographer should never forget:
the younger generation for whom he writes has a
very flimsy idea concerning the period immediately
preceding, while posterity, for whom he none the
less writes, has an even flimsier. Nothing is to be
assumed; everything is to be related.

He had reproached this historian for his inept
modesty. Modesty, wrote Goethe, belongs where
one is personally concerned. It is clear that in good
society no one should be forward; each should seem
the peer of the other. But in the case of a free,
written production we demand truth. When a man
writes his autobiography, as did Müller, and is
wholly silent as to the great influence he had had
for a certain period of time, we understand neither
the slights that he suffers again and again, nor his
victory over the obstacles that were placed in his
way.

The word *Bescheidenheit* does not suit Goethe
very well, though it is better than such antinomic
expressions as vanity and arrogance. His strength
and his art lie in the fact that, though he always
explains himself in an indirect way, he is never concerned with himself, never broods over himself,
never makes a specialty of himself, but is made to
stand out before us as a living figure in the portrayal
of the cross-fire of impressions under which he
moves forward.

He soon came to feel the difficulty of self-por-
trayal, especially in the portrayal of others who,
for a hundred reasons, dared not be named (Lili
Schönemann, for example) or concerning whom it

was impossible for him to tell the entire truth (as in the case of Karl August and his Weimar contemporaries). He limited his portrayal therefore to the first twenty-five years of his life, discontinuing it at his call to Weimar. And even of these years he published only the first three parts in succession (1811, 1812, 1814) and let the fourth part, in which Lili, who was still living, simply could not be omitted, lie unpublished. It was not published until 1831.

The book is written with calm of mind; it is also artistic. There were famous and admired autobiographies previous to Goethe's. There was in olden times, that of St. Augustine, which is a confession, the story of a conversion. In more modern times there was Jean Jacques Rousseau's *Les Confessions*, unquestionably a presupposition for Goethe's. It is an apology; it is an unveiling; it is the autobiography of a self-righteous and self-admiring cynic. This is the way I was; this is the way I felt; all of these noble feelings I nourished; all of these detestable deeds I did; yes, that is how bad I was. But I dare anyone to step forward and say: "*I* was better." Rousseau is convinced that no man living can truthfully make this assertion. On this account and in advance he calls the reader a boaster and a liar who contends that he has lived a more beautiful or more worthy life. This impressed the populace, and evoked applause from the dismayed.

In Danish literature we have the autobiographies of two poets, Andersen and Oehlenschläger. Andersen called his book *Mit Livs Eventyr* (The Story of My Life). It tells how miraculously God has led him onward and upward from poverty and obscurity to a position in which he is the peer of the most prominent, the guest of princes and kings. It first shows us how superciliously he was treated and how slighted he was of men, and then how he was recognized and admired. Goethe does not regard himself as having been under the especial protection of the guardian angel of spiritual phenomena and prodigies; and his account breaks off before he had attained to any sort of external prominence.

Oehlenschläger's autobiography is a plebeian book. It contains a loquacious account of everything possible including quite a number of valuable anecdotes. But it is a book without plan, and alack and alas, it is a book without brains.

As all the world knows, the life of the great majority of more prominent individuals is either an incessant struggle or an early surrender. Life has made them either tread-mill slaves or prisoners who cannot extricate themselves from the fine meshes of the tenacious net in which they have become hopelessly entangled either by the power of external circumstances or as a result of their own actions in days that are no more. Having reached the years of complete maturity, we see them either renouncing the attempt to attain to anything like substantial fame, or they live in a delusion, perfectly transparent to others, that they have actually approached the pinnacles of distinction. Were the better of them to sit down and write the stories of their lives we would be regaled with an account of their struggles against unfavorable circumstances that lay beyond their immediate control, or against enemies and enviers and emulators. We would see their figures in the fray.

In Goethe's autobiography, we see his life lifted up above the life of others, and all the more easily, too, since he meets with no especial animosity or opposition. Men and things submit to him. A Frenchman has said: "There are very few human beings who control life in general and their own lives in particular." In his autobiography we see Goethe's personality borne along and aloft by a degree of self-control which even in the matter of passion never yields entirely and thereby proves its ability to control life in general as well as the lives of others.

What Goethe gives us in his *Dichtung und Wahrheit* are the points of departure for the history of the evolution of his personality. It is not a story of his struggles. Previous to his twenty-sixth year he had no opponents. He does mention, once in a while, some unimportant individual such as Nicolai, but Nicolai was never a considerable opponent. His world renown was so firmly established when he wrote the account of his life that he needed neither to refer to it nor to depend upon it. Nor does he say one single word about it. The book is merely an introduction to his growth, first as a mind and then as a poet.

Let us take two important poets who lived at the same time in Denmark: Ewald [8] and Wessel. They

[8] Johannes Ewald was a combination of Edgar Allen Poe, Theodor Körner and himself. The son a clergyman, he joined the Prussian army and then the Austrian and deserted from both. When fifteen he became engaged and when his fiancée married another man he sought relief in increased dissipation. The wonderful and miraculous were his chief attractions. Of his great genius there has never been the least doubt. His "Kong Christian stod ved höjen mast," translated by Longfellow. has become a national song of Denmark. —TRANSLATOR.

came to grief from self-stupefaction. Or take great
poets from the same time, or a little later, in Europe—Byron in England, Kleist in Germany, Alfred
de Musset in France. The one voluntarily wasted
his life, the other committed suicide, the third met
the fate of Ewald and Wessel. Remember too the
numerous individuals who stranded on the reef of
self-praise from Chateaubriand to many a modern
ass, and then we will feel the real significance of
the unique feature of Goethe's autobiography : he
merely wishes to portray his development.

Among the creative minds of more modern times
there is a type of artist who has succeeded completely in producing a small but monumental work
that will stand the test of ages. We have but to
think of Daniel Defoe's *Robinson Crusoe,* Abbé
Prévost's *Manon Lescaut,* Bernardin de Saint-
Pierre's *Paul et Virginie,* Adalbert von Chamisso's
Peter Schlemihl and H. C. Andersen's[9] *Eventyr for
Börn.*

Then there is another type of artist in the case
of whom everything depends upon the effect of his
works. In this class belong such pious painters as
Fiesole, who wish to arouse reverence, and such
impious writers as Diderot, who wish to make propaganda. To this group belong all moralising and
reformatory writers. They write with a purpose.
They wish to educate or to develop or to encourage.
Of this group the greatest example is unquestionably

[9] Brandes leaves an erroneous impression by his reference to a
"little" work in the case of H. C. Andersen. His "Fairy Tales
for Children" appeared in instalments. Taken collectively, they
constitute a considerable body of "immortal" literature. His
dramas and novels may be dead; but his tales for children are
still read, and to read them all takes time.   —TRANSLATOR.

Voltaire. (Throughout the entire body of his writings, historical, scientific and poetic, throughout his witty letters, his philosophic tales, his satirical verses, and his tragedies with their clandestine thrusts, there is the sole and incessant endeavor to reform, to persuade, to arouse, and to enlighten the mind of the reader. Voltaire's aim is to function as an innovator, a renovator, and a ventilator. For him the work that he writes is a means to this end.

The rarest and most refined type of artist after all is the one whose sole and fundamental aim is to develop himself. Leonardo da Vinci and Michael Angelo are conspicuous examples; but each of them was relatively unconscious in his striving, though by no means naïve. In this regard Goethe is the modern type, the prototype. He yearns least of all for full self-recognition or self-consciousness as an artist; though he is conscious of his restless self-development, he himself is the secret and the solution of his being. He had the same experience that other great artists of this type had: The passion with which they strove to approach an inner ideal made it difficult for them to leave finished works. Think of the hundreds of different tasks with which Leonardo struggled! How long he painted on his masterpiece *Mona Lisa!* How few finished paintings he left behind as monuments of this genius of his which never ceased trying! The same with Michael Angelo. How much he tried and how much he had to give up! What a number of statues he left half finished! They stand, half bound to the marble blocks, mute and yet eloquent witnesses to the fact that it is difficult for the master to give expression

to his soul as it grows richer day by day, to his
genius that is recharged without end. But even in
his case it is not so easy to detect the restless self-
development as it is in the case of Goethe.

This is owing to the fact that Goethe was the
first great poet and writer whose life lies so completely spread out before us that in every essential
point we can see the connection between his work
and his life, or more correctly speaking between
his work and his constantly shifting human nature.
Even his artistic or scientific works, otherwise of
less value, are interesting because of the insight they
give into the life of the soul of a very great man.

From the point of view of criticism in earlier
times, the history of literature connoted something
about books; it had to deal with books. The author
of these lines, however, has the weakness and the
strength to be more interested in the man than in
his book. He likes to look through the book into
the man back of it. If the man himself is meritor-
ious and deserving of respectful study, then even
one of his less important works is instructive, for
it reveals his personality. And it is, after all, the
personality that constitutes the really great work
of art.

Little Denmark has been relatively rich in renowned talents. Thorvaldsen [10] and Oehlenschlä-

---

[10] Brandes's attitude toward Thorvaldsen is that of all dependable critics of the present. Thorvaldsen was remarkably successful
in his imitation of the Pagan spirit. When he attempted to imitate and reproduce the modern spirit he failed, not entirely, but
partly. His statue of Lord Byron is a case in point. Originally
intended for Westminster Abbey, it was set up in the library of
Trinity College, Cambridge. The general public knows him probably best for his "Night" and "Morning," reliefs which he is said
to have modeled in one day.   —Translator.

ger [11] were both very great talents, though no one can truthfully call them great men. If we go through their art, and then on back to the men behind it, we meet in both cases wholesome, vivacious, richly endowed, dispassionate beings who never rise very high, who never go very deep, who never show that they have anything of the fountain-like in them; nor of the duplicate and reënforced foundation. And we return to their works, beautiful as the best of them are, and enrapturing as the effect of their individual creations may be.

When Goethe undertook to write his life, he found it ill advised and impossible to depend entirely on his memory. He had to proceed much as he proceeded when he wrote the lives of others, of Winckelmann and Hackert. He endeavored first of all to supply himself with material. An acquaintance of his in Frankfort, I. H. Schlosser (not to be confused with Goethe's brother-in-law, who died in 1799) gave him some information concerning his paternal city, and sent him books which he might need for the description of the Frankfort of his childhood. Fritz Jacobi and Knebel told him what

---

[11] Adam Gottlob Oehlenschläger (1779-1850) played a great rôle in the rejuvenation of Danish literature. Danish romanticism, if not modern Danish poetry, began with his *Guldhornene* ("The Golden Drinking Horns"), after which he wrote a long series of dramatic works. Influenced by Germany, he in turn had his influence on the romantic school in Germany. Aside from his poetization of Northern themes, he did much, in conjunction with Thorvaldsen, to revive the antique. His "Correggio" was written in German while he was in Rome. In his *Hrolf Krake* (1828) he has one character (Hjalte) represent Denmark, another (Bjarke) Norway, another (Vöggur) Sweden, and in this way he made a plea for an ideal Scandinavianism. His wide acquaintance with the literary men of his age in various parts of the world did much to make Denmark known abroad. Longfellow knew him quite well.   —TRANSLATOR.

they remembered. He went carefully through an entire series of volumes on the affairs of the Court at Wetzlar. He was forced to regret that he had destroyed some of his own private papers. His letters to his sister he had had sent back to him. He took it upon himself to leaf through old numbers of the *Göttinger gelehrte Anzeigen,* and of Nicolai's and Wieland's critical magazines, in order to visualize to himself the judgments that had been passed upon him by his contemporaries of the preceding generation. For the portrayal of his childhood and his early youth, Bettina had supplied him with everything she had learned from the stories told her by his mother. He made use of this material in an unconcerned fashion though various parts of it bear the stamp of her embellishing fancy. And in not a few instances he depended upon his memory which played him false in little things, a fact that called forth spiteful and foolish attacks.

The depiction of people and places is without exception happy. As is usually the case with Goethe, his women are more sharply conceived and better reproduced than his men, though several of his male portraits are unsurpassable. The description of the literary condition in Germany at that time is unquestionably beyond reproach so far as the Germans are concerned, but there is no picture of the spiritual physiognomy of Europe at the moment Goethe started; Germany's spiritual life at that time was not especially interesting.

In the composition we notice with displeasure the tendency mentioned above to draw parallels between situations that had actually been experienced and corresponding ones in books. We notice also the art, perfectly natural on the part of a dramatist and here carried out at great length, of preparing us for everything that is to follow, making the basis clear of that which is to be developed, and warning us of approaching events. We notice also another dramatic agency that is employed in Goethe's dramas, namely, the bringing on of personalities who are supposed to complete, to complement, each other (as Egmont and Oranien, Tasso, and Antonio). It is perfectly plain that Herder and Goethe, Lenz and Goethe, Merck and Goethe, Lavater and Basedow, are all meant as contrasts. And finally we notice that tendency which, as we have already seen, had become more and more pronounced in Goethe's art, to see and to hold fast to the typical. He portrays those parts of his life that the reader knows from his own life. He generalizes the particular incident so that it becomes doubly interesting. The individual event becomes a symbol.

CHAPTER XXIX

KARL AUGUST AND NAPOLEON: 1813

IN May, 1812, Napoleon stopped for some time in Dresden while on his way to Russia. Karl August had a conversation with him and deferentially advised him not to undertake the Russian campaign. Through his daughter-in-law, Maria Paulovna, he was closely related to the Russian imperial family. Napoleon paid no attention to his advice; he cherished, and not without cause, deep distrust for the Duke of Weimar.

Six years previous to this conversation Napoleon had imposed a tax of 2,200,000 francs on the little duchy as a condition of peace. It was done because Karl August had participated in the war. Moreover, the Duke in company with the other Ernestine dukes, had to place a regiment, *Herzöge von Sachsen,* at his disposal. This regiment took part in various campaigns, fought in Tirol and Spain and now had to prepare to fight against Russia. Up until November the regiment lay near the Baltic where it suffered so severely from the snow fields of Lithuania that the majority of the men died, or were taken prisoners.

On December 15, 1812, Napoleon came in all quietness through Weimar on his hurried sled trip. Formally, his standing at the court was the very best. He had even, in 1808, invited himself to be

its guest when he came from Erfurt. But he had,
as a result of the fact that some malicious remarks
on the part of Karl August had been brought to his
attention, made it incumbent upon Davoust to open
all letters to and from the ducal family.

Napoleon's distrust was so deep-seated that, when
an attempt was made on his life at Schönbrunn in
the fall of 1809 (by the young Friedrich Staps), he
held fast to the belief that Karl August was the
instigator.

Nothing however was farther from Napoleon's
mind than unreservedly to reveal this distrust. For
that he was far too completely in control of himself.
He felt and knew that the prudent thing to do was
to show all manner of attention to the members of
the *Rheinbund* regardless as to whether they were
more or less hostile to him or whether their country
was great or small. He received Karl August's
second son, Bernhard, in Paris. He appreciated the
young man's bravery. After the battle of Wagram
in 1809 he personally decorated the seventeen-year-
old son with the star of the Legion of Honor, and
though his parents prevented his participation in
the Russian campaign by sending him on a compara-
tively long journey to the South, Napoleon was all
amiability toward him. The Prince remained in
Paris for four months.

But in the spring of 1813 the war broke out anew.
The King of Prussia instituted his defection and the
Prussian people rose up against foreign dominion.
Karl August's heart was with Prussia, but as one
of Napoleon's least powerful vassals, he pretended,
under duress, the greatest sort of affection for the
Emperor. The first request that the French Am-

bassador, St. Aignan (March 14, 1813) made on
the Saxon courts was that they should re-equip their
military contingent, the former having been destroyed in Lithuania.   One is amazed, at the present,
at their lack of strength.   The combined forces of
the Saxon courts amounted to 800 men.   Weimar
had almost no officers.   On March 30, 376 men
marched out from Weimar under the leadership of
a certain Major von Lyncker toward the Thuringian
Forest.   Of these 200 were recruits; they remained
at Berka by the Ilm; the others were led to Ruhla
near Eisenach.   On April 3 the forces of Sachse-
Gotha-Altenburg, Sachse-Meiningen, and Sachse-
Hildburghausen joined the forces from Weimar and
formed *one battallion* the companies of which were
distributed among three small towns.   Only ten days
later about fifty Prussian Husars and cavalrymen
pressed forward to Ruhla.   They captured the entire battalion without resistance and led them to
Blücher's headquarters where they voluntarily became incorporated in the Prussian army.

Nothing more painful could have befallen Karl
August in his relation to Napoleon, who already
distrusted him.   His position became even more
difficult when the rumor (a baseless one) found
credence that a company of Cossacks who had put
some exhausted French soldiers to flight were in
actuality disguised students from Jena.

And we must add that Karl August's own vacil-
lating rashness made his situation still worse.
When a squadron of Prussian Husars under Major
Blücher, the son of the general, entered Weimar,
the Duke invited the Major to dine with him.   During the dinner the report was brought in that a very

considerable number of French soldiers were marching against Weimar. Blücher was obliged to rise
from the Duke's table in order to oppose the latter's allies. On that same evening the French General Souham entered Weimar, and now it was *his*
troops who were to be billeted on the town and
looked after generally. The Duke's confidential
agent on this, as on many other occasions during
these years, was the resolute and shrewd Privy
Councillor, later Chancellor, Friedrich von Müller.
But he had been so imprudent as to decipher a code
to two Weimar officials who, in a letter which the
French outposts intercepted and read to the Commandant of the place, had said that the French
were the pest, the Prussians were the physicians.
The French general became enraged and the entire
ducal family came within a hair of being made prisoners. The two officials just barely escaped being
shot down as traitors. As the result of a great deal
of trouble and not a little boldness, von Müller
succeeded in a personal conversation with Napoleon
in appeasing his resentment. During an audience,
however, Napoleon called the Duke his unquestioned
foe and characterized him as being "the most restless Prince in Europe" (*le prince le plus remuant
de l'Europe*) who never tired of spinning and weaving intrigues against him. The seditious speeches
which the professors in Jena delivered to their students were moreover made known to Napoleon, so
that he threatened to burn Jena that same evening.
Von Müller directed his thoughts into other chan-
nels by showing the Emperor that he was running a
great risk of forever blurring the fame that was
immortal because of his conduct at the battle of

Jena in case he now committed such a gruesome act against the town.

When Karl August came to Erfurt the next morning to pay his respects to Napoleon he was by no means received in an unfriendly way; the Emperor assured him that when he came to Weimar he would pay the Duchess a visit. He did so the next day, April 28. When he arrived at the castle he paid, according to an eye-witness, the young Eduard Genast, not the slightest bit of attention to Karl August, who stood at the foot of the stairs, but went straight to the rooms of the Duchess. When she begged him to show mercy to the two officials on whom the death sentence had been pronounced, he made the prompt reply: *Je le vieux bien, et je suis charmé de pouvoir faire une chose qui Vous soit agréable, Madame!* When he left, Karl August and his son accompanied him on horse. During the ride the Emperor again noticed him and talked with him and his escort cordially and at great length.

But the very next day Napoleon made Karl August feel his hard hand, as is evident from the beginning of the following letter from the Duke to his near friend, King Friedrich August of Saxony:

The Emperor and King seemed to be in some doubt as to the feelings that Your Majesty cherishes toward him and expressed the wish, that Your Majesty would declare himself openly; His Majesty *commanded* me to repeat his very words to you: The King of Saxony must come out frankly and say whether he is for me or against me. He cannot complain of my conduct toward him; I have done everything for him. But his action at Torgau was equivocal.

The King of Saxony sent Napoleon an humble communication, and all the more promptly since he had learned of Napoleon's victory at Gross-Görschen. The French again had the largest part of Saxony in their possession, and on his arrival in Dresden Friedrich August found that also there it was French troops who formed the espalier along his route.

After his victory at Bautzen, Napoleon made severe demands, in Dresden, on Karl August. In the place of the contingent that the Prussians had captured, he was naturally supposed to form a new one. But this was a small matter in comparison with the burdens imposed upon him by the support of the Napoleonic army that was marching through Weimar and his obligation to improve the fortress at Erfurt (aside from supplying it with provisions). For three months in succession little Sachse-Weimar (with 120,000 inhabitants) had to feed 600,000 men and an unknown number of horses.

To all of this must be added the difficulties placed in Karl August's way by the Lützow *Freikorps* and the swarm of Cossacks when they attacked French troops on Weimar territory. Napoleon believed (or acted as though he believed) that the Duke was an accomplice and made him responsible for any injury his soldiers suffered within the confines of Weimar. The Duke was obliged to humble himself in order, if possible, to ward off anger. Read this congratulatory communication to the man he hated, after the battle at Bautzen:

Since my very ardent prayers (*mes voeux fervents*) for the success of Your Majesty have been heard, I praise divine mercy therefor and lay my most submissive congratultaions. Sir, at your feet. Would that Your Imperial and Royal Majesty would condescend to accept the expression of mv

profound submission (*les èmanations d'une profonde sou-
mission*) and of the affection I have consecrated to Your
Majesty.

In the course of only three weeks (March 27—
April 19) Sachse-Weimar, aside from feeding the
army as usual in the four different stations at Eisenach, Weimar, Buttelstedt, and Jena, was supposed
to supply Erfurt with 200,000 pounds of meat, 100,-
000 rations of biscuit bread (*pain biscuité*), 100,000
rations of ordinary biscuits, 10,000 hundredweight
of meal, 200,000 bushels of oats. Concerning the
last item, it was as a matter of fact impossible to
scrape up more than 11,000 bushels in the entire
country. For the building of the fortress at Erfurt,
they were supposed to supply at the same time,
15,341 logs, and 153 wagons and 1940 redoubt
workers per day.

During all this misery, the idea ripened in Karl
August's brain of appealing to Napoleon to promote
him from Duke to Grand Duke in compensation foɪ
this socage, since a few strips of land had been
added to Weimar, including Blankenhagen in the
domain of Erfurt and some other Erfurt enclaves.
Every morning while in Dresden Karl August put
in his appearance at Napoleon's levees in order to
state his wish and to make it clear to the Emperor
that he would be in a better position with this higher
rank to give satisfaction as the middle-point in Thur-
ingia which the French army then needed, and so
on. Napoleon merely replied: *On ne m'avait pas
dit que vous désirez cela,* which was neither "yes"
nor "no," and therefore equivalent to "no."

In the meantime Karl August amused himself as
a genuine child of the eighteenth century splendidly

in Dresden, then a sort of Paris and in which a quite diversified worldly life had been developed. From there he went to Teplitz where he took his usual cure and where he met not simply Goethe but also many members of the Austrian peerage and his son, the crown prince, as well as his daughter-in-law, Maria Paulovna. The new battalion that the French government had requested had in the meantime been raised. Berthier had given the suggestion: *L'Empereur ne connaît d'autre attachement que de se prêter à ses volontés.*

"Our contingent," writes the Weimarian Minister von Fritsch, August 3, is *au grand complet, i.e.,* 800 men have been raised; a commander, an adjutant and 8 officers have charge, and the most of the soldiers can march moderately well. Under fire, however these heroes might become more dangerous for their neighbors and officers than for the enemy." The fact is they could not shoot.

For Karl August however the all-important question was the securing of the title of Grand Duke. He had a petition drawn up in which it was said that the House of Weimar, which had once been so brilliant, had lost little by little in the course of centuries, until it had sunk below other royal houses above which it formerly towered. To Napoleon he addressed these pathetic words:

Would that it might correspond at once to His Majesty's magnanimity and political interests to restore the ancient splendor to a princely house which deserves a place alongside of the house of the Medicis in that it has made liberal use of all the means in its power to beautify art and benefit literature, while it has at the same time favored science by making itself a place of refuge for the illustrious men of the nation.

Should this idea succeed in arousing His Majesty's interest, and should His Majesty have the good grace to accord the idea a place in the extended series of great questions that are now concerning him in this period of reconstruction, His Majesty would soon be convinced that among all of his allies there is none that is more zealous, more grateful, more loyal than the house of Weimar which boasts, incidentally, of having furnished French history with some famous heroes. (The reference is probably to Bernhard von Sachse-Weimar. It could hardly refer to Moritz von Sachsen, since he did not descend from the house of Weimar.)

By reason of the special hope that this petition would be granted, a hope based on the near kinship to the Russian Court, it was a question of interesting Russian in the dynasty of Weimar; Maria Paulovna was appointed to win over the Zar, her brother, to the project. Young and sprightly though she was, she did not appeal to the ambitious ruler as being sufficiently energetic.

Karl August went to Ilmenau where he unexpectedly met Goethe, who had likewise been highly invigorated by his stay at the watering place. On the very next day, he went on a four-hour ride with his Duke.

On July 13, Karl August had written from Teplitz to Voigt: "Goethe is as if new-born." The festivities for Napoleon's day (August 15) had been held in Dresden on August 10. Goethe had come to Dresden in order to be present. The city was illuminated. He walked about in the crowded streets for several hours, and as the letters from that period show, spent the rest of his time in the art galleries. On August 11, he climbed up the two hundred and thirty steps of the tower of the Church of Our Lady in order to see the sunset. His birthday was cele-

brated in Ilmenau. In a letter to Christiane he
described the homage that was done him, including
the concert given late in the evening in the open air.
This was the contribution of the town council. On
the following evening there was a ball. Goethe
returned to Weimar on September 2.

Karl August was, to be sure, disheartened by
Napoleon's victory at Dresden, assured though he
was as to the eventual outcome of the war since the
allies were overcoming the French generals one by
one. At the same time he invited the Commandant
of Weimar, Colonel Seguy, to his Court, and accorded the French officers who chanced to be passing
through the town the most cordial reception.

On October 10 the Austrian army marched into
Weimar and it was even better received. Karl
August wrote to the Zar and asked him for 2000
cossacks for his protection in case Napoleon should
elect to march from Saxony through Weimar. But
on the night following October 21 a colonel of the
cossacks had Karl August called from his bed in
order to tell him of the decisive victory that the
battle of Leipzig had brought the Allies. At first
the Duke was unwilling to believe the Colonel since
he had no written evidence of the victory; he distrusted him and believed that he was really in the
service of the French and had come to take him
away as a hostage. Karl August was, however, soon
enlightened as to the true state of affairs and French
troops in the immediate vicinity of Weimar, near
Ettersburg, were defeated in an engagement by
Russian and Prussian cavalry.

On October 24 Emperor Alexander, his brother,
Konstantin, and their escort of diplomats and gener-

als, arrived at the castle in Weimar; and on the next day Emperor Franz of Austria came. The little castle could hardly contain all the lofty lords. Karl August began again to use all his energy to obtain the promotion he so passionately longed for. Maria Paulovna was again made an especial agent; a petition was again sent in, this time to Emperor Alexander who, however, was unwilling to make any definite promise. The troops of the Allies poured into the town in masses. The victors were hungry; there was an incalculable amount of plundering in Eisenach and other places. Goethe's assurance that his fate was highly to be praised in comparison with that of many others rested on the fact that he escaped being plundered, though he had a great deal to suffer from the many high and exacting Austrian officers. With Count Colleredo-Mansfeld at their head, they lived for three days in his house. According to his diary his house had to be *cleaned* on October 26.

The distress of the civilian population increased. Contagious diseases, especially typhoid, spread. The Duke was in extreme financial embarrassment which had to be met by a loan. He entered into an agreement with the allied forces, placed a few thousand men at the disposal of their army, took over the command of the third German army corps, and united with its leaders in forcing the French out of Belgium. From here he went to conquered Paris and took the cure on the way home at a bathing resort in Aix-la-Chapelle. In Paris he urgently requested Alexander to confer upon him the title of Grand Duke. The latter referred him, however, to the Congress in Vienna then about to take place.

'I he Duke went to Vienna in person and spared no pains to secure the title so ardently longed for and the slight increase in territory corresponding thereto. He succeeded.

CHAPTER XXX

GOETHE AND THE ORIENT; *West-Oestlicher Divan;* MARIANNE VON WILLEMER

ON December 1, Goethe wrote to Sara von Grotthuss: "Everything again echoes with want and misery." A few days later he complains to Knebel over the fact that "accounts come to us from all sides concerning the death of excellent people." It was typhoid infection making its way into the towns and villages that lay next to the roads along which the armies had marched.

Goethe had just then finished the three parts of *Dichtung und Wahrheit* referred to above. The passionately enthusiastic rise of Young Germany against Napoleon, brought on by defection, did not move him; it did not inspire him to song. He said time and time again:

Is it in accordance with my nature to write war songs while sitting in my room? Out near the watch fires where at night the horses of the enemy's outposts are heard neighing, I could feel a certain desire to do just that sort of thing. That, however, was not my life and my affair but the life and the affair of Theodor Körner. His war songs clothe him excellently. War songs would have been to my unwarlike nature and unwarlike mind a mask ill-fitted to my face. I have never been affected in my poetry.

He experienced, after the manner of strong minds, a deep inclination to keep himself and his

ideas untouched by the surf which was dashing up
around him; he had to bury himself in something
with which none of the people about him were occupied, but which could captivate, develop, and en-
rich him himself. And so, in 1813, he plunged into
Oriental poetry. Even in early youth Goethe had
felt attracted by it. He had read the Old Testament time and time again with as much critical acumen as he could then command, at any rate with independent conception. He understood Hebrew. As
late as 1797, midway between *Hermann und Dorothea* and *Faust,* he had written a treatise, *Israel in
der Wüste,* which betrays much thoughtfulness.

Through Herder he had already come into contact with Asiatic poetry, and had long known something about Hafis. But in 1813 the Orientalist
Hammer, from whom Herder expected most, had
published a translation of Hafis's *Divan* in two
stately volumes. It was Hammer who initiated
Goethe into the study of the nature of Western
Asia. Though he taught himself Arabic and a little
Persian, he did not in any way come in touch with
the richer poetry of India. It was Hafis first and
foremost who enraptured him.

He zealously rejects the mystic interpretation of
Hafis's poems:

> Sie haben Dich, heiliger Hafis,
> Die mystische Zunge genannt
> Und haben, die Wortgelehrten,
> Den Werth des Worts nicht gekannt.
>
> Mystisch heissest du ihnen,
> Weil sie Närrisches bei Dir denken
> Und ihren unlautern Wein
> In Deinem Namen verschenken.

The translation he had in mind could not compete with the later, and excellent, one by Daumer through which Hafis became so dear to the readers of the next generation. But his penetration into the spirit of Hafis was adequate. He soon came to feel perfectly at home in the wealth of Persian poetic art, due, no doubt, to the fact that he saw historical resemblances between his own age and that of Hafis. As Hafis had poetized his joy in existence, his delight in life, at a time when Timur-i-Leng inspired peace-loving and peaceful people with fear by his campaigns of conquest, so he himself was living in an age of revolution in which a powerful conqueror had burst old political bonds and welded new ones which in turn were being rent asunder.

After the battle of Leipzig Goethe found a genuine fountain of youth for his lyric genius in the poetry of the Orient. He was the first to introduce it into German literature. These studies were, to be sure, interrupted by the necessity of glorifying contemporary events pleasing to Weimar in theatrical performances, festival plays and topical poems. This occupied his time and used up his energy at the beginning of 1814. But in July of that year he went to Wiesbaden, and Frankfort, in order to live for himself and compose for his personal enjoyment. Only a few individual poems from the lyric masterpiece of later years, the *West-Oestlicher Divan,* were written down when, in the fall of 1814, he received, through his acquaintance with Marianne Willemer, the decisive impulse to complete his work.

Willemer, an active and well-to-do citizen of Frankfort, had for many years stood in a friendly relation to Goethe. He had, as a young banker, in 1788, supplied Merck with a loan of four thousand gulden for the payment of which Karl August went security. This was done at Goethe's request. When Christiane Vulpius came to Frankfort in 1797, and 1806, to straighten out the affairs of Goethe's mother, Willemer was, on both occasions, one of the few who were really attentive and helpful to her. He was a forceful writer on Enlightenment and popular deistic philosophy. He wrote several weak dramas, occupied himself a great deal, as an admirer of Pestalozzi, with the problems of education, and eventually became one of Börne's collaborators on *Die Wage*. He was highly respected as a business man and as a Frankfort senator; and he took part for a time in the management of the theatre. The Prussian government granted him the title of *Geheimrat;* the Austrian government honored him with a diploma of nobility. He had been twice married and had three daughters and one son. In 1797, when but thirty-six years old, he became a widower for the second time. His oldest daughter, Rosette, was married in 1799 to the distinguished patron of art, Johann Städel.

Marianne Jung was born at Linz in Austria, 1784. In the fall of 1798 she came with her mother to the theatre at Frankfort. She became a member of the ballet when only fourteen years of age. In the rôle of a little harlequin who crept out of an egg she enchanted Clemens Brentano who memorialized her in his portrayal of the young dancer, Biondinetta, in his *Romanzen vom Rosenkranz*. Her talent for singing and acting awakened attention, her amiability won her friends. Among her ad-

mirers was Willemer who, as a member of the theatre boards, became acquainted with her and thought
of adopting her, charming child that she was.

First, however, he wanted to find out whether
she had a good heart. He disguised himself as a
peddler, took a large piece of satin with him, and
offered his wares at the house where Marianne lived
with her mother. When the women wouldn't buy,
he began to weep and related a heart-rending story
of the misfortunes that had reduced him to poverty.
Thereupon both mother and daughter began to weep
too; they bought the satin. Not long afterward,
Willemer, who had repaid the mother all the income she had received from her daughter's talent,
took the sixteen-year-old girl one evening after the
performance to his home, had her reared with his
own daughters, and gave her a thorough musical
education.

From a poem which Clemens Brentano, in 1803,
addressed to Marianne one can see that he was at
the time very much taken up with her. He taught
her to play the guitar and one day when she struck
a wrong note, he told her in his forcible and bitter
way that her position in Willemer's house was a
false one, whereupon she burst into tears. Willemer
fell into a rage over Brentano's remark and called
him a snake whom he had warmed at his bosom.
The following Christmas he had himself, among
other gifts, packed in a chest and dumped at Marianne's feet. There was as yet no mention made of
marriage.

The living of the beautiful young singer at the
home of a widower naturally afforded opportunity
for all manner of derogatory comment; but Mari-

anne was otherwise received on the best of terms in
the entire Willemer circle. She was the favorite
of the Bethmanns, appreciated by the young geogra-
pher, Carl Ritter, and associated constantly with
Bettina Brentano and the latter's sisters. When
Willemer, in 1810, started on a trip to Switzerland
and Italy he took Marianne and his daughters along
with him.

The German authors who have written on Marianne von Willemer, such as Th. Creizenach and
Hermann Hüffer, have proved in zealous German
fashion how unthinkable it is that there existed any
intimate relationship whatsoever between Marianne
and Willemer before marriage. Individual expressions by Goethe sound otherwise. After an absence
of seventeen years, Goethe came to Frankfort, July,
1814, travelled from there to Wiesbaden where he
remained a month, was the guest of the Brentano
family for the first week in September, stopped again
in Frankfort at the home of old friends for two
weeks, from where he went on September 24 to
Sulpiz Boisserée in Heidelberg. Three days after
his departure the fifty-year-old Willemer entered
into marriage with the now twenty-nine-year-old
Marianne. It is not improbable that Goethe en-
couraged him in this action; the position of Marianne had become more exposed since the daughters
had married and left home, and Goethe uses the
following strong expression about the marriage:
Rettung der jungen Frau and calls it *eine grosse
sittliche That Willemers*. His attitude toward the
newly married couple was most cordial. In October,
1814, after his return from Heidelberg, he was
often at the beautiful villa of the Willemers, *Die*

Gerbermühle, near Frankfort. He won the hearts
of the daughters of the house by his amiability and
susceptibility to impressions. We have indisputable
proof of this in the enthusiastic portrayal of his
personality from the pen of the oldest daughter,
Rosette Städel.

In Frankfort nothing at all was done in honor
of Goethe. In order to punish, in a jesting way, his
former colleagues in the management of the theatre for their indifference, Willemer inserted in a
suburban newspaper a description of an elaborate
Goethe celebration in the theatre. He spoke of a
decorated box, prologue, gala performance of *Tasso*
and crowning of Goethe on the stage with wreaths
from the busts of Vergil and Ariosto. The description was in truth copied by numerous German papers, later recopied from them, and incorporated in
some of the older Goethe biographies.

The poet's relation to Marianne took on a new
and more cordial character in 1815. After a prolonged sojourn in Wiesbaden he came, on August
12, to Frankfort and immediately went out to *Die
Gerbermühle* where he lived until September 8. The
character of the intimacy between the man of sixty-
six years and the woman of thirty grew to be fine,
rich, and warm. She had already written some
verses, including a number of poems on current topics. Now, in the course of a few weeks, she developed into a real poetess. Indeed the few verses
she addressed to Goethe during this brief period
are of so great value that it is not excessive praise
to refer to her as the most gifted poetess Germany
or Austria has produced.

Of evenings Goethe would read aloud from his poems, or Marianne would sing his songs as they had been set to music: *Kennst du das Land,* and *Der Gott und die Bajadere.* According to Goethe's own statement she sang the latter "as beautifully and feelingly as it can be sung," though he did not like to hear it from her lips: He fancied, as he remarked to Sulpiz Boissérée, that this legend of a dancing girl who is elevated to a lofty existence, through love to be sure and yet in a most painful way, would affect her too strongly, and remind her too much of her own lot. The assertion is adequate proof that Marianne's own life, in her younger days, on the stage and in the home, was exposed to unenviable temptations.

One evening Goethe read aloud a series of new love poems; Willemer fell asleep; his young wife, who was listening, placed a yellow, turban-like scarf over her head. In this way she entered into the spirit of the rôle of Hatem's Oriental friend. There follow a multitude of half modern, half Oriental poems of the highest rank from him to her and her to him. On the longest day of the year he had addressed the poem to her beginning *Süsses Kind, die Perlenreihen,* which was not published until 1837. The hatred of the cross to which it stands a witness induced him to postpone its publication. She wore a cross on a pearl necklace; as a Mohammedan he is passionately vexed thereby:

> Diese ganz moderne Narrheit,
> Magst du mir nach Schiras bringen!
> Soll ich wohl, in seiner Starrheit,
> Hölzchen quer auf Hölzchen singen?

He compares her with King Solomon's many wives
each of whom tried to convert him to her idol:

> Isis' Horn, Anubis' Rachen
> Boten sie dem Judenstolze—
> Mir willst du zum Gotte machen
> Solch ein Jammerbild am Holze!

But he closes with the declaration that he will not
seem more cantankerous than Solomon. Even the
Mexican idol, Vitzliputzli, would become a talisman
for him if worn on her heart.

The first poem that Goethe now directs to Marianne is the one that begins: *Nicht Gelegenheit macht
Diebe, sie ist selbst der grösste Dieb,* and which
closes with the remark that he detects mercy in her
shining eye, and in her arms rejoices over the happiness of renewed youth. It is in this poem that he
says he is impoverished. She replies with the poem
Hochbeglükt in deiner Liebe in which we have the
following: "Don't jest in that way! Don't talk
about poverty! Does not love make us rich? When
I hold you in my arms no one's happiness is greater
than mine."

The poems containing Suleika's question and Hatem's answer concerning the ring which he gave her,
but which slipped from her finger in a dream and
fell into the Euphrates, is the next poem which
Goethe produced during his sojourn at Marianne's
home and revolves in all probability around a question she really put to him, for the poem closes with
these words:

> Also träumt'ich. Morgenröthe
> Blitzt ins Auge durch den Baum.
> Sag' Poete, sag' Prophete!
> Was bedeutet dieser Traum?

The expression *sag' Prophete* is evidently intended for *sag' Goethe!* The answer reminds Suleika of how the Doge of Venice became espoused to the Adriatic, and closes with the assurance that Suleika has espoused Hatem to her river, her terrace, her grove, and that here his mind shall be consecrated to her until the very last kiss.

On the same day that Goethe left Marianne's home and came to Heidelberg, he wrote to her the beautiful, unrhymed, dithyrambic poem, *Die Schön umschriebenen,* and so on. He admits that he praises himself for the love and happiness he owes her, for this self-praise is a stench only to the jealous; to friends it is a rich perfume. She overwhelms him with happiness when she throws her passion to him as she would throw a ball so that he can catch it and throw her his ego in return. He sends her poetic pearls which her passion's powerful surf washed up on the shore for him who stood on life's desolate strand. With it she adorns her neck, her bosom!

A few days later, during Goethe's stay in Heidelberg, where Marianne and Willemer were to meet him, she composed the exquisite song of longing entitled, *Was bedeutet die Bewegung?* Goethe incorporated it in his *Divan* with just a few, negligible, and in part not even felicitous textual emendations: "What does the motion mean? Does the east wind bring me glad tidings? The fresh fluttering of its wings cools the heart's deep wounds. It plays caressingly with the dust and whirls it up into light clouds, and so on, but its gentle whisperings brings delightful greetings to me from my friend. Even before these hills grow dark I shall be sitting quietly at his feet. Let the east wind continue on its course; may it serve happy men and sorrowful; here, where the high walls glow, it finds the one so much in love:

Ach, die wahre Herzenskunde,
Liebeshauch, erfrischtes Leben
Wird mir nur aus seinem Munde,
Kann mir nur sein Atem geben.

The changes Goethe made are slight indeed. Among them there is one improvement: *Bringt der Ost mir frohe Kunde* in the place of *Bringt der Ostwind*. He has also made two other changes which only tend to lessen the value of the original: *Diene Freunden und Betrübten* in the place of *Diene Frohen und Betrübten*. And he felt called to make the following changes in Marianne's stanza:

Marianne
Und mich soll sein leises Flüstern
Von dem Freunde lieblich grüssen;
Eh' noch diese Hügel düstern,
Sitz' ich still zu seinen Füssen.

Goethe
Und mir bringt sein leises Flüstern,
Von dem Freunde tausend Grüsse;
Eh' noch diese Hügel düstern,
Grüssen mich wohl tausend Küsse.

Marianne's rhyme is better, just as the picture she sets forth is more beautiful. The song as a whole is an imperishable masterpiece.

The following morning and evening Goethe wrote, in Heidelberg, two of his most excellent poems to Marianne. The first is the chestnut poem, moulded with noble simplicity about a single visualization. The introductory stanzas depict the leafy chestnut tree with the prickly green fruits cradled on the swinging boughs. The last show how the brown kernels ripen in the shell until it bursts:

> Doch immer reift von innen
> Und schwillt der braune Kern.
> Er möchte Luft gewinnen
> Und säh' die Sonne gern.
>
> Die Schale platzt, und nieder
> Macht er sich freudig los;
> So fallen meine Lieder
> Gehäuft in deinen Schoos.

The diction has at once the extreme facility of the folk song and the refined verbal conciseness and simplicity of the classical song. On the very same day he wrote this poem which differs completely in style and content:

> Ist es möglich! Stern der Sterne,
> Drück ich wieder Dich ans Herz!
> Ach was ist die Nacht der Ferne
> Für ein Abgrund, für ein Schmerz!

The poem, grand in its porportions, unfolds with massive splendor from this fundamental feeling of the unnatural anguish of separation. In order to explain it, an entire theory of world creation is portrayed; we see disunion, dissolution, and distance arise in accordance with God's plan; we perceive the importance of love is everything. There is a wonderful Michel Angelo-like grandeur in this stanza:

> Als die Welt im tiesften Grunde
> Lag an Gottes ew'ger Brust,
> Ordnet er die erste Stunde
> Mit erhabner Schöpfungslust.

Und er sprach das Wort: Es werde!
Da erklang ein schmerzlich Ach!
Als das All mit Machtgebärde
In die Wirklichkeiten brach.

It sounds like an interpretation of a painting in the Sistine Chapel on the creation of the world.

Everything was silent, everything was gray in gray; then God created the dawn, which unfolded from the darkness a harmonious play of colors, and all things that at first stood apart from each other, now sought each other in mutual attraction:

Sei's Ergreifen, sei es Raffen,
Wenn es nur sich fasst und hält!
Allah braucht nicht mehr zu schaffen,
Wir erschaffen seine Welt.

There is in these lines a genuinely creative heat, the tremendous power of the all-embrace.

From these Heidelberg days there is furthermore the antiphonal song between Hatem and Suleika, beginning

Locken, haltet mich gefangen!

It is dedicated to the beautiful brown serpents entwined about her head. In this he stresses the glowing youth of his heart despite his gray hair. It reads:

Nur dies Herz, es ist von Dauer,
Schwillt in jugendlichstem Flor;
Unter Schnee und Nebelschauer
Rast ein Aetna Dir hervor.

That the poem is purely European and, despite its Oriental dress, entirely personal in its conception

and content, is revealed by the fact that the word
Hatem is inserted instead of Goethe which would
rhyme perfectly in this stanza:

> Du beschämst wie Morgenröthe
> Jener Gipfel ernste Wand,
> Und noch einmal fühlet *Hatem*
> Frühlingshauch und Sonnenbrand.

The following beautiful poem in reply is by Marianne and not by Goethe:

> Nimmer will ich Dich verlieren!
> Liebe giebt der Liebe Kraft.
> Magst Du meine Jugend zieren
> Mit gewalt'ger Leidenschaft.
> Ach, wie schmeichelt's meinem Triebe,
> Wenn man meinen Dichter preist!
> Denn das Leben ist die Liebe,
> Und des Lebens Leben Geist.

It is nothing short of amazing that a young
woman who, previous to these weeks, had never
produced anything other than jesting or jeering little
poems for the amusement of her friends or relatives,
should all of a sudden rise up to Goethe's heights
in this masterful way, adapt herself to his style, and
remain on a level with him.

During those days she wandered around with
Goethe through the ruins of the Heidelberg castle
and out about the castle itself. In the dust on the
edge of the castle fountain Goethe wrote her name
with his fingers in Arabic letters. Concerning this
he says in his poem that he no longer writes symmetrical rhymes on paper as smooth as silk, no longer
encloses them in golden vines, no, he writes them
in the moving dust and yet the strength with which

they are written endures and forces its way down to
the very centre of the earth:

> Dem Staub, dem beweglichen, eingezeichnet,
> Ueberweht sie der Wind; aber die Kraft besteht,
> Bis zum Mittelpunkt der Erde
> Dem Boden angebannt.

It was on September 24, while taking a walk by
the castle, that Goethe thus wrote Marianne's name
in human memory.   A few hours later, the Willemers returned to Frankfort.   Goethe and Marianne
never saw each other again.   In a poem dated September 26 he placed these deep words on her lips:

> Volk und Knecht und Ueberwinder,
> Sie gestehn zu jeder Zeit:
> Höchstes Glück der Erdenkinder
> Sei nur die Persönlichkeit.

On September 28 she wrote in her home her other
immortal masterpiece, the poem of longing and be-
reavement which she addresses to the west wind and
which, though it assuredly cannot be placed by the
side of Shelley's magnificent ode on the same subject, belongs to those verses which the Germanic
people will not cease singing for centuries.   It begins with the familiar lines:

> Ach, um deine feuchten Schwingen
> West, wie sehr ich dich beneide!
> Denn du kannst ihm Kunde bringen
> Was ich durch die Trennung leide.

There is a tenderness here such as is not to be
found in any of Marianne's other poems, a pain of
regret and languishing, and a fear of causing her

beloved grief by talking of her own sufferings. The west wind cools her tear-reddened eyes:

Doch dein mildes, sanftes Wehen
Kühlt die wunden Augenlieder,
Ach, für Leid müsst' ich vergehen,
Hofft ich nicht, wir seh'n uns wieder.

In both of the stanzas quoted Goethe has changed the text a little. The last one sounds better in his emendation:

Sag ihm, aber sag's bescheiden:
Seine Liebe sei mein Leben;
Freudiges Gefühl von beiden
Wird mir seine Nähe geben.

In October Mariane sends Geothe a poem in ciphers which they had agreed to use. From this Goethe forms the beautiful and intensely passionate poem beginning

Dir zu eröffnen
Mein Herz verlangt mich.

The close of the poem contains woman's burning erotic love:

Mein Leben will ich
Nur zum Geschäfte
Von seiner Liebe
Von heut an machen,
Ich denke seiner,
Mir blutet's Herz.

Kraft hab ich keine
Als ihn zu lieben
So recht im Stillen.
Was soll das werden!
Will ihn umarmen
Und kann es nicht.

But the poetic account of the two approaches its fullest, its most imperishable expression, in the prodigious poem with which Goethe closes the *Buch Suleika,* the song in which he ascribes characteristics

to his sweetheart that remind one of the hundred
names believers give to Allah. Not even in the
warmest days of his early youth did Goethe ever
write anything more charming than this love poem:

In tausend Formen magst Du Dich verstecken,
Doch, Allerliebste, gleich erkenn' ich Dich;
Du magst mit Zauberschleiern Dich bedecken,
Allgegenwärt'ge, gleich erkenn' ich Dich.

The last two stanzas of the poem run as follows:

Wenn am Gebirg der Morgen sich entzündet,
Gleich, Allerheiternde, begrüss' ich Dich;
Dann über mir der Himmel rein sich ründet,
Allherzerweiternde, dann athm' ich Dich.

Was ich mit äusserm Sinn, mit innerm kenne,
Du Allbelehrende, kenn' ich durch Dich;
Und wenn ich Allahs Namenhundert nenne,
Mit jedem klingt ein Name mit für Dich.

Goethe and Marianne von Willemer kept up their
correspondence throughout the rest of his life, in
other words, for seventeen uninterrupted years. In
March, 1831, Goethe decided to return all of her
letters to her. He enclosed in the package a little
poem and a note in which he begged her to leave
the package untouched "bis zu unbestimmter
Stunde," that is to say, until his death. He left
the package lying, however, for fully eleven months;
he did not send it to her until a month before his
death, on February 10, 1832. A few weeks later
he received Marianne's promise that she would conscientiously preserve the package. Then he wrote
to her, just once more and for the last time, on February 23. On March 22 he breathed his last.

The little poem that was sent with the letters reads as follows:

> Vor die Augen meiner Lieben,
> Zu der Brust, der sie entquollen
> Einst, mit heissestem Verlangen
> So erwartet, wie empfangen—
> Zu der Brust, der sie entquollen
> Diese Blätter wandern sollen;
> Immer liebevoll bereit,
> Zeugen allerschönster Zeit.

The octogenarian feels anew, even here, the tension and longing with which he always expected these letters and the joy with which he received them.

Let us compare for a moment, in our thoughts Marianne von Willemer with Bettina von Arnim, her near acquaintance. Each is thirty years old. In the life of each Goethe marks an epoch. In the presence of each he stands as the senescent man in the presence of a very young woman. Bettina feels attracted to him strongly and fantastically, just as he feels attracted to Marianne. Each became a poetess of rank. But where Bettina tries to encircle her head with a halo of glory by usurping unto herself the honor for some of Goethe's very best sonnets, Marianne gives him, without a moment's hesitation, the most beautiful poems she ever produced. He publishes them under his own name, and does her the honor of recognizing them as being the equal of his own. He was so rich and great that he was not dishonored by so doing; on the contrary, he conferred honor when he took. Not until several years after her death was the secret brought to light. But in one of her poems she uses these beautiful and touching words to Goethe concerning her verses:

Wohl, dass sie Dir nicht fremde scheinen:
Sie sind Suleika's, sind die deinen.

Bettina was like the resplendent bird that comes flustering and comes blustering; Marianne's being was the attraction that beauty and grace and a very great talent exercise when they work together, in harmony, and when they work quietly, peacefully. This explains those so significant words in her poem to the west wind: "Tell him, but tell him modestly, that his love is my life."

CHAPTER XXXI

DUALISM IN GOETHE'S FACULTIES

THERE was in Goethe, as there is in various other minds of first rank, a double faculty: There was the one that gilds things over; and there was the one that sees things soberly, unmercifully, just as they are. His being is like a cord woven together of two threads: reality's understanding and reality's glorification. It was easy to inspire him; it was not difficult for him to be sagacious.

Nature laid him out after a harmonious plan. He took pleasure in life and delight in men. But as to his unreserved freedom from illusions, even as a young man, that drama of his entitled *Die Mitschuldigen,* written in his extreme youth, is abundant evidence. And we have even more testimony to his strength of character in this connection in his attitude toward the French Revolution. He who once upon a time said that we have but one alternative, that of being either anvil or hammer, could naturally place but little confidence in those people who wished to emancipate the entire human race.

It was his inspiration for nature, his enthusiasm for it, that gave him a feeling of security. And poet that he was, nature was not indifferent to the fate of man. Quite the contrary: nature, as he felt it, stood opposite man as a beneficent power. In his visionary treatise entitled *Die Natur,* 1780, he said: "Nature brought me into life; it will also lead me out. I put my trust in it; let it rule over me, for it will not despise its own work. It is not I that talk about it. No, everything that I have said, true or false, it itself has said; it is responsible for all; all merit belongs to it." Nature spoke a similar language, years later, in Swinburne's *Hertha*:

> I the grain and the furrow,
> The plough-cloven clod
> And the ploughshare drawn through
> The germ and the sod,
> The deed and the doer, the seed and the sower, the dust
>   which is God.

It was this intuitive and fundamental view of life that constituted a bulwark for Goethe against the rising tide of bitterness. For this tide rises in all vigilant human souls. And if one's character be really strong, and one's eye really sure, so that he is in a position soberly to deduce correct results from his own personal experiences, he is mortally apt to tie up in a joyless harbor laden with a cargo of contempt for human kind.

Bitterness arises in Goethe also, a deterrent to which was his life in common with Schiller whose nature was antipodal to his own. Yet when he, in speaking of Schiller's struggle for advancement, says in his memorial poem to the author of *Wallenstein,*

> Damit das Gute wirke, wachse, fromme,
> Damit der Tag des Edlen endlich komme,

this so fundamentally Schiller-like characteristic was what Egmont calles "a strange drop in his blood:" he did not have an especially strong faith in this future in which the noble dominates. We have seen him, however, at this same period making a big concession to optimism, to Schiller, to his native country, and to the idyllic strain in his own nature by the dignified and wholesome poem *Hermann und Dorothea*. Thereupon he glides over into the mood of renunciation which we have already had occasion to observe.

But he takes a decisive turn in *West-Oestlicher Divan*. In this resignation has disappeared; joy in life has triumphed. The poets of Western Asia had brought this about. He conquers, not merely the general oppression of old age, but also the specific melancholy superinduced by the war. *Buch Suleika* is a copious and joyous testimony to the power and enrichment of life. There is, too, not even a faint tang of gentle softness in these love songs.

Manly seriousness characterizes the *Divan* from beginning to end. Bitterness is neither excluded from it nor restrained in it; it is merely confined to the space allotted it by the poet. It is the drop of quinine in the wine. The *Buch des Unmuths* is an instructive counterpart to the *Buch Suleika*. In it Goethe has assembled once for all his feeling of dissatisfaction and spirit of resentment. The verse fits in with that of the *Buch der Betrachtungen:*

> Was bringt zu Ehren?
> Sich wehren.

In one of the poems he portrays the apparent good will of the Germans and their actual animosity toward him. The last two verses read:

> Sie lassen mich alle grüssen
> Und hassen mich bis in Tod.

With an insight free of illusions into conditions as they really were, and with an unmistakable appreciation of the hatred they felt toward him, and the hypocrisy with which they concealed it, he set forth in the final supplement to the book his own self-esteem—that armored weapon which enabled him to face the worst with calm:

> Was? Ihr misbilligt den kraft'gen Sturm
> Des Uebermuths, verlogne Pfaffen!
> Hätt' Allah mich geschafft zum Wurm,
> So hatt' er mich als Wurm geschaffen.

It is also in this book that, under the title of *Wanderers Gemüthsruhe,* he indited the outburst, profound to the point of madness, which revealed what he had endured from the rabble of his time, and how he had raised himself up and above mere disgust at its vituperative mouthings:

> Uebers Niederträchtige
> Niemand sich beklage!
> Denn es ist das Mächtige
> Was man Dir auch sage. . . .
>
> Wanderer! Gegen solche Noth
> Wolltest Du Dich sträuben?
> Wirbelwind und trockner Koth,
> Lass sie drehen und stäuben.

But he never allows himself to be overcome by his scorn for mankind. In prosperity and adversity he preserves his spiritual superiority and lets his wisdom pertaining unto things of this life at last come out in these simple words:

> Wonach soll man am Ende trachten?
> Die Welt zu kennen und nicht zu verachten.

Up to the very end he continues to exercise his talents in all possible fields; he cultivates his mind as one cultivates his garden. He feels how necessary it is to have a general survey of history in order to understand the present:

> Wer nicht von dreitausend Jahren
> Sich weiss Rechenschaft zu geben,
> Bleib' im Dunkeln unerfahren,
> Mag von Tag zum Tage leben!

The great men who die young remain forever fresh in our memories as young men. Those who approach old age lose, as a rule, as time goes on, a great deal of their attraction. They often turn against many things that inspired them in their youth. They dry up inwardly or, like so many artists of second rank, they become senile virtuosos. They live surrounded by the wreaths with pale ribbons that once were bestowed upon them.

Goethe never loses a minute in thinking over his greatness or his renown. He feels as Voltaire did when he called our mind a flame which must be kept alive with all the means at our disposal. He was old even when a young man, for he had in those years that are ordinarily the years of visions, and visions only, a keen and sober sense for the reality of everything that is natural, even for that which is wholly affected, which is a mere leading astray of real nature. He never went out of his way for the base or the undeserving. Every fundamental line in the jeering physiognomy of Mephistopheles was drawn by a young man between twenty-three and twenty-five years old.

And when old in years he was still young in soul;

for he had preserved alongside of his powers of observation the ability to be enraptured, to be inspired, to love and to worship unmoved by all his experiences, disappointments and bereavements. The dualism of his natural gifts gave him at once his precociousness and his inextinguishable ability along the line of self-rejuvenation.

CHAPTER XXXII

Epimenides Erwachen: A FESTIVAL PLAY

ON May 7, 1814, Iffland, as director of the National Theatre in Berlin, sent a request through Kirms, second in command to Goethe in theatrical affairs, to the great poet asking him as the first man of the German nation to lend his assistance to the theatre in Berlin by writing some drama which, occupying if possible only about twenty minutes, might serve as a curtain-raiser at the gala performance that was to be given when, as was to be expected, the King of Prussia accompanied by Emperor Alexander came, in about four weeks, to Berlin. It was a question of doing honor to the Russian Emperor and "the rare friendship" that bound him to Prussia's King. Emperor Franz of Austria, whose participation had been so effective, would naturally have to be remembered; there would also have to be some reference to the Crown Prince (Bernadotte) of Sweden.[12]

Goethe was staying at that time at the new sulphur bath of Berka a few miles from Weimar. He

[12] Jean Baptiste Jules Bernadotte was born at Pau, France, in 1763, and died at Stockholm in 1844. From 1794 to 1809 he was a French general. In 1799 he was French minister of war. In 1804 he became a marshal of France, served with distinction at Austerlitz in 1805, and was elected crown prince of Sweden in 1810. In 1813 he commanded the army of the north against Napoleon. From 1818 to 1844 he was King of Norway and Sweden.
—TRANSLATOR.

found the request entirely honorable; dismayed however as he was by the brevity of time, he answered
at first reservedly.   But a few days later he had
already fixed upon his idea and sent in his program
for a work on a relatively large scale.   It soon became evident that there was no great haste; they
could give the poet ample time.   The performance
was arranged tentatively for October 19, the anniversary of the battle of Leipzig.   But on September
22, Iffland died suddenly and the performance was
postponed until March 30, 1815, the anniversary of
the entry into Paris.

It was perfectly natural that Iffland should direct
his request to Germany's greatest poet.   To whom
else could he have gone?   Heinrich von Kleist, the
man best adapted to the solution of the task, had
taken his own life, when thirty-five years old, on
November 21, 1811.   Theodor Körner, next to
Kleist, the poet most deserving of such honor, had
fallen, when scarcely twenty-two years old, in an
engagement on August 26, 1813, the same day on
which he had written his famous *Schwertlied*.

Goethe was not well suited for the task.   He had
not participated in the military rise of the German
people, had not hated Napoleon, was not a Prussian,
had always been far away from Berlin, not to speak
of the theatre of Berlin.   It was impossible for him
to express, without affectation, the feelings of Prussian patriotism that were to fill a work such as had
been requested.   If ill-fitted on general principles
to write to order, he was especially unfit to execute
this particular order.

It is odd indeed that the very motif to which the
task directed his powers of imagination was in

actuality neither this nor that topic pertaining to
the history of Germany, or more accurately speaking, to the history of Prussia (such as Kleist had
taken in *Der Prinz von Homburg*), but to a theme
from Grecian mythology, and to a nondescript
figure at that—to Epimenides. We know nothing
of him except that he slept away, as the result of
an especial fate, an entire period of his life, and
oddly enough, found thereby, sage that he was, his
power as a seer reenforced.

If there was one occasion for which ancient
Greece was not appropriate this was it. But at this
period of his life Goethe, despite the fact that he
was just now beginning to concern himself with
Oriental poetry, was so eager to see everything
from the Greek point of view that he had to do that
even in this case. The same passion for ancient
Hellenism made itself felt much later in the North.
When Christiansborg Castle burned down in 1884,
Denmark's most famous architect, Theophilus Hansen,[13] returned a year later from Vienna, where he
was then living, to Copenhagen with a plan for the
rebuilding of the castle in which he—vastly over-
estimating my influence—tried to interest me. The
plan was for a long, low building in the style of pure
ancient Greek such as he had employed in the public
buildings he had erected in Athens. I said with a
smile: Must everything be Greek here too? He

---

[13] Theophilus Hansen (1813-1891) studied at the Academy of
Art in Copenhagen until 1838, when he went to Athens, where he
remained for eight years and became an instructor at the Athenian
Institute. In 1846, Ludwig Förster brought him to Vienna, where
he remained, with interruptions, until his death. He was the
architect of some of the most noted buildings in Greece and Austria. See: "Theophilos Hansen und seine Werke." By Niemann
and Feldegg: Vienna, 1893. —TRANSLATOR.

answered quite seriously: Yes, everything *must* be
Greek.

That is precisely the way Goethe felt. He wished
above all to avoid anything that was distinctly modern, such as the Prussian uniforms of that time. On
this account he stipulated that the soldiers of his
drama should wear the costume of the ancient Order of St. John which, according to his fancy, looked
"nobler." Iffland had contended that the Prussian
people "would not recognize their honor-crowned
soldiers in this disguise." Having taken this pre-
caution, he received the permission to use the latest
Prussian cavalry uniform. In the frame of Epimenides this uniform must have created an impression similar to that made by the soldier in Berlin
who stands in the Greek guard house in Unter den
Linden wearing a Prussian *Pickelhaube.*

Goethe had arranged his prelude in such a way
that it portrayed a European rather than a national
German liberation. He could consequently utilize
Epimenides as a cipher in a sign language that would
be perfectly intelligible to Europeans. But the symbolic figure was not a requirement, nor was it clear.
Goethe had to guard against the possibility of making Epimenides, the seven-sleeper, stand for the
King of Prussia who had hesitated so long about
giving the countersign for a rebellion. It is more
reasonable to suppose that he had himself in mind
when he depicted Epimenides: He had been inactive
for so long, and now that Napoleon had been conquered, he took it upon himself to glorify the victors. He did not however wish to depict himself
as having been asleep during the critical era through
which he and his contemporaries had just passed.

He had in truth lived through it with his senses on the alert; he had been active in a marked variety of ways.

He caused a decidedly strong effect on the stage by having Epimenides, on awakening, become astonished at finding everything so different from what it had been when he fell asleep. He brought to light and service, in truth, the entire stock of experience that is at the command of one who knows the theatre from the practical side. Epimenides having fallen asleep, and the martial music having pealed forth, he directed that all lights on the stage be covered with yellowish red glass so that the theatre might be flooded with a reddish gleam of fire—the unpropitious sign of the horrors of war.

Furthermore the characters are allegories: the demon of war, the demon of oppression, the demon of cunning, all sorts of genii, and finally as leading characters, Faith, Hope, and Charity; of these *Charity* is to call forth the idea of the Emperor of Austria and his patriarchal relation to his people, *Faith,* the idea of the zealously believing Emperor Alexander, and lastly *Hope* in the garb of Minerva, but with the face of the deceased Queen Louise, is to represent Prussia. In this way Faith, Hope, and Charity become now once and for all great powers. England as *Steadfastness* receives a modest place in their vicinity.

Love refers to the Emperor of Austria with the words:

> Ich suche Den mit liebevollen Blicken,
> Der liebevoll bei seinem Volk verweilt,
> Der treuen Seinen neubelebt Entzücken
> Mit offnem, holden Vaterherzen theilt.

Faith refers to Alexander and the burning of Moscow:

> Zum Ungeheuren war ich aufgerufen,
> Mir dienten selbst Zerstörung, Blut und Tod;
> So flammte jüngst an meines Thrones Stufen
> Der Freiheit plötzlich furchtbar Morgenroth.

There is no lack of flattery for the mediocre Friedrich Wilhelm III: *Hope* contends that all three sisters live inspired by his good fortune:

> Ich will gestehn den Eigennutz, o Schwestern!
> Für jedes Opfer fordr' ich meinen Lohn,
> Ein selig Heute für ein schrecklich Gestern,
> Triumphes-Wonne statt der Duldung Hohn:
> So hab ich's ihm versprochen, ihm gegeben,
> Von diesem Glück beseelt wir alle leben.

It was only in the year 1815 that anyone in Berlin could see Faith, Hope, and Love for himself in the figures of Russia, Prussia, and Austria; and it certainly does not increase Goethe's renown that he as a poet for a set occasion had to become the official spokesman for this idea. The effect is wholly ludicrous when this legendary figure from ancient Greece discusses Frederick II of Prussia:

> *Epimenides:* Und wir sind alle neugeboren,
> Das grosse Sehnen ist gestillt,
> Bei *Friedrichs* Asche war's geschworen
> Und ist auf ewig nun erfüllt.

As a soldier's chorus Goethe applied the virile war song from his *Pandora*, parts of which have already been quoted. But since it did not fit in with the time, he wrote a new warrior's chorus with

a refrain-like repetition of Blücher's nickname of
Marshall *Vorwärts* and directly referring to him:

> Und so schreiten wir, die Kühnen,
> Eine halbe Welt entlang;
> Die Verwüstung, die Ruinen,
> Nichts verhindre Deinen Gang
> Hinan!—*Vorwärts*—Hinan!
> Und das grosse Werk sei gethan!

This song was naturally more effective at the time
than any other element in the drama.   It was meant
to be popular and it was, though it did not harmonize with the style of the drama in general.   How
different was the homage that Goethe paid to
Blücher two years later when he wrote in lapidary
style the inscription on his monument in Rostock!

> In Harren und Krieg,
> In Sturz und Sieg
> Bewusst und gross!
> So riss er uns
> Von Feinden los.

It is distinctly pathetic to see Goethe in *Epimenides* so completely approving of the vulgar German
conception of Napoleon as the representative and
emissary of the Devil that he has his genii sing:

> Doch was dem Abgrund kühn entstiegen,
> Kann durch ein ehernes Geschick
> Den halben Weltkreis übersiegen,
> *Zum Abgrund muss es doch zurück.*
> Schon droht ein ungeheures Bangen,
> Vergebens wird er wiederstehn!
> *Und Alle, die noch an ihm hangen,*
> *Sie müssen mit zu Grunde gehn.*

Since Goethe himself belonged to those who felt
attracted to Napoleon, this exulting certainty, that

all of those who are still attached to the fallen
Emperor on the island of Elba must eventually come
to grief, does not especially become him in the eyes
of posterity.

The superiority of the work lies wholly in its
lyric and linguistic phases. There is tremendous
verbal power in the very first words of Epimenides:

> Uralten Waldes majestät'sche Kronen,
> Schroffglatter Felsenwände Spiegelflächen
> Im Schein der Abendsonne zu betrachten
> Erreget Geist und Herz zu der Natur
> Erhab'nen Gipfeln, ja zu Gott hinan.

There is in *Epimenides* a well written stanza which
gives allegoric expression to Napoleon's defeat in
Russia. It begins as follows:

> Von Osten rollt Lavinen gleich herüber
> Der Schnee—und Eisball, wälzt sich gross und grösser.

At the close of the stanza England and Sweden
receive their coveted compliments, though Goethe's
geographic memory is a bit defective in that he has
The Belt represent Bernadotte:

> Vom *Ozean,* vom *Belt* her kommt uns Rettung,
> So wirkt das All in glücklicher Verkettung.

There are, moreover, a number of beautifully
written stanzas in which freedom is glorified. These
words are put on the lips of *Hope* with a great deal
of sense for theatrical effect:

> Nun begegn' ich meinen Braven
> Die sich in der Nacht versammelt,
> Um zu schweigen, nicht zu schlafen,
> Und das schöne Wort der Freiheit
> Wird gelispelt und gestammelt,

Bis in ungewohnter Neuheit
Wir an unsrer Tempel Stufen
Wieder neu entzückt es rufen
           (mit Ueberzeugung, laut)
Freiheit!
           (Gemässigter)
                              Freiheit!
(Von allen Seiten und Enden Echo)
                              Freiheit!

It is however only painful to consider the sort of freedom which the year 1815 inaugurated for Germany (as for Europe). Freedom from French supremacy undoubtedly, but at the same time the worst condition of bondage, both spiritual and political, which the nineteenth century has ever known.

The German public was very naturally displeased with *Epimenides* as falling far short of the expectations of a festival play that was supposed to glorify the fatherland and victory, and to be what the Greeks called an *egkomion*. Neither can it be denied that, compared with Aeschylus's *Persians* and Shakespeare's *Henry V*, it was a complete fiasco. But the work was written to order; Goethe struggled in this case with a task which he could avoid only with difficulty and could not solve at all. *Epimenides* reveals the limitations of his talent, and the weaknesses of his character.

CHAPTER XXXIII

CHRISTIANE'S DEATH; AUGUST'S MARRIAGE; GOETHE AND BYRON—GOETHE AND ULRIKE VON LEVETZOW; *Marienbader Elegie*

ON June 6, 1816, Christiane died after prolonged and painful suffering. Her convulsions became so heart-rending toward the end of her illness that her servants fled in terror-stricken distress. She had been gradually sinking for an entire year, worn out by her anguish and perplexed by her household worries. These had recently become more burdensome than ever, since the woman who had been her chief support married Dr. Riemer.

Goethe's grief was intense; he locked himself up in his room where he gave way to violent sobbing. He wrote this heart-felt verse:

> Du versuchst, o Sonne, vergebens
> Durch die düstren Wolken zu scheinen,
> Der ganze Gewinn meines Lebens
> Ist, ihren Verlust zu verweinen.

The truth is, Goethe had never ceased to appreciate Christiane's real value. In her he had a reliable, faithful, modest, kind-hearted wife—just as a wife was supposed to be in the conception of an ancient Greek.

We have a proof, of its kind, even of the physical attraction that she had for him in the poem entitled *Das Tagebuch*, 1810. This poem is not included in his works; it is coarse and massive rather than salacious or indecent; it contains some thoughts that are beautiful, though it has in it one stanza that is written in remarkably poor taste in that it is a com-

posite of the vulgar and the blasphemous: It depicts a *stranded* effort on his part to embrace a
woman who is not his wife. Through the invocation
of good intentions and German thoroughness it is
possible to interpret the poem, after all, as an homage to the woman who bore him his children; and
this is the way it has been interpreted in Germany.
But Goethe paid homage to Christiane in more
charitable and becoming ways. In 1817, his son
August was married to Ottilie von Pogwisch, a
young woman of an aristocratic family. She was
quite fascinating and had unusual social ability, as
a result of which she made an amiable hostess in
Goethe's home. But she was by nature restless,
giddy, changeable, capricious, and wasteful. Her
husband had some talent for business, the special
aim of which was to make advantageous use of his
father's productions and secure for himself a liberal
inheritance. But he was always very much oppressed by his father's superiority, got along poorly
on this account with his wife, and eventually fell a
hopeless prey to the drink habit. By means of
patronage he secured, when still a young man, a title
and position; but he was quite devoid of any sort
of efficiency.

In 1816, Lord Byron rose up on Goethe's horizon.
The master read with interest Byron's *Corsaire* and
Lara. And in 1817 he began to perceive the mysterious relation in which he stood to that contemporary mind which, since the disappearance of
Napoleon from Europe, concerned him more than
any other mind of his time. A young American
had presented Goethe with a copy of Byron's *Manfred*. With astonishment and living interest Goethe

saw for the first time how his own poetry had affected a great mind of another people which, incidentally, was amply independent and as unlike his own as possible. He saw that Byron had assimilated his *Faust* though he had changed its motives; he was astonished at the despair that lay so far from his own being, the murky flames of which shot out from *Manfred* toward him. He introduced the work and the author to the German reading public, though he was credulous enough to take up with and spread the romantic legend that had just then been started concerning Byron: He was supposed to have fallen in love with a woman from Florence; this woman had been murdered by her husband; and the following night the husband was found dead on the street though suspicion for the murder could not be fixed upon any definite individual. Byron had left Florence and was now dragging these ghosts around with him in his soul.

Goethe translated Manfred's despondent and world-weary monologue, and from this time on he remained in constant touch with Byron and wrote articles on his *Don Juan* and *Cain*. Byron, feeling a profound admiration, sent Goethe his *Sardanapalus* with this dedication:

To the illustrious Goethe.
A stranger
presumes to offer the homage of a literary vassal to his liege
lord
the first of living writers
Who has created the literature of his own country
and illustrated that of Europe.
The unworthy production which the author ventures to
inscribe to him is entitled
Sardanapalus.

Byron's next tragedy, *Werner,* brought another dedication to the German poet: *To the illustrious Goethe by one of his humblest admirers this tragedy is dedicated.*

In 1823, a young Englishman by the name of Sterling brought Goethe a message from Lord Byron, then about to leave in order to dedicate his last strength to the Greek Revolution. Goethe gave him the poem which reached Byron in Leghorn and in which a heartfelt emotion is expressed:

> Ein freundlich Wort kommt eines nach dem andern
> Von Süden her und bringt uns frohe Stunden;
> Es ruft uns auf, zum Edelsten zu wandern,
> Nicht ist der Geist, doch ist der Fuss gebunden.
>
> Wie soll ich Dem, den ich so lang begleitet
> Nun Etwas Traulichs in die Ferne sagen?
> Ihm, der sich selbst im Innersten bestreitet
> Stark angewohnt, das tiefste Weh zu tragen.
>
> Wohl sei ihm doch, wenn er sich selbst empfindet!
> Er wage selbst sich hoch beglückt zu nennen.
> Wenn Musenkraft die Schmerzen überwindet;
> Und wie ich ihn erkannt, mög er sich kennen!

And again six years later, after Byron's death, Goethe wrote a little poem in his honor, which begins:

> Stark von Faust, gewandt im Rath
> Liebt er die Hellenen;
> Edles Wort und schöne That
> Füllt sein Aug' mit Thränen.

The man does not exist who does not willingly and gladly grant Byron, living and dead, the honor that is due him. Moreover, he fully deserved Goethe's interest by reason of his filial relation to him. Goethe gave him, too, a place in the second part of *Faust*. But the fact remains that Lord Byron did not understand German; that he had no knowledge of *Faust* at first hand; that he had indeed none of Goethe in general.

On the other hand, it is a melancholy fact that Shelley's name never occurs in Goethe's works; that the great lyricist lived and died unknown to him. It is not simply that Shelley, by reason of his exalted genius, was worthy of appreciation by the individual who first used the word *Weltliteratur;* he had entered into his life in a quite different way; he had entered into the spirit of *Faust* in a way that was closed to Lord Byron. In 1822, he translated the *Prolog im Himmel* with the antiphonal song of the angels. He also gave a masterful reproduction of the scenes on the Brocken in the Harz. But with all this, it seems to have been written down in the book of fate that Shelley was not to receive the recognition due him while living.

In 1819, Goethe celebrated in complete stillness his seventieth birthday while riding in a carriage from Hof to Karlsbad. He received of course many congratulations. Even Frankfurt did him honor by arranging a gala performance in his absence.

He had now come to that point in life where it was natural for his friends of equal age to disappear, while the great personages with whom he had come in touch and to whom he had stood so near were no longer living. In 1819, Fritz Jacobi and Fritz Stolberg died. Napoleon's death took place in 1821, Byron's in 1824, Charlotte von Stein's in 1827, while in 1828, Goethe, then almost eighty years old, was struck by the death he felt so deeply, that of Karl August. In 1830, the Duchess Luise and his son, August Goethe, died, the latter in Rome. It fell in short to his lot to survive those who had meant so much to him. Time and time again he was obliged to collect himself and overcome his grief by work.

II

In the year 1822 Goethe once more burst forth in erotic passion. Scarcely had his heart burned out when it caught fire again. The one phœnix had gone up in flames, another had arisen from the ashes. In 1806 Goethe had become acquainted with Frau Amalie von Levetzow, the memory of whose charm had never departed from him. In 1821 he saw her again in the company of her parents with her three daughters, Amélie, Bertha, and Ulrike. This was only for a short while, in Marienbad. But when he returned to the bath in the summers of 1822 and 1823 he was constantly with the Levetzow family. The youngest daughter Ulrike had charmed him; he felt as happy as possible in the family's company. In 1823 the attraction grew into a passion. He had not, as a twenty-one-year-old man, loved Friederike Brion more vehemently than he now as a seventy-four-year-old-man loved Ulrike von Levetzow. At the mere sound of her voice far away on the street he seized his hat and hastened out.

There was a child-like expression in her brown eyes and well formed mouth; and in accordance with the fashion of the time she wore her brown hair in short curls. I must confess, in passing, that to judge

from the portraits, both her mother and her two
sisters were more beautiful than she, however young
and sprightly she herself may have been. And yet,
it is not the degree of beauty that decides a passion.
When Amélie one day asked Goethe whether he
liked her dress he said: "Ulrike's is prettier." The
answer is typical. Ulrike still remembered that
reply in her ninety-fifth year (she died unmarried
when she was almost a hundred years old) and remarkably enough, Goethe jotted down in his note
book the fact that the dress was of checkered Scot-
ish material.

There is only one point in which Ulrike's memory,
seventy-seven years after the event had taken place,
and just like a woman, played her false: She insisted
that her relation to Goethe had never been other
than that of a granddaughter to her grandfather.
What she affirmed is true; Goethe was seventy-three
years old when she, seventeen years of age, became
acquainted with him; but his passion was as ardent
as that of a young man and it left her by no means
unmoved. It is utterly unthinkable that she lived
without being kissed and was a stranger to caresses.
The picture of her daily reception of him in the
poem entitled *Elegie* bears the full stamp of authenticity:

> Wie zum Empfang sie an den Pforten weilte
> Und mich von dannauf stufenweis beglückte,
> Selbst nach dem letzten Kuss mich noch ereilte,
> Den letztesten mir auf die Lippen drückte:
> So klar beweglich bleibt das Bild der Lieben
> Mit Flammenschrift ins treue Herz geschrieben.

It seemed to Goethe that Ulrike was necessary
for the continuation of his life. He decided to make

her his second wife; and even before he had assured
himself of her consent—and that of her mother—
he took steps to put his house in order for her reception. He had in the very beginning, in letters from
Marienbad and Karlsbad whither he had followed
the Levetzows, betrayed his secret to his daughter-
in-law in covered words, though they were transparent to her. But when in the interim between his
two visits to Marienbad he appeared before his son
and told him his intention of entering into a new
marriage, painful scenes occurred in which Ottilie's
sister, Ulrike, also took part. August, who saw
himself threatened in this way of the enjoyment of
the inheritance to which he was soon to fall heir,
turned the raw side of his nature toward his father,
so much the more since he was also irritated by
Ottilie, who felt extremely ill disposed at having a
mother-in-law in the house who was much younger
than she. August threatened to leave his father's
house, a move which Goethe certainly could have
endured. The son gave his tongue free play. Children not infrequently regard their parents as existing for their sake and theirs alone.

Up to this point the young girl had, however,
certainly not taken her relation to Goethe seriously.
She had just come home from a boarding school
in Strassburg, had read Voltaire and other French
authors of that time, but she had never read a word
of Goethe, in whom she saw His Excellency, the
famous Minister. When Goethe accordingly asked
the Grand Duke to woo for him, and the latter
carried out the commission, both the mother and
the daughter were surprised and considered the affair almost as a joke.

Karl August assured them that Goethe was quite in earnest. He told Ulrike that she would be the first woman in Weimar, that he could confer upon her all possible marks of distinction, and that she would not need to be separated from her people. He would give them a well furnished house in Weimar. To the mother the Grand Duke gave the assurance that he would care for Ulrike's future. Since she in all probability would survive Goethe, he would settle an annuity of 10,000 thalers upon her.

Frau von Levetzow, who had firmly made up her mind never to persuade her daughter to get married, asked Ulrike whether she was inclined to accept the offer that had been made her. She said that she would in case she were thereby fulfilling a wish of her mother. Frau von Levetzow said that Ulrike was far too young for her, as her mother, to wish to see her married; but the offer was so complimentary that she would have to decide for herself.

The daughter gave a negative reply on the ground (according to what she said seventy-seven years later) that Goethe already had a married son in the house whom he did not wish to dislodge. Regardless, however, as to what the ultimate reason for her final decision was, the filial affection that she cherished for Goethe had in all probability an insufficient amount of the element of abiding passion.

It was a hard blow to Goethe. His forced renunciation touched his heart. In February 1823 he had been very ill; he had a convulsive cough and steady pains about his heart (*Pericarditis*). He was often unconscious and delirious. After his return home from his sojourn at the watering place in November,

he became so ill that his friends despaired of his
life. His cough and fever returned, he again had
pains about his heart as a result of an inflammation,
and in addition to all of this he lost his courage and
his eagerness to work. Reconvalescence was a slow
process.

As an evidence of the passionate experience of
those years, the familiar poem entitled *Die Aeolsharfen*, a poetic conversation between him and Ulrike, and *Trilogie der Leidenschaft*, with especial
reference to the *Marienbader Elegie*, are and remain monumental among Goethe's productions. In
the *Aeolsharfen*, 1822. which gives expression to
the pain at parting when neither can live without
the other, and in which the grief on her part is as
pronounced as it is on his, the most beautiful part
of the poem is the comparison of his sweetheart
with the rainbow, a wonder that is always new and
always equally joyous:

> Ja, Du bist wohl der Iris zu vergleichen,
> Ein liebenswürdig Wunderzeichen,
> So schmiegsam herrlich, bunt in Harmonie
> Und immer neu und immer gleich wie sie.

The little poem entitled *Die Aussöhnung* was addressed to the distinguished Polish pianist Frau
Marie Szymanowska, who had been with Goethe at
Marienbad in 1823; she was accompanied by her
sister Fräulein Kasimira Wolowska, whose praises
he also sang. She visited him in Weimar, and Frau
Szymanowska's beautiful playing had an assuaging
effect upon the poet's rent soul. It was she who six
years later gave Adam Mickiewicz and Odyniec letters of introduction to Goethe, and thus brought

about an acquaintance between Poland's greatest poets and Germany's.

The introductory poem, entitled *An Werther,* was the last part of the trilogy to be written (1824). It contains a portrayal of the melancholy conditions of human life. It is beautiful and dignified. But the poem entitled *Elegie* is the one in which everything depends in fact on the psychological and poetic. It should be read line for line for its melancholy is deep, its life experience is rich, and the expression, though somewhat abstract, is free from flourishes; the despair is unveiled as it rarely is in Goethe's works. No attempt is made to veil the anguish.

The portrayal of how he was received into Paradise, of how blessed he felt there, and of how terrible it was to be driven out, is exquisite:

> Der Kuss, der letzte, grausam süss, zerschneidend
> Ein herrliches Geflecht verschlungner Minnen:
> Nun eilt, nun stockt der Fuss, die Schwelle meidend,
> Als trieb' ein Cherub flammend ihn von hinnen;
> Das Auge starrt auf düstrem Pfad verdrossen.
> Es blickt zurück, die Pforte steht verschlossen.

It seems to him now as though his sealed heart had never been opened; despondency, repentence, self-reproach, and sorrow fill it. Is the landscape in its beauty, or the vault of Heaven in its grandeur, no longer existent? He sees nothing but *her* form as an airy phantom in space. He recalls, how, in her presence, he was what men regard as pious. In beautiful verse he gives the meaning of the word:

> In unsers Busens Reine wogt ein Streben
> Sich einem Höhern, Reinern, Unbekannten
> Aus Dankbarkeit freiwillig hinzugeben,

Enträthselnd sich den ewig Ungenannten:
Wir heissen's: fromm sein!—Solcher sel'gen Höhe
Fühl' ich mich theilhaft, wenn ich vor ihr stehe.

She is to him the one who disposes of *yesterday* as
uninteresting and of *tomorrow* as that of which we
know nothing; she implores him to view the present
with joy and determination. But he cannot. The
moment he is separated from her all is misery; his
heart is filled with trouble; his spirit knows neither
will nor decision. He has lost the cosmos; he has
lost himself. The gods have doomed him to destruction.

Thus it seemed to him in his mood of profound
depression: The gods had doomed him for the
time being to intensified loneliness, and to increased
mental activity, not in communion with men who
were approximately his equals and from whom he
could learn, but with his spiritual inferiors; with
those who, faithfully receiving, seized with avidity
and preserved the thoughts and ideas that came to
him as a result of conversation. The gods doomed
him, in other words, to conversation with Eckermann. For it was precisely at this time, in the year
1823, that Johann Peter Eckermann, an indigent
young man with a reasonable love for the art of
the spoken word, came to him, and offered him his
services. After having taken part in the wars
against Napoleon, Eckermann had studied Klopstock and Schiller, though he eventually found his
ideal in Goethe. He went on foot from Göttingen
to Weimar, was received by Goethe and retained by
him as an apprentice. Goethe had been impressed
by his manly seriousness, his feminine dependency,

and his receptivity. With him Goethe talked for
years, not so much for the moment as for posterity,
and he even read Eckermann's notes through—
which somewhat vitiates the impression for us—and
gave a part of them his personal approval.

CHAPTER XXXIV

Zahme Xenien; Invektiven—Sprüche in Prosa

It had been a long while since Goethe had had
acquaintances from whom he could learn. The last
instance in which such a fate befell him was when
Sulpiz Boisserée came on from Cologne and paid
him a visit. He and his brother Melchoir had taken
upon themselves the task of doing honor to Old
German art. They had collected the mediaeval
statuary and paintings which, on the abolition of
monasteries and charitable institutions, were thrown
on the market in great masses, or they were treated
with such scorn that out of altars table-tops and
window-shutters were made.

Boisserée reminded Goethe of his youthful enthusiasm for the Cathedral at Strassburg. This
was his means of interesting him at present in the
Cathedral at Cologne. He had persuaded Goethe
to sit for hours in the thorough study of Old Dutch
and German art; he had held him to it in fact until
he was saturated with a Van Eyck.

He never found it entirely possible, however, to
convert Goethe to his way of thinking. Goethe remarks in his apothegms that the dry and naïve, the

413

rigidly demure and scrupulously righteous, in primitive Northern art can also be found in the oldest works of the Florentines and the Venetians. The most that can be said in his favor is that he broadened Goethe's horizon.

This, however, was a long while ago, fully ten years previous to the moment under consideration. At present Goethe is the giver; a Heinrich Meyer could do no more than agree with him; an Eckermann could merely give the clue for a conversation. The value of Eckermann's work is not to be disparaged; nor are the kindred works of Chancellor von Müller, Falk, Riemer, and Soret. These works all stand as evidence of Goethe's extraordinary many-sidedness. But the communicator has on the one hand merely the value of an interviewer; and on the other hand it is injudicious to overlook the fact that every conversation noted down in this way is of necessity colored by him who wrote it, and is on this account quite unreliable.

Of infinitely greater value than the conversations with Eckermann and the others, all of which are now splendidly arranged in chronological order, and thus made easily accessible, in W. von Biedermann's large work entitled *Goethes Gespräche*, are the short apothegms in verse and prose written by Goethe himself. They constitute a rich source of knowledge pertaining to the master's ways and means of thinking during his later and more mature years.

The few in verse are partly basic thoughts concerning life and the world in general, partly polemic sallies aimed at literary foes and assailants. The first—the *Zahme Xenien*—have the greatest value.

Some of them contain incontrovertible wisdom. There is this one, by way of illustration:

> Gut verloren—Etwas verloren.
> Musst rasch Dich besinnen
> Und Neues gewinnen.
> Ehre verloren—Viel verloren!
> Musst Ruhm gewinnen,
> Da werden die Leute sich anders besinnen.
> Muth verloren—Alles verloren!
> Da wär es besser, nicht geboren.

Others defend freedom of thought as over against importunate religionists and nationalists. Goethe asserts his Pantheism in this forceful verse:

> Was soll mir Euer Hohn
> Ueber das All und Eine?
> Der Professor ist eine Person,
> Gott ist keine.

He makes the unforgetable and eternally true remark concerning knowledge, ability, and inherited emotional nature:

> Wer Wissenschaft und Kunst besitzt,
> Hat auch Religion;
> Wer jene beiden nicht besitzt,
> Der habe Religion.

Along exactly the same line we have this verse of freedom:

> Den deutschen Mannen gereicht's zum Ruhm,
> Dass sie gehasst das Christenthum
> Bis Herrn Karolus' leid'gem Degen
> Die edlen Sachsen unterlegen.

He expresses his contempt for Philistinism in the
monumental lines:

> Was ist ein Philister?
> Ein hohler Darm,
> Mit Furcht und Hoffnung ausgefüllt,
> Dass Gott erbarm!

He pours out the full beaker of his scorn over the
Nationalists who made propaganda for the word
Deutsch being written *Teutsch* and for the entire
debate concerning this pitiable question.

> An die T. . . . und D. . . .
> Verfluchtes Volk! Kaum bist du frei,
> So brichst Du in Dir selbst entzwei.
> War nicht der Noth, des Glücks genug?
> Deutsch oder Teutsch, Du wirst nicht klug.

From precisely the same point of view he expresses (in contrast to his own weakness in *Epimenides*) his disgust for the patriotic derision of
Napoleon:

> Ich kann mich nicht bereden lassen,
> Macht mir den Teufel nur nicht klein!
> Ein Kerl, den alle Menschen hassen,
> Der muss was sein.

Of essentially psychological and symptomatic interest are the minor polemic poems against Kotzebue, Merkel, Böttiger, Spazier, Pustkuchen, and
all the rest of them, whose spiritual livelihood consisted in the persecution of Goethe and whom he
hated according to their just deserts and yet not
enough to allow their attacks to go unnoticed. As
it is they have become unforgetable through his
rejoinder, while all the praise they heaped upon each

other at the time would never have kept their names from oblivion.

Goethe amused himself by calculating that if he could live a hundred years longer, healthy and satisfied as he had been for the most part, Merkel (also the enemy of Tieck and the Schlegel brothers), Spazier (Baggesen's guide in *Labyrinthen*), and Kotzebue would not have any rest in all that time. but would daily write a pasquinade against him which would give no less than 36,500 not counting the intercalary days:

> Gern würd' ich dieses holde Wesen
> Zu Abend auf dem Abort lesen,
> Grobe Worte, gelind Papier
> Nach Würdigkeit bedienen hier.

The tone is furthermore this:

> An Schmierern fehlt's nicht, nicht am Lob der Schmierer
> Der rühmt sich selbst, Den preiset ein Verleger,
> Der Gleiche den; der Pöbel einen Dritten.

To be sure Goethe did not himself publish a single verse of his *Invektiven;* they were gathered together and given out after his death.

II

The same applies to the no fewer than 1055 *Sprüche in Prosa,* this treasure-house of wisdom which, with a few individual exceptions, lay untouched while Goethe was living. His grudge against the public had become so great that he was wholly out of patience with it; he no longer bore any sort of relation whatsoever to it. The hatred of his own age that had seized upon him is probably best shown by the fact that when he finally, as the result of extraordinary exertion, finished the second part of *Faust,* between the middle of the year 1827 and July 1831, he sealed the manuscript with seven seals and laid it aside in peace and quiet for posterity, fully convinced that his contemporaries would simply misunderstand it and make all sorts of maliciously stupid remarks about it.

Goethe's apothegms in prose are, though not worked out in pointed form, of no less value than Pascal's famous paradoxical *Pensées* or La Rochefoucauld's and Chamfort's sharp and witty desultory thoughts. Unlike Pascal, there is no *à priori* taking sides in Goethe's apothegms with some supernatural power. Unlike La Rochefoucauld, Goethe brings to light no great zeal to scent out and lay bare human egotism. Unlike Chamfort, he does not express his contempt for and hatred of men in caustic form.

His standpoint is that of a man who, in mental superiority, surveys all human life, becomes the servant of no particular dogma, is in the power of no mood or passion, but by virtue of his innate greatness calmly looks down upon things as they actually are from his lofty heights above.

When, once in a long while, he does concern himself with religious questions, he does so, not after the fashion of Pascal, in the anguish and passion of self-torment, but with peaceful profundity. He says: Piety is not a goal but a means of approaching the highest state of civilization through the cleanest mental serenity. Consequently those people who set up piety itself as the goal are for the most part hypocrites. He does combat the value of asceti-

cism. He simply says, laconically and with biting
ridicule: The Hindoos in the desert vow that they
will eat no fish. When he touches upon the Bible,
he says: There is a great deal of wrangling concerning the advantage and the harm that have come
from the spread of the Bible. Harm comes from
the spread of the Bible when it is used, as it has
been, dogmatically and fanatically; good comes
from its spread so long as it is used humanly and
as a source of knowledge.

With his profound experience as to what it means
to each individual to be able to work and mature in
peace, Goethe could not help but look with fear and
disquietude upon the newspaper literature which
was just then beginning to flourish. It was only
in its infancy at the time, but it was even then doing
its part by way of hindering the serene growth of
individuals and making the progress of great men
difficult. He writes:

The greatest misfortune of the age lies in the fact that it
never permits anything to mature; it consumes the present
moment in the coming one; it lives forever from hand to
mouth; it never gets anything done. We already have newspapers for the various hours of the day. Everything that
one plans, everything that one simply has on hand or in one's
mind, everything that is still far from completion, is dragged
out into publicity. No one dares be happy or sorrowful
without thereby creating a pastime for the others. Do the
fortunate really believe that the unfortunate person should
be allowed to die decently and in order as the old gladiators
used to die before the eyes of the Roman rabble?

It is not infrequent that Goethe portrays his own
character. He writes: I keep a good many things
to myself, for I would not discomfort other people.

I much prefer to let them rejoice where I am annoyed. The greatest happiness is produced by that which improves our defects and corrects our mistakes. As a rule it is a man's knowledge that determines what he shall do and what he shall leave undone. There is, therefore, nothing more terrible than to see ignorance in action. The greatest respect that an author can show the public is never to do what it expects of him, but what he, following such light as he has at that stage of his development and with regard to the development of others, looks upon as being right and useful. The active man tries to do what is right; whether right happens thereafter is not his affair. Writing history is a means of getting rid of the past. Instead of contradicting my remarks, they should act in my spirit.

Thus his apothegms run. Concerning the incessant accusation of self-praise to which he was forced to listen he writes: They say that self-praise stinks; it may be true. But as to the odor of alien and unjust censure, for that the public has no nose.

Goethe's practical wisdom induces him at times to note down small, everyday, but strikingly correct experiences such as this one: We never really become acquainted with people when they come to us; we must go to them in order to find out what they are really like. But his method of noticing the most important traits of character is quite different. In the *Xenien* he had often expressed his detestation for those people who were simply incapable of recognizing the good sides of someone else. Here he writes: Face to face with the great superiority of another person there is no other means of safety but love. He had always found the lack of ability to recognize greatness a wretched characteristic. Here he says: There is a proverb according to which no man is a hero to his valet. This comes from the fact that it takes a hero to appreciate a hero. There is no doubt at all but that the valet fully appreciates his equals.

While pondering over the reasons why great men perform such marvelous deeds, he gives expression to this apparently paradoxical idea: To live in the idea is equivalent to treating the impossible as though it were possible. In this way events arise at which the world is astonished for a thousand years.

In deep appreciation of the difficulty encountered by the man of action when he tries to take into consideration all the things that the spectator feels are justified, he utters this profound and boldly formulated thesis: The man of action is always conscienceless; it is only the observer who has a conscience. He takes consolation in the rigid coherency of his own life: That man is happiest of all who can bring the close of his life into connection with the beginning.

Remembering the great amount of time that he has wasted trying to teach and educate people who were impervious to instruction he writes: Not everyone to whom one makes fruitful remarks becomes thereby productive. It often happens that something that is old and well-known occurs to him. While he recalls how many men he trained who never thought of doing anything else but tripping him up at some later time, he writes this rich and pithy sentence: I stumbled over the roots of the tree which I myself had planted. Pausing to reflect

on the number of times he has been mistaken in
men, he forms this weighty judgment: One is never
deceived; one merely deceives one's self.

In leisure hours, and therefore in many of his
aphorisms, reminiscences of his opponents have
risen up before his mind and he has been astonished
to find that they did not have, so to speak, distinct
physiognomies but in their triviality they resembled
each other like drops of water. He expresses this
politely: You all have the same nature, like the
sea, to which one gives various names but which is
all salt water together.

He is reminded of the jealousy of his enemies.
He repeats in his own name Ottilie's aphorism:
There is no greater consolation for mediocrity than
this, that genius must die. He remembers how these
men have toiled in order to give their calumniations
the appearance of superior and nourishing wit: You
have whipped the dirt to see if it would not become
cream. And yet they received the names that they
have from themselves: Filth glitters when the sun
shines.

He found no support from the public which soon
became accustomed to him and tired of him: A
rainbow that stands for a quarter of an hour no
longer attracts the attention. He balances up his
account with his own age: The present generation
is of too little value for us to do anything for *it*.
We must work for the past and for the future, that
is to say, we must try to recognize the merits of
the past and increase the worth of the future.

But despite all his dissatisfaction he does not
complain of his lot. It can to be sure befall one
that he be soundly flailed by fate, but ruthless fate

crushes only the straw: the grain never feels it and springs lustily about on the threshing floor.

He knows full well that the others wish to harm him, but he doubts their ability: The empirical-moral world consists mostly of bad will and envy. The really wretched take an interest only in malevolence; there are people who simply cannot go astray for they never undertake anything reasonable. But this does not lead them to anything.

In the relatively small number of reflections that Goethe has devoted to literature, he strikes at not a few of his countrymen's besetting sins. He remarks, for example, that the Germans (but not only the Germans) have the gift of making the sciences *inaccessible,* and that certain of their books seem to have been written, not that we may learn something from them, but that we may see that the author was *erudite.* He expresses his detestation for the literary vulgarity that claims to be humor: There is nothing so base but that it will appear humorous if expressed with grimaces. He jests with the activity of translators: Translators are to be regarded as zealous matchmakers who praise a half veiled beauty as being exceedingly amiable. They merely awaken an irresistible longing for the original.

He cries out with the vehemence of his youthful days against the so-called patriotic art: There is no patriotic art, there is no patriotic science. Both art and science need and belong to the whole world.

He explains why he—and for this he had been roundly abused—prefers to pass judgments on foreign rather than on German literature. This is owing to the fact that one in a foreign country (presumably) pays no attention to his judgments, and one cannot be impolite at a distance. But in the very presence of people one feels as little inclined as one does in good society to say anything offensive, and a disapproval is always regarded by an author as an offense.

He defends himself against the charge that his writings are unclear. He who wishes to reproach an author for being unclear must first look into his own mind and soul and see how things are there. Even an exceedingly distinct work is illegible in the twilight.

He jests with his countryman's intolerable boasting about German *Gemüth,* which was denied him: The Germans should not pronounce the word *Gemüth* for thirty years; in this way a new *Gemüth* would gradually arise. As it is the word simply means being tolerant with weaknesses including one's own.

And last of all he makes this illuminating remark concerning reading and learning: We really learn only from those books which we cannot criticise; the author of a book we can criticise would have to learn from us.   (From *Sprüche in Prosa,* Nos. 41, 42, 138, 332, 23, 163, 38, 46, 64, 76, 99, 104, 113, 369, 389, 391, 343, 162, 133, 106, 577, 476, 124, 392, 148, 79, 584, 183, 208, 210, 930, 71, 108, 258, 485, 601, 705, 299, 293. And apparently also from Nos. 125, 345, 72, 130, 316.)

CHAPTER XXXV

Faust, PART II; IMPRESSIONISM OF STYLE

DESPITE Goethe's quite late remark to Eckermann and others to the effect that the second part
of *Faust* was in and on his mind for at least a half
a century, he seems in his youth to have considered
what we now call the first part of the poem as a
complete whole in itself. Nothing with regard to
the theme in the original work points to the fact
that there was any thought of continuing it. It is
not until the years 1797-1801 that the plan shows
a glimmer of continuation. A few details were
worked out: the Baccalaureus scene, which however
really belongs to the first part, and which contains
the constantly recurring derision on the part of
Goethe with regard to that particular sort of originality which derives from total ignorance of what
has already been produced by others. We have
also the beginning of the *Helena* section, which is
now the third act, and which had been submitted to
Schiller.

It was not until 1806 that Goethe interpolated
the scene of the wager between Faust and Mephistopheles in the first part, which made a continuation
not merely possible but obligatory.

The essential thesis of the oldest, the real *Faust*
lies first in its threefold sally against the rhetori-
cians with their belief in the historical rules of ora-

tory, these "jingling-tingling" fools who can neither feel nor speak in a simple, straightforward manner; secondly against the pedantic investigators and writers of history with their belief that the past can be called to life without poetic sense; and finally against the censors of society with their imbecile persecution of thinking heretics, of the few who have been aware of some truth which they are forbidden to utter and who, consequently, have been crucified and burned from the time of Arild on. The author of this *Faust* feels that he is the liberator from the cold and outward rhetoric of the preceding age and of Germany's first historic drama. He feels also that he is the celebrator in song of that old and great and mystic heretic—Prometheus.

In the scene in the witches' kitchen, interwoven in Italy, 1788, there is a revelation of classic paganism in the attack against the Trinity:

> Es war die Art zu allen Zeiten,
> Durch Drei und Eins und Eins und Drei
> Irrthum statt Wahrheit zu verbreiten.

As has already been pointed out, Faust sees in the magic mirror a lovely woman who lies couched after the fashion of Titian's Venus in the Tribuna of Florence. She is perhaps a Helena form. The scene closes with these significant words by Mephisto:

> Du siehst mit diesem Trank im Leibe
> Bald Helenen in jedem Weibe.

If Goethe has given his Italian heroine in the *Römische Elegien* the name of Faustina, there now arises before his mind another heroine with a name far more familiar to antiquity, and she it is with whom he wishes to provide his rejuvenated Faust. In order to reach perfection, final development, the acme of culture, the Gothic Faust of legend, just like Goethe himself, had to be espoused to the Antique. Marlowe, the *Faustbuch,* and German tradition pointed him the way: Faust conjures up Helena from the lower world and makes her his beloved. From the point of view of antiquity, Helena was the personification of beauty.

Think of the significance that this detached conceit from the age of the Renaissance had for Goethe! What a symbol this Helena became for his basic view that had been in the process of development for an entire generation! When Gretchen, the little Gothic girl, was dead, her place could be worthily filled only by the very queen of beauty from ancient Hellas, by that queen who in her own person represented the ideal for whose sake Goethe now stood alone, but to which he will remain forever true. And somewhat earlier than the time at which he collects all his energy in order to work on *Faust,* he completes, during the years 1825-1826, the third act of the work and ascribes to it, as an independent whole, the significant title of *Helena,* a title he afterwards removed.

Critics, who (like Orlando's horse in Ariosto), aside from some respectable characteristics, have the unfortunate one of incompetency, have contended that Goethe was incapable of reproducing the external world. This ability, which developed more and more in his lyric poetry as years went on, made the art of his old age impressionistic, which it had never been in his youth, and induced him to develop a new and astounding originality.

His *Divan* forms the transition to his new lyric, descriptive style. Here, for example, from the *Buch Suleika* is a verse so thoroughly saturated with golden, red, and green colors that it reminds one of the coloring of Rembrandt:

> Schau, im zweifelhaften Dunkel
> Glühen blühend alle Zweige,
> Nieder spielet Stern auf Stern,
> Und smaragden durch's Gesträuche
> Tausendfältiger Karfunkel.

But it is in the second part of Faust, elaborated with incessant, indefatigable work during the years 1827-1831, that is to say, from the time he is seventy-eight to the time he is eighty-two years old, that his new style comes to the fore. It transcends his former style just as the style of the old Titian transcends that of the young Titian, or as Beethoven's ninth symphony towers above all the other symphonies (Richard Hamann: *Der Impressionismus in Leben und Kunst.*)

The second part of *Faust* is in reality only lyric poetry. Its fascination lies in the verbal art with which Goethe attempts to reproduce all sensations: Auditions from the slightest whisper to the rolling thunder, visions in all shades from the variegated world of color, which he had so carefully investigated, the flaming, the sparkling, the gleaming, the dazzling, that which billows and floats in light, and that which wavers and quivers; odors in all degrees of fresh scent, perfume, refreshing fragrance, irritating effluvia down to rank stench. When for example Goethe has Mephisto depict Hell, he obviously had in mind the strong smell of sulphur; he

has Mephisto introduced with a remark to the effect
that the devils began to cough:

Die Teufel fingen sämmtlich an zu husten,
Von oben und von unten auszupusten;
Die Hölle schwoll von Schwefelstank und Säure.

The sense of feeling also finds expression here
both with regard to the gliding, and to the heavy
and solid:

Wie war die Welt mir nichtig, unerschlossen,
Wie ist sie nun seit meiner Priesterschaft
Erst wünschenswerth, gegründet, dauerhaft!

At times Goethe, just as the German romanticists,
intermingles various senses: The light has sound,
or the sound has odor. So overrefined have his
never obtuse senses become. Homunculus's light
not only shines but sounds:

Mephisto: Lass deine Leuchte, Kleiner, tönend scheinen!
Homunculus: So soll es blitzen, soll es klingen.
(Das Glas dröhnt und leuchtet gewaltig.)

Or still more refined: color-impression, sound-im-
pression, and odor-effect are blended:

Von buntesten Gefiedern
Der Himmel übersäet,
Ein klingend Meer von Liedern
Geruchvoll überweht.

Heaven is as it were concealed back of the variegated plumage of birds, and a resounding, strongly
odorous flow of song rushes in from over yonder.
The very first scene in the second part of *Faust*
mixes programme-like sensations: The light not
only dazzles, but creaks, rattles, booms, and is con-

ceived of as the music of the trumpets and bassoons.
Ariel sings

> Tönend wird für Geister-Ohren
> Schon der neue Tag geboren.
> Felsenthore knarren rasselnd,
> Phöbus' Räder rollen prasselnd,
> Welch Getöse bringt das Licht!
> Es trommetet, es posaunet.
> Auge blinzt und Ohr erstaunet.

Thereupon follows Faust's description of the sun-
rise and his comparison of it to the satisfaction of
hope and desire. Goethe here, as throughout this
entire period, in aversion to the worn-out small
change of the language, coins new, concise, and effective words such as *Erfüllungspforten—flügeloffen*.
He shows how passionately, despite his years, he
conceives of the fullness of life in the fulfilled desire:

> So ist es also, wenn ein sehnend Hoffen
> Dem höchsten Wunsch sich traulich zugerungen,
> Erfüllungspforten findet flügeloffen.
> Ein Flammenübermass; wir stehn betroffen.
> Des Lebens Fackel wollten wir entzünden,
> Ein Feuermeer umschlingt uns, welch ein Feuer!
> Ist's Lieb, ist's Hass, die glühend uns umwinden,
> Mit Schmerz und Freuden wechselnd ungeheuer?

The monologue ends with the description of the
waterfall and the rainbow above it, so that we feel
the moisture, the spray, the foam, and the splendor.
Lastly the philosophy of this style is given in the
significant words that this colored radiance is all
that we can grasp of life:

> So bleibe denn die Sonne mir im Rücken!—
> Der Wassersturz, das Felsenriff durchbrausend,
> Ihn schau' ich an mit wachsendem Entzücken
> Von Sturz zu Sturzen wälzt er jetzt in tausend,

Dann abertausend Strömen sich ergiessend
Hoch in die Lüfte Schaum an Schäume sausend.—
Allein wie herrlich, diesem Sturm entspriessend
Wölbt sich des bunten Bogens Wechseldauer
Bald rein gezeichnet, bald in Luft zerfliessend,
Umher verbreitend duftig kühle Schauer!
Der spiegelt ab das menschliche Bestreben.
Ihm sinne nach, und Du begreifst genauer:
Am farbigen Abglanz haben wir das Leben.

Even in the first part of *Faust* he says of the snail
that it is guided at once by sight and touch and
smell:

Siehst du die Schnecke da? Sie kommt herangekrochen;
Mit ihrem *tastenden Gesicht*
Hat sie mir schon was *abgerochen.*

Goethe succeeds in giving us, in this his last stage
of development, what the art of painting cannot
give because of its very nature, the momentary
shifting of the vision of light and color and the quiv-
ering in motion itself:

Blinkend, wo die Zitterwellen
Ufernetzend leise schwellen.

Or take this bit of fireworks:

Irrfunkenblick an allen Enden,
Ein Leuchten, plötzlich zu verblenden.

Or this, which, as Hamann has strikingly said, reminds us of Velasquez's *The Lance:*

Die Piken blinken flimmernd in der Luft
Im Sonnenglanz durch Morgennebelduft.

Or this beautiful night, a nocturne which is more
than Whistler-like, an invocation directed to the

stars, beseeching them to shine down upon the Nereids frolicking in the sea:

> Blicke ruhig von dem Bogen
> Deiner Nacht auf Zitterwogen,
> Mildeblitzend Glanzgewimmel;
> Und erleuchte das Getümmel,
> Das sich aus den Wogen hebt!

Note how much sympathetic observation of the color-accustomed and color-loving eye there is in the following words concerning the light billows which rise and swell along the dark shore:

> Siehst auf und ab lichtgrüne, schwanke Wellen
> Mit Purpursaum zur schönsten Wohnung schwellen?

What an immeasurably great artist this octogenarian was! Consider how with changing, ever striking expression he depicts the skulking and hulking of a fog cloud through space, as viewed from a high mountain:

> Ein dunkler Nebel deckt sogleich den Raum.
> Er schleicht sich ein, er wogt nach Wolkenart,
> Gedehnt, geballt, verschränkt, getheilt, gepaart.

The artistic pith and power of the last expression is matchless. There is a tone depiction of corresponding vigor. We hear the wind whistling in the rushes along the shore, in the weeping willows, in the aspen foliage:

> Rege dich, du Schilfgeflüster,
> Hauchet leise, Rohrgeschwister,
> Säuselt, leichte Weidensträuche,
> Lispelt, Pappelzitterzweige!

Goethe far surpasses the German romanticists in sound effect which, incidentally, was their specialty.

He anticipates the song of the Rhine maidens by Richard Wagner in the line: *Wir säuseln, wir rieseln, wir flüstern Dir zu.* He has powerful stanzas with almost pure A-sounds:

> Waldung, die schwankt heran
> Felsen, sie lasten dran,
> Wurzeln, sie klammern an,
> Stamm, dicht an Stamm heran.

On the other hand, the song of the sirens, they who worship all the gods of the universe, contains nothing but O-sounds:

> Wir sind gewohnt
> Wo es auch thront,
> In Sonne und Mond,
> Hinzubeten; es lohnt.

It is in truth in its verbal, descriptive, and musical skill that the second part of *Faust* is so instructive, so aesthetic, so suggestive, and stands on such a high plane. And the artistic is after all the chief desideratum. The demonstration of the rational element of the poem, its plan, the clarification of obscure passages, and of what Goethe has mystified into it, consciously or in the interests of his art— all this furnishes topics for professors of literature in Germany and North America to lecture on. This is admittedly an essential phase of the business, but it is of far less interest to us.

From a purely intellectual point of view, there are a number of unsatisfactory features in the construction. The point that was to be proved was indeed the fact that the angels can save him who constantly strives—which is equivalent to saying that he is

deserving and should not be lost.   But unfortunately
this is precisely what Faust has not done: He has
neither striven nor acted.   He has made, with the
assistance of Mephisto, some worthless paper money
for use at the Court of the Emperor, and he has
arranged a series of Court festivals.   This can
hardly be called striving.   He has brought Helena
up to the world of men.   This, however, though
an act, is an act in the interests of amusement rather
than in those of diligent service.   And he has robbed
Philemon and Baucis of their little home.   This is
an act, but an unreservedly reprehensible one.   And
after this career, he is to be redeemed by the inter-
cession of a woman whom he has treated with undisciplined cruelty, and then abandoned for ever
and a day.   In this which was supposed to represent
the logic of the work, real logic is quite far off, and
altogether thin if found at all.

Faust derides the idea of studying the far-away,
the world beyond, as though he were speaking in
the name of the poet himself:

> Nach drüben ist die Aussicht uns verrannt,
> Thor! wer dorthin die Augen blinzelnd richtet,
> Sich über Wolken Seinesgleichen dichtet.
> Er stehe fest und sehe hier sich um!
> Dem Tücht'gen ist die Welt nicht stumm,
> Was braucht er, in die Ewigkeit zu schweifen!

There is then immediately revealed to us the
Roman Catholic Heaven with the angelic choir, the
choir of penetential sisters, the blessed youths, the
*Mater gloriosa, Pater ecstaticus, Pater profundus,
Chorus mysticus, Pater seraphicus*, even down to
St. Francis of Assisi, whose church Goethe once dis-

dained to see.   There is not much here to offer
lovers of logic.

And yet, when the mystic choir voices its dark
concluding stanza, we are filled with a mood as
though we heard a Pagan-Christian Sibyll's words
of wisdom; by virtue of the lofty art of the poet,
these almost impenetrable words have remained engraved in the memory of generations:

> Alles Vergängliche
> Ist nur ein Gleichnis;
> Das Unzulängliche
> Hier wird's Ereignis;
> Das Unbeschreibliche,
> Hier ist es gethan;
> Das Ewig-Weibliche
> Zieht uns heran.

This entire world of legend was nothing but a
symbol.   The inadequate—inadequate as is every
human work—here come most nearly being satisfactory, indeed it even marks an epoch.   The indescribable—in the sense of inexhaustible—takes
place here before our eyes.   The eternally feminine,
the maidenly, the maternal, the enigmatic, attracts
us just as the lap of nature attracted Goethe's manhood, and as partly *die Mütter,* partly Helena, attracted his Faust.

CHAPTER XXXVI

Helena; THE THIRD ACT, THE FIRST PART TO BE WRITTEN—FIRST ACT—SECOND ACT— FOURTH AND FIFTH ACTS

THE third act of the second part of *Faust,* the poem originally entitled *Helena,* was the first one to be written. It constitutes more or less of a whole; it is relatively complete in itself. Study it, and it shows, without unusual difficulty or the arts of exegetic interpretation, what Goethe intended to make the kernel, the heart, of this great new work of his. That is, it makes this point clear to him who has followed and examined the historical development of Goethe's own soul. As we have already intimated, the kernel was the marriage of the legendary Gothic hero to the antique ideal, the symbolic history of that stage of development in the life of the leading character in which he, precisely like the poet that created him, conjured up and worshipped the Hellas of days gone by.

By this time, reflection had dislodged the naïveté in Goethe's works which had made him such a spiritual force in the days of his youth. The power of imagination was still luxuriously rich, the inventiveness extraordinary. Of conceits and apercus there

436

is no end. But we have already had occasion to
see how the ability to portray *individual figures* has
been swallowed up and lost to view by the tendency
to delineate *the typical*. In the second part of
Faust everything has become symbolism. The figures derive their value, not from their individual
and personal psychology, but by virtue of the lyric
expression in which they clothe their inner soul.
Here is depth; for here is thought ingeniously
worded. Here is beauty; for here is lyric poetry in
which an art that is rare rejuvenates the language
and widens the reproduction of nature to hitherto
unapproached boundaries. But the ability to form
figures, to create characters, has weakened. The
seer no longer says, and that with vigor, *this is;*
quite the contrary: the brooder appears on the
boards with his explanatory *this means*. These figures are not compact but transparent; one sees
through them into the meaning back of them. They
give their own meaning. They are not even pictures: they are symbols. They are not of flesh
and blood so that they can be embraced or hewn
down or pierced through. They are ghosts that
disappear before a puff of wind or magic word.
They vanish in the mists that enshroud them. The
entire work is so eldritch that the illusion is often
destroyed by the poet himself through the voluntary
introduction of a participating personage whose un-
reality is altogether obvious.

We find ourselves before Menelaos's palace in
Sparta. Helena appears, having returned home
from conquered Troy, accompanied by her maid-
servants, a chorus of captured Trojan women. The
time is far distant when Goethe had his Iphigenie

speak in modern iambic pentameters. Helena speaks
in rigid, weighty classic trimeters; the cadence of
her speech is heavy, though solemn, and beautiful.
The chorus joins in precisely as in an old Greek
tragedy. But a figure appears which brings an
alien and ugly element into this welter of beauty
arisen from the lower world; it is a tall grim woman,
Phorkyas by name, who sets herself up as the direc-
tress of the palace during the queen's absence. With
her raucus and domineering voice, she not simply
frightens the captured girls who accompany Helena,
but even dares to remind the queen of her past in
a way that cannot help but be quite painful to her.
Helena sublimely sets her aright, though she still
refuses to acquiesce. She is Mephisto himself in the
garb of a woman.

When the queen steps across the threshold in order once more to take possession of the palace, and
to bring the gods their due sacrifice, Mephisto, as
Phorkyas, tells her that she herself is the victim!
Menelaos has given the command that she shall be
sacrificed with the polished ax that lies at the foot
of the altar, while her hand-maidens shall without
exception be hanged.

Helena resigns with calm dignity, though she cannot forego asking whether there is not some way
out of this situation. Phorkyas enlightens her by
saying that there is; and from the answer we are
reminded that we are all of a sudden no longer in
the time of ancient Greece, but in that of the Middle
Ages. There lies nearby a strongly fortified and
beautifully fitted out castle inhabited by a strange,
warlike race ruled over by a great and intelligent
chieftain.

Mephisto at once sends Helena and her followers to the inner court of the castle. After the servants and squires have marched down in a long procession to the bottom of the steps, Faust comes slowly and pompously, wearing the knightly court costume of the Middle Ages and extends to Helena his lavish homage. He leads along with him, in chains, the keeper of the tower, Lynceus, who should have announced her coming but forgot to attend to his duty. In beautiful verses Lynceus defends himself with, to be sure, a gallantry unknown to ancient times: Helena's beauty has so blinded him that he neglected to blow the horn that hung by his side; as an infatuated lover he brings her chests full of treasures, pearls, and precious stones. Some of his courtesies are a bit antiquated, as when he has the ruby turn pale in comparison with the blush on her cheek—it is difficult to conceive of Helena as being so brick-red. His use of the word egg-drop as a circumlocution for pearl is, however, beautiful; the homage implied in it at least gives the reader the impression of the queen's remarkable beauty:

> Nun schwanke zwischen Ohr und Mund
> Das Tropfenei aus Meersesgrund;
> Rubinen werden gar verscheucht,
> Das Wangenroth sie niederbleicht. . . .
> Denn Du bestiegest kaum den Thron,
> So neigen schon, so beugen schon
> Verstand und Reichthum und Gewalt
> Sich vor der einzigen Gestalt.

With the proneness to artistic double reflection such as we have already noticed in Goethe, and which the German Romanticists developed into a

formal system, the poet has Helena become astonished at the rhymes in Lynceus's speech; she asks
what this is, what it means:

> Erstaunen trifft mich, fragen möcht' ich viel.
> Doch wünscht ich Unterricht, warum die Rede
> Des Manns mir seltsam klang, seltsam und freundlich.
> Ein Ton scheint sich dem andern zu bequemen,
> Und hat ein Wort zum Ohre sich gesellt,
> Ein andres kommt, dem ersten liebzukosen.

And now the dialogue between Faust and Helena is
continued in rhyme verse.

Spiritually and physically the two come nearer
and nearer together. The chorus sings—and says—
that they are sitting right out in the presence of the
people, shoulder to shoulder, knee to knee, hand in
hand. That Goethe's ability to depict the mutual
erotic intoxication is no longer that of his youth is
seen in the dialogue between Faust and Helena:

> *Helena:* Ich fühle mich so fern und doch so nah,
> Und sage nur zu gern: Da bin ich! Da!
> *Faust:* Ich athme kaum, mir zittert, stockt das Wort,
> Es ist ein Traum, verschwunden Tag und Ort.
> *Helena:* Ich scheine mir verlebt und doch so neu,
> In Dich verwebt, dem Unbekannten treu.
> *Faust:* Durchgrüble nicht das einzigste Geschick!
> Dasein ist Pflicht, und wär's ein Augenblick.

When Menelaos and his army threaten to make
a sudden attack, Faust mobilizes his military force
and here, where Faust after the victory divides his
land among those who have been true to him, Goethe's lyric poetry once again rises as high as it has
ever risen in descriptive strength. We have for

example these lines from Faust in his conversation
with his generals:

> In Stahl gehüllt, vom Strahl umwittert,
> Die Schaar, die Reich um Reich zerbrach,
> Sie treten auf, die Erde schüttert;
> Sie schreiten fort, es donnert nach.

Or consider this description of the countries' stock
of cattle and their flora

> Vertheilt, vorsichtig, abgemessen, schreitet
> Gehörntes Rind hinan zum jähen Rand;
> Doch Obdach ist den Sämmtlichen bereitet,
> Zu hundert Höhlen wölbt sich Felsenwand.

The picture of the tread of the oxen in the first line
is vivid and veracious. In the following stanza the
oak and the maple are portrayed with equal warmth:

> Altwälder sind's! Die Eiche starret mächtig,
> Und eigensinnig zackt sich Ast und Ast;
> Der Ahorn mild, von süssem Safte trächtig,
> Steigt rein empor und spielt mit seiner Last.

We have seen how strongly the relation to Byron
concerned Goethe; it was a filial relation in which
the English Lord placed himself with regard to
the author of *Faust*. In Goethe's estimation, and
according to the idea prevalent at the time, Byron
was the greatest poet of Europe after Goethe himself. If later generations have found that Byron
was overesteemed in countries other than England
to the extent that there were in England in his day
such poets as Keats and Shelley who, from a purely
artistic point of view, were superior to him, there
is nevertheless not a shadow of a doubt but that
he alone had historical and political influence of

the first rank; and that he was the only one who
created schools in three or four different countries.
Byron's brave determination to bring personal and
economic help to struggling Greece, even more than
his beautiful death, moved Goethe profoundly. He
felt a desire to glorify his young and brilliant col-
league, and since he had gradually become accustomed to looking upon *Faust* as a station and depot
for everything that captivated him, it lay near to
him to erect a monument to Byron in *Faust* itself.

He conceived, consequently, the singular idea of
having the tender association between Faust and
Helena result in the birth of a son, a young genius,
without wings to be sure, but springing up like a
faun, or like a chamois leaping and bounding from
cliff to cliff. Euphorion's ambition is similar to that
of Icarus: He wishes to rise up above the earth,
to move back and forth, unrestrained, free, through
the air. For the time being there is no mountain
peak that is too high for him.

All of this is allegory. There is sound sense in
it too when Euphorion—the son of Achilles in the
legend—is supposed to be the son of Faust. But
it becomes unclear when Byron is also supposed to
be the son of Helena. For just as it is clear that
Byron descends from the Danish Normans (the
name is *Björn*), from Shakespeare and Pope and
Voltaire and Rousseau, just so is it clear that there
is nothing in his life that leads back to *ancient* Hellas. His relation to Greece consists of his valiant
effort to convert it into a *new* Hellas.

Goethe obviously saw him in a different light from
that in which we see him. What we admire most
in Byron the artist is the wild humors of *Don*

Juan; in Byron, the man and statesman, it is his bold
spirit in unbroken rebellion against sham, hypocrisy
and coercion.   These are not the features that enraptured Goethe.   He saw in him a young Apollo,
a figure gloried by a Hero's death, with a halo of
poetry, or the crown of Greece, about his head.   And
consequently he has—rather peculiarly—Mephisto
himself pronounce these inspired words upon him:

In der Hand die goldne Leier, völlig wie ein kleiner Phöbus,
Tritt er wolgemuth zur Kante, zu dem Ueberhang; wir
        staunen,
Und die Eltern vor Entzücken werfen wechselnd sich an's
        Herz.
Denn wie leuchtet's ihm zu Häupten?   Was erglänzt ist
        schwer zu sagen,
Ist es Goldschmück, ist es Flamme übermächtiger Geister-
        kraft?
Und so regt er sich geberdend, sich als Knabe schon ver-
        kündend
Künftigen Meister alles Schönen, dem die ew'gen Melodien
Durch die Glieder sich bewegen; und so werdet Ihr ihn
        hören.

As characteristic of Byron, Goethe places these
lines on the lips of Euphorion:

> Das leicht Errungene
> Das widert mir;
> Nur das Erzwungene
> Ergötzt mich schier.

Lines such as these express the contrast between
the vigorous instinct for nature in Goethe's being
and the defiant element in that of Byron.   Thus
far the poetic illusion, in so far as adventurous and
fantastic traits can illude, is preserved to a certain
extent; it had to be.   But when Euphorion, in his

first attempt at soaring high up through space, falls
to earth and is crushed, and when the chorus, which
consists of captive Trojan women from the castle
of King Priam, strikes up a dirge that can allude
to just one person, to George Noël Gordon Byron,
then we feel quite beyond the age, and quite beyond
Faust. It is characteristic of Goethe, and significant
too, that in this poem, as everywhere else, it is
Byron's placing himself above and beyond custom
and usage, law and order, that concerns him, and
that shows him to be more than reconciled with the
defense of Missolunghi. Goethe has allowed himself to be a trifle misled by his faith in the imbecile stories concerning the deceased. The real
kernel of Byron's nature was not the kernel for
Goethe.

When the dirge on Euphorion is ended, Helena
returns once more to the lower world, and the entire
episode would be at an end if the chorus, which
remains behind and is now characterised as consisting of the nymphs of trees, mountains, springs,
and vineyards, had not given voice to the concluding
couplets, concerning which it is difficult to decide in
which of them Goethe's new lyric style makes itself
felt most characteristically. Note, however, especially the amazingly picturesque and musical portrayal by the dryads of the way in which they guide
the sap of plants and struggle with twigs, leaves,
flowers, and fruits:

Wir in dieser tausend Aeste Flüsterzittern, Säuselschweben
Reizen tändelnd, locken leise wurzelauf des Lebens Quellen
Nach den Zweigen, bald mit Blättern, bald mit Blüthen
　　　überschwenglich
Zieren wir die Flatterhaare frei zu luftigem Gedeihn.

Fällt die Frucht, sogleich versammeln lebenslustig Volk und
    Herden
Sich zum Greifen, sich zum Naschen, eilig kommend, emsig
    drängend,
Und wie vor den ersten Göttern, bückt sich Alles um uns
    her.

The act concerning Helena ends, then, with nature hymns in which Helena and her son are entirely
forgotten; it even disembogues in a wild festival
of Dionysus, in which Silenus and the bacchantian
followers with cloven ram's feet tread morality under foot, drink to excess, and whirl about with muddled senses—just as the Hellas tragedy of antiquity
was followed by a satyr play.

II

The new Faust poem is grouped around the Helena climax. After a beautiful elf-song, and a dignified monologue by the awakening Faust, the details
of which have just been reviewed, the scene opens
before an imperial palace in which Mephisto is court
fool, since his predecessor, after drinking himself to
death, had to be carried off. From the replies of the
courtiers as well as from the emperor's conversation
we derive the impression of a great empire in the
process of dissolution. We feel at any rate that we
have to do with a state that is without currency.
Money is lacking on all sides. A medium of exchange is to be had nowhere. Mephistopheles
makes the point that the empire's soil is full of treasures which were buried in former times out of fear
of the enemy. Asked how they are to be brought
to light, how they are to be realized, he says:

Through the natural ability and, intellectual power
of a talented man, of a spiritual leader. In reply
the benighted chancellor remonstrates as follows:

> Natur und Geist—so spricht man nicht zu Christen.
> Deshalb verbrennt man Atheisten,
> Weil solche Reden höchst gefährlich sind.
> Natur ist Sünde, Geist ist Teufel;
> Sie hegen zwischen sich den Zweifel,
> Ihr missgestaltet Zwitterkind.

In the meantime Mephistopheles promises to pro-
cure for the emperor and court just as much money
as they wish. Many contend that his promises are
the effusions of a charlatan, the catch-phrases of a
trickster. But he remains steadfast to his assertion
that the earth has an abundance of riches in hiding.

At this point, and for this reason, the action is
interrupted by a stupendous court carnival the description of which weakens the coherency of the
drama, though it gave Goethe an opportunity to
say a huge number of things that had been on his
mind for years. It opened the way for a discussion
of the varied conditions of life and the numerous
professions by which life is made a reality. He
said all he had to say about gardeners, male and female, who develop the world of flowers. He commented on wood cutters, pulchinellos, niggards, parasites, drunkards, mothers who wish to get rid of
their daughters, a mass of mythological figures,
graces, parcae, furies and so on *ad infinitem*. For
a while Faust and the plot are wholly forgotten.
This is not in the interest either of art or of dramatic economy, especially at this point where the
very exposition of the drama is involved.

Mephistopheles has by no means lost his satiric wit with years. When the court wishes to acquire the treasures of the earth without effort and cannot understand that the grape must first be ripened and then pressed to produce wine, Mephistopheles says:

> Wie sich Verdienst und Glück verketten,
> Das fällt den Thoren niemals ein;
> Wenn sie den Stein der Weisen hätten,
> Der Weise mangelte dem Stein.

The impressionistic force of the style is, without exception, striking and pleasing: Goethe's senses were sharpened with years and the feeling of his sovereignty over the language increased at the same time. He coins new words and expressions in order to reproduce down to the minutest detail the external as well as the internal reality. Thus for example the parasites say:

> Da brät's und prudelt's.
> Da kocht's und strudelt's.
> Der wahre Schmecker,
> Der Tellerlecker,
> Er riecht den Braten,
> Er ahnet Fische.
> Das regt zu Thaten
> An Gönners Tische.

He is as ingenious as he has ever been in his life. What a glorious conceit it is for example that, when the furies are introduced, it turns out that the true furies are beautiful, well formed, friendly, youthful —and none the less malignant, deceitful, passionately backbiting, creating mischief and discontent wherever they go. No better than they is the masculine abuser by profession, Zoilo-Thersites, who reviles everything that succeeds:

> Doch wo was Rühmliches gelingt,
> Es mich sogleich in Harnisch bringt,
> Das Tiefe hoch, das Hohe tief,
> Das Schiefe grad, das Grade schief,
> Das ganz allein macht mich gesund,
> So will ich's auf dem Erdenrund.

At the carnival the Emperor appears in person as the great god Pan; we are again moved by the finesse and wonderful power in the aromatic verses sung by the nymphs in his honor:

> Auch unterm blauen Wölbedach,
> Verhielt er sich beständig wach;
> Doch rieseln ihm die Bäche zu,
> Und Lüftlein wiegen ihn mild in Ruh.
> Und wenn er zu Mittage schläft,
> Sich nicht das Blatt am Zweige regt.
> Gesunder Pflanzen Balsamduft
> Erfüllt die schweigsam stille Luft . . .
> Wenn unerwartet mit Gewalt
> Dann aber seine Stimm' erschallt
> Wie Blitzesknattern, Meergebraus,
> Dann Niemand weiss wo ein noch aus. . . .

Through the aid of Mephisto, Faust now supplies the Emperor with paper money, approximately as John Law, in 1716, came to the assistance of the Regent of France, the Duke of Orleans, with his banknotes. Mephisto adds a number of witty cynicisms concerning the power that notes bestow, especially on women.

In order that Goethe might abandon all this extraneous and irrelevant discussion and revert to the real pith, substance, and theme of the poem, it is necessary to have the Emperor seized with a sud-

den impulse to see Helena and Paris before him as
a spiritual apparition. Faust requests Mephisto to
produce them. The latter replies that the entrance
to the Pagan world can be made possible only by
Faust's visiting *Die Mütter,* stern and lofty goddesses like the Norns, though conceived of as beings
who command the innermost workshop in which
Mother Nature performs her familiar deeds. They
rule over the forms of things and men. Their
thrones stand upon the ground which is beyond time
and place, in a never trodden expanse.

This fancy is surely one of Goethe's most charming and profound. It is, however, such ideas as this
that have given rise to the dolt-like observations
concerning *Faust,* Part II. We are told that it is
altogether incomprehensible. The same was said
of Beethoven's symphonies and Wagner's operas
when they first appeared. The symbolism is in truth
easy to grasp; it is also extremely enjoyable. Note
this alternation of speeches

> *Faust:* Wohin der Weg?
> *Mefistofeles:* Kein Weg! Ins Unbetretene,
>   Nicht zu Betretende; ein Weg ins Unei
>   betene,
>   Nicht zu Erbittende. Bist Du bereit?—
>   Nicht Schlösser sind, nicht Riegel wegzu-
>   schieben,
>   Von Einsamkeiten wirst umhergetrieben.
>   Hast Du Begriff von Oed' und Einsamkeit?
> *Faust:* ... Musst ich nicht mit der Welt ver-
>   kehren?
>   Das Leere lernen, Leeres lehren?—
>   *Sprach ich vernünftig, wie ich's angeschaut,*
>   *Erklang der Widerspruch gedoppelt laut;*
>   *Musst ich sogar vor widerwärt'gen Streichen*
>   *Zur Einsamkeit, zur Wildernis entweichen.*

It is Goethe himself who speaks through Faust—
and he does so with marked distinctness.   It seems
to him, and justly so, highly preposterous to ask
him whether he knows the wilderness and solitude
when he never could utter a rational word without
hearing the bellowing of fools against him, until he
finally took refuge in the loneliness of human contempt.

While Faust descends to *die Mütter* the scene is
prepared in the palace for the catoptric images of
Helena and Paris.   A Doric temple forms the
scenery; this fact gives an architect, whom Goethe
momentarily wishes to deride, opportunity to emphasize the excellence of Gothic architecture, which
the poet, plainly enough out of politeness to the
Boisserée brothers, allowed in his time to be considered as coördinate.   The apparitions appear and
Faust becomes so jealous of Paris and wants to
hinder him so passionately in his abduction of Helena, that the entire performance ends with an explosion.

III

The second act brings us back to Faust's study of
the first part.   Mephisto again finds the old mantle
in which he inspired the student with awe, and from
which a chorus of insects now comes forth buzzing
a droll song by way of greeting.   It was here that
Goethe had the brilliant idea of having Faust's
former Famulus, the noble Doctor Wagner, become,
during Faust's absence, the first man in the world
of scholarship.   He is the diurnal augmenter of
wisdom.   Around the lecture platform on which

he shines, there have gathered huge swarms of erudition's devotees. The fame of no man can compete with his. He has even outshone and darkened the name of Faust himself.

It is in this old room that the student from the first part appears as baccalaureus, now grown into an original genius with jubilant conceitedness; he uses phrases from Fichte's philosophy in order to dazzle by his youthful greatness. Here it is that we again find our old Doctor Wagner, the pedant who has now gone in for natural science, and who is on the point of creating a human being by artificial means.

This merry idea Goethe held on to and carried out with energy since just at this time, by a queer coincidence, a namesake of Wagner, Professor J. I. Wagner in Würzburg, had insisted that chemistry simply must succeed in creating a human being through the process of crystalization. The idea, moreover, came from the Middle Ages; during the Renaissance it was championed by Paracelsus, who considered it possible to create human beings without the natural process, through alchemy, somewhat as in our own day F. T. Marinetti has expressed the hope of eventually being able to create "his mechanical son" solely as the fruit of his will. And even during the Middle Ages this delicate human being in the laboratory glass was given the name of Homunculus, the name that Goethe has preserved.

When Homunculus comes to life in the glass flask with the longish neck, his gaze falls at once on Faust who, stupified, has been sleeping since the explosion. As he reads the sleeper's thoughts he begins his personal life with the above quoted monologue, which portrays Leda and the Swan, the an-

cestors of Helena. Homunculus finds it necessary
to divert Faust, and since the latter is already acquainted with the romantic world of ghosts from
his trip to the Brocken, this newly born, precocious
gentleman suggests that he strike up an acquaintance with the classical world of ghosts by way of
contrast.

In his own mind Goethe had quietly decided to
work out a parallel between the first and the second
part of *Faust,* in so far as this could be done. The
witches' sabbath on Walpurgis Night of the first
part was to correspond to the classical Walpurgis
Night of the second part. Wagner is to remain at
home. He still has something to do by way of
brooding over the old *pergamenta* that feed his
mind. Faust, Mephisto, and Homunculus, the latter of whom floats through the air and guides the
others on the way with light from his glass flask,
all set out at the same time.

Thessalian sorceresses, griffins, pismires, sphinxes,
sirens, nymphs, Chiron the centaur, pygmies, cranes,
lamiae, all sorts of fabulous beings meet the trav-
ellers as they journey in the dark over the Pharsalian
fields. At the song of a siren, which flatters the ear
but leaves the heart cold, Goethe was in all probability thinking of Rossini's music which did not correspond to his German taste.

Faust loses himself in great classical reminiscences: As a means of resistance against the song
of the sirens, Odysseus had himself bound to the
masts of the ship and his ears stopped up. Otherwise Faust is concerned only with Helena; he asks
the sphinxes whether they have seen her. Resting
on the banks of the Peneios, he sees before him once

more the vision that Homunculus described; the
swan approaches Leda and her hand-maidens. This
is the mystic pairing that resulted in the genesis of
Helena. He also meets Chiron, who had raptur-
ously borne her on the back of his steed when she
fled with her brothers from a band of robbers:

> Da sprang sie ab und streichelte
> Die feuchte Mähne, schmeichelte,
> Und dankte lieblichklug und selbstbewusst.
> Wie war sie reizend! Jung, des Alten Lust!

Goethe once more amuses himself by shattering
all illusions. He has Faust ask: She was only seven
years old? And Chiron replies: I see, *Die Philo-
logen* have deceived you as well as themselves.

We have here a repetition of Mephisto's uncanny
relation to the witches from the first part. The
lamiae give him no peace; nor he them. These old
Greek vampyres are portrayed, incidentally, just
like ultra-modern women. Mephisto characterises
them as follows:

> Man weiss, das Volk taugt aus dem Grunde nichts:
> Geschnürten Leibs, geschminkten Angesichts,
> Nichts haben sie Gesundes zu erwidern,
> Wo man sie anfasst, morsch in allen Gliedern. . .
> Mann weiss, man sieht's, man kann es greifen,
> Und dennoch tanzt man, wenn die Luder pfeifen.

The old philosophers are found here; they have
arisen from the dead. They discuss, as above mentioned, the problem of the genesis of the earth. In
an invocation of Artemis, Anaxagoras has these delightful lines:

> Du Brusterweiternde, im Tiefsten Sinnige,
> Du Ruhigscheinende, Gewaltsam-Innige!

It is annoying to find, as is usually the case in Goethe's works, the Greek and the Latin names of the gods so confused, so chaotically arranged. Artemis is called *Diana, Luna, Hekate.* In like fashion sphinxes sing four lines in which the Greek name for the sun, *Helios,* is paired with the Latin name for the moon, *Luna.*

In this section Goethe has vigorously asserted, through Thales as his mouthpiece, the Neptunian conception of the genesis of the earth. In flowing verses he has Italian and Lybian snake exorcists sing the praise of the sea:

> In stillbewusstem Behagen
> Bewahren wir Cypriens Wagen
> Und führen beim Säuseln der Nächte
> Durch liebliches Wellengeflechte
> Unsichtbar dem neuen Geschlechte
> Die liebliche Tochter heran.

Thales, however, as the champion of the theory that the earth was formed through the rising and falling of the sea, becomes the leading character at this juncture. He sings a song of praise to the water as an element. It sprang from the depths of Goethe's soul; and it is a happy product of his genius:

> Heil, heil aufs Neue!
> Wie ich mich blühend freue,
> Vom Schönen, Wahren durchdrungen.
> Alles ist aus dem Wasser entsprungen!
> Alles wird durch das Wasser enthalten!
> Ozean, gönn' uns dein ewiges Walten!
> Wenn du nicht Wolken sendetest,
> Nicht reiche Bäche spendetest,
> Hin und her nicht Flüsse wendetest,
> Die Ströme nicht vollendetest,
> Was wären Gebirge, was Ebnen und Welt?

Following this geological interlude, we have the central act originally entitled Helena. It was the first to be written. It has already been discussed.

IV

The fourth act of the drama is the least interesting. As happened not infrequently in the Middle Ages, an anti-emperor rose up against the real emperor. We become witnesses to a campaign and a defeat during which the magic arts of Faust and Mephisto turn the scales in the favor of the imperial power. The enemy is so completely hallucinated by sorcery that he sees running water on all sides, which makes a firm foothold impossible.

As a reward, Faust demands from the Emperor all the coast land of the empire, and such parts of the land itself as can be wrested from the sea. The Emperor confers titles of distinction on his deserving followers, and grants them positions of trust and honor. But he allows himself to be hopelessly intimidated by the archbishop, who requests and receives penitence and concessions from him because he dared to misuse his power to the extent of liberating a heretic who had already been bound to the stake which, in accordance with an order direct from Rome, he was to set on fire instantly and without mental hesitation. The truth is, we find precious little in this entire political act to arouse human sympathy or chain the reader's interest, whereas an inordinate number of gripping scenes and songs have been fused together in the sublime and singular fifth act.

Faust has become the ruler over a vast stretch

of land situated by the sea, wrested from the sea,
as was Holland or Venice, with extensive trade and
the wealth of a sea power. He is very old; he has
become morose and domineering. Philemon and
Baucis, the venerable and innocent old couple, occupy a little home surrounded with linden trees;
they obstruct Faust's view and consequently annoy
him, somewhat as the mill at Sans Souci irritated
Frederick II, or as Naboth's vineyard aroused the
avariciousness of King Ahab. Faust has offered
the two old people a better home within his realm;
but they cling to their own property. Faust then
orders Mephisto to dispossess them by force. Mephisto and his servants carry out the order in the
rudest sort of fashion They burn the little house,
and the old couple, noted for their gentleness and
fidelity, are burned with it. Here, as so frequently
in Goethe's work, the consequences of a deed, reprehensible and yet *per se* pardonable, become
terrifying.

Lynceus, the guardian of the tower, is a witness
to the atrocity from his high seat of activity. His
monologue belongs to the most beautiful of the
lyric parts of the entire tragedy. It begins:

> Zum Sehen geboren,
> Zum Schauen bestellt,
> Dem Thurme geschworen,
> Gefällt mir die Welt.
> Ich blick' in die Ferne,
> Ich seh' in der Näh'
> Den Mond und die Sterne,
> Den Wald und das Reh.

From the ashes of the little house there arise
four avenging ghosts, four gray women, in the per-

sons of whom Goethe has condensed romantic terrors. Their names are *Mangel, Schuld, Sorge,* and
Noth. And *Noth* has a brother whose name is *Tod;*
he follows at her heels. The scene between Faust
and these four weird creatures is one of the deepest
and most emotional, not simply of *Faust* but of
poetry as a whole. There is poetically clarified
anxiety and depressing knowledge of men in every
single line. The fear of old age, torture, and death
is expressed magnificently; this it was that Maeter-
linck was to vary half a century later and thereby
bring fame to his name.

What Faust says and what the four old women
say in return embraces the terrifying tragedy of
every wretched human life. The uncanniness begins
to make itself felt at Faust's very first words:

> Vier sah ich kommen, drei nur gehn;
> Den Sinn der Rede konnt' ich nicht verstehn,
> Es klang so nach, als hiess es—Noth,
> Ein düstres Reimwort folgte—Tod.
> Es tönte hohl, gespensterhaft, gedämpft.

Faust regrets his relation to magic; he would
be most happy if he could forget all the words of
witchcraft he ever knew. But this point (in which
Hermann Türck has seen the leading idea) has for
me less interest in comparison with the universally
human content of the monologue:

> Wenn auch *ein* Tag uns klar vernünftig lacht,
> In Traumgespinnst verwickelt uns die Nacht!
> Wir kehren froh von junger Flur zurück,
> Ein Vogel krächzt. Was krächzt er? Missgeschick.

Infinitely tragic is the following dialogue between
Sorge and Faust, which ends by *Sorge's* breathing

into Faust's eyes and blinding him. He feels night
and darkness welling up about him; but his courage
is not crushed. He calls in his servants and sets
them to work; his far-reaching plans must now be
realized. He demands order and industry; he
wishes to hear the sound of hoes and spades. There
is a swamp that must be drained; a dwelling place
must be created for countless men in the future.
And while the Lemures, that is to say, the wretched
shades of the deceased, dig Faust's grave by torch-
light in the fore-yard of the palace, Goethe, with
exalted and profound irony, leads him to believe
that the work has been begun on the plan he has
always had in mind, the embankment against the sea,
creating thereby a happy life for generations to
come, in lee and shelter against the storm and protected from the onrush of the ocean. From his lips
there come now the most beautiful truths; and over
them glide at the same time the expression for the
most incurable illusions. He speaks such truths as
this famous one:

> Das ist der Weisheit letzter Schluss:
> Nur dur verdient sich Freiheit und das Leben,
> Der taglich sie erobern muss.

He resigns, in that he confuses the sound of the
spades that are digging his grave with the sound of
the tools that are making fertile a stretch of land,
to the sad illusion that he is preparing a glorious
future. When he, in the anticipation of this, enjoys
the highest moment he shall—by an artificial interpretation of his words—have lost the wager of his
youth with Mephisto, the wager that he himself,
and the readers too, have long since forgotten. He
sinks back while the Lemures catch him and stretch

him out on the earth. His remarks seem more those
of Goethe than of Faust, and in the reading world
they have lost, and not without reason, every trace
of the ironically despairing shadow which the situation casts over them:

> Solch ein Gewimmel möcht' ich sehen,
> Auf freiem Grund mit freiem Volke stehn
> Zum Augenblicke dürft' ich sagen:
> Verweile doch. Du bist so schön.
> *Es kann die Spur von meinen Erdetagen*
> *Nicht in Aeonen untergehn.*

There follows the struggle, after the fashion
of Mediaeval tradition, between the devils and the
angels for the soul of the departed; Goethe has
elaborated it with a deal of energy. He has not
even shuddered from such a disgusting feature as
the depicting of the paederastic lusts that arise in
Mephisto at the sight of the nude angels' bodies;
but in individual strophes of the angels' song, the
metre of which is supposed to recall the angels' song
on that first Easter morning, the song that prevented Faust from committing suicide, are on the
same high level on which the poet moved when a
young man.

While the angels, the clarified Gretchen among
them, scatter roses over Faust's body, and the devils
seek to get possession of his soul, they sing these
beautiful verses:

> Rosen, Ihr blendenden,
> Balsam versendenden!
> Flatternde, schwebende,
> Heimlich belebende
> Zweigleinbeflügelte,
> Knospenentsiegelte,
> Eilet zu blühn!

Frühling entspriesse
Purpur und Grün!
Tragt Paradiese
Dem Ruhenden hin!

We have already seen to what extent the second part of this sublime creation lacks unity and coherency, though it was written without interruption. It has in truth not much more unity than the first part, which was written at odd intervals, as the spirit moved, and as time allowed. The anxiety as to whether Faust's soul will be accepted in the Catholic Heaven has undeniably been thrust into the background, so far as the reader is concerned, throughout the long period during which no one has thought about it, but during which the possibility of an espousal between him as a German from the period of the Renaissance and Helena as a Grecian woman of olden days has seemed to be the kernel of the poem.

Goethe has produced a very strong artistic effect by reaching back, at the close of the tragedy, to the very problem that was always presented and solved in the Mediaeval Mysteries. Posterity has been struck by the manner in which Goethe's voice seems to drown out that of Faust in the closing words:

Es kann die Spur von meinen Erdetagen
Nicht in Aeonen untergehn.

And yet it is by no means certain that the words were not written naïvely and with poetic honesty, and intended as the expression of the dying Faust's hope. When we recall other lines written by Goethe that are equally strong and equally unaffected, lines that betray a hearty distrust in posterity, one feels a bit shaky as to the confidence that here seems to be expressed in the generations that are to come after us. Incidentally, Goethe wrote also this stanza:

Nach kurzem Lärm legt Fama sich zur Ruh,
Vergessen wird der Held so wie der Lotterbube.
Der grösste König macht die Augen zu,
Und jeder Hund bepisst gleich seine Grube.

There is a remote possibility, however, that Goethe conceived of himself as constituting an exception to the general rule he laid down in these verses.

CHAPTER XXXVII

GOETHE, CUVIER, AND GEOFFROY DE SAINT-
HILAIRE—GOETHE AND THE GERMAN PUBLIC—
GOETHE AND FRANCE—GOETHE AND ENGLAND

GOETHE's intellectual interests were just as keen
and vigorous after his eightieth year as they had
ever been. He followed with real suspense the dis-
pute then being waged between Cuvier and Geoffroy
de Saint-Hilaire; he was delighted when it came to
an open rupture in the meeting of the French Scientific Society on July 19, 1830, that is, less than two
weeks before the outbreak of the July Revolution.
The question under discussion had to do with his old,
old belief in the mutability, and possibility of development, on the part of all beings and species. The
theory had been rejected during his entire life. Now
he saw it taken up by Saint-Hilaire and defended in
opposition to Cuvier's theory of the finished species,
the species that cannot and does not evolve. He
lived, therefore, to see his favorite idea come out
victorious in scientific debate.

Soret has related the charming anecdote of how
Goethe, at the former's visit on August 2, 1830,
received him in great excitement with the words:
"What do you think! What is the news from Paris!
The volcano has broken out!" Soret thought that
Goethe was speaking of the political revolution
which, in reality, impressed him as being of but quite

negligible importance. His mind had really been
aroused by the scientific revolution that was then
well under way. Soret writes:

Nouvelles inquiétantes de Paris; j'ai un bon coq-à-l'âne
avec Goethe à leur sujet; je lui fais visite dans le courant de
l'aprè-diner: Eh bien! s'ecrie-t-il, que pensez vous de cette
grande affaire? Violà tout en combustion, ce n'est plus une
affaire à huis clos, le volcan vient d'éclater!—La chose est
terrible, me suis-je mis à répondre; une aussi misérable
famille donne bien peu d'espoir, appuyée d'un aussi misérable
ministère. On finira par les chasser.
Mais je ne parle pas de ces gens-là, que m'importe! Il
s'agit de la grande querelle entre Cuvier et Geoffroy.

By virtue of his spiritual vigilance Goethe overcame the troubles of age, severe attacks of illness,
and death which ravaged round about him, as well
as the jubilees which belong to the terrors of old
age—the fiftieth anniversary of his arrival in Weimar, the fiftieth anniversary of Karl August's reign,
and so on. It was this, too, that assuaged the feelings of loneliness after so many friends had departed—his Duke, his son, and the women who had
once stood near him. For several years he devoted
himself to the completion of *Faust—das Hauptgeschäft,* the appellation under which it at that time
alone appeared in his diary. When the work was
finished, packed up, and sealed without its occurring
to him for a second to publish it, he felt satisfied and
at ease; he had received a vacation. He was no
longer to write in his diary: "Das Hauptgeschäft
bedeutend gefördert." His time was now his own;
he could use the days that were left him as he willed.
Numerous they were not. July 22, 1831, Goethe
wrote in his diary: *Das Hauptgeschäft zu Stande*

gebracht. . . . Alles rein Geschriebene geheftet.
Precisely eight months later, March 22, 1832, he
breathed his last after a week's illness. On the
day of his death he felt so ill that he could not remain in bed; he wished to rest in his easy chair, the
arm chair which even now stands in the little room
in the Goethe house where he sat when he died. His
dead body, according to contemporary testimony,
was surprisingly beautiful.

II

On July 17, 1777, Goethe wrote, with a captious-
ness that is characteristic of immature minds, this
celebrated little poem to Countess Auguste von
Stolberg:

> Alles geben die Götter, die Unendlichen,
> Ihren Lieblingen ganz;
> Alle Freuden, die unendlichen,
> Alle Schmerzen, die unendlichen,
> Ganz.

Though the thesis seems to have found confirma-
tion in his own life, his familiar words to Eckermann, January 27, 1824, are equally true:

> I have always been regarded as having been specially
> favored by fortune. I am not inclined to complain of my
> lot, or bemoan my career. But in actuality it has been noth-
> ing but toil and trouble. I can truly say that in all my
> seventy-five years I have not had four weeks in which I was
> really happy. It was the incessant turning and lifting of a
> stone that had to be lifted and turned once more. . . . The
> claims upon my time, within as well as from without, were
> far too numerous.

It was not long after Goethe's death that K. von
Conta was speaking of him to his friend Heinrich

Meyer. Conta told Meyer that Goethe was the happiest mortal that ever lived. Meyer denied it stoutly. He insisted that the discomfort which Goethe had been obliged to undergo, at times through his own action, was more than outweighed by the happiness he may have enjoyed. Meyer also made the point that the excess of praise which men occasionally showered upon him motivated the bitterest injustice a man's heart can suffer in that it inspired his opponents to criticism and censure that were all the more caustic.

It would seem that Goethe was not influenced by the painful incidents that befell him in a material and external way; but it only seems so. Silence is rarely the antidote to suffering, and in Goethe's case never. His lips were sealed but his heart was hurt. There is irrefutable truth in Eckermann's statement. Fate was not hostile to Goethe along lines and in fields that are easily described. But as a thinker with an original mind, and a poet with a matchless imagination, he was not the favored child of fortune; his lot cannot be regarded as an enviable one.

What we are pleased to call the public is, all things taken into consideration, a power the stupidity of which can never be fathomed. Goethe's case was unique; his misfortune was without equal. In the first place, his people constituted anything but a united nation. In the second they were so far behind in general development that there was no native standard by which to measure a mental force or an activity such as his. His public was without an organ for free beauty; there was no mouthpiece for liberal art. For centuries the ideal had been

accessible to the public in no form other than the
moral or the moralizing. The apostles of Enlightenment who had been his predecessors, and who had
had their own hard fight with orthodoxy, had never,
even in their poetry, advanced beyond the point
where they disseminated utilitarian truths. The
men of *Sturm und Drang,* who wished to become his
allies, merely revelled in sentimentality, and wielded
their blunt and heavy pens in the cause of common-
places. We have but to think of Lenz. And yet,
his public was quite unable to make an appreciable
distinction between him and them, between a Goethe
and a Lenz.

When therefore voices were raised in older civ-
ilizations, particularly in England, in zealous proc-
lamation of the disjointed, the fragmentary, the
stylistically uncertain elements in Goethe's works,
someone should have had the grace of liberality to
remark that intelligent support on the part of the
general public is one of the prerequisites to creation.
Without it the author feels abandoned by his friends
and surrendered to his foes. He cannot write with
ease and distinction. Feeling absolutely alone, he
gives up his task when only half completed, or even
earlier. He finds it possible to complete it only
through the expenditure of excessive will power
when he knows in advance that it is not going to
meet with a cordial response on the part of those
who did not write it, but who might reasonably be
supposed to read it. Goethe knew that his public
stood on a low level, so low that it could be inspired
only patriotically, only by hearing the nation to
which it by chance belonged praised, preferably at
the expense of other nations. Or it could be moved

only through sentimentality, by reading the stories
of the agonies of love in the hearts of the young.
And there were, truth to tell, only three times in
his life when Goethe had his public solidly with him
and behind him: When he published *Götz*, when
he published *Werther*, and when he published *Hermann und Dorothea*.

The public at that time, as always, was accustomed to look to its leaders to see what it should
think. But on this occasion, for once, the leaders
left the public—and Goethe—in the lurch. Lessing was a stranger to restraint in his malignant
criticism of *Götz* and *Werther*. He was beside
himself with wrath when he read brave Wieland's
epistle in praise of Goethe. Klopstock, who survived Lessing by so many years, invariably treated
Goethe's poetry with ironic or overt contempt. He
had called his *Iphigenie* a *stiff* imitation of the
Greeks; he scorned the theme in *Hermann und Dorothea* on the ground that it was inadequately exalted
for epic treatment. He uttered the most pitiable
witticisms on and against the nine muses who sing
in rustic taverns. Nor did he fail to avail himself
of the opportunity to tell Goethe that it was he who
could not write German. This happened when
Goethe wrote his epigramme against the German
language. Klopstock spake as follows:

Die deutsche Sprache

Goethe, du dauerst mich, dass du mich schreibst? Wenn
     du mich kenntest,
Wäre dir dies nicht Gram. Goethe, du dauerst mich auch!

The friendship between Goethe and Schiller
aroused Klopstock's cordial embitterment. He in-

formed the two gentlemen that they were square-
toes from whose mouths exuded nothing but self-
praise.   One epigramme begins:

Afterahmer und Original sind sonst sich was ungleich,
Dennoch gleichen sie sich, *Schüler und Gothe,* die Herrn!
Kaum dass der Eine des Eigenlobs Trompete vom vollen
Mund absetzt, so ergreift sie der Ander' und bläst.

From the very beginning of Goethe's life in Weimar, he was regarded in the German reading world
as dead to literature; he was at any rate forgotten.
In his *Charaktere deutscher Dichter und Prosaisten,*
two volumes, K. A. Küttner, the literary historian,
rejoices to record the fact that "little by little, and
gradually withal, the overwhelming praise that
drunken admirers have lavished upon Goethe is
dying out."

Nor dare we overestimate the satisfaction that
the Court in Weimar could give Goethe, and still
more cautious must we be about the alleged appreciation he enjoyed on the part of its members.   Six
months after his arrival, Charlotte von Stein de-
scribes, in a letter written in French to the physician Zimmermann, the Ducal family in the following
words:

A ruler who, at odds with himself, discontented with
the world about him, places his very life in jeopardy day
after day, and this despite his naturally weak constitu-
tion; an even sicklier brother; a morose mother; a dis-
gruntled wife.   Good creatures all of them, but of harmony in this family—not a trace.

We have already seen what difficulties ensued
from living with Herder.   In a letter from Goethe
to Lavater, written in September, 1780, we read:

"Herder continues to make his own life and the lives of those about him bitter." Before he had gone very far on his career, Goethe lost Merck, of whom we read this significant note in his diary of July 13, 1779: "Since he is the only person who thoroughly understands what I do and why I do it, and yet sees everything from a different point of view, a gratifying certainty and assurance arises between us."

Charlotte von Stein's criticisms of Clärchen, the *Römische Elegien,* and *Wilhelm Meister* show that she never had the faintest conception of Goethe's art; that she could not possibly be the ideal public which he persistently tried to find in her. That Christiane could not constitute an ideal audience lies on the surface. So far as she is concerned we did not need, in order to convince ourselves of her lack of ability to appreciate Goethe, the jocose observation which Oehlenschläger alleged to have heard from Goethe's own lips: "Es ist doch wunderlich, die Kleine kann gar kein Gedicht verstehen."

In short, no human being eager for a reputation of sanity, can ever maintain that Goethe enjoyed the appreciation from his fellow citizens that spurs an author on, creates in him a burning desire to write, and enables him to execute the plans his genius has designed. Indeed there were even times when the master, old or young, looked upon Weimar itself with troubled eyes. The question having arisen as to whether his foster-son, Fritz von Stein, should enter the service of Prussia or that of Weimar, Goethe wrote to the boy's mother, his quondam friend: "Anyone who wishes to *live* and see what the world looks like, should stand aghast at the thought of service in a petty state as he would shudder at the sight of *an open grave."* And yet, Karl August was more enlightened than any prince in Germany at that time.

That even Schiller was at first ill calculated to appreciate Goethe's art is proved by his preposterous criticism of Egmont. It was only under the impression of the master's personality as seen at close range, and of his purely personal good-will, that Schiller lifted himself up, as it were, above the level of his own life and that of his century and became the great promoter of Goethe into which he eventually developed. But by his partnership with Schiller, Goethe did anything but incur the favor of the German public. The rising up of the two men against common opponents was explained by that marvelous factor dubbed public opinion in some such fashion as the following: The noble Schiller, who loved the true, the beautiful, and the good, has been led astray by Goethe, as heartless as he is shameless, by Goethe whose immorality even liberal Herder, the friend of his youth, condemned without reserve. (Herder to Knebel, August 5, 1887, concerning *Die Braut von Korinth*: "Priapus as a pagan youth priapises, in this ballad, a cold and heartless corpse into the living warmth of passion.")

That Schiller, after he had finished *Wallenstein,* considered himself in all good faith as Goethe's equal, and ceased looking up to him by way of understanding him, is in no way surprising. His own endowment, which belonged so wholly to the eighteenth century, made it difficult for him to appreciate that in Goethe which not merely extended beyond his century, but was independent of all time.

It was indeed Rahel who led the way toward an understanding of Goethe; she had no misgivings and but few false judgments. Later came Bettina, then the Schlegels. They pointed out the contrast between Goethe's poetry and Schiller's rhetoric. They felt, for a time at least, a really sincere reverence for Goethe. But it was only for a time. At the very beginning of the nineteenth century, their attitude underwent a complete right-about-face. Indifference was followed by hostility. It was the tubercular Novalis who first made the grand discovery that *Wilhelm Meister* is mere prose. His second invention lay in the formula: As a poet Tieck is different from and greater than Goethe. This final break between the author of *Faust* and the rejuvenators of *die wunderbare Märchenwelt* was brought on by Goethe's treatise on Winckelmann. In a letter to Fouqué, A. W. Schlegel called it a "sin against the Holy Ghost." Friedrich Schlegel maintained in all seriousness that Fouqué's *Der Zauberring* was, next to *Don Quixote* (*Wilhelm Meister* and *Die Wahlverwandtschaften* are no longer taken into account), the very best of all novels.

As a sort of Apostles Creed on the part of the Romanticists, the view became more and more general that there was a poet who would some day— the day was not specified—dethrone Goethe and enthrone himself. This poet was Ludwig Tieck. Immermann, the ally of Heine, wrote on November 28, 1831, these glorious words to Tieck: "Methinks the domain of real poetry begins where Goethe (with a few exceptions) stops."

Admiration for Goethe was contrary to the spirit

of a North German on general principles. Without being more moral than the men of other races,
the North German places a high value on, and he
wishes to see portrayed, *moral,* that is to say, bi-
sected beings in whom the intellectual wages a stub-
born war against the sensual. Nothing interests
him less (as is the case with a Northerner in general) than *nature,* nature without dualism, without
the schism between pleasure and duty, nature as an
all-embracing unity. If nature were worshipped
without restraint and with no feeling of shame, what
would the preachers have to preach about? Who
would wish to receive their words of consolation?

In his *Der Fall Wagner,* Nietzsche says: "We
are familiar with Goethe's fate in morally sour, old-
maidenish Germany. Goethe has always been repellent to the Germans; honest admirers he has
found only among Jewesses." We have seen what
Pustkuchen had to say in his *Wanderjahre.* A
little later, Vogler and Köchy wrote the even more
venomous book entitled *Goethe als Mensch und
Schriftsteller.* And when Romanticism was setting
and Liberalism was rising, Goethe became the especial target. To aim at it and hit it was to carry
off the big prize. Wolfgang Menzel was the master
marksman. It is impossible for an individual of
today to realize the weight that was attached at
that time to his history of German literature; there
are two volumes; Tieck is lauded to the skies. But
in this work called *Die deutsche Literatur* (1827),
Goethe is treated with all the contempt known to
envy and born of prejudice. Menzel finds him lacking in morality, in love of country, in love of liberty,
and in religion. Goethe has flattered all the preju-

dices and all the vanities of the age. He has three
different brands of personal vanity. He has no
poetic *genius;* he does have *talent;* but it is devoid
of inner durability; it is a hetæra who has her price
for everyone. Goethe has, too, marked "ability to
make his readers his accomplices." He loved to
swim with the stream and on the surface, like cork.
He made himself the servant of every weakness
that chanced just then to be in vogue. Under the
polished mask of his works there lies concealed a
refined lust for sensuous pleasures. His poetry
shows the materialism of the modern world in full
bloom.

As we have mentioned before, in the discussion of
Die Braut von Korinth, Menzel catalogued six different types of voluptuousness in Goethe. He went
through his works seriatim in order to measure them
with his moral-national yardstick. In case it was
impossible for him to show up any instances of real
immorality, he preferred charges against him on
the ground of his lack of originality. *Hermann
und Dorothea* was disposed of as a sheer and mere
imitation of Voss's *Luise.* In truth, says Menzel,
Goethe was original only in *Faust* and *Wilhelm
Meister;* and he was original here because he imitated himself. Moreover, he borrowed, as a
younger man, from Molière and Beaumarchais,
from Shakespeare and from Lessing, whereas his
later "iambic tragedies" were merely "the fruits of
his contest with Schiller."

And such a book the Germans read! And such
a book Heinrich Heine commended! But Heine
soon found it convenient to keep poles removed
from Menzel. As to Börne's politically well founded

though in actuality insane attacks on Goethe, we
have already spoken at length in another place (in
"Main Currents," vol. VI). Gervinus's moral-
political conception of literature led to an idolization of Shakespeare at Goethe's expense. To understand Goethe was not given to Gervinus.

It is highly significant that in every single instance
in which Goethe modestly called attention to his
limitations, to some inadequate phase of his talents,
his opponents leaped at the confessions with un-
curbed ecstasy. Incapable themselves of finding defects, or appreciating real merit, they made a great
ado out of these statements from the poet himself.
And despite the obligatory admiration for Goethe
in literary circles, the clerical opposition to him was
not disarmed until quite recently; it has indeed not
been completely demobilized at this very day. On
the hundredth anniversary of his birth, in 1849,
everyone was so preoccupied with the revolution
and the reaction that the celebration passed by almost unnoticed. Politics at that time swallowed
up every other consideration. It was not until after
the founding of the German Empire that *Goethe
Philologie* gained a firm foothold in Germany. Since
then the study of Germany's greatest poet has been
developed into a formal system. The homage that
is done him has become a service in the temple. It
is a matter of consecration or hands off.

III

There was something in Goethe's character that
made it impossible for him ever to become universally popular. He was too great, too inaccessible,

to be admired with reason by more than the minority. If his renown has spread throughout the entire world, and if it can at this moment be said to be unshakable and indestructible, this does not mean that his works have won such legions of readers as have the novels of Walter Scott or those of the elder Dumas. It merely means that those who know art and appreciate literature in their noblest manifestations have imbued their fellow countrymen with faith in his superiority. Every now and then his incomparable genius is taken to task for this or that. But the charge is invariably weak; it is full of holes and falls apart on being handled. It comes about as the result of just one thing: The skeptic has made unto himself a weapon from his own ignorance and irrationality. Goethe has entered the phalanx of the earth's most excellent minds.

While still living, he was known, and his works were appreciated, by individuals in the majority of the larger, and smaller, literatures, Scandinavia not excepted. A study of Goethe's significance for Denmark has been made in another place ("Samlede Skrifter," vol. I, page 266 ff.: *Goethe og Danmark.*) But from these lesser literatures he never received one single impulse that expanded his soul or enlightened his mind. In order to become world famous, he was obliged to make an impression in France and England. This he succeeded in doing while quite young. But the knowledge of him beyond a little circle was so slight and one-sided that it cannot be said to have been of much value.

It was *Werther*, soon translated into French, that gave Goethe a hearing in France. But even this worked out in such a way that for the next forty years the French persisted in calling him "the author of Werther." The expression encompassed their knowledge of him. By his *Werther* he had made, along with Rousseau, Young, and Ossian, a lasting impression on French literature. It was done into French by Count Schmettau (Aubry), Deyverdun, Henry de la Bédoyère, Sevelinges, imitated by Nodier, remodelled by Chateaubriand (as *René*), by Sénancour (as *Obermann*), defended by Madame de Staël in her book *On Germany*, and copied by Frau von Krüdener (in *Valérie*). At last it occurred to the French that Goethe had written a number of other things besides *Werther*. But his mental pliability confused them for a long time. They were accustomed to find an author at that particular spot where they had left him. They were always certain never to find Goethe there. When Benjamin Constant visited Goethe in Weimar, he was astonished to find him utterly indifferent to the attitude of the public and in no way concerned about the circulation of his own works. Even Constant had an eye single to the external effect.

The mere name of *Götz von Berlichingen* was, for men of the old classical school, the sign to laugh. Even as late as 1825, Auger acted in the French Academy as though the thing were unpronounceable. But on some of the leading French Romanticists the work made an indelible impression. One of these was Prosper Mérimée. He had turned to Goethe with deference and confidence. Goethe abused his trust. He unveiled his *nom de plume;* he announced him as the author of the *Illyrian Folksongs*. Mérimée was vexed; but he was inspired by scenes from *Götz;* the valiant scenes in his *La Jac-*

quérie show it. Ludovic Vitet also came under the spell of *Götz;* the excellent scenes in his *Les Barricades* prove it.

The younger set who wrote for the *Globe* were introduced to Goethe through Victor Cousin who visited Weimar in 1817 and again in 1825. Also, and especially, by Jean Jacques Ampère, who came to Weimar in 1827, remained there for months, and eventually came to a full appreciation of Goethe's originality.

Hermann und Dorothea, Wilhelm Meister and *Die Wahlverwandtschaften* had been translated as early as 1800, 1802, 1810. The character of Faust was a cryptic puzzle to the French—at first. But *Faust* was again and again translated. Its influence on Edgar Quinet's *Ashasvérus* is unmistakable. *Hermann und Dorothea* was imitated by Victor de Laprade in his *Pernette.* *Werther* was parodied on the French stage, while *Clavigo* was revised and performed time out of mind.

Goethe's lyrics were frequently translated by the Romanticists, each poem many times; the *mot juste* was not easy to find, but the search was pleasing. Charles Nodier even translated the poem on the violet:

> La violette ingénue
> Au fond d'un vallon obscur
> Déployait sur l'herbe émue
> Son frais pavillon d'azur.

Der Fischer was translated several times:

> L'onde frémit, l'onde s'agite,
> Tout près du bord est un pêcheur.
> De ce beau lac le charme excite
> Dans l'âme une molle langueur.

Emile Deschamps laid before Goethe his translation of *Die Braut von Korinth;* it won the poet's approval:

> Un jeune homme d'Athène à Corinthe est venu.
> C'est la première fois.   Cependant il espère
> Chez un noble habitant, vieux hôte de son père,
> Entrer comme un ami trop longtemps inconnu.

It was A. Stapfer who gave the best translation of Mignon's song of longing:

> Ne la connais-tu pas, la terre du poète
> La terre du soleil, où le citron mûrit,
> Ou l'orange aux tons d'or dans les feuilles sourit?
> C'est là, maître c'est là qu'il faut mourir et vivre,
> C'est là qu'il faut aller, c'est là qu'il faut me suivre,

Théophile Gautier has even tried to reproduce a few lines of *Wanderers Nachtlied:*

> Pas une feuille qui bouge,
> Pas un seul oiseau chantant.

As an older man Gautier was dominated in general by the idea of Goethe's olympian deportment, as it was then called.   His entire collection of *Emaux et Camées* is written in Goethe's spirit, and under the influence of Goethe's *Divan.*

Enthusiasm for Goethe gradually took hold of the thinking and aesthetic youth of France.   They outdid each other in their eagerness to show him homage.   David d'Angers made a journey to Weimar in order to complete a bust of Goethe.   Hector Berlioz sent him the score of his excellent but fantastic work entitled *Eight Scenes from Faust* (in the translation of Nerval).   This letter begins as follows:

Dans l'atmosphère de gloire, où vous vivez, si des suf-
frages obscurs ne peuvent vous toucher, du moins j'espère
que vouz pardonnerez à un jeune compositeur qui, le coeur
gonflé et l'imagination enflammée par votre génie, n'a pu
retenir un cri d'admiration.

Though Victor Hugo mentioned "the great Goethe" in his inaugural address on being admitted to
the Academy, as the one at whose death German
thought paled in retirement, Hugo never actually
appreciated Goethe; he found him "cold and egotis-
tical." His brother-in-law, Paul Foucher, published,
on the contrary, a hymn to Goethe, in 1830, that is
replete with passionate admiration. Its concluding
lines run:

Nos gloires à tes pieds naissent, luttent, s'écroulent;
Pour leurs flots expirants ton roc est un écueil,
Ces vagues d'un instant, qui sur sa base roulent,
Le rendent plus splendide et plus luisant à l'oeil.

The death of Goethe was regarded in France as
the most far-reaching literary event in Europe since
the death of Lord Byron. In Paris, Lesguillon's
Méphistophélès, inspired by *Faust,* was to be performed for the first time just as the news of Goethe's
death arrived. The performance was introduced
by an *Homage to the Spirit of Goethe* (Hommage
aux mânes de Goethe) which began as follows:

Lorsque nous méditons au theatre, en silence,
L'oeuvre qu'à votre arrêt nous offrons aujourd'hui,
Un cri de mort vers nous s'élance:
    Goethe n'est plus! Goethe! celui
Qui, depuis soixante ans, de victoire en victoire,
    Promenant son front radieux
Toujours jeune et nouveau, se berçait dans la gloire
    Comme le soleil dans les cieux.

When Auguste Barbier, at that time living in Rome, received the news he united in beautiful verse his homage to Goethe with his homage to the former capital of the world which then lay in ruins.

> O Goethe! O grand viellard, prince de Germanie!
> Penché sur Rome antique et son mâle génie,
> Je ne puis m'empêcher, dans mon chant éploré,
> A ce grand nom croulé d'unir ton nom sacré.

Geoffroy de Saint-Hilaire's intimate relation to Goethe in his last years has already been touched upon. In June, 1836, he read a paper before the French Academy on Goethe's scientific works in which he honored him, first and foremost, for his having fixed the hypothesis concerning organic unity.

Among the numerous Frenchmen who were permeated with Goethe's spirit after his death, and who emphasized his superiority over his age, the two greatest have yet to be mentioned. There is Ernest Renan, akin to Goethe by his spiritual adaptability which takes in all history, and his marvelous sense for the primitive and refined ways of feeling. And there is Hippolyte Taine, descended directly from Goethe through his rare powers of understanding, his ability to mould into one natural and mental science, and his practical, enthusiastic, and natural feeling for art and insight into the ways of art.

That Goethe had an ideal public in the newer France is shown by the various translations of *Faust*. There is Stapfer's forceful and Saint Aulaire's less successful renderings, both of the year 1823, the interesting translation of 1828 by Gérard de Nerval which won Goethe's approval, Henri Blaze's which, like the others, partly in verse and partly in prose, was done with assistance from Weimar in the year 1840, Henri Bacharach's prose of 1873, Alexandre Laya's in verse, likewise from 1873, A. Maussenet's, intended as a text-book, in 1879, which tries solely to reproduce the German text, which Maussenet frequently misunderstood, Marc-Monnier's talented but incomplete one of 1875, August Daniel's painstaking and conscientious one of 1881, which is, however, embarrassed by the verse form, Georges Pradez's good metrical one of 1895, and finally the best of all by François Sabatier, published after the translator's death. Sabatier's rank as an artist will be felt by anyone on reading his version of the *Zueignung*:

> Mes nouveaux chants ces âmes plus n'entendent
> A qui ma voix a dit mes premiers chants;
> De tant d'amis se dispersa la bande,
> L'écho premier s'est tû depuis longtemps!

> Mes plaintes à des inconnus descendent,
> Tous leurs bravos pour moi sont un tourment;
> Et ceux à qui mes chants avaient su plaire
> S'en vont errant, s'ils vivent, sur la terre.

.(Fernand Baldensperger: *Goethe en France;* Martha Langkavel: *Die französischen Uebertragungen von Goethe's Faust.*)

IV

By way of picturing the poetic grandeur of Shelley as contrasted with that of the French, we need merely to refer to his translation of the angels' song which opens the prologue to *Faust*.

The sun makes music as of old
  Amid the rival spheres of Heaven,
On its predestined circle rolled
  With thunder speed; the Angels even
Drew strength from gazing on its glance,
  Though none its meaning fathom may;—
The world's unwithered countenance
  Is bright as at creations day.

This translation dates from the year 1822; it was done consequently just before Shelley's death.

It was not the great English poet, however, but a zealous writer of prose who introduced Goethe as a mental force to the English public; and oddly enough, it was a writer with senses keenly alive to spiritual excellence but woefully lacking in the finer feeling for great poetry. Richard Garnett has well said, apropos of the essay on *Faust* by Thomas Carlyle in the *New Edinburgh Review* of April, 1822, that in a letter by Shelley, written in the same month, there is embodied, in just five lines, more and richer insight into *Faust* than there would have been in five volumes from the hand of Carlyle in the unripe and dyspeptic prose he used in the essay. Carlyle was too impatient; he was too eager to disseminate newly acquired information. The people of Germany have nevertheless always been justly grateful to Carlyle for the work he did by way of making Goethe known in England.

Born December, 1795, he began the study of German in February, 1819. Madame de Staël's book *De l'Allemagne* had attracted his attention to Germany, just as it had attracted the attention of thousands of others. He was on the point of taking up mineralogy, and felt constrained to become acquainted with the ideas of the German mineralogist Werner in the original. His friend of that time, Edward Irving, procured him a lexicon; he had a German grammar sent on from London to Scotland. As he tells John Murray in a letter written August 4, 1820, he soon had the impression that a new Heaven and a new Earth had been revealed to him through his penetration (it was not deep then) into German literature.

He read Jean Paul whose influence on his style is most marked. Jean Paul called forth his Scotch humor and provided his otherwise somewhat monotonous prose with vigorous arabesques. He read Fichte whose influence is easily discernible in his fundamental viewpoint according to which the world of experience is merely a cloak for the divine idea, and true life consists in placing one's personality at the service of mankind.

But Carlyle's interest in the spiritual life of Germany soon centred around Goethe, despite the fact that it would be difficult to find two personalities more dissimilar. If we except hatred toward chaos, they had hardly a feeling in common. What Carlyle saw in Goethe was the liberator from the merely negative and destructive toward which he himself was at first inclined. He yearned for a great living model who had found peace after a tremendous inner struggle. He had found one in Goethe. Years later he said to Emerson: "He is the only genuine soul of profound depth and wide range that I have found in Europe after search through the records of generations." He also wrote to Goethe himself the significant words: "I can never forget that it is you to whom I owe the unspeakably precious thought that *Ehrfurcht* is possible. Seeing this, I no longer guess and deny; I believe and know."

It was not admiration for Goethe as an artist and a poet that had captivated him. He lacked the feeling for poetry and had a poor ear for verse. His criticisms of Wordsworth, Keats and Shelley, together with the iambic pentameters scattered throughout his translations from German, are incontrovertible witnesses on this point. It was Goethe's personality that charmed him. He said to Sterling: "The existence of this man was for me the message of the evangelists. It ransomed me, I believe, from disaster, inward and outward."

Goethe, who understood everything, was after all quite well aware that Carlyle's attention was not drawn to the purely artistic. One day he remarked (July 25, 1827) to Eckermann that Carlyle, curiously enough, with regard to his criticisms of German writers, "had their spiritual and moral kernels in view; these he regarded as all-important." To Carlyle, poetry was a means of sensualizing the rational. In actuality he clung to the theories from the days of Pope or Lessing.

He published, after considerable interest in Schiller's *History of the Thirty Years War,* a *Life of Schiller.* It is a book of no great consequence. Then he went in for Goethe with all his heart. Though he did not think highly of *Wilhelm Meister,* he translated it into English. In September, 1823, he wrote a letter in which he betrays his Scotch impatience: "Goethe is the greatest genius of the last century and the greatest ass of the last three." But by and by the work and the man won him entirely. He asserts that not for six years has he found so many thoughts in any one book. Shortly after Goethe's death (July, 1832) he wrote his Essay on Goethe for the *Foreign Quarterly*. This was an event in England at that time. There is only one unfortunate thing about it: the essay is a mediocre funeral oration; it is nothing more; from it nothing is to be learned.

But the thick volume of correspondence between Goethe and his apostle across the Channel has not lost its value for the present generation. Carlyle's letters are beautiful because of their profound respect. Those from Goethe do not number more than a dozen; and Eckermann writes at times for his chief. But what Goethe says is deep; his judgments carry weight; they betray vast understanding, and a richness of heart that even a novice can grasp and like. By the mere touch of his spiritual personality, Goethe had initiated Carlyle into life and literature. He won in him, also, a sworn supporter among the English people—a people that is highly developed and noted then, and for a long time before then, for its conservatism.

The beautiful, almost paternal, relation to Byron, evoked by and based on the deferential homage of the otherwise defiant Lord, could not win the hearts of the English to Goethe. Byron had had his own troubles with his countrymen. The misunderstanding between him and them existed even after his death. Emerson's admiration made a lasting impression in North America, though it was not given out until after Goethe's death. His essay entitled *Goethe, or the Writer,* is, truth to tell, irrelevant talk and nothing more. It is immeasurably pretentious and quite void. But the superior, violent and

domineering Scotchman, Thomas Carlyle, who
would tolerate no opposition and soon acquired the
habit of nailing his judgments so fast that they were
allowed to stand unquestioned and uncontested, became in the years 1823-1832 the redoubtable mouthpiece of German thought, and especially of Goethe's
thought, on British soil. He wrote a score of books,
essays and translations. The same man who coined
the term *hero-worship* introduced into the Anglo-
Saxon world the cultivation of Goethe as a hero.
And like a good and trusted general, he won the
battle for his emperor.

At Goethe's death, the word *Weltliteratur*, which
he himself had coined, had become a reality. And
he himself, thanks to the united efforts of others,
had become the centre of this *Weltliteratur*.

CHAPTER XXXVIII

The Tree of Life, and the Tree of Knowledge

DURING his entire life, Goethe bewildered the reading world through his adeptness at transformation and rejuvenation. First he was Prometheus; then he was the Olympian Zeus. First he was an insurgent; then he was the royal sage. First he was the poet of passion; then he was nature's great, serene interpreter.

There have lived unforgetable personages whose gifts lay exclusively in an extraordinary ability to create life. There have been sculptors such as Donatello, painters such as Rembrandt, Musicians such as Mozart, poets such as Alfred de Musset. They created and handed down to generations after them works that are richly blessed with life, that bubble over with life. The judgments they have passed outside of their own fields, however, do not interest us. Toward the doctrines they homaged we are indifferent. They had an adequate knowledge of the inner and outer world, of man's nature and man's heart. They never theorized on these subjects. Their creations live. That is more than enough. And it is enough for us.

The tree of life is not the tree of knowledge.

And there are minds from which we have received uninterrupted instruction: An astronomer like La-

487

place who discusses the most difficult problems so that all men may understand them; a scientist like Alexander von Humboldt whose wisdom is all-embracing and imparted with delightful clarity; a natural scientist like Charles Darwin, who, with enrapturing modesty, posited an ingenious substitute for the belief in final causes, and as an explanation of the origin of species; a historian like Augustin Thierry who is recondite and yet, despite all romanticism, intelligible, entertaining and informing. These men have great knowledge and great wisdom. They have sought and found. But they neither try, nor are they able, to create characters that live and move.

The tree of knowledge is not the tree of life.

Goethe is not like the men of either of these two classes. He has the ability to form characters; from the clay of art he can create men and give them life. He has also the gift of the investigator. He explains the cosmos, the genesis of the earth, the formation of plants, the inner connection of the skeleton, the true nature of art. He is at once a fountain of life, and an inexhaustible fountain of knowledge.

In the Eden of art and science he has revealed to men, the tree of life and the tree of knowledge are one.

END OF VOLUME TWO

INDEX

Aeschylus, II 318, 399
Agoult, Comtesse Marie d', I 349
Alembert, Jean d', I 77; II 247
Alexander I, II 269, 363, 391, 395
Alexander the Great, II 14, 87
Alfieri, Vittorio, I 281
Alcibiades, I 87, 95
Alphonso II, I 398
Ampère, Jean Jacques, II 477
Anacreon, I 95
Andersen, H. C., I 396, 399; II 309, 345, 348
Angers, David d', II 478
Anna Amalie, I 236, 255-280, 309, 314, 318, 320, 366, 402, 497; II 21, 195, 203, 217, 239, 253
Aretino, Pietro, II 17
Ariosto, I 141, 398, 449; II 372, 427
Aristophanes, I 366, 368
Aristotle, I 125, 176; II 330
Arminius, I 284
Arnim, Bettina von, II 10, 383
Arnold, Gottfried, I 70, 149
Assisi, St. Francis of, I 443, 467; II 434
Auerbach, Heinrich, I 294
Auger, Louis Simon, II 476
Augereau, P. F. Charles, II 250
August, Duke of Gotha, II 189
Augustenborg, Duke F. C., II 58-60
Augustinus, Aurelius, II 345
Augustus, I 469

Bacharach, Henri, II 481
Bacon, Francis, II 332
Bacon, Roger, II 332
Bagger, Carl, I 396

Baggesen, Jens, I 89, 247, 368; II 58-61, 131, 416
Bahrdt, Carl Friedrich, I 161
Baldensperger, Fernand, II 481
Balle, Nicolaj, I 217
Balsamo, I 453; II 32
Bang, Herman, I 361
Barbara, Duchess of Ferrara, I 398
Barbier, Auguste, II 480
Barthélemy, Jean Jacques, I 77
Basedow, Johann Bernhardt, I 234, 235; II 353
Batsch, August, I 479; II 77
Bayle, Pierre, I 449
Beaulieu, General, I 253
Beaulieu, Henriette von, I 253
Beaumarchais, Pierre A. C. de, I 37, 137, 220-229; II 107, 473
Beccaria, Cesare Marchese de, II 299
Beck, Heinrich, II 41
Becker, Christiane, II 107, 198, 203, 206, 210
Becker, Heinrich, II 204, 210
Bédoyère, Henry de la, II 476
Beethoven, I xiv; II 428, 449
Behrisch, Ernst Wolfgang, I 53, 57, 58, 59, 106
Bellomo, Joseph, II 196, 197, 203
Bentham, Jeremy, II 296
Berendis, Hieronymus, II 242
Bergmann, Torbern, II 271
Berlichingen, Götz von, I 129, 131, 143, 149, 457; II 35
Berlioz, Hector, II 478
Bernadotte, II 391
Bernhard, Carl, I 396
Bernini, Lorenzo, I 92
Bernhard, Duke of Sachse-Weimar, II 362

489